JAMES AGEE REDISCOVERED

JAMES AGEE
REDISCOVERED

The Journals of
Let Us Now Praise Famous Men
and Other New Manuscripts

EDITED BY
MICHAEL A. LOFARO
AND
HUGH DAVIS

THE UNIVERSITY OF TENNESSEE PRESS / *Knoxville*

Copyright © 2005 by The James Agee Trust.
All Rights Reserved. Manufactured in the United States of
America. First Edition.

This book is printed on acid-free paper.

Agee, James, 1909–1955.
James Agee rediscovered: the journals of let us now praise
famous men and other new manuscripts / edited by
Michael A. Lofaro and Hugh Davis.—1st ed.
      p. cm.
Includes bibliographical references and index.

ISBN 1-57233-355-3 (alk. paper)

  1. Agee, James, 1909–1955—Manuscripts.
  2. Agee, James, 1909–1955. Let us now praise famous men.
  3. Agee, James, 1909–1955—Notebooks, sketchbooks, etc.
  I. Lofaro, Michael A., 1948–
 II. Davis, Hugh, 1965–
III. Title.

PS3501.G35A6 2004
813'.52--dc22   2004002716

For Anthony L. and Helen W. Lofaro
—MAL

To my parents, Bill and Susan, and my wife, Linda
—HD

CONTENTS

Let Us Now Praise Famous Men
Journals and Drafts

JOURNAL 1 ────────────────────────────

JOURNAL 2 ────────────────────────────

JOURNAL 3

JOURNAL 4

ESSAYS AND DRAFTS

POETRY AND NOTES ON POETRY

FILM TREATMENTS AND RADIO PLAY

NOTES, FRAGMENTS, AND OUTLINES

FICTION

INTRODUCTION

Even for a modern writer, [James Agee] was extraordinarily self-destructive. He was always ready to sit up all night with anyone who happened to be around, or to go out at midnight looking for someone: talking passionately, brilliantly, but too much, drinking too much, smoking too much, reading aloud too much, and in general cultivating the worst set of work habits in Greenwich Village.

—Dwight Macdonald

He was a very hard and constant worker. He was at all times at work on one or more projects of his own and was always dissatisfied with himself for not getting more of his own work done. So the waste of talent is perhaps not so much a real waste (i.e., not having done enough writing) but a discrepancy between the talent and the tasks to which it was put. That, too, I think is largely debatable.

—Mia Agee

When James Agee died at the age of forty-five, he had become for a small but rapidly growing cult of followers an icon of the uncompromising artist, raging against the establishment, tragically out of step with his time. Dwight Macdonald christened him a literary James Dean. Feeding this myth was the fact that at the time of his death in 1955 all his major works were out of print or not yet published—commercial

First epigraph: Dwight Macdonald, "Death of a Poet," *New Yorker* 33 (November 6, 1957): 216.

Second epigraph: Mia Agee, with Gerald Locklin, "Faint Lines in a Drawing of Jim," in *Remembering James Agee,* ed. David Madden (Baton Rouge: Louisiana State UP, 1974), 155. Rpt. in 2nd edition, ed. Madden and Jeffrey J. Folks (Athens: U of Georgia P, 1997), 222.

failure represented the unimpeachable sign of unappreciated genius. With David McDowell's Pulitzer Prize–winning edition of *A Death in the Family* in 1957, however, the time for recognition had come, and posthumous reconstruction of the Agee corpus began in earnest. In addition to the reissue of *Let Us Now Praise Famous Men*, which in 1960 found the audience that had eluded it in 1941, selective volumes of Agee's screenplays, film criticism, poetry, short prose, letters, and journalism appeared over the next three decades, along with scattered pieces of fiction and juvenilia.[1] Although Agee counted several of the editors of these works as friends, it is certainly ironic that a writer so devoted to the integrity of the individual artist has had the canon of his established works shaped to an uncommon degree by the hands of others.

In one sense, the present volume, *James Agee Rediscovered: The Journals of* Let Us Now Praise Famous Men *and Other New Manuscripts*, is a continuation of the project of building Agee's legacy. What makes this book different, though, is the degree to which Agee speaks in his own voice, without the editorial intrusion and selection that have characterized earlier collections. Included here for the first time are Agee's notebooks as he wrote them, a combination of working drafts and personal journal entries—with all the self-conscious posturing, maudlin self-laceration, stunning insights, wicked satire, enigmatic asides, and mundane lists left in place, providing fascinating evidence of a sensitive, unsettled, and wide-ranging mind. Also included with the seven journal-notebooks are dozens of previously unpublished poems and drafts, essays, and film treatments, as well as notes and drafts covering a dizzying range of subjects and genres.

Agee's excesses are in full view. Of the "Alabama trip," for instance, he writes:

---

1. Posthumously published works and collections of works by Agee include: *A Death in the Family* (New York: McDowell, Oblensky, 1957); *Agee on Film*, vols. 1 and 2 (New York: McDowell, Oblensky, 1958 and 1960); *Let Us Now Praise Famous Men*, intro. Walker Evans (1941; rpt. Boston: Houghton Mifflin, 1960); *The Letters of James Agee to Father Flye*, ed. James H. Flye (New York: George Braziller, 1962); *The Collected Poems of James Agee*, ed. Robert Fitzgerald (Boston: Houghton Mifflin, 1968); *The Collected Short Prose of James Agee*, ed. Robert Fitzgerald (Boston: Houghton Mifflin, 1968); *James Agee: Selected Journalism*, ed. Paul Ashdown (Knoxville: U of Tennessee P, 1985); and *Agee: Selected Literary Documents*, ed. Victor A. Kramer (Troy: Whitson, 1996).

> In all the ways in which the South is peculiar to itself and distinct from all else it lay out there ahead of me faintly shining in the night, a huge, sensitive, globular, amorphous, only faintly realized female cell, towards which in determined speed, winding and gliding upon rails as upon the always fortuitous and perfect and beautiful pre-shaping predestination (like the music that remains wound up in silence to be played beyond the slow eating of the needle into the disk) carrying my little mind and its hungers and intentions, this sperm-shaped, strong-headed, infinitesimal train was traveling to pierce and, in my infinitesimal yet absolute terms, to fertilize. (J 1.1)

Those already familiar with Agee's prose will recognize the periodic style, the hypnotic cadences, the convoluted metaphors, the self-indulgence. More compelling, though, is the content: beginning with this entry, the journals provide an almost complete record of the genesis of *Let Us Now Praise Famous Men,* not only early drafts of passages that were later published but also an extended narrative of the time from Agee's receiving the assignment at *Fortune* to his arrival in Alabama. Agee's account of his initial excitement—which he literally interrupts mid-sentence to compose a love letter—takes a sudden turn, ending in an account of a League for Southern Labor fundraiser that climaxes in a denunciation of the hypocrisy of the "sincere enough young women who got a thrill out of hearing an imported negro tell how he had been beaten up and burned with matches" (J 1.6) that is shocking in its intensity. "A couple of grosses of dildoes and a few hard kicks in the ass," he concludes acerbically, "would reduce the revolutionary movement to something more like its proper size" (J 1.6).

The reader soon feels the rhythm and motion of the rail and road as Agee describes traveling by train from New York to Chattanooga and on to Birmingham by car. Though these passages were excluded from the final version, it is obvious that for Agee writing the journey south was essential, both practically and symbolically, to the process of shaping the work that eventually became *Let Us Now Praise Famous Men.* Furthermore, fragmentary notes and letters about the trip identify people and places that will allow future scholars to construct a more comprehensive itinerary than is now available.

As well as providing invaluable access to Agee's creative processes through working drafts, these notebooks and other manuscripts offer a glimpse into his turbulent personal life. For example, in what are apparently notes regarding his health after several heart attacks beginning in 1951, Agee writes under the heading "non-physical sources of trouble": "My work as a rule involves a lot of tension. Not as a rule when it is going best—but distinctly so, on the way there, & sometimes there. It can be very important sometimes to ride a spell out, and I've always done so: have good stamina for that. Dangerous now?" Sadly, by answering this question with another, Agee shows himself aware yet all too oblivious of consequences: "It is extremely unnatural to me to avoid strains, strong feeling, what is known as trouble—should I try to?" (N 31).

Clearly a part of this "trouble," Agee's relationships with women are also the subject of many revelatory passages, some coldly analytical:

> [Alma] explained, more level than has been usual, that by mind she agreed with me in every detail, most of it even in advance of everything I said (by which I measure her unconsciousness of the size of the thing, and of what motivates her), and that all her forms of depression, from small to extreme, were always pure feeling, her mind still knowing I was right (and often enough hating me for it) (J 4.2)

and some wildly emotional:

> Dirty sex in this face. It is not congruent with fucking or even masturbating but with very vain, cockteasing flirtation. As if sex, her looks, and your desire (the latter assumed by her) was a joke between herself and you in which, of course, you were bound to be the loser, with a public standing by and catching on, and laughing at you. I hate women who are professional beauties and confident of their beauty. (J 4.4)

One of the more poignant story lines in the journals covering 1937 and 1938 follows the development of Agee's affair with Alma Mailman and the concurrent deterioration of his marriage to Olivia (Via) Saunders. Many of the details of these relationships are only now available. Agee's letters to Alma—which he writes to his journal, knowing he will not send them—are full of the insecurity, infatuation, frustration, and hyperbole of a new love. "Do you think of me dear?" (J 1.5) Agee asks early on, and he pleads, "If what we have is to die, let it have had the best our hearts and intelligence could give it, let it not die under a mass of fears and half-truths and runnings-away" (J 1.12). There are moments of exquisite tenderness in these letters: "So that I'm often so suddenly & unexpectedly taken by happiness that it comes out in a laugh & in tears in my eyes before I know what has hit me. Then remembering, I know it is you, and think of you" (J 2.11). These sentiments stand in stark contrast to his thoughts concerning Via: "But I do not feel a thing. Only sadness; love for you; pity for you. What have I let you in for. Work; aging; poverty; no children; no sexual love; so much indifference" (J 2.2). Complicating matters is the fact that Agee met Alma through Via's family, and entry J 2.13 describes a meeting between the two women after the affair is in full bloom.

Alma did not merely replace Via, however, as later entries make clear. Writing while staying with the Saunders family towards the end of their marriage, Agee recalls:

> There was a night, not at all long before our marriage, when all doubts of it struck me the hardest they were able and I told Via of them, saying, how do I know what I am doing; and I was deeply sad, for her and for me, and near or in tears. She took my hand, then my head against her, then drew me away and looked at me with all her gentle sweetness and love, and tears in her eyes, and the slightly drawn, radiant smile of her purest emotions, and said, let not your heart be troubled; several times, very gently; and still deeply sad and loving, we both were, I was drawn into this religious faith and peace. (J 4.9)

But then he admits, "I do not often more than half-think of either Alma or Via. When I do, it is seldom with any warmth or happiness of Alma, and it is with sadness and love of Via, but a love a good deal helped by the situation and the imminence" (J 4.10). He realizes that there will be no reconciliation "unless all my center of desire, which probably I have in part deliberately killed, were shifted from Alma and renewed toward her" (J 4.10). He adds, "If there is any dignity and meaning in love, it certainly isn't within the scope of reason or sense" (J 4.10). In one of the most somber entries in the journals, Agee and Via divide their possessions before moving out of their apartment. Agee follows this with a strangely clinical letter to his mother detailing the planned divorce proceedings and arguing the case for his love for Alma. By this point he has already reached an unfortunately prescient conclusion to the triangle he has created, however: "What will become of her; what will become of me; what will become of this girl I love; I have no idea. But it seems unlikely that any of us can come to any good" (J 4.12).

While the journals indicate Agee's interest in labor and race relations and foreground his literary influences, they also contain a few surprises that will allow scholars to flesh out the picture of his life as well as his work. That Agee, at least in the late 1930s, was "a great deal more a communist than not" (J 1.4) is evident in passages such as this, from a draft of a previously unpublished letter to Father Flye:

> You think of the set-up as labor, capital, and government, making their adjustments as best they can, with the supremely important thing observance of and just administration of the law to the individual instance. I think of it as inevitable and literal <u>war</u>, in which, again inevitably, government and capital stand together against labor. Much as I may dislike the fact, there can be no sacred rules in war, and if strikers occupy the sacred property of their employers I rejoice as in the capture of an enemy fortress, only more so, for I have no enemies in any war but this kind. And if great sections of the law-abiding populace approve this rupture of law, I am glad again, for my side can in the long run never win without breaking the laws as they stand, the laws being against them; and this general approval shows a growth of insensitiveness toward my enemies, and of understanding of my friends, which is very encouraging in the very fact that it weakens the meaning and stature of government as it is. (J 2.17)

Poems such as "Fight-Talk" and "Collective Letter to the Boss" satirize public figures of all political persuasions, from Huey Long to Franklin Roosevelt and William Randolph Hearst. It is also evident that he followed the trial of black Communist Angelo Herndon. Rather than following any party line, the political sensibility of the poems and essays collected here emanates from the core of sympathy that made Agee, unwilling to tolerate hypocrisy in any form, an untiring defender of the powerless and downtrodden.

In addition to new works in several genres by Agee, this volume also lends insight into his views of other writers. Thomas Wolfe hovers over these pages, as it to be expected, but his presence in Agee's thoughts is perhaps even more pervasive than has been recognized. From the very first paragraph of his working drafts of *Let Us Now Praise Famous Men* Agee wrestles with Wolfe's influence:

> It is hard to know whether or not to skip the train. We could simply say that it did all the things Thomas Wolfe says a train does, and let it go at that. Wolfe has pretty thoroughly covered the subject, and whatever you may think of him or say against him, and much of it may be true, it will do none of you any harm to remember that Wolfe is a greater writer than a lot of neater writers ever will be.
>
> My present trouble is, that I am as badly a victim of train-love as Wolfe is or anyone else. (J 1.1)

A year later, Agee's anxiety and ambivalence over Wolfe are still strong:

> I know that Wolfe troubles me a great deal. He is a stupid man as well as a good and innocent one, and his stupidity gives me a feeling of cheapness or guilt or shallowness for whatever forms of understanding I have that he lacks. I am fond of him, and would I think like his friendship, and exactly in that proportion. I also want to avoid him, and certainly a part of this avoidance is a form of cowardice I cannot afford. (J 4.7)

Agee also pays tribute to Proust, Joyce, Hemingway, and André Gide. In early 1938, as he was struggling to find a form for *Let Us Now Praise Famous Men,* Agee turned to Gide's *Travels in the Congo*[2] and was "disturbed as you are bound to be when you find even minute aspects of your mind, and methods, and technical ideas, anticipated or cut across" (J 4.4). This bit of information opens *Let Us Now Praise Famous Men,* usually read both in the tradition and as a radical critique of other Depression-era documentaries such as *You Have Seen Their Faces,*[3] to intriguing new possibilities for interpretation. Critics hoping to make sense of Agee's complex mix of technical innovation and proletarian sensibility must now consider the implications of *Let Us Now Praise Famous Men* as a colonial travel

---

2. André Gide, *Travels in the Congo,* trans. Dorothy Bussy (New York: Knopf, 1929).

3. Erskine Caldwell and Margaret Bourke-White, *You Have Seen Their Faces* (New York: Modern Age Books, 1937).

narrative, an approach that may do much to illuminate Agee's identifi-cation with and distance from the sharecroppers for whom he speaks and also silences. That Gide's modernist ennui, fascination and repulsion for the exotic, and racial condescension exerted a pull on Agee is apparent as he resolves, "I must not touch this book again until I have finished mine" (J 4.4). Even more telling is that he was unable to keep the reso-lution. Despite these varied influences, Agee's most succinct formulation of his own aesthetic is unusually visceral and simple: "I guess I don't care much what I am moved by, so long as I'm moved" (J 5.4).

Scattered throughout the journals are unsent letters, reading lists, comments on movies and books, meditations on art, and plans for future projects, and all show Agee's restive mind at work. A detailed descrip-tion of lurid crime-scene photographs from a pulp detective magazine continues for several pages. Enthusiastic notes on Charlie Chaplin—"A movie could be made of his hands alone" (J 5.6)—merge into melan-choly self-criticism. A draft of a response to an article on *The Grapes of Wrath* written for the journal *Films* in 1940 may be Agee's first extended movie review and anticipates his work of the next decade in the genre for which he would become justly celebrated.

In addition to journals and working notebooks, this volume includes essays, poetry, film treatments, and other bits of writing. Although these vary widely in quality, the best of them constitute a sig-nificant and lasting contribution to the Agee canon. "America! Look at Your Shame!" is arguably his most powerful piece of non-fiction, as its recent publication—as soon as it came to light—in the *Oxford American* and *Harper's* confirms.[4] The unpublished (and unfortunately incomplete in manuscript) preface to *Permit Me Voyage*,[5] part review and part dis-quisition on "God vs. Art," is as insightful a portrait of the young poet as any since written. Many of the poems collected here are drafts of lyrics, but there are a number of topical satires that are quite different in style and content than the bulk of his published poetry. Also of inter-est are several examples of automatic writing, a surrealist technique

---

4. James Agee, "America, Look at Your Shame!" ed. and intro. Michael A. Lofaro and Hugh Davis, *Oxford American* 43 (January/February 2003), 34–39. This essay was reprinted as "After the Riots" in *Harper's* 306 (June 2003): 27–31.

5. James Agee, *Permit Me Voyage* (New Haven: Yale UP, 1934).

Agee used to generate ideas and poetic phrasing. A short film treatment concerning "one version of the ancient dream of an Earthly Paradise" of the Polynesian Islands, written with Manuel Conde, is a clear precursor to *Noa Noa*.[6] As with the drafts of *Let Us Now Praise Famous Men*, Agee's painstaking revisions of his comments on Walker Evans's subway photographs demonstrate that the seemingly effortless prose of the introduction to *Many Are Called*[7] is in fact the product of a tenacious pursuit of precisely the right word.

As a novelist, poet, critic, journalist, and screenwriter, Agee left a body of work so varied and all-embracing that it defies easy classification, and the present volume supports his well-deserved reputation for maddening complexity. The editors have attempted to produce a reasonably coherent, readable text from the diverse collection of Agee's manuscripts that will be both accessible to the general reader and rigorous enough for scholarly reconstruction. Where we have succeeded is testament to the power and relevance of a writer whose voice continues to resonate, in new and remarkable ways, a half-century after his death.

While we owe a debt of gratitude to many for the help provided in bringing this volume into print, we wish to note that grants from the John C. Hodges Better English Fund and the Professional Development Fund of the University of Tennessee have provided the time needed to complete some of the research and editing. We also wish to recognize the special contributions of Dr. James B. Lloyd, Research Consultant, and Mr. D. Strong Wyman, Special Collections, both of the University of Tennessee Libraries; the professional staff at the Harry Ransom Humanities Research Center, University of Texas, Austin; Mr. Jeff L. Rosenheim, Associate Curator of Photographs, The Metropolitan Museum of Art, New York City; and Mr. Paul Sprecher, the Trustee of The James Agee Trust. Their help and encouragement have made our work easier and far more enjoyable.

—*The Editors*

---

6. James Agee, *Noa Noa*, in *Agee on Film*, vol. 2. 1–148.

7. James Agee, Introduction to *Many Are Called* by Walker Evans (Boston: Houghton Mifflin, 1966).

THE LIFE AND TIMES OF JAMES AGEE

Although James Agee (1909–1955) lived through one of the most turbulent periods in American history, the intensely personal nature of his writing—even on such major national concerns as the plight of sharecroppers during the Great Depression or the dropping of the atomic bomb at the end of World War II—has tended to obscure the political and cultural contexts within and against which he was working. But Agee, like all artists, was a man of his time and was engaged, intellectually and emotionally, with major currents of the early to mid-twentieth century.

Born in Knoxville, Tennessee, November 27, 1909, James Rufus Agee grew up in Fort Sanders, a well-kept neighborhood containing a mixture of modest homes and Victorian mansions. Originally West Knoxville, the area had been annexed only a decade before, and its manicured lawns and middle-class mores contrasted sharply with Knoxville proper, a rough-and-tumble manufacturing and distribution center known for its saloons and brothels. It had little of the bourgeois gentility exhibited by Rufus's maternal grandparents in *A Death in the Family*, Agee's largely autobiographical novel set in the years from his birth to his father's death and funeral in 1916.[1] Before citywide prohibition in 1907, saloons and brothels lined the streets of downtown Knoxville, a city of around 32,000 inhabitants, and even after Tennessee became a nominally dry state in 1909, the ease with which "Jay Follett," Agee's fictional father, procures a drink in the novel, son in tow, at a crowded downtown speakeasy subtly attests to the extent to which the city deserved its reputation for a casual disregard for the law. Street violence, prostitution, disease, poverty, and racial tension—which culminated in a 1919 race riot that left seven dead and hundreds injured—were all a part of Knoxville in the first decades of the twentieth century,[2] a part which the lyric nostalgia of a work such as "Knoxville: Summer of 1915," which was added by the editor to *A Death in the Family* to create

---

1. James Agee, *A Death in the Family*. New York: McDowell, Oblensky, 1957.

2. For more on Knoxville in the early twentieth century, see Michael J. MacDonald and William Bruce Wheeler, *Knoxville, Tennessee: Continuity and Change in an Appalachian City* (University of Tennessee Press, 1982).

a sleepy southern atmosphere, tends to conceal. The father's obvious attraction to the seedier side of Knoxville life that Agee hints at in the novel is perhaps emblematic of the darker and self-destructive aspects of his father's personality, and of his own.

The respective backgrounds of Agee's parents, Hugh James (Jay) Agee and Laura Whitman Tyler Agee, also provide historical commentary on larger issues. Laura's father, Joel Tyler, had moved south from Michigan for health reasons and invested in land in East Tennessee, hoping to capitalize on railroad construction and the booming timber industry. He was a co-owner of Ty-Sa-Man, one of the many machine shops in Knoxville producing the implements that sustained rapid economic growth in the region around the turn of the century, a growth centered on extractive industries such as coal mining and timber harvesting primarily financed by outside investors. Although the Tylers were northern, well educated, thoroughly bourgeois, and progressive (in *A Death in the Family*, Joel reads the *New Republic* and "Aunt Hannah" reads the *Nation*), to imply that Jay Agee was their opposite in every way is mistaken. Jay, from La Follette, Tennessee, in the Powell River Valley about forty miles north of Knoxville, did not have a university education, but he was hardly an ignorant hillbilly, and his family included doctors, lawyers, small business owners, and teachers. He worked for the U.S. Post Office in Panama during the construction of the Panama Canal, and he and Laura married there in 1908. After returning to the States, he worked for the Louisville and Nashville Railroad in Corbin, Kentucky, before moving back to Knoxville for a job a Ty-Sa-Man. His desire for and willingness to make a financial stretch to purchase a Model T Ford signals his quest for the markers of upward social mobility and testifies to his obvious attraction to the possibilities of movement afforded by new technology. At the same time, however, his death after losing control of his car on May 18, 1916, is also an indication of the double nature of the transportation revolution that was irrevocably transforming the lives of all Americans.

Three years after her husband's death, Laura enrolled her son James in St. Andrew's, a boarding school administered by Episcopal monks on the Cumberland Plateau near Sewanee, Tennessee. Although she rented a small cottage on the grounds of the monastery, she limited her visits with her son, hoping that he would benefit from a strong male influence. It was here that Agee began a life-long friendship with one of his teachers, Father James H. Flye, and became thoroughly immersed in the Anglo-Catholic rituals he would so meticulously evoke in his 1951 novella, *The Morning Watch*.[3] Agee's letters to Father Flye, which cover a period of thirty years, were published in 1962 and are a remarkable testament to Agee's restless intelligence. His constant probing of aesthetic and ethical questions, all within the context of deep love and respect for his friend and mentor, offer indelible insight into the restive mind of a complex and sensitive artist.

After a year back in high school in Knoxville and a trip to England and France with Father Flye, Agee moved north to Rockland, Maine, with his mother and her new husband, Father Erskine Wright, a former rector at St. Andrew's. Agee attended Phillips Exeter Academy in Exeter, New Hampshire, where he wrote fiction and poetry and won a prize for an essay on international trade. From Exeter he went on to Harvard in 1928. By all accounts, Agee's charisma and infectious energy were well suited for the heady intellectual climate, and he took full advantage of opportunities by reading and absorbing Chaucer and Shakespeare, Virgil in the original, Whitman, Hopkins, Hart Crane, Donne, Coleridge, and many more authors besides. He also studied Joyce and Dostoyevsky— particularly *Ulysses* and *The Possessed* under I. A. Richards, the philosophical father of New Criticism. The summer after his sophomore year he worked as a migrant farm laborer in Nebraska and Kansas, stepping out of his privileged position to glimpse the ravages of the Great Depression first-hand and perhaps developing the sensibility that would later shape *Let Us Now Praise Famous Men*.[4] In 1931 he was elected president of the *Harvard Advocate,* where he published a parody of *Time* magazine[5] and the first installment of "John Carter," his long Byronic satire.[6] Agee was forced to censor certain parts of "John Carter," but the *Advocate*

---

3. James Agee, *The Morning Watch* (Boston: Houghton Mifflin, 1951).

4. James Agee and Walker Evans, *Let Us Now Praise Famous Men* (Boston: Houghton Mifflin, 1941).

5. *Harvard Advocate* 163 (March 1932), inclusive.

6. James Agee, "Opening of a Long Poem," *Harvard Advocate* 163 (June 1932): 12–20.

was issued with thick black marks over the offending lines, granting the poem, as with *Ulysses,* the type of artistic credibility that can only come from being deemed unfit to print.

Just as important as his literary influences, Agee became acquainted through his tutor, the noted Shakespeare critic Theodore Spencer, with the family of Dr. Arthur Percy Saunders, a professor of chemistry at Hamilton College in Clinton, New York, and a renowned horticultural-ist. The Saunders home was host to a modern salon, where artists and musicians, poets and scientists cultivated an atmosphere of gracious liv-ing and devotion to high culture. Agee endeared himself to the family by playing the role of drawing-room Marxist and roguish bohemian, even-tually marrying Dr. Saunders's daughter Olivia in 1933 and becoming close with her mother as well over a number of extended visits through-out the decade. However, it was also at the Saunders salon that he met Alma Mailman, a young violinist taken in by the family as a project, her father lacking the money for full development of her talents. As his mar-riage to Via crumbled and he began an affair with Alma, who became his second wife in 1938, Agee knew, as his journals make clear, that he was betraying not only Via, but her family and all they represented.[7]

Upon graduation from Harvard in 1932, Agee went to work at *Fortune* magazine on the recommendation of Dwight Macdonald, a fel-low Exeter alumnus with whom he had initiated a correspondence based on their mutual passion for movies. Founded in 1930 by Henry Luce, *Fortune* was intended as an uncritical celebration of American business, but the 1929 stock market crash and advent of the Great Depression obviously demanded a more nuanced approach. Under the guidance of managing editor Ralph Ingersoll, a talented group of left-leaning writers and photographers including, in addition to Agee and Macdonald, Archibald MacLeish and Margaret Bourke-White, pro-duced socially aware studies of economic issues, including the New Deal, as well as world events and American culture. Agee, for instance, wrote articles for *Fortune* on industrial pollution,[8] the decline of the

---

7. See the "Introduction" to this volume for a more complete account of Agee's relationships with Via and Alma.

8. James Agee, "Smoke" *Fortune* 15 (June 1937): 100–102, 130. Reprinted in *James Agee: Selected Journalism,* ed. Paul Ashdown (Knoxville: U of Tennessee P, 1985), 130–38.

Italian aristocracy under Mussolini,[9] and the role of the automobile in the emergence of an eclectic and thoroughly American roadside economy.[10] Although Agee never again lived in the South for any substantial period of time, he returned to write stories on the effect of the Tennessee Valley Authority's transformation of the landscape and the lives of the region, one of which contains a visit to TVA headquarters in Knoxville,[11] and on tenant farmers in Alabama, which, though never printed in *Fortune,* eventually became *Let Us Now Praise Famous Men.* Agee's later piece on the end of World War II for *Time*[12] was one of the earliest and most powerful examinations of the implications of the atomic bomb. "The promise of good and of evil bordered alike on the infinite," he wrote, "—with this further, terrible split in the fact: that upon a people already so nearly drowned in materialism even in peacetime, the good uses of this power might easily bring disaster as prodigious as the evil." The essay also has a regional connection —the atomic bomb was developed in part at a secret facility at Oak Ridge, Tennessee, twenty-five miles from Agee's boyhood home.

While he considered magazine work an economic necessity and a distraction from his higher literary calling, Agee wrote for Luce publications more or less continuously for eighteen years. Some devotees of Agee's work have seen this as a failing, as a waste of his energies on commercial publications. The simple fact was, however, that such employment provided the financial means (as movies would later) for Agee to support himself and his family through writing and provided a necessary base from which to pursue his literary art. Agee's association with Luce placed him squarely within the commercial world as a small part of a publishing empire that was to have a profound impact

---

9. James Agee, "Roman Society," *Fortune* 10 (July 1934): 68–71, 144–50. Rpt. in Ashdown, 30–41.

10. James Agee, "The American Roadside," *Fortune* 10 (September 1934): 53–63, 172–77. Rpt. in Ashdown, 42–62.

11. The TVA articles are "The Project Is Important," *Fortune* 8 (October 1933): 81–97 (rpt. in Ashdown, 1–18) and "T.V.A.," *Fortune* 11 (January 1935): 93–98, 140–53 (rpt. in Ashdown, 63–96). The visit to TVA headquarters overlooking Market Square appears in the latter.

12. James Agee, "Victory: The Peace," *Time* 46 (August 20, 1945): 19–21. Rpt. in Ashdown, 160–61.

on American culture. At a time when the country was moving from a production- to a consumption-based economy, largely dependent on advertising, and transformations in media and transportation technology were giving rise to a more homogenized national culture, Luce anticipated, exploited, and perpetuated all these trends. He founded *Time,* a nationally distributed news digest with broad appeal, in 1923, and though his distinctive editorial voice was easily parodied (by Agee, for instance), it spoke to millions. *Fortune,* which initiated the use of high-quality photography as a complement to literary prose as a conveyer of information about capitalism, was an ironic precursor to the New Deal photo-text documentary that provided social welfare to out-of-work artists. *Life,* a photography-oriented weekly founded in 1936, practically created the genre of photojournalism and spurred advances in print, production, and paper technology, which were quickly adopted by Madison Avenue and insinuated even deeper into the national consciousness.

On the agitated political front of the 1930s, it was clear that though MacLeish had praised Agee's 1934 poetry collection, *Permit Me Voyage,* for its apolitical stance,[13] Agee had not only become engaged politically but had also moved decisively to the left by the second half of the decade. This political engagement is strikingly evident in the journals published in this volume, which cover the period from 1937 to 1941. The failure of the New Deal to stave off an economic downturn in 1937 seemed to sound the death knell for liberal democracy, and many intellectuals felt that the stark choice facing the West was one between Communism and fascism, a conflict then being played out in the Spanish Civil War. Agee attended pro-Loyalist speeches and films and his first instinct after receiving the *Fortune* assignment on sharecropping was to contact a Communist labor organizer.[14] Despite his self-characterization as "a great deal more communist than not" (J 1.4), Agee also recognized the hypocrisy of organizers' exploitation of the plight of southern blacks to advance party interests. Agee's attitudes towards African Americans have received very little attention, but certain passages in this volume are worth noting: "We are living in their ancient history. In their histories and social memory,

---

13. James Agee, *Permit Me Voyage* (New Haven: Yale UP, 1934).

14. See journal entries J 1.4 and J 1.6 in this volume for Agee's account of receiving the assignment.

when they are the dominant race and culture, this will be the period of emergence: 1800–2000 A.D.: and these records, for instance, and any movie or written records of their living, will have an almost holy character" (J 5.1). The brutally honest essay "America! Look at Your Shame!" (E 1) depicts Agee's excruciating response to an encounter on a New York City bus with racism embodied in a group of menacing southern servicemen during World War II. "[T]hat night the flogging," an enigmatic throwaway line referring to a Ku Klux Klan murder in Florida from a 1936 itinerary that also mentions Franklin Roosevelt, black Communist Angelo Herndon, and actor Bill "Bojangles" Robinson, shows just how seamlessly Agee absorbed and processed seemingly unconnected events around a nexus incorporating race, politics, entertainment, and economic deprivation (N 20).

Agee was even more disturbed by the incipient fascism embodied by populist demagogues such as Huey Long and radio priest Father Coughlin and understood, as they did, the immense political implica tions of newly emergent mass media.[15] Luce's *March of Time* newsreels used actors to recreate actual events, blurring the line between fact and fiction—but no less disturbingly so than the films and images manufactured by supporters of both sides in the Spanish Civil War. Virtually all of Agee's Greenwich Village peers in the late 1930s worked for mass-circulation magazines, produced propaganda such as photographs for the Farm Security Administration and plays for the Federal Theatre Project in support of New Deal programs, or exhibited at elite cultural institutions such as the Museum of Modern Art. Photographer Walker Evans, Agee's collaborator on *Let Us Now Praise Famous Men,* did all three. Agee himself wrote glorified advertising copy: his caption for a *Fortune* spread on glass products that begins "The clear amorphous honey born of hard sand, potash, lime, and fire" in any other context could be considered a prose poem.[16] Agee's meditations on photography in these notebooks—whether on lurid and mesmerizing crime-scene shots in pulp detective magazines (J 4.4) or Evans's austere,

---

15. See, for instance, the poems "Major Douglas" (P 27), "Dialog" (P 28), and "Collective Letter to the Boss" (P 50) in this volume.

16. "Jewel Spread," *Fortune* 14 (August 1936): 70.

"straight style" subway photographs (N 1)—reveal an awareness of and ambivalence about the power of the visual image to shape mass consciousness, for good or ill.

Within and against this dynamic confluence of politics, technology, media, and aesthetics, Agee published *Let Us Now Praise Famous Men* in 1941. Originally assigned to produce an article on white sharecroppers for *Fortune*'s "Life and Circumstances" series, Agee and Evans, who was under contract to Roy Stryker's Farm Security Administration at the time, traveled to Alabama in the summer of 1936 to find an appropriate family and stayed for eight weeks doing research. Perhaps the most salient fact to consider about the two artists' respective approaches is that while Agee actually lived with the "Gudger" family, Evans stayed in a hotel in town. The piece Agee wrote on the experience was so completely unpublishable that the magazine released it to him. Over the next five years, he wrote and revised—for the most part deep into the night in a farmhouse in Frenchtown, New Jersey, where he had moved with Alma—and struggled to "recognize the stature of a portion of unimagined existence, and to contrive techniques proper to its recording, communication, analysis, and defense."[17] The result—"a book only by necessity" (J 6.3)—is an intense and complex examination of not only its putative subject matter but also the act of perceiving itself, in all its potency and self-deception. Prefaced by a series of uncaptioned Evans photographs, *Let Us Now Praise Famous Men* both follows in the tradition of Depression-era photo-text collaborations such as Dorothea Lange and Paul S. Taylor's *An American Exodus*[18] and utterly undermines them, calling into question their (and its own) assumptions and techniques and castigating unexamined liberal pieties. Part anti-documentary documentary, part formalist experiment, part jeremiad, and part anti-journalistic primal scream, *Let Us Now Praise Famous Men* challenges readers as it challenges itself and implicates them in its confession. It

---

17. *Famous Men*, x.

18. Dorothea Lange and Paul S. Taylor, *An American Exodus: A Record of Human Erosion* (New York: Reynal and Hitchcock, 1939). Other books in this genre include *You Have Seen Their Faces* by Erskine Caldwell and Margaret Bourke-White (New York: Modern Age Books, 1937) and *Twelve Million Black Voices: A Folk History of the Negro in the United States* by Richard Wright, with photo-direction by Edwin Rosskam (New York: Viking, 1941).

would have to wait for civil rights activism and the advent of the "New Journalism" in the early 1960s to find its audience, though, since it sold only six hundred copies upon publication. Despite Agee's plea, "Above all else: in God's name don't think of it as Art,"[19] it is ironically marketed as "The American Classic" today.

After the tumultuous thirties and the disappointing reception of *Let Us Now Praise Famous Men,* Agee generally settled into a new career as a film critic.[20] Or, rather, he transformed the genre of film criticism through an informed and highly literate yet unapologetically subjective treatment of a medium for which he had a long-standing enthusiasm. In typically contradictory fashion, he did so in two diametrically opposed publications: *Time,* from 1941 to 1948, where he also wrote features, beginning in 1945, and, more importantly, the *Nation,* starting in 1942. Whereas Luce proclaimed that individualism and initiative were inaugurating an "American Century" in 1941,[21] the *Nation,* under Freda Kirchway, took a pro-Stalinist editorial line; in 1937 Dwight Macdonald had written a series for the *Nation* on Time, Inc., accusing it not only of allowing the advertising department to corrupt news selection and exploiting its secretarial staff, but also of barely disguising its fascist sympathies. Agee, whose office mate at *Time* was Whittaker Chambers, seems not to have noticed the contradiction or to have cared. Writing as a self-professed "amateur,"[22] he praised emotional honesty wherever he could find it and decried Hollywood pretension, whether artistic or moral. W. H. Auden, in a 1944 letter to the editors of the *Nation,* called Agee's movie column "the most remarkable regular event in American journalism today" and assigned it to "that very select class . . . of newspaper work that has permanent literary value."[23]

Notable for their perception and generosity, Auden's comments also point to the crucial intersection of high and middle-class cultural

---

19. *Famous Men,* 12.

20. See *Agee on Film,* vol. 1 (New York: McDowell, Oblensky, 1958) for a collection of Agee's movie reviews and other essays on film.

21. Henry R. Luce, "The American Century," *Life* (February 17, 1941): 61–65.

22. James Agee, "Films," *Nation* 155.26 (December 26, 1942): 727. Rpt. in *Agee on Film,* vol. 1, 22–24.

23. W. H. Auden, "Letter to the Editor: Agee on Films," *Nation* 159.21 (November 18, 1944): 528. Rpt. *Agee on Film,* vol. 1, epigraph.

forms that defined the second half of Agee's artistic development. While *Permit Me Voyage,* with its sonnet sequence and epithalamium, and *Let Us Now Praise Famous Men,* with its modernist formal extremism and impenetrability, embodied elitist assumptions about literary value, over the course of the 1940s Agee gravitated toward more popular forms of expression. His near-endorsement of nonresistance to evil in *Let Us Now Praise Famous Men* in 1941 gave way to disgust with the moral paralysis of the intelligentsia in the essay "America! Look at Your Shame!" contained in this volume. The essay, a personal indictment of homefront racism in the context of World War II, grew out of coverage of the 1943 Detroit race riots and anticipated the Civil Rights movement by highlighting the contradiction between the America's fight for freedom overseas and the oppression of a significant part its population at home. In describing her situation, a black woman in the essay articulates Agee's message on racism: "Just might bout's well be Hitluh, as a white man from the South" (E 1).

By 1950 Agee had rejected many of his previously held highbrow attitudes, equating popular art with action in "Undirectable Director" and elevating John Huston's films to the status of "good art" because they require of their viewers "the responsibilities of liberty."[24] In a 1930 letter to Father Flye, Agee had expressed his desire to create an "amphibious style" of writing that would combine poetry and prose in an unprecedented way.[25] Twenty years later, he defined himself as a religious "amphibian" in a *Partisan Review* seminar on the postwar religious revival, disclaiming formal religion but not its spiritual benefits.[26] This both-and-neither individualism characterizes a good deal of his approach to politics as well. Long associated with the left—the same issue of *Partisan Review* in which "Knoxville: Summer of 1915" appears also contains a long letter from Leon Trotsky on the state of art after the revolution[27]—

24. James Agee, "Undirectable Director," *Life* 29 (September 18, 1950): 128–45. Rpt. in *Agee on Film,* vol. 1, 319–31.

25. James Agee, *The Letters of James Agee to Father Flye,* ed. James H. Flye (New York: George Braziller, 1962), 48.

26. "Religion and the Intellectuals: James Agee," *Partisan Review* 17.2 (May–June 1950): 106–13.

27. Leon Trotsky, "Art and Politics," *Partisan Review* 5.3 (August–September 1938): 3–10. Agee's "Knoxville: Summer of 1915" appears on pages 22–25.

Agee was untouched by the various anti-Communist trials, hearings, and blacklists of the late 1940s and early 1950s. He could eulogize FDR as commander-in-chief while lamenting the wartime destruction of a Benedictine abbey; he recognized the "vigor and promise and individual generosity of the American soldier," who could be "homesick and purposeless and often misbehaved," as well.[28] One of the few to defend Charlie Chaplin from charges of anti-Americanism after the release of *Monsieur Verdoux,* Agee was probably alone among his intellectual circle also to defend Whittaker Chambers's charges of Communist espionage against Alger Hiss in the congressional investigations that brought a first-term congressman named Richard Nixon to the public eye.

Though diametrically opposed in almost every way, both Agee and Senator Joseph McCarthy, the vigorously anti-Communist chairman of the Subcommittee on Investigations, came to appreciate the power of television, which, though barely a decade old in the early 1950s, was already beginning to transform culture and politics. The broadcast of McCarthy's hearings on Communist infiltration of the army in 1954 exposed his bullying tactics and prosecutorial overreach to a nationwide audience, destroying his political career and damaging the efforts of more rational anti-Communists for decades. Less seriously, and having more to do with national self-image than national security, Agee's adaptation of Carl Sandburg's biography of Abraham Lincoln for the Ford Foundation's *Omnibus* television series was a critical and popular success but drew the ire of historians. After the series aired in 1953, Agee faced off with Columbia University history professor Allan Nevins in a debate, also televised on *Omnibus,* on Agee's considerable use of poetic license in his depiction of Lincoln. Though Agee defended himself on the grounds that there are "two kinds of truths,"[29] what was really at stake was not so much his right to interpret history but the fact that his interpretation had been so widely disseminated to an audience disposed to receive it uncritically. As a cultural gatekeeper whose position relied on the stability of history and historical fact, Nevins understood the danger that Agee represented as an artist who had embraced popular

---

28. James Agee, "Europe: Autumn Story," *Time* 46 (October 15, 1945): 24–25. Rpt. in Ashdown, 164–68.

29. Laurence Bergreen, *James Agee: A Life* (New York: Dutton, 1984), 374.

forms and had little regard for institutional authority. Agee now had access to a powerful new medium that could circumvent the control that Nevins and other guardians of traditional written knowledge formerly exerted.

In the meantime, Agee's personal life continued to take new turns. His first son, Joel, was born to Alma in 1940; she soon left him, took Joel, and went to Mexico, accompanied by photographer Helen Levitt. He married Mia Fritsch in 1944, after she gave birth to a premature son, who died soon afterward. In 1946 Julia Teresa (Deedee) was born to Mia, followed by Andrea Maria in 1950 and John Alexander in 1954. Despite his intellectual commitment to personal responsibility—he believed that the true meaning of the atomic bomb was "that each man is eternally and above all else responsible for his own soul"[30]—Agee was an erratic father. Perhaps because of this instability, or perhaps because he was newly attuned to the importance of childhood experience through his role as a parent, children are the focus of much of his work of the late forties. Along with Helen Levitt and Janice Loeb, he made *In the Street,* a documentary film about children in Harlem in 1945, and he wrote the commentary for *The Quiet One,* Levitt's award-winning documentary film about a juvenile delinquent in Harlem in 1948. While undergoing Jungian analysis, beginning in 1945, he composed *The Morning Watch,* a guilt-wracked fictional recounting of a Maundy Thursday ritual he had experienced at St. Andrew's, which was published in the elite journals *Botteghe Oscura* and *Partisan Review* before appearing in book form.[31] In 1948, his last year as a reviewer for *Time* and the *Nation* and first as a screenwriter, he also wrote most of *A Death in the Family,* which focused upon his perceptions of his life through the age of six. Although after Agee's death David MacDowell successfully edited the manuscript to conform with literary standards of the mid-1950s (it was published in 1957 and won the Pulitzer Prize for Fiction the next year), he obscured Agee's development of the relationship between his childhood fictional self, Rufus, and Rufus's father through chronological displacements and elision of important chapters and scenes. Also disguised by the editing is the degree to which

---

30. "Victory: The Peace." In Ashdown, 161.

31. *The Morning Watch* appeared in its entirety in 1950 in *Botteghe Oscura* 6 (339–409) and in March–April 1951 in *Partisan Review* 18.2 (137–66, 206–31).

the novel marks Agee's transition to screenwriting, with its continuity developed through many short scenes and emphasis on dialogue.

For the last five years of his life, Agee wrote exclusively for the movies and television, and, given the collaborative nature of the media, his major works are adaptations. He wrote adapted screenplays of the Stephen Crane stories "The Blue Hotel" in 1948 and "The Bride Comes to Yellow Sky" in 1952 under contract to Huntington Hartford. The screenplay for *The African Queen,* which he adapted along with John Huston, who had to finish it after Agee's first heart attack in 1951, was nominated for an Oscar. He also wrote the screenplay for *The Night of the Hunter,* directed by Charles Laughton. His most original screenplay is *Noa Noa,* based loosely on Paul Gauguin's diaries, but it was never produced.[32] In the script for an *Omnibus* television series on Lincoln he inserted himself—as he had with *The Bride Comes to Yellow Sky*—as the town drunk. Whether one reads any psychological meaning into this or not, by the middle of the decade Agee's health had severely deteriorated, and his inability or unwillingness to give up drinking, smoking, and other bad habits exacerbated the problem. On May 16, 1955, he died of a heart attack in a New York City taxi, two days short of the anniversary of his father's death, thirty-nine years before.

In his too few years, Agee lived more than most men do in many more. From the early tragedy of his father's death to his education in privilege at Harvard, from radical politics in Greenwich Village to commercial success in Hollywood, from sharecropper's shack to the Chrysler Building, Agee strove to apprehend and communicate each experience as truthfully as possible. In an apparent attempt to connect more completely with his audience, he rejected the detached aestheticism of his early poetry and the formal high modernism of *Let Us Now Praise Famous Men* in favor of direct engagement through the power of the popular media of mass journalism, television, and film. As a particularly sensitive

---

32. The screenplays for these five films are collected in *Agee on Film,* vol. 2 (New York: McDowell, Oblensky, 1960). Agee's manuscript for *The Night of the Hunter* has recently been discovered. Longer and more detailed than the shooting script published in *Agee on Film,* it puts to rest the claim that Laughton found Agee's work unusable and points instead to a productive collaboration between the two.

observer of and participant in the complex culture and politics of the Great Depression, World War II, and the beginning of the Cold War, Agee was also perfectly positioned to comment upon the contradictions of his age, even as he exemplified them. In the journals, drafts, poetry, film treatments, fragments, and other materials collected in this volume, Agee both provides a panoramic, albeit sometimes fragmented, window upon this world and forces the perceptive reader to engage its major issues, its profound problems, and the rollercoaster of emotions that constitute an existence vibrant with life.

A JAMES AGEE CHRONOLOGY

1909 James Rufus Agee is born November 27 to Laura Tyler Agee and Hugh James Agee in Knoxville, Tennessee.

1916 Agee's father is killed in an automobile accident on May 18.

1919–24 Agee attends St. Andrew's School, near Sewanee, Tennessee, where he begins a life-long friendship with Father James H. Flye.

1924 Agee attends Knoxville High School. His mother marries Father Erskine Wright and moves with him to Rockland, Maine.

1925 After traveling with Father Flye in England and France during the summer, Agee enrolls in Phillips Exeter Academy in Exeter, New Hampshire.

1927 Agee is elected editor of the *Exeter Monthly* and president of the literary Lantern Club.

1928–32 Agee attends Harvard University.

1929 Agee spends the summer working as a migrant farm laborer in Nebraska and Kansas

1930 Agee is introduced to the salon of Dr. Arthur Percy Saunders, whose home in Clinton, New York, is a center of culture, science, and art.

1931 Agee is elected president of the *Harvard Advocate*.

1932 On the recommendation of Dwight Macdonald, Agee begins work as a reporter at *Fortune* magazine.

1933 Agee marries Olivia (Via) Saunders, January 28.

1934 *Permit Me Voyage* is published in the Yale Series of Younger Poets with an introduction by Archibald MacLeish.

1935–36 On leave from *Fortune* from November 1935 to May 1936, Agee lives with Via in Anna Maria, off the west coast of Florida, also visiting New Orleans and St. Andrew's. He writes poetry and completes "Knoxville: Summer of 1915," published in *Partisan Review* in 1938.

1936 On assignment for *Fortune*'s "Life and Circumstances" series, Agee travels with photographer Walker Evans to Mills Hill,

Alabama, where he lives with a family of sharecroppers for eight weeks from June to August. *Fortune* rejects the article Agee produces on the experience.

1937   Agee begins an affair with Alma Mailman, a friend of the Saunders family.

1938   After his divorce from Via in November, Agee marries Alma on December 6.

1939   Harper and Brothers rejects "Cotton Tenants: Three Families," Agee's revision and expansion of the *Fortune* sharecropper article. Agee begins reviewing books for *Time* magazine.

1940   Agee begins an affair with Mia Fritsch, a researcher at *Fortune*. Alma gives birth to his first son, Joel, on March 20. Later that year Alma leaves Agee and goes with Helen Levitt to Mexico, taking Joel with her.

1941   Houghton Mifflin publishes *Let Us Now Praise Famous Men*. Agee begins reviewing films for *Time*.

1942   In December Agee begins reviewing films for the *Nation*.

1943   Agee writes but does not publish "America! Look at Your Shame!"

1944   On July 30 Mia gives birth prematurely to a son, who dies soon afterwards. Agee and Mia marry in late August.

1945   Agee begins writing features for *Time;* films *In the Street* with Janice Loeb and Helen Levitt.

1946   Mia gives birth to Julia Teresa (Deedee), Agee's first daughter, November 7.

1948   American composer Samuel Barber's *Knoxville: Summer of 1915,* for soprano and orchestra with text by Agee, debuts in Boston. Agee leaves *Time* and the *Nation* and writes his first full-length screenplay, an adaptation of Stephen Crane's "The Blue Hotel," under contract to Huntington Hartford. He also writes most of *A Death in the Family,* which is published posthumously.

1949   *The Quiet One,* a documentary film by Helen Levitt, for which Agee writes the narration, opens; it is named Best Film at the Venice Film Festival. His "Comedy's Greatest Era" appears in *Life* magazine (September 3).

1950	Agee's second daughter, Andrea Maria, is born, May 15. Agee goes to California to write the screenplay for John Huston's *The African Queen*. "Undirectable Director," Agee's portrait of Huston, appears in *Life* (September 18).
1951	On January 15, Agee suffers his first major heart attack and is hospitalized. Huston finishes the screenplay for *The African Queen;* the screenplay is nominated for an Academy Award. Houghton Mifflin publishes *The Morning Watch*, Agee's novella based on experiences at St. Andrew's.
1952	Agee is commissioned by the Ford Foundation to write a television script on Abraham Lincoln for *Omnibus*. Agee adapts another Stephen Crane story, "The Bride Comes to Yellow Sky," for Huntington Hartford.
1953	Agee writes the screenplay for *Noa Noa*, based on Paul Gauguin's diary.
1954	Agee writes the screenplay for *The Night of the Hunter*, directed by Charles Laughton. John Alexander, his second son, is born, September 6.
1955	On May 16, Agee dies of a heart attack in a New York City taxi. He is buried in Hillsdale, New York.
1957	*A Death in the Family*, edited by David McDowell, is published by McDowell, Oblensky.
1958	*A Death in the Family* wins the Pulitzer Prize for Fiction. McDowell, Oblensky publishes the first volume of *Agee on Film*, a collection of reviews and essays.
1960	McDowell, Oblensky publishes the second volume of *Agee on Film*, a collection of screenplays. Houghton Mifflin reissues *Let Us Now Praise Famous Men* with a new preface by Walker Evans and additional photographs. *All the Way Home*, Tad Mosel's stage adaptation of *A Death in the Family*, opens on Broadway; it later wins the Pulitzer Prize for Drama and a Drama Critics Award.
1962	George Braziller publishes *The Letters of James Agee to Father Flye*.
1963	The screen version of *All the Way Home*, starring Jean Simmons and Robert Preston, premieres in Knoxville.

1965   *A Way of Seeing,* a book of photographs by Helen Levitt
        with an essay by Agee, is published by Viking.

1968   Houghton Mifflin publishes *The Collected Poems of James Agee*
        and *The Collected Short Prose of James Agee,* both edited by
        Robert Fitzgerald.

1974   *Remembering James Agee,* edited by David Madden, is
        published by Louisiana State University Press.

1979   The James Agee Film Project produces *Agee,* a film by
        Ross Spears.

1985   University of Tennessee Press publishes *James Agee: Selected
        Journalism,* edited by Paul Ashdown.

1988   Houghton Mifflin reissues *Let Us Now Praise Famous Men*
        with an introduction by John Hersey.

1992   *James Agee: Reconsiderations,* edited by Michael A. Lofaro, is
        published by University of Tennessee Press.

1996   *Agee: Selected Literary Documents,* edited by Victor A. Kramer,
        is published by Whitson Publishing Company.

1997   The second edition of *Remembering James Agee,* edited by
        David Madden and Jeffrey J. Folks, is published by University
        of Georgia Press.

2005   University of Tennessee Press publishes *James Agee
        Rediscovered,* edited by Michael A. Lofaro and Hugh Davis,
        and the second edition of *James Agee: Selected Journalism,*
        edited by Paul Ashdown.

A NOTE ON EDITORIAL MATTERS
AND METHODS

In 1988 the Special Collections Library at the University of Tennessee purchased the papers of David McDowell, publisher and editor of James Agee's posthumous novel *A Death in the Family* and former head of The James Agee Trust. In addition to documents relating to McDowell's life and publishing business, the papers contained approximately six hundred pages of mostly handwritten Agee manuscripts: three bound journals, two unpublished chapters of *A Death in the Family,* and an extensive collection of poems and drafts of poetry, particularly of "John Carter," Agee's unfinished Byronic epic. Though scholars have long been aware of some of the related manuscripts, The Agee Trust only recently granted the rights to make these new Tennessee materials and those from the Harry Ransom Humanities Research Center at the University of Texas available. The manuscripts relating to *A Death in the Family* and "John Carter" will be dealt with in subsequent works. In this volume we attempt a comprehensive treatment of the Tennessee materials and supporting manuscripts from the Texas collection and from The Agee Trust.

As this volume was assembled from original material in various states of completion from several sources, it has required a fairly elaborate editorial method. The editors' primary consideration has been producing a readable text, and we have organized the material so as to highlight what seems most relevant to general readers and scholars alike. We have also made silent corrections throughout and have listed all these and other changes in an appendix at the back of the book so that an interested scholar or reader can reconstruct the original.

The journal-notebooks are arranged chronologically. Journals 1 and 2 can be dated to 1937, and Journal 3, which consists of a loose sheet of paper that was inserted at some point into a notebook containing notes on "John Carter," provides an outline for the material in them relating to *Let Us Now Praise Famous Men.* We have followed this outline in determining the order of the first two journals. Journal 4, which, like the previous three, is owned by the University of Tennessee Special Collections

Library, dates to early 1938, and Journal 5, provided by The Agee Trust, to later that year. Journals 6 and 7, from the Ransom Center, date from spring or summer of 1940 and late 1940 or early 1941, respectively. The editors have numbered individual entries based on natural breaks and given them titles based on the first few words.

The other sections and the works within them are not arranged chronologically but by completeness and coherence and are also given working titles by the editors. For instance, in the "Essays" section, "America! Look at Your Shame!" is obviously a finished work of high quality and so is placed first. The "Nathanael West" and "Brecht's Almanac" essays are about the same length and at roughly the same stage of completion, and so follow. The notes to "The Ordinary Sufferer" come last.

In the "Poetry" section, three prose pieces related to Permit Me Voyage and "John Carter" precede several examples of automatic writing, some of which are followed by the poems generated from that particular exercise. With three exceptions from Texas, all of the poetry comes from Tennessee's Special Collections and, except for the "John Carter" material, is written on loose pages filed in no discernable order. Although it is impossible to determine the exact order of composition of the poems, they are written on paper of four different colors: brown, white, orange, and blue. The brown pages, which include most of the automatic writing, can almost certainly be dated to Agee's leave of absence from Fortune magazine and his stay in Anna Maria, Florida, from November 1935 to April 1936. The white and orange pages, though perhaps not all from Anna Maria, were also probably written in 1935–36. Poems are arranged by the color of paper, with typescripts coming first within each internal division. The one poem on blue paper, "Twitch off the tune of night," was written earlier, probably in 1933 or 1934. The Texas poems are much later, dating from around 1947.

The arrangement of the "Film" (with the exception of the radio play, which comes last) and "Notes: Fiction" and "Notes: Miscellaneous" sections follow the logic of relatively complete pieces preceding more fragmentary ones.

In the interest of establishing context, the editors have annotated Agee's references to people, places, books, movies, and events, and drawn attention to passages in this volume that have some bearing on

Agee's other works. These annotations are covered in footnotes. As Agee often refers to people by initials or nicknames, however, it has not been possible to identify everyone, and some references remain unknown or obscure. Head notes give a summary overview of the contents of each section.

Agee's miniscule handwriting is notoriously difficult to read, and his constant revisions and idiosyncratic use of punctuation—not to mention the normal deterioration of manuscripts over time—make producing a reading text in print that does not sacrifice the integrity of the original something of a challenge. With the exception of a few apostrophes inserted for clarity, we have retained Agee's punctuation, including his placing of commas outside of quotation marks and using colons and semicolons interchangeably. Briticisms are also retained. Silent corrections of misspelled words (*Delacroix* for *Delaxroix,* for instance) occur throughout the reader's text and are indicated in the appendix. Words, letters, and assigned manuscript page numbers inserted by the editors for clarity are indicated by brackets in the reader's text.

Though some passages in the manuscript are heavily revised, with a number of insertions, deletions, and transpositions, the clean version in the text does not call attention to them. In Journal 4 (entry J 4.5), for instance, beginning on manuscript page 41 and continuing to page 42, the clean text reads:

> And I would be a liar and a coward and one of your safe world if
> I should fear to say the same words of my best perception, and of
> my best intention.
>
> Performance, in which the whole fate and terror rests, is
> another matter.

Turning to the appendix of silent corrections at the end of the book, the reader will find the same passage as it appears in the manuscript:

> J 4.5
> [41–42]
>> And ~~I do not~~ {{insert from top margin: *I would be a liar and
>> a coward and one of your safe world if I should*}} fear to say
>> the same words of my best perception, and of my best
>> intention. ~~Performance is another matter.~~

> Performance, in which the whole fate and terror rests,
> is another matter.'

J 4.5 and *[41–42]* indicate the position of the passage in the text, that is, the fifth entry in Journal 4, beginning on manuscript page 41 and continuing onto page 42. (Although manuscript page numbers are indicated on the right margin in the text, they are on the left in the appendix to facilitate ease of reading. Also, Agee sometimes wrote on the backs of pages but sometimes only the fronts and sometimes skipped pages; blank pages are therefore numbered in the text and grouped together when there are large numbers of them. Where there is only one loose page, it is not numbered.) ~~Strikethrough~~ indicates words crossed out (usually with a single line) by Agee. Double braces indicate that Agee has written *I would be a liar and a coward and one of your safe world if I should* in the top margin and drawn a line from this phrase to the space in the sentence before *fear. Performance is another matter* has been written and crossed out. (All words in italics within double braces are Agee's.) The editors have also removed the single stray quotation mark after *matter* in the second paragraph.

Similarly, the clean text for the second paragraph in J 6.5 reads:

> A record (in photographs and in writing) of the daily living of three white families of cotton tenant families, with whom the authors lived:

In the appendix, the same passage looks like this:

> J 6.5
> [65]
>   ~~To whom it may concern:~~
> A record [Agee's brackets follow:] [in photographs and in writing] of the daily ~~living~~ {living} of three {white} families . . .

Since Agee has deleted *To whom it may concern,* there is no indication of it in the reader's text. Agee's brackets have been changed to parentheses to avoid confusion with other editorial insertions. Single braces indicate that *living* is rewritten above (as is usual with Agee) the deleted *living* and is to be inserted in the sentence, as is *white,* which is written above the space between *three* and *families*. Since there are no further corrections, ellipses end the excerpt in the appendix. All materials are handwritten manuscripts unless otherwise noted.

A key to the editorial system heads the appendix at the end of this volume, and more detailed explanations are included where necessary. It is our hope that this methodology will provide readers with texts of James Agee's manuscripts that are easily accessible and enjoyable, while at the same time clearly documenting, in the interest of stimulating further textual scholarship on these works, the decisions made in producing this edition.

Let Us Now Praise
Famous Men

Journals
and Drafts

These journals cover the years 1937 to late 1940 or early 1941 and contain entries concerning personal matters and drafts of parts of Let Us Now Praise Famous Men and other works. Although entries are presented in the order they were written, the material in the journals is not arranged chronologically—or according to any system other than Agee's own predilections. Journal 1 begins, for instance, with Agee's description of his train journey south in the summer of 1936 followed by notes on how to approach the experience; in entry J 1.4 he begins the narrative of the Alabama trip again, but at a different point, at the moment of receiving the assignment. He interrupts this section for a letter to his mistress, Alma Mailman, and then resumes the story a few pages later, mid-sentence. The journal continues with other letters to Alma and another attempt at introducing the sharecropper book and ends with a letter to Archibald MacLeish, an editor at Fortune, audaciously proposing that Agee and Walker Evans be given free rein to produce their own parallel version of the recently launched Henry Luce publication Life as a lesson in the possibilities of magazine photography. While there is little to be found here in the way of a straight linear development of a single narrative or idea, the portrait that emerges is that of a sensitive, if somewhat anarchic, and engaging personality.

A similar amalgamation characterizes the second journal. It is filled with notes, proposals, extended drafts on the Alabama trip, personal entries, and letters on movies, books, politics, and the loss of love. The third journal provides an outline for the material in the first two journals related to what eventually became Let Us Now Praise Famous Men, most of which was not published. Journal 4, from 1938, is the most personal and self-conscious in the volume, as Agee struggles both with the problem of literary influence and with the collapse of his marriage to Via Saunders, which was complicated by his close relationship with her family. Race, aesthetics, writer's block, Charlie Chaplin, and the interpretation of dreams are among the subjects addressed in Journal 5. Journals 6 and 7 include notes and long drafts of recognizable passages from Let Us Now Praise Famous Men, as well as what is probably Agee's first extended movie review. For readers interested in the genesis of Let Us Now Praise Famous Men, these journals are an invaluable resource; more generally, they provide a fascinating window into the life and mind of an artist at a critical time in his creative development.

For more information on Agee during the time of the composition of these journals and the other works published here, please see "The Life and Times of James Agee" in the introductory section of this volume.

JOURNAL 1

[J 1.1: *LUNPFM* Draft:
"It is hard to know whether or not to skip the train"]

It is hard to know whether or not to skip the train. We could simply say that it did all the things Thomas Wolfe says a train does, and let it go at that. Wolfe has pretty thoroughly covered the subject, and whatever you may think of him or say against him, and much of it may be true, it will do none of you any harm to remember that Wolfe is a greater writer than a lot of neater writers ever will be.

My present trouble is, that I am as badly a victim of train-love as Wolfe is or anyone else. Any given trip on a train, or the memory or thought of any given trip, gets me excited. Am I then to lay off the subject simply because it has already been handled, and out of an underhanded fear of comparison? Or am I, thanks to similar prides and fear, going to try to shoot the works. I think not and I hope neither. But I will try to write a little about this train trip.

All right. This was the long sort of train that is used to go long distances up and down or across the face of a continent. It went at a good, high, steady speed and

it did not make all the stops. It was handled by an engineer, a fireman, and a train crew whose names I do not know, but they were, as I was not, parts of this creature, and every quarter of a mile of the trip was familiar to them in idioms of their own. I had no part in their life or in the life of the train, and they had no part in mine. I was just one of several hundred passengers. I had no part in their lives either, nor did they have any in mine; and we were all being rapidly, loudly and impersonally taken from one place to another, not in a big electric leap but over a certain number of miles and inches of contiguous land which, again, lay out all around us in the terms not of ours nor of the train's but of its own life and, shallowly grown up upon it as a summer's crop, the city and town and country life of the people who lived on it. The great dominant in this trip was motion and the noise and look and feeling and odor of motion special to a train as distinguished from all other forms

of transport and special moreover, to this sort of continent-eating train
and, in fact, to

[3]

this particular train, starting in summer at dusk, going through the night
and the next day, on this particular trip, carrying these particular people
to their particular destinations on their several particular divergent
sometimes deducible never truly determinable errands, of which mine
was one, the only one I knew of, the one I cared most for. This motion
and its manifestations were sustained a long way beyond the power of
the most heroic art; and every slowing and every stop partook much
more of motion than of stasis, just as a silence in music partakes very
powerfully of sound, and enhances it.

Riding one train, or thinking of it, one's perceptions and images
are likely to multiply and diverge even more than normally. I shan't pretend to give all of mine; only a few.

One was this.

A train is large at the head; slender and whiplike in all its length. This
train was going South. It was into the South that it was taking me. I
was born there, and much more than loved that country, and now, a
young man, with five senses and a mind, with

[4]

hunger, and curiosity, and some passionate and some dispassionate feelings and ideas about earth and heaven, I was going down there again to
see and understand what I might be able to. My thoughts and my excitement were for any detail of the south for its own sake and on its own
merits, but also, or, rather, through an extension of that very fact, and
not so pretentiously as may seem but earnestly, what I was caring for,
and what I was being drawn into a peculiarly good opportunity to try to
see, was the farthest and commonest, most unanswerable questions of
human and earthly and universal destiny, human art, human life. What
lay ahead of me was in a sense familiar to me, for my childhood had
been spent in it and half my ancestry was of the very depths of it; but
what lay ahead was also mysterious to me, in its own terms and in those
terms by which the mere next hour of any part of a life is mysterious.
And what I was seeing and thinking of this train, in one of its aspects,
was this.

In all the ways in which the South is peculiar to itself and distinct from all else it lay out there ahead of me faintly shining in the night, a huge,

[5]

sensitive, globular, amorphous, only faintly realized female cell, towards which in determined speed, winding and gliding upon rails as upon the always fortuitous and perfect and beautiful preshaping predestination (like the music that remains wound up in silence to be played beyond the slow eating of the needle into the disk) carrying my little mind and its hungers and intentions, this sperm-shaped, strong-headed, infinitesimal train was traveling to pierce and, in my infinitesimal yet absolute terms, to fertilize.

This idea of the train (like all such) was come at swiftly and simply, rather more like a movie image than anything else, with the added advantage, which a movie lacks, of my complete physical and mental involvement in the image; and with each recurrence (each being also in a light peculiar to it and different from the others) it brought the complete satisfaction of a poetic image, or more accurately of the memory of a face or a breast or a sweetness of smiling which you love, the form of voice, the reaction to a situation or idea, of a good friend.

Then there were other ways.

[6]

The extreme narrowness of a train's (as of any human) journey and experience. This train is running on rails which are set a strict, small number of feet apart. They are inch by inch so continuous a thousand miles that you could only rarely insert a razorblade between their joints. They are lifted and drooped and twisted sometimes to the shape of the land, sometimes they sliver and sometimes even they bore their way straight through this shape; they are almost inconceivably narrow and rigorous and frail upon the scope of the land; they are what a train runs on. From their blunt beginning-ending under the great shadows of the Pennsylvania Station they project their long evolvement and continuance of curves, lifts, falls and straightaways in one great suspension whose support is not land but their own personality and special function, out over, bridging, a gulf of land whose speed, purpose, existence is otherwise from their own; and it is out onto and along the unfurlings

over space of this strict frailness and musical, riverlike delicacy of pre-
destined steel that at high speed and with daring hoots and roars

[7]

the confident train sinuously dashes, all but imperceptibly crawls, on the
greatness of the land, between the remote stars, the intense sharp glands,
of the cities. I would lay out the course of these rails like a heroic line of
plainsong, and swarming upon the exactitudes of its memory, bring the
wavelike yet likewise narrow roaring of the train.

Or I am a reeking and red clay, and huge, field, and there is a rumor
of iron at my horizon and the rumor swells and the dot enlarges and
squares up real with a round eye at middle and racketing more giganti-
cally reams, rants, blinds, brains, the lengths of its great speeding weight
upon me, while, beneath each speeding wheel, the butt-ends of ties yield
into cinder clay and the clay trackside weeds shudder, like a sped-up
movie shot and with a reduction of noise as sudden as the cracking of a
whip the last end of the last car flashes over and brained, bruised, like the
running of distraught ants when the hill has left my hill I recollect and,
in the now diminishment and now extinction of the train I reassemble,
restore, myself into the silence, the weight and composture of

[8]

clay, the integrity, of my own terms, scarcely tickled, crept merely, by a
lousage of crops. Miles down the line the vanished whistle blows, and I
am disturbed only as a dog is disturbed by memories in a dream, and there
are other parts of me which feel none even of this gentle disturbance but
who, a child awake in bed under the night or a sad human being who has
never extricated himself from the first elementary traps of circumstance,
the bondages of place and of people, are at the same time increased and
comforted in their wonder and in their sorrow; for the whistling of a train
in the depth of the night surpasses every effort of music, and, above all,
after the preparation of the two long, lifted notes and the short note, in
the lingering, softening, mournfully land-caressing falling and failure of
the iron yet streamlike last note, is one of the bravest, noblest and most
lonesome sounds that can ever have found expression.

[9]

This train, traveling its narrowness on the face of the earth in the
night in all its noises, the shaded, peopled and sleeping earth opening

before it like a flower and flowing, fleeting, fainting past, drawn down to little and lost, lost, out of the streaming of its speed and out of its noises gives forth, at intervals, a spontaneous yet classic statement of the situation and of its feelings, like the speculations of Catholics, or the phrase which a negro will sing over and over again; and this statement, this lyric song, this prayer, this bursting of steam, this griever, this solacer, so wise, sad, rough, above all brave twice over, though in foreknowledge of its ending, sinks in its ending note out of all speech, for speech no longer can express what its wisdom and its bravery have shown it, and its close is less a statement, or a question, than the meaning of a mother over her weeping child, or the subdued noises a negro or a poet may make when he sees standing all around him and upon all creatures and all the earth more wonder and deep trouble than the earth, his kind or he can bear and yet who is bearing them: something of the whole, real, shape and nature and unrelentment

[10]

of the human condition and the situation of the earth in nature and of nature, seen, faced, borne: and yet this is nothing but the noise a dutiful and unconscious train makes in the course of its hurry, and you hear the metal noises, its wheels and its hurry even though these lie far beyond your actual ability to hear, and it is these things which are beautiful about the whistling of a train and which help to give it its greatness.

[J 1.2: *LUNPFM* Draft and Notes: "This was first one trip, not like any other"]

This was first one trip, not like any other. By this time I had been on many trains and many trips, so there was nothing new to me about it; a basic feeling was one of being back in the old rut.

In this sort of pleasure and excitement, I must try & set up the state of mind.

It is calm, in a sense, and relatively light and agile. Your mind and senses are working hard, clear, and very seriously, yet their vigilance is not solemn but is a vigilance similar to that a young man walking a street has for the girls he sees: a vigilance which checks on everything immediately.

[11]

There is a certain, definite amount of narcissism in it. A sense of comedy. A thing which Hemingway has expressed and which comes under the influence of Hemingway. A certain cheapness about it if you like, but not by any means so cheap as you may think; for it is the avid, watchful, trained, economical eye partly of the artist and partly of the human being, more interested, in the course of its travels, in technic than in emotions. It is likely to be capable of developing something not far short of a sense of glory out of so simple an ache as sitting in a train or walking around a new or a once familiar city, or going in and ordering a drink, or reading a back number of Judge[1] in a club car, or acting in some way true to its present special and false to its essential situation. Yes it is certainly liable to streaks of smugness. For a certain amount of it depends on self-consciousness and on self-confidence. The satisfactory feeling you sometimes get of your body in your clothes, your way of walking, watching and speaking; a time when you trust yourself and your analysis; a state of mind which self-mistrust destroys sometimes for a worse and sometimes for a better. It is a state of mind which can be sustained through many that are "better" than it is; for there is much that is serious and solid about it.

[12]

All this started in New York. It took me suddenly by train to Chattanooga; by car south into Alabama, round and round and round, becoming more and more serious.

————

This is among other things a straight narrative. But it is not just a narrative, and is bound to break the rules of narrative time and again to give an account of things for their own sake.

An accounting of the train for instance in no way advances the narrative and indeed obstructs it. By mere tricks the narrative could be given suspense: by lack of them it would sag. It will sag I think, for I am here more against tricks than for them.

————

1. *Judge* magazine was founded in 1881 by a group of artists who defected from *Punch,* its closest rival, and featured timely satire and high-quality drawings. *Judge* folded in 1947.

I am telling it, much of it, from at least two planes at once. As it was when it happened: as it is now, thinking of it. This is liable to confuse. It was a chance of giving musical thickness; and it happens to be just that much nearer than the literal truth. Only by great skill in art could the latter result instead of the former. And entirely aside from my lack of such skill I don't at all know that I want to use it here.

Yet again, I do want to tell the "truth." And the truth was, that none of these things sagged

[13]

or even confused each other; nor do they in my memory; but were continuously intense, exciting, full of suspense. So perhaps by every possible trick I should try to make them so here.

The picaresque state of mind: always intensified by situation.

This can so easily slacken into a dogged telling of things in the past because they happened.

A thing past is drawn almost immediately into a distance where it reappears all at once, economically, in the form of images and movements or odors or tastes: and these are as valid a part of the truth as the thing was in the extension of its present. As for instance: the tunnel image of the train. And: the train entering Bristol in full dawn. And for that matter, actual detail, such as the drinks in the diner; getting off at Washington to phone Walker.[2] Breakfast with Holt.[3] Stopping in Knoxville. The southern air of the train & passengers. The summer heat.

There is a way of handling this in which its varieties and contradictions are rich direct and understandable and in which all their talk would be needless; the

[14]

thing would be explaining itself.

Some use of third person.

Everything is extremely clear to me as images, incidents, essences.

The French word for perfume is wisely chosen, and is I think characteristic of the French.

---

2. Walker Evans (1903–1975), American photographer with whom Agee collaborated on *Let Us Now Praise Famous Men*.

3. Thad Holt was the Alabama state director of the Works Progress Administration. Holt is very likely "Harmon" in *Let Us Now Praise Famous Men*. See J 1.6.

What I am interested in is infinitely less myself than what by chance I saw. Such as the band concert in Chattanooga. And yet that requires— how much?—my presence and my feeling of amusement, joy and shy- ness. Espionage. Like watching lovemaking through a window, was nearly everything we did.

The constant presence of this one person I or he and of his feelings & of what he saw is bound to be maddeningly tiresome to a reader and even to me, writing it. This tiresomeness isn't true to the fact for my constant presence was to me neither tiresome nor necessarily exciting. The device is or should be chiefly the constant presence of a thinking & feeling camera. How can such a device be worked. I did not feel smug or self-interested: I was too busy

[15]

and too interested in what I saw.

What I saw was so damned good at all times.

The way I saw it and the way I felt is just as significant as it is, too. It would be significant if I were God or a genius. It is significant also in that I was simply & exactly what I was.

[J 1.3: *LUNPFM* Notes: "list places & incidents largely"]

list places & incidents largely, much longer than I have.

———

In recall, an incident or place can return whole immediately which as it happened took time. It returns independent of you & your feelings at the time it happened. It is already condensed & digested into some- thing like the difference between art & actual occurrence. It moves you not to break it down into what actually happened but to give it even more edge.

———

In a sense & on an important matter I am a schizoid. The strong ten- dencies toward the poetic, musical, religious, "sublime" on one side; on the other, watchful, somewhat hardboiled, light, narcissistic. In recall & the attempt to write I tend strongly toward the former, which falsi- fies the latter.

In much of this trip, above all its 1st sections, the basic state of mind was the latter.

This and the technique for handling it is almost the most important

[16]

thing I have to work out if I am to get anywhere with writing this.

The basic tone must be this but it must be transparent and thus capable of every variation & analysis needed.

[17]

[J 1.4: *LUNPFM* Draft:
"We got back from the south late in May"]

We got back from the south late in May, after seven months leave. We had spent most of that time in one place on the west coast of Florida, a week in New Orleans, a last month with some old friend of mine at the school I used to go to in Tennessee.[4] I mention these places because we needed money again now, so I reported immediately at Fortune.

I had left there with the understanding I might come back full time as before or might, if I progressed, try working on occasional stories on a wordage rather than a salary basis. Eric[5] asked me which I preferred by now and I said I wanted to try to occasional.

They set me back to work on a piece on State Fairs which in an American Scene phase I had suggested two years before, and which I had done some work on the summer before, and which had been killed. I now no longer felt any enthusiasm for it and so I was glad enough when three or four days later it was once again killed, though I knew the chances were fair I would get something that would be less fun and bring me less money.

For the time being I was assigned a straight utility piece, a blurby-like caption to stand in beside a Gerlach color spread

---

4. From November 1935 to April 1936 Agee and his first wife, Olivia (Via) Saunders Agee, vacationed in Anna Maria, Florida, spending a few days in New Orleans and stopping at Agee's alma mater, St. Andrew's School, near Sewanee, Tennessee, to visit Father James Flye before returning to New York. See N 20, note 34.

5. Eric Hodgins (1899–1971), who replaced Ralph Ingersoll as managing editor of *Fortune* in 1935 and served in that capacity until 1937, gave Agee the Alabama sharecropper assignment that became *Let Us Now Praise Famous Men* and probably killed the article he produced on it.

[18]

on jewels⁶ which in my opinion stank. So did my caption: very routine commercial-poetic prose. It wasn't all that hard work but it took and wasted enough time not to be by any means worth the forty dollars that was the best it could bring in. So I didn't mind; but I hoped for a better break on the next assignment.

Along about the twentieth of June I got it, by all odds the best assignment I have ever had, and the only one I have a hundred per cent worked to do. I was asked if I wanted to take on a family piece on sharecroppers, for the September or October issue, depending some on schedules, which weren't yet crystallized, and some on how much time it would take to research and write it. Eric thought it could be a swell piece and that I could have more fun out of it than out of anything since the TVA stories.⁷ That was putting it mildly so far as I was concerned.

It won't be possible to make them all clear, for such things depend on what your whole life has been, but I had better try to lay down some of the reasons why this job appealed to me so much.

For me, I love to travel around in a car anyway; everything to do with that and with seeing new cities and new country and people or things and places of a kind I have seen before or that I have[n't] seen before. Everyone who is interested in an

[19]

art or in living is bound to be seeing all he can anyway, but as a rule a lot of your time has to be spent earning a living and your whole apparatus gets dulled in the process, and it is seldom that you get paid for doing what you most want to do, and the chance is likely to open up your brain and your senses, your sense of pleasure, your sense of "reality", as wide as they every get.

Also, I was born in the south. I spent my first fifteen years about equally divided between a Tennessee city and Tennessee mountains, and since then I had lived north and had seen the south very little, not at all until two years before. In a limited, entirely unstudied way I knew

6. "Jewel Spread," *Fortune* 14 (August 1936): 70. Photographs by Arthur Gerlach.

7. "The Project Is Important," *Fortune* 8 (October 1933): 81–97 (rpt.in Ashdown, 1–18); "T. V. A.," *Fortune* 11 (May 1935): 93–98, 140–53 (rpt.in Ashdown, 63–96).

a good deal about the south in terms of some of its parts, and I a great deal more than loved this country.

My father was of mountain people who were tenant farmers. My mother was Michigan born, raised in the south; she was of middle-class, somewhat cultivated, small capitalists. My father died when I was six and though I spent some lucky years in a mountain school most of my life had been middle-class. I have always more resented this fact than not, and have to a degree felt cheated and irreparably crippled of half or more than half of what I am.

I am not quite such a fool as to think anything can ever

[20]

really be "done" about this sort of thing; but here was about the most that could be done.

Also I am in any case a great deal more a communist than not. Most of the things I felt about the assignment on this score must be self-evident.

Also, though I knew the south, the Tennessee mountain-city-valley aspects of it, I knew little or nothing about the cotton country, beyond a rough idea of the look of it and an even sketchier idea of just what the situation was there, beyond what I had got out of Tobacco Road, some passages in Faulkner, and a few meetings of the Committee for the Defense of Southern Workers,[8] the purpose of which, raising money, was all right enough, but which leaned pretty tiresomely on such words as terrorism and fascism and which by the cheap uses of the word had already made me unable to hear, say or think "sharecropper" without a certain amount of nausea.

The winter before, I had started a novel and had sketched a play and pieces of a couple of movies on the subject, projecting all I could from the mountain stuff I knew, and had given them up in self-disgust.

[21]

Here was a chance to see more than I otherwise could have short of learning how to be of use as an organizer, a thing I had considered but never done anything about.

---

8. The Committee for the Defense of Southern Workers was an auxiliary of the International Labor Defense of the Communist Party later absorbed into the League for Southern Labor. See J 1.6, note 18.

Also, I was intensely interested to learn all I could about the unions, especially the straight communist Sharecropper's Union;⁹ and here was my chance on that, too. I knew I could get help and could get all this stuff. I intended to research and write three pieces: the first on the family, the second a generalized piece, a big fatassed analysis of the situation and of cotton economics and of all Governmental efforts to Do Something about It, which latter I was quite sure could beautifully hang themselves in their own rope; and the third a straight union piece, starting with inch-by-inch process of a couple of organizers opening up new territory, leading that on through night-riding et cetera, and mushrooming it into a history of both unions.

So an hour later I submitted the following memo.

QUOTE.

[22]

The next few days were spent reading up on it, shooting off my mouth about it, and trying to locate Walker Evans and Bob Smith and Beth Mitchell.¹⁰

It will be worthwhile making a note of this:

For reasons I have tried to make clear, all of which of course, when I was offered the story, opened up full force and simultaneously, like a well-prepared-for, struck chord, I was within a few seconds as shifted in state of mind as I might have been if I had changed personalities. Every sense cleared about three hundred per cent and stood up on its hind legs waving its feelers. My mind became capable of running all directions at once and of synchronizing its findings; it became at the same time hard and capable of analysis and of poetry. And like the release of a spring or the opening of a sluice I became owner of a kind of energy I am other-

---

9. The Communist-backed Sharecroppers Union (also known as the Share Croppers' Union) was founded on August 6, 1931, in Tallapoosa County, Alabama, by former members of the all-black Croppers' and Farm Workers' Union, which had dissolved after a series of white vigilante attacks and the arrest of several dozen of its members.

10. Smith and Mitchell have not yet been identified; the names are possibly Communist Party pseudonyms.

wise capable of only in drinking, driving or love, and of a kind of self-confidence I am almost never capable of under any circumstances. A translation, I suppose, from a mildly depressive into a strongly manic yet semi-controllable state. Not very controllable, except in a fully matured man, which I was not. It was centrifugal, and not to be restricted to my work. With a good deal of a sense of parody I went through a lot of the mannerisms of the big [continued on manuscript page 27]

[23]

[J 1.5: Letter to Alma Mailman]

Alma.[11] This is just to tell you the usual. How much I love you. I am trying tonight, for few reasons I have any respect for, to exercise the word was going to be self control. At that juncture though, the cat knocked a vase off the table, waking up Via[12] in a howling rage against him and, after the noise & discussion of my wiping up after the brat, putting water back in the vase &c, putting self-control out of the question. The chances are slender you would be in or awake now; it is 12.40; after so depriving you of sleep for 2 nights I won't quite have the brass to try to see you again anyway—i.e. tonight—and as I've said it is impossible anyhow. So now I am just writing to relieve my mind, such as it is. I would so much wish to be seeing you and talking with you and better yet lying quiet as we were last night.

[24]

My sweetest Alma don't you know how far beyond doubt and reversal this is? Can you be as beautiful and kind to me as you are and have these doubts? Writing you is no damn good. I am so full of thoughts and remembrances of you and nothing but you is good now. All I want to write you I couldn't even say most of for it is all nothing but a list of things

---

11. Alma Ruth Mailman (1912–1988), Agee's second wife. Agee met Alma shortly before his marriage to Via Saunders at the Saunders residence in Clinton, New York, in 1933. Agee and Alma began having an affair in 1937 and were married December 6, 1938, after living together for almost a year in Frenchtown, New Jersey.

12. Via Sauders Agee, Agee's first wife. Via and Agee were married January 28, 1933, and divorced in November 1938.

which are you yourself and how fine in all ways you are to me, and this would embarrass you and also in course of time bore you to hell with the very thought of me. It's in terms of all of your body and mind and way of being, and all of that goes into details which would take me the rest of the week just to list. Why the hell do I write you. I can never mail it so you would get it in the morning, and by afternoon I hope so to see you myself. Also I fear your reactions and thoughts, both to a letter and on their own, without a letter. I wonder Alma whether you miss me at all. I do you, so much that it seems literally impossible now to be going to sleep without you. It may be odd to you that I am

[25]

not at present as you asked me if I was, sick of the sight of you. Don't make me laugh. Maybe theoretically it is odd and maybe not but in any case I'm far from sick of the sight of you. What I want is no time of day or night away from you. Are you sick of sight of me though, Alma. Sweetest love you were not last night when you might have been. Do you think of me dear? I mean am I at all on your mind, do you at all think of me with any happiness and love or affection, during a day, and want at all to see me? Are you ever glad at all, when the BUZZER makes its snotty sound, in thinking it may be me, or do you always think O Christ, <u>that</u> again. Two nights ago you said a thing that made me very happy—that you love to see me. I know you meant it my darling but you may of course and even must only have meant it at the time. Are you really happy to see me? My sweet heart I <u>do</u> know how bound you are to feel another side of it, don't think I don't, but it means so much to me that you do at all love me. The hell with this letterwriting. I want to see you. I will not even

[26]

try to see you tonight. Alma my dear, sweet love I hate this thought of your lying there, all that is so dear to me, alone, that I will not be near tonight except in my thoughts that you will know nothing of. I can't tell you how much I hope and count on seeing you tomorrow night, Friday night, and if not then, then Saturday, or Saturday too. I want so much to spend a day with you peacefully, and a day and a night and a week and of course I mean my life, but I retain just sense enough to know that is impossible (or is it?), which makes it even more needful to see you now. Bless you heart, and mind and body. Goodnight.

Jim.

Whether you like it or not I can't help, you are like a bride to me and that in my feelings is literally what you are to me.

[27]

[J 1.6: *LUNPFM* Draft: "We got back," cont.]

[continued from manuscript page 22] executive or the stage newspaper man, smacking down names, memos, new ideas, recommendations, phone numbers a dozen a minute and phoning half a dozen people at once and reading up background by day, sleeping about four hours a night, drinking much more than usual with much less than the usual effect, and as full of the wish and practice of letting everybody I like at all about it as a young man gets who is pretty crazily in love and who has lost every sense of the value of conservation of energy and of pessimism. There was incorporated in this a fairly strong current of narcissism: business of wearing hat at angle, throwing feet around on desk, and feeling in general like a combination of Ernest Hemingway and Sergei Eisenstein.[13] My bladder was overstimulated and it was necessary on an average of three times to the hour to leave my desk and drain it, or to look up and down the corridors for a friend who wanted to drink, take a cup of coffee, or talk, or just to get out of my office and wander in a walk that was a stiff, only slightly muted truck-style dance, snapping the four fingers of each hand rapidly against the palm over and over again, or spreading my fingers so wide and straight that the stretched skin burned on the bone, sculpturally conscious of and enjoying, the feeling of the trunk of my body lifted above my legs, the face held-in a little at all times, and once in a while breaking loose into a grin I could

---

13. Innovative Soviet film director (1898–1948).

[28]

not control. Every girl in the office was suddenly attractive to me. I felt capable of proliferating the face of the earth and as if that would be a very sound idea if there were a little more time.

I was specially anxious to locate Beth Mitchell because she is a party member whose work is in the South and who for a while if I remembered rightly had worked with the union in Tallapoosa County Alabama.[14] In any case she could tell me who to see.

Bob Smith was a friend of hers, a communist too, a New York newspaper man. He had never been south but had organized the Defense Comm. [and] could and I felt would put me onto some people too.

Walker Evans, the photographer I mentioned in the memo, was in my opinion the best photographer alive. He had for the past year been traveling on the government payroll, making most of the time the pictures he wanted to make. Where he was now neither I nor his sister[15] in Washington nor Ben Shahn[16] in New York, with whom he shared an apartment, had any idea of, and this got me very worried, for I had no wish to be let in for a stranger who would turn up a lot of Dramatic shots

[29]

and a lot of slick posed candids, and this unless I could locate Walker was bound to happen.

Bob Smith thought it could be good and was anxious that I wait over into the next week when Beth and a number of other more directly concerned people would be up for the Communist convention. There was no telling about this in advance, though: Fortune had already made Arrangements with Thad Holt[17] and the idea was that I should if possible go down with him from Washington or in any case meet him South and be under his guidance and power of contact. So when I was to start was to me a matter of unknown chance.

---

14. Tallapoosa County, the scene of several violent episodes at Camp Hill in 1931, was the organizing base of the Sharecroppers Union. See J 1.4, note 8.

15. Jane Beach Evans Brewer (1902–1964).

16. Ben Shahn (1898–1969), Lithuanian-born American social realist artist and photographer, who, like Walker Evans, worked for the Farm Security Administration.

17. See J 1.2, note 2.

One evening I went to a big stink of the League for Southern Labor[18] in an Italian restaurant on 13th street. The Defense Committee had been absorbed into this organization while I was South, so there were a good many familiar faces, chiefly of sincere enough young women who got a thrill out of hearing an imported negro tell how he had been beaten up and burned with matches and out of shaking his hand, which badly embarrassed him. This was an annual dinner at $4.25 a plate. The meal alone lasted three hours. I got there after the end of it

[30]

when they had moved upstairs to collect money. Not much came of that, either. Though more of these people were moderately poor than really poor, or rich, or well-to-do, I felt as I saw them smiling with sweet unselfconsciousness through the ten and five and two-dollar phases of appeal, and beginning dutifully to rustle in their pouches when it got down to mention of a dollar, that quite a number of these bitches were here for the ride.

This was the night of the Louis-Schmeling fight[19] and about sixty per cent of those present were not such utter frauds but what they tuned in and kept quiet and listened, all of course in perfect confidence of the result. A dozen or so of them were negroes and it was sad, sickening and complex to see what was happening to them as the rounds wore on; and it was a good deal of fun, of a disgusting sort, to watch the eyes of certain of the negrophiles. It was God knows a shocking fight.

After that there was some singing, and in this context there was something unfortunate about the way it was staged. I kept thinking of children being cheered up and of the band playing Nearer My God to Thee as the Titanic foundered.

A serious, rather complacent pale young Jew with a

---

18. The League for Southern Labor, formed in 1935 in Chapel Hill, North Carolina, by a group of intellectuals including playwright Paul Green and historian C. Vann Woodward, later became the Southern Committee for People's Rights. The New York chapter of the SCRP had approximately one hundred members, including Thomas Wolfe.

19. On June 19, 1936, German boxer Max Schmeling knocked out Joe Louis, who was at the time undefeated, in the twelfth round in New York.

[31]

fair baritone that was stale with overtraining led off with a number
called So They Burn Babies in Alabama. That was all there was to it,
for that matter: They burn babies in Alabama, news item. This hot tip
was passed in the dialect affected by the sort of whites who call Negroes
darkies. The music was roughly an amalgam of folk at fourth remove
and of Schonberg,[20] with lots of cultivated discords in the accompani-
ment and a grand-pause after which the baritone let ding fortissimo on
some dialect word with political coloration, I forget just what.

Nearly everyone seemed to be a good deal cheered up. Louis might
lose but they are still burning babies in Alabama. Pippa Passes[21] out quietly by the rear.

After this some mimeographs were passed around and once again
the Hebe led in song.

It had been some screaming jackass's idea that since this was a gathering less of real left wingers than of lowneck liberals the tactful thing
to sing would be the marching song of the Farmer Labor Party.[22] I will
say in favor of plenty there who had nothing else visible to recommend
them beyond,

[32]

if you wish, bedroom eyes which dissatisfaction with had given a class
angle and reasonably nice pairs of tits that needed manhandling, that
they were just a shade to[o] embarrassed to take hearty part in this song.
I wish I had the words and tune. Bob Smith, who was supposed to be
running this show, kept muttering sing the International,[23] fuck you,
sing the International, and quietly chanting shit, shit, shit to the tune.

After that the singing broke up. There was wine and beer. It was
here now that I remember it that Bob gave me the Tarrant City[24] address.
We went to a bar and had two more drinks and I went home.

---

20. Arnold Schönberg (1874–1951), Austro-Hungarian-born composer.

21. A reference to Robert Browning's dramatic poem *Pippa Passes,* which contains the lines "God's in his heaven— / All's right with the world."

22. The Farmer Labor Party was founded in 1920. Broadly socialist, the party
fielded presidential candidates in 1920, 1928, and 1932, but never garnered significant support nationally.

23. "The *Internationale,*" the anthem of the socialist working class.

24. Tarrant City, Alabama, an industrial suburb of Birmingham, was a center
of Communist organizing in the state in the 1930s.

When all was said and done this 5-hour plethora of tortoni and political bellyrubbing cleared about twenty-nine dollars in at best indirect behalf of 9 million people who have never eaten fresh meat.

They burn babies in Alabama so you bitches can sit around and sniff the bacon. A couple of grosses of dildoes and a few hard kicks in the ass would reduce the revolutionary movement to something more like its proper size.

[33]

A natural act done in an unnatural world, has a certain unnaturalness forced upon it (and this must be accepted as part of the bargain) but is in any case more natural than capitulation to the unnatural.

[34]

[35]

[J 1.7: *LUNPFM* Notes: "On the porch"]

On the porch.

We got back to town late in May.
    the winter before.
    the shape in the mind.
    home.   friends.   back to work.

[36]

[37]

[J 1.8: Letter to Alma Mailman]

Wednesday night.

Well my sweet friend it is only twelve hours since I left you and already (in fact, every minute since I saw you go in the door) the yeast is working. Lying still this afternoon late, when everything relaxed into place and perspective, I saw plain as glass how simple and harmless the whole thing was and what fools we had been in our respective ways— how by that foolishness we had complicated it and ourselves beyond any hope of understanding any of it except the deadness and despair our foolishness had created out of it. Each in our own way, we were making the mistake of feeling it was significant that we had no feelings.

The minute we put ourselves where our attention might be drawn from ourselves (Nick's),[25] things cleaned up very far. Oh, sure,

[38]

a dozen or hundred things come into it dear; and we need better understanding as we need God himself; but let's skip it. Because of our stupidity and the nervous complexity we had got ourselves into, every current in us was capable of short circuiting every other, and the burn and stench were awful. It became much too complicated for some minds to bother with too closely; for it could still entangle. When in quiet joy and certainty how clear and simple it was, I felt impulse to write you of it this afternoon, I made that mistake of bothering too closely, and got half entangled again. There is a streak of melancholia and of dead inept despair in me that can ruin me, and I run along its edge in any such complication. Ruth,[26] at the worst

[39]

we feel, the most dead, or the most angry, or the most cold, in God's name let us be kind, and compassionate, and fully ready to be open toward each other, whenever it is clear the other needs it. We must be these things even when we have to make a fight in ourselves to be them.

And let us be more mature; and again, _try_ toward maturity. _Not_ to regret and _not_ to worry nor assign it great power of meaning over feelings we lack when we lack them (_every_ time we have managed to relax out of this, we have come through into clean, plain sense); and if we _are_ silent in a way that troubles either of us, or if in any other way one of us is troubled, and the other guarded, then plain patience and openness and kindness. At our worst of all we are yet two living human beings, and at that worst we

[40]

are each in pain, acute or stony; and we must break through whatever the obstructions are, and look straight in each other's eyes, and know this clearness and kindness until it possesses us once more. Alma, my lovely Ruth, pray for me dear, and for our life. You are the most beautiful in creation, to me. God be in your beauty tenderly through this night.

---

25. Nick's Tavern, a jazz club in Greenwich Village.
26. I.e., Alma.

I must see you soon—not for long, but to know we have kindness and the love that is in kindness toward each other.

Probably I should not send this. I have a feeling that communication from me will vitiate your own recharging process. Good night anyway.

[41]

Sweetheart: NOTHING to say. I'm nearly sure I won't send this: I think maybe that a lack of these notes might help to sharpen your own appetite to something nearer mine—also that sending them may dull it. Also that sooner or later, for all we can do, our appetite will become less eager and likewise my need to speak to you by note when I can't otherwise, & that time will be better if I haven't too badly abused my need at present—just as it will be both better and far later if we continue to take care to see each other less often that we want to. To hell with that. One more hour's desperate fight with Via. God damned if I will go into it. It is both and neither of our faults: mine much more, if anyone's, stemming from the fact that we are married and that I am essentially dead against the marriage: which, for that mater, is not my fault either. Her ability to exaggerate and distort things I try my damnedest to tell her honestly, drives me nuts. We are too many ways different to each other to ever

[42]

manage to live together without some choice between dishonesty & friction—& too much of either to make life worth the trouble except conceivably on her account, and, not being in love with her, and at present shaky with desperateness after bathing with her, her account doesn't cut whatever ice it ought as against mine. Sorry for this. It is full of self-pity. I said I had nothing to write you of. I meant by that how much I love you: and can't say a tenth I'd wish I could. I've got to tell you Alma. In your dear face and eyes I see the person sweetest and most beloved to me on earth, beyond any power to be reasonable about it, and <u>know</u> that all our lives are bound together, that you are the person I want in all my life to be near to as to no one else. It is the strength of this feeling that makes me so unable to write you and so foolish when I see you, & is what I mean when I say that I feel

[43]

drastic, or that I wish we were married. I have got to tell you the whole of this feeling, and can't, because it goes beyond anything I can say. It

is the same I mean when I say, how I wish I could <u>do</u> something for you.
I look at you in a full sense of your beauty and dearness to me and in a
keen sense of living and death, and know how your lovely face and
being and body belong in not just the present but all of my life. Yet I
know, this is a feeling anyone is sure to have in love; and that love can
very possibly harm itself and drain away, leaving nothing of it but regret
or pity. God defend us. There is <u>everything</u> we must watch with
patience, honesty, and all possible intelligence, and care for each other,
and see what comes of it. Meantime I know so closely and well, even
in thought, in many ways and how dearly I love you. That is more joy
to me than I can tell you: and that we should be one thing with each
other all the rest of our lives seems

[44]

natural and inevitable, and sweet to me, beyond any boundaries of
more Common sense. I know how we must only watch and take care
my darling. But I had to try to tell you this other, that has nothing to
do with taking care. Alma if I threw aside all that second thought and
simply followed the impulse I feel so strongly, I would by now have
begun a child in you, because I love you so much. (That again is assuming you could wish it, which I have no reason to assume & do not
assume or dream of; I'm only again telling what I feel.) Good night.
God bless you always.

Jim

[45]

[J 1.9: Letter to Alma Mailman]

Ruth: with control, I keep emotional words out of this. I enclose
a letter. If you feel that reading it will at all dilute any such feelings of
fondness or aliveness for me or you may begin to have, please postpone
reading it. There's nothing in it that necessarily would: simply the
sound of my own voice, which I wince to think of.

Also I will soon <u>have</u> to know, what feelings you have or haven't
towards me, simply as something to go on. I may have to before you
get this. Forgive me my trespasses.

Oh, <u>love</u> me, Alma, all you can, stay with me, know we are bound in <u>all</u> together, most seriously—you are dearer to me than my life. I know, because in thought of losing you I actively and passionately do not want to live.

[46]

[47]

[J 1.10: *LUNPFM* Draft: Introduction]

The following is a short record of the lives of three families of cotton tenants. They live on Mills Hill, about seven miles from Moundville,[27] in Hale County, in west central Alabama, in the United States, in the fourth decade of the twentieth century. They represent nine million other human beings, white or black, who are cotton tenants in similar houses, wearing similar clothes, eating similar food, working in similar fields, responsible to similar landlords, living similar lives, and dying similar deaths, all over a stretch of land sixteen hundred miles wide and three hundred miles deep. And they have much more than they lack in common with

[48]

[49]

all but a very negligible fraction of the two billion human beings who at present carry human existence on the surface of this planet.

They are therefore not News; unless the poverty and the deprivation and the distortion which makes up human life itself is News. And they are not easily to be helped. Not by fatherly landlords, nor by liberal county agents, nor by state and national schemes of Rehabilitation nor by Bankhead Bills[28] nor by the abolition of tenancy itself. The very least that can really help them is a thoroughly successful and thoroughly

---

27. Mills Hill is "Hobe's Hill" and Moundville is "Cookstown" in *Let Us Now Praise Famous Men*.

28. The Bankhead-Jones Act of 1937 established the Farm Security Administration, replacing the Resettlement Administration and shifting the New Deal's agricultural policies towards extending rehabilitation loans to farmers, granting low-interest, long-term loans to enable selected tenants to buy family-size farms, and aiding migrants, especially through establishing labor camps.

communist revolution, and even the communists, in proportion to the relative strength and

[50]

[51]

depth of their knowledge, suffer dangerously from over-confidence and from delusions of completeness.

So that what you are seeing and reading here: is one thorough and entirely authentic record of one contemporary expression of an old and plain matter: the human predicament.

[52]

[53]

[J 1.11: Letter to Alma Mailman]

My Ruth: In Jesus' name take this into your heart soul and body and know it is <u>serious</u> as life and death: We <u>must</u> <u>understand</u> each other better and to hell with how much time or trouble it takes. Some of the time the problems seem so innumerable and your realization and understanding of them and of their seriousness so dim and passive, that I am desperate for the only out, to knock my brains out a soon as possible. **Oh, <u>what</u>** in God is the use writing, talking, hoping, trying at all. **Nothing** is any hope or use if you will not take it <u>hard</u> into your heart, the

[54]

desperate seriousness of treating this thing right—so hard into yourself that passiveness and flabbiness are out of the question, are physically impossible to you.

I know I'm difficult as hell Ruth. But I have got patience, short of utter despair and insanity—if you want any dream of how much patience. I beg you to realize what it means to have known you these months and to have listened ten thousand times over to those idiocies you have picked up, which I know by heart and ad nauseam as the platitudes of a stinking and voraciously soul-suicidal world, and

[55]

to have kept my reason at all.

God <u>damn</u> it have you no heart for learning at all?

[56]

[57]

[J 1.12: Letter to Alma Mailman]

My own Ruth: I serve journal notice.

Oh, will you in Jesus' name take into your heart the seriousness of trying to understand and clean yourself of what is wrong and can destroy us and your own soul, so hard into your heart that passiveness, flabbiness, all, is out of the question, a physical impossibility, except the most intense sense of need and responsibility, and energy and hunger to attack it. Oh will you take my hands hard and look me in the eyes and work, with me, actively, with all your heart and all the best that is in you, regardless of Feeling Good and with regard only for goodness and truth, and without fear?

Because if you can't or won't, God

[58]

help your soul, only God can't, it's up to you; and if you can't, how shall I keep my brain in one piece?

If what we have is to die, let it have had the best our hearts and intelligence could give it, let it not die under a mass of fears and half-truths and runnings-away. That latter is more guilt than anyone can afford to carry through a lifetime.

You are the best and most beautiful woman I have ever known or ever care to know, why is it you must also be the particular one to carry this massive inability to understand what you are letting yourself do.

[pages 59–88 blank]

[89]

[J 1.13: Letter to Archibald MacLeish]

Dear Archie:[29] Tell me what you think of this idea.

Sitting in and writing captions, as a sort of half-member of the staff, is not a very good idea. Stuff would be fed back and forth too fast, with

---

29. Archibald MacLeish (1892–1982), American poet, was a writer and editor for *Fortune* from 1929 to 1938. See E 2, note 2.

too continuous compromise at too great frequency. What might be good ideas would in their inceptive stages be killed, or diluted, or confused, much as if one talked too much of a work before writing it, or showed sketches and drafts to friends.

This is the more true because the limitations of Life[30] as it stands are basic, and not to be superficially changed or much helped, springing as they do from limitation of depth and incisiveness of THEORY, or INTUITION, of what a picture is.

[90]

[91]

Many suggested changes would be accordingly drastic.

Therefore this suggestion:

That Walker Evans and I be set up to office space and to ease and choice in getting news pictures, COMPLETELY INDEPENDENT of the weekly production of the issue, and in our work COMPLETELY INDEPENDENT of detailed responsibility to any editor, for two or, better, three months, as an experimental department. We would of course submit work long and probably often before that, but the whole point would be, that we should work out our ideas of what a picture magazine—or a given article—or a given page—should be, entirely on

[92]

[93]

our own, submitting each job only when we consider it finished or of definite and full relevance to others—, and submitting it on a take-or-leave basis. I.e., unless we want to on a specific piece, it becomes the property and business of the editors and staff to revise and compromise it: no further concern of ours. This latter on the theory that nothing is more destructive to the production of good ideas and good work than detailed and repeated compromise of them to some other's, or others', taste, by those who first had them.

Out of this Life might get ideas, and articles, they could well use, during the whole course of the experiment. (Again, they

---

30. *Life* magazine was founded in 1936 by Henry Luce (1898–1967), whose media empire also included *Fortune* and *Time*.

[94]

[95]

might not.) At the end of that time they might or might not find, that they had possibilities of better a perhaps rather different magazine. And might or might not want to make the change.

They also might, or might not, see it as possible that Evans and I could from time to time, IF UNHINDERED, furnish them something they could find useful and usable. Such work could be by-lined or otherwise set apart as or if they wished. Immaterial to this end.

I think such a scheme could at very least give out some useful ideas and very probably some

[96]

[97]

forms of vitality they have not hit on and would find they'd be glad to have. I also somewhat respect that our ideas of what a picture magazine could and should be would essentially and as a whole differ sufficiently from their own, that they would be unlikely to accept it as a whole. That would be all right too. I feel definitely sure the experiment would be worth their while.

I speak of Evans for two reasons.

1.) Two men strike many ideas out of each other which one alone might miss and which three or more could make chaos of.

2.) He has the best eye I know,

[98]

[99]

and the forms and ramifications of brain in & behind it that would inevitably go with that. Along with that, or an inevitable part of it, the cleanest and strictest THEORY, meaning KNOWLEDGE, of what an eye and a camera is; of what it does and can and cannot do. Meaning among other things: a great freezing and cleansing of all "art" and "dramatic" and of the plethoric and flabby ends of Leica photography.

We should be able to do this for 75 dollars a week each.

JOURNAL 2

[J 2.1: Notes: "Not by any stratagem of hands"]

Not by any stratagem of hands.
Sweated in patterns.
Pierced tissue patterns, rolls of bad music to play on the body.
The Harlequin family.[1] The grace of the woman's hand and the man's
head.
In the crow, the hand. The deep drawn beak.

————

In a morning crowd, the tall ladder slatting itself up.
Negro fat child of nine in brown close coat and close cloth helmet of
brown.
Trunk full of big yellow boxes in a certain light, drawing away down a
blue street with space around it.
Proud sighted.
Branched valleys. The vines of valleys. Water trellised on mountains.

[2]

[3]

There in the ring where name and image meet.
Leaving the furnaces gasping in the impossible air.
    these intelligible dangerous marvels.

————

the measuring of the world.
some possible dream. military silence. surgeon's idea of pain.

————

——

[4]

[5]

The street & house.
West End Blues[2]   Knoxville passages?

———————

1. Pablo Picasso created a number of harlequin-themed works; Agee is
probably referring to *The Family of Saltimbanques* (1905).
2. Written by Joe "King" Oliver, "West End Blues" was recorded by Louis
Armstrong in 1929. See J 4.18, note 56.

"Forgotten Men" film.[3]
Rovers—
Man's Fate[4]
Tenant Farmers.

Dryness of wheat sound. Wind $\rightarrow$; wind $\swarrow$; 2 opposing winds lighting a great reef of wheat.

West End: dew-wet iron.

Rooster—

West End: all in 1 mind?

[6]

[7]

Salty Dog.[5] Screen solid black. It ends on unresolved guitar chord.

Starlight. Drop cameras among black treetops on scarcely less black sky. The camera, in ensuing shots, is in steady descent. Heavily leafed treetops; other tree shapes; solitary tree; descent catching roof trees of houses and of stores; on one house, it concentrates; roof; walls; front view; dog asleep in porch; hens heavy on roost;

[8]

[9]

Salty Dog or what. The great heaviness, tenderness, richness and impersonality of the night. The trees are black and hypnotized in it. City streets are empty a half hour on end. One man is moving; his feet are dry and loud on the pavement. In all the South there is only one whippoorwill, but he seldom stops for breath and he is audible everywhere.

---

3. *The Street of Forgotten Men* (1925), directed by Herbert Brenon, concerns professional beggars in the Bowery.

4. André Malraux's novel *Man's Fate* (*La Condition humaine*), which concerns a Communist uprising in Shanghai, was published in 1933. In 1939, Agee wrote a movie scenario from the novel that was published in the inaugural issue of the journal *Films*. See J 6.2. note 2, and "Man's Fate" in *Collected Short Prose*, 205–17.

5. In "Notes and Appendices" in *Let Us Now Praise Famous Men*, Agee recommends Salty Dog Sam's "New Salty Dog" and "Slow Mama Slow." "Salty Dog Sam" was one of many pseudonyms of bluesman Sam Collins (1887–1949).

There is also a slow creek that talks neither to itself nor to anything else. It lies along among the roots of bushes and trees, within its banks.

[10]

[11]

Is Auden's language his own or a new one.

———

V and J and V in a line.

———

divergent.

———

59. circular wall Combray.[6] Town has broken but not cast shell of former perfection. What things shaped its present structure. i.e., as simple as, a hill, a creek.

[12]

[13]

another picks up the new cigaret: smokes it.

———

Katov is lying right beside Kyo;[7] separated from him by the vast expanse of suffering:
    (Katov's head)
But joined to him
but joined to him:

————————————————————

————————————————————

sitting, slouched: pin-point pain in left side & in sole of left foot. Without there being any pain between there was nevertheless clear feeling of the pain transmitted in a straight line between, regardless of the structure of bent leg (it wd have seemed same between any 2 points.)

[14]

[15]

"not the desire for fame which produces a finished piece of work, but the habit of laboriousness."

————————

6. Combray, modeled on the village of Illiers in central France, is the fictional setting of one of Marcel Proust's childhood vacation homes in *Remembrance of Things Past* (1913–27).

7. Katov and Kyo are primary characters in Malraux's *Man's Fate*. See note 4.

every baby may be counted on to do the best he can. and I had better, as a crutch, get myself into as near as I can a baby state of mind.

the other end of it is, to become much more deliberate and conscious of what I am trying to do than I am.

[16]

[17]

End of Alabama book: series of reprises—musical form, elliptic.

————

[J 2.2: Journal Entry:
"goodnight. I look strongly in your eyes"]

goodnight. I look strongly into your eyes,[8] and at your face from below as you lean over; and see the depth of the creases, like broken necklaces, around your throat, which I must not have looked at so closely for two years. Your face as you lean over, the hair fallen around it, smiling, is your face as it was in times of absolute joy in each other. It is also the face of Dorothy[9] and of my mother. Misshapen by the odd hanging of the flesh in this abnormal position, and in a sense "motherly", as over a child at the breast who must be looked down into the face of by tucking in the chin, creasing the neck and cheek; and with a smile. Also as your blouse falls away I see your underclothing, which is worn now; when have I earned enough to get you any better; and your throat in the round fall of your breast. The skin

[18]

[19]

of your throat as I put my hand on it is fine, crepe-like, yet faintly rough. I feel your body, at the breast and side and down the back and along the buttocks and the thigh (I am still looking into your eyes and smiling, trying to truthfully and yet not to make you unhappy). We had made a not at all definite agreement to go to bed together tonight. I am think-

————

8. This entry is apparently addressed to Via.

9. Agee began dating Dorothy Carr when he was a senior at Phillips Exeter, and they continued to correspond and see each other intermittently until 1930. See J 4.3, note 19.

ing of that, and I know you are thinking of it. I know too that you are being careful not to mention it, because you know that nervously, psychologically, emotionally, that does the possibility harm in me. You are in a sense waiting for me to make the move; and you are already very nearly sure I won't make it. So am I. As I look at you, and caress you, and hold you close against me, I do not feel a thing, sexually. Not that I am trying to; but I am wishing that I might. But I do not feel a thing. Only sadness; love for you; pity for you.

[20]

[21]

What have I let you in for. Work; aging; poverty; no children; no sexual love; so much indifference. Here is your hand: the wedding ring on it. A narrow hand. It is red and rough both palm and back; scarred and split by knives, water, the cat, accidents and steady frictions of work. I care for a working and not for a cultivated hand, and I know in what ways it is "good" that your hand and your life are so: but I know and care also in what ways it is sorrowful; and I would be glad if I had not brought these things on you. I know how strongly you feel that some conscious "effort" could be made, sexually, whether I feel it or not; that in the course of the effort or, the repeated effort, I would feel it. It seems a wrong thing to strain over, to make an effort over. The idea makes me sick at my stomach. Maybe you are right though. But as it is, I know only an effort, if

[22]

[23]

anything, could bring it; and I know that I am not making the effort, and that other nights will be like this. I would give anything on earth to feel sexual love for you, sexual excitement over you. Though your body is not attractive to me and though it is even hard for me to look at it, lately, I know very well that it is a good body, one indeed that I love as I do not in the least love certain others that I am attracted to. But I am unable to feel anything. The more that I realize my inability to feel any sexual excitement, except in the regret of memory, the more strong, and tender, not excited, nowhere near tears, this amalgam of pity and sorrow and care and respect for you becomes: so that in a sense I come to love you, and your body, and all about you, very much. So that it is with a certain truth and frankness

[24]

[25]

that I can look at you so steadily, and so put my hands on you, embrace you tightly, and kiss you, and feel out with my lips the roughness and hardness of your hand. And yet neither of us is fooled by any of this. We have no sense, even, of the Judas kiss about it. There is a little, but we know where that belongs and why it is there. We know what this is, very well, and keep looking at each other, and smiling, with more love even than sorrow. After a while, long after I have made the tentative experiments which I have known would bring no help, and long after you have known it is hopeless, you speak what for a while you restrained, saying, smiling, very slightly joking, "Let's go to bed some time soon", and I say "yes; let's"; and you say, "I want to." Shortly after that you go, and I stay up and read. But instead of reading, I write

[26]

[27]

this.

I don't see that there is any help for this sort of thing. It is perfectly quiet but it is final, and without hope.

Perhaps in some part my anesthesia comes of the continuous subconscious resistance not against you but against marriage. Perhaps if that were yielded, relaxed into, we would be happy together. It seems beyond control or unraveling, now.

Perhaps too, this very dead kind of love in time generates its own heat, enough to make fire of its own. That has happened once or twice. It might even become good. But at best it seems a sad thing to sustain two lives on, and to raise a family out of.

Your gentleness, sweetness and courage,

[28]

[29]

all that you do so determinedly that you are unaccustomed to. And saddest of all, how brightly and like a child your face and your smile fill with happy light, when I warm you with the thinnest semblance of the love you need, and that I wish I were giving you.

[30]

[31]

[J 2.3: *LUNPFM* Notes: "One thing I had better do"]

One thing I had better do is, list and slightly develop those recalls which I will be most uneasy over if I don't unload. The drive to the sawmill, for instance; the negro singing there; the mules in the swampy grove of pines and saplings. The red, flooded swamp: thick trees, heavy foliage, the sun striking brilliantly through; early afternoon: the tremendous noise of frogs. The fox call: pure excitement. Goodnight; goodnight; goodnight Mary; goodnight. The walk outside Green's house, at night.

Another thing: list and analyze those things which I want to do and which can't be done in this book. And those things which can.

I want for instance, more than almost anything else, to write a long piece which will from start to finish be organic, exciting development.

[32]

[33]

I want to write musical structures. The musical continuum of Schubert.

Another thing: Things here offer themselves variously to various keys and kinds of writing. As nearly as possible discover and tabulate their tones and rhythms.

Hearing music clears up to me, complexities and tones which were otherwise lost.

Now, writing for myself, I lose all leverage. I had it for verse awhile, in borrowing tones; for Fortune awhile because it was a job for someone else.

Music can carry a tone and feeling out completely, many times, things scarcely different. Writing can do so only by describing & in describing it loses everything of embodiment. When writing tries to

[34]

[35]

embody anything "elevated", it has apparently to generalize, and in that, repeats itself.

If I could only make up my mind whether I want to do this book. When I sit down even this near it, with pencil and paper, it seems worthless. When I withdraw a little from it, it seems necessary. I see and feel its variety clearly, and all at once: because it is a part of memory and thought. Why do I lose that when I come nearer it. One obvious reason: I become concentrated on some one small piece, and the piece fattens and loses all its quality, and drags the rest down with it. It seems worthless for just the reasons which at other times make it seem good: variety, formlessness, anti-art. But there is nothing I want so much as to make any given part of it a work of art.

I become just what I am now: sad, desperate, feeble minded, paralyzed.

[36]

[37]

One trouble. In this book I am wanting to tell "the truth": and am denying myself the only ways I have of telling it: the means of art. I am writing & thinking of it in terms which are totally slack excepting the wish to convey something & understand it as nearly as possible; and I am not wanting to convey but to embody.

What should be movie. What should be landscape. Music. Analysis. Straight narrative. Poetry. Still life.

[J 2.4: *LUNPFM* Draft: "Can a train trip be had in one sentence"]

Can a train trip be had in one sentence.

The rails lay out unbroken from New York through Chattanooga and along the rails in a steady shuffling, creaking, leaving, decorated by bells, whistlings and brief stops, the train took me, starting early one evening and leaving me behind, at Chattanooga, about four the next day: the strong June light broken on the buildings, the people at many speeds. The taxi driver,

[38]

[39]

who said he was the youngest in the city, took me a short cut across the bumping railroad tracks to the Read House,[10] medium priced, the second best hotel in town.

The Read House was twelve stories of rather new brick. Outside it looked like a tinted postcard. Inside it looked like a color photograph. Big walnut service desk. Bus-terminal type floor, of polished peanut brittle. Machine made persian rugs, dark reds and purples. Potted palms. Posters of movies. Indirect lighting behind green and cream colored lalique glass. Smooth elevators, like sitting on the cushions in a pneumatic chair. Negro help mostly pale coffee, apparently chosen to harmonize with plum colored uniforms. Bellhop turns on fan, opens windows, opens door to toilet:

Now I am alone.

I look out the window from the fifth floor and see what I can of the city; shadows darkening and lengthening but still a lot of daylight.

[40]

[41]

All the signs. The gliding tops of autos, trucks, and busses, the asphalt, blue in shadow, pale grey-gold in the slicing sunlight; the orchestration of motors; the sharp hiss of air brakes. Noise, and smoke. The smell of a hotel room and the smell of a city I knew in my childhood. Friends of mine, and boys who beat me up, came from the slums of this town. The mothers of two were whores. My great-aunt established her convent here. Down the street when I was twelve, on my way back to school, I stopped in between trains to see West of the Water Tower[11] with Glenn Hunter, May McAvoy, Ernest Torrence and George Fawcett. I came in at ten minutes of one. I stayed through two showings, came out at five, ate a hot dog, saw The Flying Dutchman,[12] by rushing, got back for the 7 o'clock showing, stayed through till eleven, spent the night on a bench

---

10. The Read House Hotel, a ten-story brick and terra cotta building at 827 Broad Street in Chattanooga, opened in 1926 and is still in operation.

11. A film directed by Rollin S. Sturgeon, 1924.

12. A film directed by Lloyd B. Carleton, 1923.

in the Union Depot, and got to school late next morning. My mother was worried to death and I was seriously whipped at the school.

The carpet in this room is green with a

[42]

[43]

sober, small, black pattern. All hotel carpet feels richer than it looks. It is laid on some thick cushion that makes it feel richer under the leather just than it looks. It goes all the way to every wall and it is nailed down with a bright brass strip. Under the glass top of the narrow desk is a calendar with ads.

The glass in the bathroom is green celluloid.

The fan swirls at the centre ceiling.

I am extremely happy. I have been happy all along but now it catches at me in a rush. The very thought of cheap to middle-price hotel rooms and of the look of the streets of all cities except huge ones can make me as happy as the greatest art.

---

[44]

[45]

This driving, in unknown country, in the blazing light, was in many essential ways more like fumbling your way through a huge and unknown house, with no matches, in pitch darkness, trusting to your ears and your sense of touch alone.

We were doing this on back roads, new to us, west and south of Tuscaloosa; sand and clay roads, damp where they were steadily shaded. We made fair speed. There was then a thing which stopped us as dead as would the sudden appearance of a child in front of the car.

On our left was thick, green woods, impossible to see through. On the right, a swamp. It was not more than a hundred yards wide, but it stretched back farther than we could see.

[46]

[47]

There must have been swamp even to begin with, but not to this amount; the water was the wrong color. Evidently a creek had flooded.

The water was backed up deep enough so that it was just short of flush with the road. Trees, with trunks black with humidity, stood up thickly out of the water, but well spaced enough so that it was possible to see perhaps a hundred yards back into the woods. As far as you could see, there was this same motionless (but not stagnant looking) deep but bright, orange water. It was only shortly after noon, the most blazing kind of day, but the foliage was so heavy there was almost no freckling of sunlight. The sun got through only in spaces where there were no leaves at all: in those places, it

[48]

[49]

shot down on the water with stunning but motionless brilliance. The rest was dark as leaf-mold, and smelt like that.

From all over, in this little patch of darkness in the glaring day, came a roar of frogs so strong that your face vibrated with it; and this noise was enormously sustained. It was a great deal louder than anything I have heard at night.

Fumbling as rapidly as we could along an unknown back road we were brought as short by this as if a child had suddenly appeared a yard in front of the car, and we must have stayed a half hour, without speaking more than twice, before it was possible to go on.

But best about this is, that that roaring and ringing of frogs had been [continued on manuscript page 53]

[50]

[51]

[J 2.5: Letter to Walker Evans]

Dear Walker—Damned stupidity thinking the letter returning Burroughs'[13] letter contained nothing but that, delayed opening it till today, & note among other things I wd have wanted to answer that you spoke of spending weekend with us. Sorry. Do so next time you are up, will you? In spite of hopes I keep having I suppose it is really doubtful that I'll get to Washington. Money, money. (Who could ask for anything more.) Re-saw Peppermill[14] and it seemed much better than before. The

---

13. Floyd Burroughs, "George Gudger" in *Let Us Now Praise Famous Men.*

14. *The Peppermill,* Erika Mann's antifascist cabaret with sketches and lyrics by Klaus Mann, Ernest Toller, W. H. Auden, and others, opened in New York on January 5, 1937.

Eternal Mask[15] is no more than fair on any strict standard; first half of it is very good on the day by day standard. Second half is partly interesting but almost entirely muffed. Or do all German nuts have that style of fantasy since Caligari[16] was made.

[52]

Thanks for the typings of the letters. I enclose further notes from various Tingles.[17]

And by the way why shd I have asked for Burroughs letters back— all there are as much yours & in your keeping as mine. The Tingle letter for its first day still carried some of the old aroma. I never had nostalgia in the form of nausea before. I am wondering whether (A) the money order got through to Burroughs and (B) whether he passed it on to Tingle & Fields.[18] No mention of it yet anywhere. I give no damn for mention needless to say but I am curious did they get it.

Seeing some German movie Hamlet[19] tonight and the Last Laugh.[20] Fairly consistent feelings these days of insecurity & depression, thanks to paralytic inability to do sustained work. I must develop extreme ability to kick my own ass.

See you soon I hope—

Jim

---

15. Werner Hochbaum's film *Die Ewige Maske* (1935) was released in America as *The Eternal Mask* in 1937.

16. *The Cabinet of Dr. Caligari* (*Das Kabinett des Doktor Caligari*), directed by Robert Wiene in 1919, is a classic of German film expressionism.

17. The Tingles are the "Ricketts" family in *Let Us Now Praise Famous Men*.

18. Bud Fields, "Bud Woods" in *Let Us Now Praise Famous Men*.

19. This 1920 silent version directed by Sven Gade and Heinz Schall stars Asta Nielsen as a female Hamlet disguised as a boy.

20. *The Last Laugh* (*Der Letzte Mann*), directed by F. W. Murnau in 1920 with cinematography by Karl Freund and Robert Baberske, revolutionized the use of the camera as a mobile instrument. *The Last Laugh* and *Hamlet* were shown together as a Museum of Modern Art program entitled "The Film in Germany: The Moving Camera" on January 24, 1937.

53

[J 2.6: *LUNPFM* Draft:
"Can a train trip be had in one sentence," cont.]

[continued from manuscript page 49] going on all that day and would keep going on all in one unbroken breath, and would have been there if human beings had never existed.

[J 2.7: *LUNPFM* Notes: "The fox"]

The fox. The noise of hydrogen exploding when a match is held to the mouth of a test-tube. It has about this note and tone and sharpness, <u>if</u> the hydrogen is stepped down, softened, quieted, about one half. It sounds as much like a bud as like a furred animal, only after a lot of listening are you sure it is an animal, and you never understand why you are sure. Without resounding an echo, it has a tremendous illusion of echoing power: the silence after it is very full of suspense. The noise itself is exciting nearly to the point of fear with mystery: I don't know any wilder noise in the woods; more

entirely alien to human existence; nor with half as much implicit contempt. (The contempt is implicit, though, not real; it is like seeing into the secret life of Negroes). Staccato. —— — — — : — — : — ▯ .

Silence.   The frogs.

A long way off: silence: much fainter:

— — — — : — — : — —— .

Set up as musically, or artificially, as you like.

Dependence of words, like film cutting, on context. From the wave-sound in variations, was able to begin a use of words with a maybe new quality: childish, & primitive, ppp, opening of a huge buildup as in 9th finale, the orchestral preparation for tenor solo. Verbal-musically (& philosophically) much more strong general principles cd be drawn from this fact than I have drawn.

[56]
[57]

Alabama: tone, pace, bulk, cut, develop detail.
    hold to the specific. Let any generalizations grow out of it.

[J 2.8: Journal Entry: "Running low on cigarets"]

Feb. 11. Running low on cigarets got out machine & rolled some Prince
Albert. First draw brought back very strongly the solitary 3 days,
returned to Harvard before vacation ended, during which I first really
caught on to the Brahms 4$\underline{\text{th}}$ Symphony. What it brought back was not
the symphony and only very faintly the place; it was the exact quality
of excitement which I had chiefly over the works in part over loneliness
and over Dorothy Dart[21] (whom through, I was in love with because of
the 4th Symphony).

———

My late night rounds of these streets watching for the lights of friends:
a dog checking up on his pissing posts.

———

Why didn't the P[rince] A[lbert] recall last summer? Because too recent
& because I was not then & am now in love? Why not Kansas 1929?[22]
Because I was not in love?

[58]
[59]

[J 2.9: Letter to Brick Frohock]

Dear Brick:[23] It has been a hell of a while. Damned bad luck and management on the New Years time you were in town. We were in Clinton,[24]
& were wanted to stay, and were for that matter having a good time. And

---

    21. Dorothy Carr. See J 2.2. note 9, and J 4.3, note 19.

    22. In the summer of 1929 Agee worked as an agricultural laborer in Nebraska,
Kansas, and Oklahoma.

    23. Wilbur Merrill "Brick" Frohock (1908–1984), a friend of Agee's since high
school and later a professor at Harvard, was at the time teaching French at
Columbia University. He is the author of *The Novel of Violence in America* (1950)
and "James Agee: The Question of Unkept Promise," *Southwest Review* 42
(Summer 1957): 221–29.

    24. At the Saunders residence in Clinton, New York.

I thought & hoped then I was going to spend some time soon in Providence. So, wired the office to tell you latter & that we wd not be down. The wire wasn't delivered or wasn't rec'd, I forget which, till you were long gone. And since then, am now involved in a book and suppose I shan't do much traveling until I finish it, fuck it or get it very well in Hand. So, nothing to do but regret, at present.

This book is, if it gets written, a full-length workout on the Alabama trip. I'm excited in possibilities of a lot of things in it, some of them new or part new. Also am for a change a little bit better than 70 per cent. But not so damned confident but what I am afraid to talk about the book either pessimistically or optimistically,

[60]

so I will shut up. Nothing much in movies. 2 good revivals, Potemkin[25] & Frontier,[26] but I resaw neither. Spain in Flames[27] a damned well organized documentary; with some good and some goddamned good commentary (former by Dos Passos & latter by Hemingway). The Eternal Mask[28] is partly very good; dream stuff not so hot; all interesting though. Have been doing some movie scenarizing: not for money or for anyone. Now much hotter on movies than ever before, but see much fewer. Reading Proust pretty hard. Only contemporary comparable size to Joyce. Agreed or not? Auden & Malraux may become so. Celine & Silone[29] I like a hell of a lot. I very damned much hope you can get down or I up or both, soon. My present estimate & hope is I could in May. But it depends on my guts with & luck with writing this southern thing. I didn't mean "thing" in affectation: by general type it is not classifiable except as a book and I am superstitious abt speaking of it too much as a book. Hope you will write me. What are you working on. Love to Nat[30] and to you. Jim.

---

25. *The Battleship Potemkin* (*Bronenosets Poyemkin*), directed by Grigori Aleksandrov and Sergei Eisenstein, 1925.

26. *Frontier* (*Aerograd*), directed by Aleksandr Dovzhenko, 1935.

27. *Spain in Flames,* a pro-Loyalist propaganda film highlighting Fascist atrocities, by Prudencia de Pereda, opened at the Cameo Theatre in New York on January 30, 1937.

28. See J 2.5, note 15.

29. Louis-Ferdinand Céline (1894–1961), French novelist; Ignazio Silone (1900–1978), Italian novelist.

30. Natalie Barrington, to whom Brick Frohock was later married, on August 16, 1938.

[61]

[J 2.10: Letter to Father Flye]

Dear Father.[31] Tired & untalkative but thinking of you, knew how much I would love to see you. No maintaining of silence or reading of things in a letter though, so this won't make much sense. A friend of mine Walker Evans wrote me from Memphis the other day, where he was photographing flood camps,[32] that he wd have liked to see you but knew he wd lack time before he came north. I know you would enjoy his company and believe also you would more personally like him: in some ways, (more or less French-analytic amorality or moral style; kindness; curiosity; strong Francophilia) like Oliver Hodge.[33] Other ways, of course, quite different. So far as I know of or think, the best photographer in the world, and would have been & may become a first rate writer. Does no writing though. It was he I was south with last summer. I am beginning to do some writing on my own about those 8 weeks. They may turn out to be good. I am insecure and up and down badly, in recognition of my terrible lack of mental self-discipline & analysis and of my somewhat probable lack of the degree

[62]

of native born & unaquirable talent I would rather die than lack. A foolish statement this "rather die" but I am just that foolish about it. I wish we were both families living near and might see each other. Within your influence I have certain kinds of calm and at least some raw beginnings of a sense of goodness and integrity which I otherwise seem much of the time to lack. But that is foolish of me too for if these things are ever to be found or developed it must be within a given person, his own responsibility, essentially both independent of and even unhelpable by anyone else, the same as becoming a good artist (meaning writer, composer, movie maker, as well as painter or sculptor). I spoke of the poet W H Auden and read you some things. I think more & more of him and his new writing is better and better.

---

31. Father James H. Flye was a teacher at St. Andrew's School near Sewanee, Tennessee, with whom Agee developed a lifelong friendship. See *The Letters of James Agee to Father Flye*, ed. Flye (New York: George Braziller, 1962).

32. In Forrest City, Arkansas, February 1937.

33. Oliver Hodge was a student at St. Andrews with whom Agee had been tutored in French by Father Flye.

Father in my own way I know I am religious: and that the whole nerve and blood of it is love. God help me live up to toward it: i.e., make me help or beat myself into doing so.

[63]

Am still reading a great deal of Proust. Some things about him you might not care for but you would dislike none and a tremendous amount you would love I think. Somewhat special world he was looking at but one of the best minds and sensibilities that can ever have looked at anything: also, his world is not by any means so limited as it is cracked up to be: much of nature and the look of cities and the feeling of rooms and homes; most of art, especially literature and painting; and a terrific stretch and delicacy of human relationships. And a great sense of history. What I would wish would be to read him with you. If you should want to (or maybe you have but we didn't speak of him) the books are all, or anyway the first 3 or 4 of them, in the Modern Library in this order: <u>Swann's Way</u>, <u>Within a Budding Grove</u>; <u>The Guermontes Way</u>; then (I think), <u>The Cities of the Plain</u>, <u>The Sweet Cheat Gone</u>; <u>The Past Recaptured</u>.[34] I'm midway in <u>Guermontes</u>. Do you know

[64]

Pushkin's writing?[35] By hearsay, seems was a really great writer, & certainly he was not responsible for the present centenary whooping; latter however makes me pretty sick. Do people who claim to love & know poetry have to consult calendars and if so who wants their love & knowledge. Wd like to read him. That it seems wd entail learning Russian. Wdn't mind that either but almost certainly won't undertake the labor. I must quit and get to bed.
Much love to you and Mrs Flye.

Rufus

---

34. The Modern Library first editions and dates of publication of Marcel Proust's *Remembrance of Things Past* are *Swann's Way* (1928), *Within a Budding Grove* (1930), *The Guermontes Way* (1933), *The Cities of the Plain* (1938); *The Captive* (1941), *The Sweet Cheat Gone* (1948), and *The Past Recaptured* (1951).

35. The one-hundredth anniversary of Russian poet Aleksandr Pushkin's (b. 1799) death in 1937 was the occasion of great state celebration in Russia, which was mirrored in American Communist circles.

[J 2.11: Letter to Alma Mailman]

Alma my darling. This one will be fatuous if at all. Probably you won't ever see it though. There can't be anything quite as good as this state of mind, though thank God some other things, in art and the chances of walking & looking around approach it. It's the whole feeling, which you may or may not yet have lost for the first time (but I assume you have) of being alive again. So that I'm often so suddenly & unexpectedly taken by happiness that it comes out in a laugh & in tears in my eyes before I know what has hit me. Then remembering, I know it is you, and think of you. At luckiest and best we are such flimsy receptacles of this terrific damn thing that we can't hold it consistently or long. You become more and more grateful for being alive, and to the person who brings you alive. I say this sincerely and with even some knowledge at 27. God help me if I live to be 50. If I should fall in love at that age, (& again God help me if I didn't) I would break wide open with it. It is just now oc-

curing to me, Christ forbid, that this smells suspiciously like a Literary Love Letter. Perhaps because of the things I want to say, or perhaps because I am not at all sure you will ever see it. I will have I guess to take that chance. I am also overcome, or undermined, by waves of knowledge of my callowness, sloppiness of mind, laziness and lack of power. But this is of writing. I don't mean to talk of it to you, not anyway now. My sweetest Alma what would ever come near being what love is.

I am thinking of your mind and look and body and voice with such joy, gratefulness and love. It is going to be hard to sink myself as I must, much more in the book than in thought of you. Neither of these things can be postponed. Both of them mean so much to me now. God bless and be upon you my dear love and my friend. Goodness and happiness certainly exist in the world and that becomes clear in knowing you. Goodnight. I lie down beside you. But I shan't be a bother.

                                        Jim.

[67]

[J 2.12: Drafts of Poem: "Now I lay me down beside"]

Goodnight. I lie down beside you.
Now I lay me down beside[36]
You, my truest, my transient bride.
And where, upon another bed
You lie, my hand sustains your head.

O if we should before we wake
By some chance out love forsake

[68]
[69]

Now I lay me down beside
You, my transient and true bride.
And where upon another bed
You sleep my hand sustains your head.

If we should wake

[70]
[71]

[J 2.13: Journal Entry: "Out of the wish to see her"]

Out of the wish to see her an hour even among people I helped
make it that we all go. They looked at each other and it was good deal
like matches raised to heat and taking immediate light. My hands began
to tremble and I could not make them stop. I became cold in the middle
of the back, and sick in the stomach, and had to clamp my jaws to keep
my teeth from chattering. They kept looking at each other. After a
little they got to talking. I remembered over and over as I had been
doing since it had happened, how she sat and how I had felt in my lifted

---

36. Cf. "Now I Lay Me Down Beside," *Collected Poems*, 152–53. See also J 2.14.

hand the lightness and round full of the side of her breast: and, by her look, how soon she might have become in love with me.

There is nothing to say and nothing to do about this, but watch it happen or worse, not be able to watch it happen. Very likely for a little while, a few weeks more at best, things will remain as good as they are. Then they will begin to rot before their natural time, and I don't see how I can stand it. I am cold, nauseated, and my knees and hands tremble, and this is not going to stop for long, for perhaps months now. And there is some more of living gone, that might have been so good.

[72]

[73]

[J 2.14: Draft of Poem: "Now I lay me down beside"]

Now I lay me down beside
You, my friend, my love, my bride.
And where you bless a useless bed
My hand sustains your lovely head.

Though we stay this night apart,
By an illimitable art
Separation, quite undressed,
Yields me your look, your laugh, your breast.

O should our thoughts lie down to sleep
I pray the Lord our love to keep.
If love should die before we wake
I pray the Lord our love to take.

[74]

[75]

Though this lies down as all things do
At length in the large earth, the true

[76]

[77]

[J 2.15: Letter to Alma Mailman]

Alma: Goodnight my lovely Alma. I find out a bad thing of myself. Anything I think of as I do of this I can write nothing but slushy doggerel about. Which may prove either that I am no good at all or something or other about the psychology of doing or trying art: Emotion Recollected in Tranquility is I suppose the bright idea. I am in no position to do any analysis of it though. I am so griped that this Alabama book is not poetry (which it should not be) that it's hard to keep writing it. I'm pretty low about my abilities anyway, but I'll be smart to lay off that subject if I am ever to write even bad things.

I just note that 5 of the 8 sentences so far, are begun with "I". Excuse it please.

All right here go some more. I keep thinking of you, everything about you, meaning eyes, look, smile, laugh, voice, honesty, kindness, courage, mind, youngness, body, strength, and there can't be many people so beautiful, meaning at the same time admirable, as you. You are much stronger

[78]

than I am, and in a part of my thought of you, you are a young, strong and gentle mother to me. Which is balanced another way, for I also think of you in your youngness, your mixture of hard and soft, as I might of a daughter. And as of a sister too, but most of all as a girl I love and think highly of and would wish to be with and to do things for and to make happy. That you should be so very beautiful to me as you are. The most on earth I feel and am grateful for is the knowledge that I have seen you happy and that I have caused you to be, and that I've seen you look at me as people can only look who are happy and who at least somewhat love someone. This state of physical-emotional indigestion clouds things for me and I hate it, more than I can tell you: but there are some large things it does not touch: especially, love for you so strong that thinking of you I laugh with happiness in your existence. I now want plenty to see you, but will wait a while. Love to you darling, all on and around you as you sleep. Goodnight—   Jim

[79]

[J 2.16: Notes: "Scenario addenda" to *LUNPFM*]

Scenario addenda—

Probably shd be a note indicating PACE.

steady rather slow pace: with speedups like uses of triplets, 8^{ths}, 16^{ths}; broken rhythms.

In plane shots, a terrific swoop shot in which the plane leans on an angle on the uptake so that the land lists and is twirled.

in changed recapitulations, much detail to work out & much good use. An unsmiling child second, for instance, who smiled first. or vice versa. a sidelong look after a full face look. A hand to the face. Or wiping the forehead. A hand bro[ugh]t up in deceptive salutelike form; not completing it; it is accidental. A face bent over work as toward work or harnessing a mule.

auto shot 4 times over.

in 1st section, lonely houses; strong atmospheric stuff.

[80]

Lucile[37] not looking up into lens but, eyes at just downcast are lifted to level.

Dirt road: a fast car swings dust against lens.

[81]

[J 2.17: Letter to Father Flye]

Dear Father: Thank you for your letter. About the sit down strikes: in certain ways I agree with you & in others (in which I believe much more strongly) not at all. Let me start it though with the picketing idea. I remember your writing of it & we never talked of it thoroughly. You felt in effect: "generically, I have sympathy with labor and its difficul-

---

37. Lucille Burroughs, i.e., "Maggie Louise Gudger" in *Let Us Now Praise Famous Men*. See J 3.1.

ties, and agree it has the right to organize and to use this weapon of organization (depending on circumstances). But when it comes to the point of picketing a plant, and keeping or scaring or fighting off men from jobs they need and have a perfect right to, that is too much. That is unqualifiedly wrong."

But is it. Look. The only weapons labor has are organization, the very hard-won, <u>nominal</u> right to collective bargaining, and picketing. According to your belief it really amounts to this. A group of workers have a right to pull themselves out of their job and by halting produc-tion to bring the owners to terms; but they have no right to fend off those whom the owners call in to replace

[82]

them; and the owners have every right to call in these scabs. Don't you see and have to admit that in that case you have left labor merely the right to lose its job and the chance for any settlement of any terms it has asked for; you have deprived them of the weapon without which they can have no hope of winning even a part of their demands. And in that case your sympathy toward labor, and labor legislation in gen-eral, are, whether you believe so or not, quite hollow.

Sure, I have respect for private property; anyone's except my own. But you know well how abused the idea of the sacredness of private prop-erty is every day. Armed force is called out against human beings who are not legally allowed to arm and who can't afford to, to protect rights of property and the "rights" of employers to give away jobs from under men who are losing needed pay in the hope of helping themselves to a minutely better share of what they deserve. Does that make sense?

[83]

For every time law has been used in favor of labor, ten I am sure could be found when it was used precisely opposite. In other words there is nothing equitable about law, and nothing in it which labor should feel called on to observe or respect beyond immediate expediency.

Of course our basic difference on these points is this; and within your belief, if I believed it, I would agree with you. You think of the set-up as labor, capital, and government, making their adjustments as best they can, with the supremely important thing observance of and just administration of the law to the individual instance. I think of it as inevitable and literal <u>war</u>, in which, again inevitably, government and capital stand together against labor. Much as I may dislike the fact, there can be no sacred rules in war, and if strikers occupy the sacred property of their employers I rejoice as in the capture of an enemy fortress, only more so, for I have no enemies

[84]

in any war but this kind. And if great sections of the law-abiding populace approve this rupture of law, I am glad again, for my side can in the long run never win without breaking the laws as they stand, the laws being against them; and this general approval shows a growth of insensitiveness toward my enemies, and of understanding of my friends, which is very encouraging in the very fact that it weakens the meaning and stature of government as it is. I had a sleepless night so I'm probably not making this clear. I wish I could and would like later to try again.

I've been reading a book that would I think interest (and also trouble you) a good deal. I am afraid it would set you against the Communists more than you are, but I wonder. <u>In Dubious Battle</u>, by John Steinbeck.

I must get to work. I'll hope to write soon again. Much love to you both,

Rufus.

[85]

[J 2.18: Notes: "An act of 'ATMOSPHERES'"]

An act of "ATMOSPHERES"

———

World's Fair: pix & questionnaires.

———

The acts: wallpaper; train & c.

———

Parade. Black house. Band record: $\lessgtr$.

———

Film color: The mouth and nails of the woman in the allegiance dream.

[J 2.19: Notes: "<u>PHOTOGRAPH SHOW</u>"]

<u>PHOTOGRAPH SHOW</u>.

Broaden it. Organize a job on America: the land, cities, occupations, people, classes: which in fact will be not simply pro-democratic–anti-fascist but communist.

————

First in the show:

Movie: plane views of cities, wedged [?] in small & still at either side a long strip of close-shot earth. Around this earth right to left in continuous repeated frieze, a plow turns dirt into the lens.

Or: A series of coast-to-coast plane-shots, all in same direction. Either all are low or, they begin low & rise to a high arch & decline from it. Mostly land, but also a dozen perhaps cities of different sizes. Shores, mnts, rivers, plains, set up in rhythm grabbed from map of continent. About a 3-to-5-minute show, continuous. If any sound, the sound of a steady wind. At end of cast, stills of the key figures used in

[88]

the screen leaves. Stills either of political leaders or of political symbols. Then start again.

AMERICA:

Land: Cities and towns: People.

First thus: The static, pure "scenery" mixed with and superceded by agriculture; mining; lumbering.

Then: camps, farmhouses, stores, small towns.

Then: conveyance shots: food & raw materials into cities.

Then: the straight look of cities: city streets; postcard stuff.

Then: industrial: sweatshop: office work: executive offices. People going to; coming from, work.

Then: pay envelopes.

Then: much more detailed shots of housing. Streets. Facades. Interiors.

[89]

Same with people. Not by any means all of one class. Extremely important are the lower middle & middle class.

Furnishings &c are <u>very</u> important.

A section perhaps of wedding pictures.

A big section on <u>mothers</u>. Worker; lower-middle; fatass middle; upper middle & capitalist & "aristocrat".
And infants.
And children at play, school & work.
Interland of blowups of textbooks, emphasis on dullness & instillation of class prejudice and americanism. Flag Day stuff.

(This all might be run on Food Clothing & Shelter, [] WORK and LEISURE.)

A section on what feeds the bodies; what feeds the brains. Here might be chamber

[90]

of Honors. <u>Ads</u> full of sugared sex; fear; fake science; simulations. <u>Movie</u> stills: crime, sex, wealth-simulation, redbaiting, Big Godlike abstracts of the great king & queen-bee stars. <u>Sound</u>: either straight or travesty radio stuff, both music & talk; a horrible tangle of sound suffueses the show.
        NEWSPAPERS & TABS.
Men of God: straight pictures of ministers of all denominations.

Men Who Govern Us: mayors, aldermen, state legislators, Governors, Congressmen, Supreme Court, president or presidents.

Set up Class by Class?

[91]

It should by this time become apparent chiefly: that Labor is bitched; that the middle class is equally bitched and by training poisoned, more the enemy than the friend of labor; that capital & middle class do the bitching; that capital too is bitched somewhat seriously & is personally responsible only to a degree. That DA Seestem is wrong. That there are things to do to change it.

Now proceed to strikes, pickets; cops, criminals, Natl Guardsmen, beatings, killings, lynchings, fascist organizations (simply [illegible] in Hitler &c?) The function of Gov't, & of police; & of law; recapitulate the function of God; possibly break up into simple textual stuff: The Republicans believe so & so; the Democrats so & so; the Fascists thus;

[92]

the socialists thus; the communists thus. All without comment. They shd speak for themselves.

Pix of leaders, & backers, & representative rank & filers, of all political factions: again to speak for itself.

International Summary: Germany under this, France under this, Spain under this, etc, form of Gov't. Choose a few shots each carefully & unsensationally.

[93]

[J 2.20: *LUNPFM* Draft: "All the light from the sun was vertical all over the world"]

All the light from the sun was vertical all over the world. The world was visible for miles through it, yet it had the color of blazing silver. The roofs of tin and tar, and all bare glass and metal, were shining: the long bare pavements lay squared out under trembling air. I soon got over my first clumsiness with the car and began to learn its ways. Its combination of tinniness and somewhat spurious luxury & its spaciousness, and the slenderness and broad diameter of the steering wheel and the almost slippery ease with which it could be handled, were all new and pleasurable to me; so was the learning, as it always is, of the new length and breadth of this car. I picked up the numbers quickly and got out into the edges of town, gradually gathering speed as the side streets diminished in frequency and importance and obscurity and as the buildings shrank more & more to sun-blinded sheds & shops scattered along sweeps of vacant lots full of rank steaming weeds, dead cars & old tires and

[94]

bedsprings, and as the street streamed though metamorphosis more and more into road, until at length it became sumptuous, still nearly new, gleaming white, oil-streaked, four lane concrete highway, and lifted itself in a long, slow, steady curve, through surroundings now which were more filling-station and dogstand than edge of city, up the lower shoulder of Lookout Mountain, while behind me the spread and relaxation of the beautiful low-built city I felt affection for, shrank into a unit and shrank in my mirror and I was swinging round the green flank of Lookout Mountain, one of the most hackneyed postcard views in all the South, and the sharp-edged pure white curving road swam strongly up and beneath me in the tremendous silent sunshine, and I was happy. I was happy and flattened my foot and the car drew up to sixty, sixty

[95]

three, sixty five, and the road streamed under, and to the left it spilled upward in sweet curves to the crest an auxiliary that swung toward and past and on my right, treetops heavy with leaves drooped dreaming in heat and beneath, beyond, lay the fluent phrasing in that place of the red-brown, islanded, Tennessee river and in its arms glittering, the flat city and the railroad yards. The road furled and tilted in a long left curve, perfectly banked, and I drew down the weight of my hand and took it. Together the car and I, running with razor sharpness the narrow safety of the bias, were drawn strongly to the right and the river and city with the sudden lifted lean of a low wave sank off the side of this beautiful, physical curve and were gone and curve, raw rocks and clay on its embanked right, completed itself and the road prepared and leaned like a swimming fish to the right once more, and the whole of the world that surrounded

[96]

me was heavy, dusty, summer green, slivered through by the road over my speeding. I relaxed, and got eyes and body into restful focus for a few hours' driving.

Just as there are times when you are taken with the feeling, "I have been here before", "I have been saying these things in this way before", so there are in your memory places and things which attach themselves not to one but to two parts of your past. It seems to me that it was a few miles further out of Chattanooga that I came to this big, bright new bridge; yet I am sure too that there was such a bridge, in such surroundings, in country west of New Orleans; a big extravagant free bridge where Huey Long had put it and put on it his name and that of O. K. Allen.[38] Probably there is a bridge at both places, and if the landscapes are similar or even identical, that is not remarkable: for Southern riversides are very likely to look like themselves.

I am speaking of this bridge particularly, though, because in my memory it and the country and context

[97]

it stood in have a special quality of beauty to me. This will be hard to tell of because, though distinct, the memory is confused and dreamlike.

There seems to have been a long hill that I came down while the lowering country lay out in lazy motions beneath the curvings I made of the road towards the bridge. This country was still crowded with trees, yet it was much more open than not, and much more bare than covered with the crops of late June. It was a country of very poor farms and very poor houses, and weeks of rainless sunlight had scorched it into the brown and brittleness of a midsummer autumn. No one was at work in the fields; no one could be seen on front porches. On either side of this new road the land was skinned and raw, and this rawness enlarged toward the bridge, so that there was a great deal of clay, sand and white stone loose in the sunlight. As I came up very close to the bridge a road ran in from the right in a broad curve and joined mine in sudden-

[98]

ness and surprise and the distinct feeling, born partly of speed and partly of its traffic which joined ours for advantage of this bridge, of the mixed flowing of the waters of a river in the miles just below a strong tributary, where the two waters, of different strengths of flow, color, and temperature, are still shyly making intimate and delicious acquaintance before they become identical and relax once more into the laziness and uneventfulness of a single stream.

We took the bridge. It was of new concrete and new metal bright in the sun; a good, strong, big piece of engineering. We were not very

---

38. Huey P. Long (1893–1935) was governor of Louisiana from 1928 to 1932 and a U.S. senator from 1932 to 1935. O. K. (Oscar Kelly) Allen (1882–1936) was Long's secretary of state and became governor in 1932. As governor, Long built more than one hundred toll-free bridges in Louisiana. See P 28, note 20; P 47, note 45; and N 23, note 46.

heavy traffic: a few quite lonely trucks and sedans: but in our speed and in the iron noises the trucks made in the quiet and heat of noon in that abandoned country we were tremendous. Beneath us sank not water but a long stretch of hard strong land, the lonely and hazy crests of cotton-woods lifting their sporadic waves nearly to bridge level, rows of brittle and brown young corn on bare dirt, little houses, and only after that, and foolishly narrow, trivial enough to ford, the fledged and shriveled river. But our context

[99]

was the concrete and our noise and speed which it threw back intensi-fied upon us, and we were conveyed in the heat upon our narrow business of driving. This bridge was entirely of the city and of the twen-tieth century, and so were we and our way of moving and our will to speed. We cut through country that was a certain, poor, kind of twen-tieth century South and yet that was of no century but was the misused property of the sun and sky. This was not just obvious contrast, though: it had the quality and taste that happens when in your body two recalls of entirely disparate parts of your past experience intersect.

Negroes and white men who were of such country drove these trucks, casually and efficiently enough, too. Others had built this bridge and this road. And yet that only made it still more strange. For these people and this country, though they are of our century, and represent a great and ill-recognized weight not only in human existence but in history, do not belong to time as most cities and city people do.

[100]

It would be no more correct to call them primitive, a medieval, or old-fashioned, than to call them modern: they simply do not belong to time, though they must take part in it; they belong to some other order of existence: just as animals, or uninhabited parts of the earth, do not belong to time in the sense of the word.

Moreover this is not just true of any part of the country: it is much stronger in the South and has a special quality there. The South is generic, basic, primal, like my idea of what China must be or of what Czarist Russia must have been. And yet in every detail it has edge, and participation and involvement in what we think of as the present.

[101]

Long sweeping curve to the right then left around Lookout; descent; cross bridge; georgia line: to right: southwestward straightaway bearing up to due west; branch to Scottsboro; the courthouse town; spilling off curve and decline southward through Gadsden to Birmingham.

Even while you are driving, the direction you are moving in and the sense of known or unknown land or town around you is physically influential as is for instance the centrifugal pull of your body as you round a curve; and as you complete a day's driving, the sum of the directions you have taken are computed in you and satisfactory to you. For another thing you usually have a definite destination, and a double sense, got off a map, of two things; the general shape of the trip you must make to get there, and the strong sense of the straight-line placement between the place you left and the place you are going: minor curves, which balance each other, you take in your stride, (though if there are more to the

[102]

right than to the left you are sensitive to this fact); but the major deviations from the straight line cause the same wrenching that syncopation gives in music, verse, prose or conversation. You move due west for instance with a strong pull of Birmingham to the South. If you are headed South there is something of the satisfaction in moving west that there is in sailing on a broad reach as compared with running before the wind.

In memory the whole drive reduces and perfects itself chiefly into three things: the sense of movement; the sense of rhythm and phrase in the sum of the major directions taken and magnet-influences undergone; specially clear recalls of a few sights or incidents.

[pages 103–106 blank; top and bottom thirds
of pages 103 and 104 torn off]

[107]

[J 2.21: *LUNPFM* Notes: "Make no mistake in this"]

Make no mistake in this, though: I am under no illusion that I am wringing this piece of experience dry. Nor do I even want to wring it dry. There are reasons of time, judgement and plain desire or if you like whim.

Time: It took the greatest living artist seven years to record nineteen hours and wring them anywhere near dry.[39] Figure that out for yourself. I take what I am trying here seriously but there are other jobs I want still more to do.

Judgement: Though I do on the one hand seriously believe that the universe can be seen in a grain of sand, and that that is as good a lens as any other and a much more practicable one than the universe, I am again not trying any such job here. In too many other ways I simply do not think the experience was important

[108]

[109]

enough to justify any such effort; and I will consistently try to keep the effort and method in strict proportion to my own limited judgement of the importance of the experience as a whole and in its parts.

The plain desire of whim must then be self-evident: all I want to do is tell this as honestly and clearly as I can and get the damned thing done with. I would again be false to the truth if I were false to that.

Very roughly I know that to get my own sort of truth out of this experience I must tell of it from four planes:

that of recall, reception, contemplation, in medias res: for which I have set up this silence on this front porch as a sort of stage to which from time to time the action will

[110]

[111]

return.

"As it happened": the narrative at the prow as from the first to last day it cut unknown water.

------

39. A reference to James Joyce's *Ulysses*, published in 1922.

By recall and memory from the present: which is still a part of the experience: and this includes imagination, which on the other planes I swear myself against.

As I try to write it: problems of recording; which, too, are still a part of the experience.

These are of course in strong conflict. So is any piece of human experience. So, then, inevitably, is any even partially accurate attempt to give any experience as a whole.

————

It seems likely that the truest way to treat a piece of the past is to handle it as such: as if it were no longer the present.

[112]

[113]

In other words the 'truest' thing about the experience is neither that it was from hour to hour thus and so; nor is it my fairly accurate "memory" of how it was from hour to hour, in chronological progression; but is rather as it turns up in recall, in no such order, casting its lights and associations forward and backward, into the then past and the then future, across that expanse of experience.

In this case the book as a whole will have a form and set of tones rather less like those of narration than like those of music.

That suits me, and I hope it turns out to be so.

————

From the amount I am talking about "this experience", you may

[114]

[115]

very reasonably have got the idea I think it was of some egregious importance. In that case you will be disappointed as well as wrong. This was just a series of extremely various, fairly complicated, and to me interesting, things which happened to me last summer, that's all. Greater and less things have happened, even to me. And I keep speaking of it in this way simply because I am respectful of experience in general and of any experience whatever, and because it turns out that going through, remembering, and trying to tell of anything is of itself, (not because the Experience was either hot or cold but of itself, and as a part of the experience) interesting and important to me.

From any set of particulars, it is possible and, perhaps, obligatory to generalize; that is all.

JOURNAL 3

[J 3.1: *LUNPFM* Notes and Outline
of Material from Journals 1 and 2]

We got back to town after 7 months' leave.
What is anyone to say of such a country as that.
pace placement & transportation
Negroes – a note
        appendix
        story
Landlords – appendix
        Tidmore & Negro
        Tidmore quotes
        the landlords & their houses
Money –
Location – Hale County
        immediate vicinity
        Moundville
suggestions to the reader
seasons & weathers
        odors – motions –
Mrs B.[1] Mrs T.[2] Ida Ruth[3]
Fortune
Selma
Tenantry
New deal
Lucile[4] & sweeping
The death of the kittens.
Postcard found in road.
Letters to us.

------

1. Allie Mae Burroughs, i.e., "Annie Mae (Woods) Gudger" in *Let Us Now Praise Famous Men*.

2. Mrs. Tingle, i.e., "Sadie (Woods) Ricketts."

3. Ida Ruth Fields, most likely "Emma Woods."

4. Lucille Burroughs, i.e., "Maggie Louise Gudger." See J 2.16.

[2]

<u>'We got back to town'</u> –
'The minute I got this assignment' – 2
'What I wanted to do'   3, 4,
pick my own   4, 5, 6
Bob Smith   7–11
League for Labor   11–16
Walker & leaving   18–22
train notes   22–28
Chattanooga   29–30
Read House   31–36
Chat-Birm-driving   36–39
   Bridge   40–41
   driving   42

The frogs – C
on the train (blue notebook B)
clay; Lucile – Ⓐ

JOURNAL 4

[1]

[J 4.1: Letter to Adam Margoshes]

Dear Mr. Margoshes:[1] Thank you very much for your letter. I'd like to send you some work if I have any. Of that I should explain: I've written almost no verse for a while, only, once in a while, here drawn out and worked over something done a while back. So my idea of what I have unpublished that is fit to be seen is foggy and it will take me some time to find out. But I wanted to answer you immediately, and to ask you too, whether prose rather than verse could be considered. And when is the latest I might send you something. The magazine sounds good. I'll see if I can get copies at the Times Bldg Bookstore. Thank you again.

Sincerely yours,

James Agee

[2]

[3]

[J 4.2: Journal Entry: "I've tried this before"]

5 January[2] 1938

(Why did I write 193<u>4</u>?)

I've tried this before. I have no better reason today than every to think I'll stay with it long. Reading Delacroix[3] has to do with it. So has my lack of notes on the Alabama trip,[4] the New Orleans trip with Alma,[5] and for

---

1. Adam Zion Margoshes. (1917–1966), later a professor of psychology and a columnist for the *Village Voice*. See J 4.2, note 15.

2. January 6. See J 4.3.

3. Eugène Delacroix, French painter (1798–1863). *The Journal of Eugène Delacroix*, translated and with an introduction by Walter Pach, was published in a handsome illustrated edition by Covici, Friede in 1937.

4. Agee's stay with sharecroppers in the summer of 1936 that resulted in *Let Us Now Praise Famous Men*.

5. During the summer of 1937, Agee and Alma Mailman took an extended automobile trip through the South, staying in Knoxville, Birmingham, and New Orleans.

that matter any day of my life. So has my feeling about notebooks, journals, and letters in general, and my feeling of all that composed work cannot touch. This one will have every din of selfconsciousness a journal or
person can have. I had better accept that fact to start with. In writing to
or for myself, all right: but whoever may read it will come on and off my
mind. I must make my one main rule, that that shall not interfere with
candor or cause me to white wash, or force me to any more or less laziness than is at the time natural to me. But if I get literary I get literary,
and if I get selfconscious I get selfconscious.

This is Thursday. I had to count up from Saturday to know the day
of the month.

Saw Blitzstein's show[6] again last night. I am glad they have kept it
without sets. I told Alma a minimum about it in advance,

[4]

as I did of Draper,[7] and of tactics with her father. I knew she would like
it fine but what all that she would feel all the exhilaration and joy she
did feel.

After the show straight to her place (after a chocolate Sundae, she
amused by watching me in a mirror and thinking I didn't know I was
watched). Gravitation into talk of Leroy Street.[8] I dropped all gentleness
without getting mad, knowing, too, what I was letting us in for, and told
her off on all she was spoiling or hurting or confusing or making difficult
by her immaturities, and how bad it was also, that to get anything new
to her into her head I was forced to be careful and gentle, not only a great
waste of energy of us both but such a diluter of what needed to be known
that her returns to kindness, though thankful to me one way, were always
a sad signal of my hopeless defeat in another; that whether she meant it
or not she was using her goodness and kindness as a weapon against us
both. Et cetera. The full involvement of such as this is what I would care
to write. It is tough as the toughest counterpoint.

------

6. The musical *The Cradle Will Rock,* with music and lyrics by Mark Blitzstein,
opened January 3, 1938, at the Windsor Theatre in New York and ran for 104
performances.

7. Left-wing writer, lecturer, and radio host Muriel Draper (1886–1952)
appeared at a number of fundraisers for the Loyalist cause after visiting Spain
in 1937.

8. Agee and his first wife, Via, lived at 121 Leroy Street in Greenwich Village.

She got sick as hell of it; I couldn't and never can, blame her, only despair; and I made up the couch single while she

[5]

undressed, feeling this time more stonily sad than vindictive.

She explained, more level than has been usual, that by mind she agreed with me in every detail, most of it even in advance of everything I said (by which I measure her unconsciousness of the size of the thing, and of what motivates her), and that all her forms of depression, from small to extreme, were always pure feeling, her mind still knowing I was right (and often enough hating me for it). I told her, the real crisis was the obstructions between her intelligence and her feelings, in which she is in common with nearly all the world, and could we work at great length on the causes of obstruction, the importance of non-obstruction, and all she defaulted through it. Yes, and she meant it. I told her also: To whatever degree you are not as angry at these things in yourself at least as I am, that is an accurate measure of your lack of understanding of what it is about. But she doesn't really understand it. It would take about the length of an analysis for her to and no one can be blamed for that. In her own terms and dimensions as they stand, she is one of the best things I know. I was realizing this again

[6]

as I lay with her. In every way I can feel favorable to mothers, I could care to be son to the best that is in her.

We started lovemaking on a fine, steady, human-animal but somewhat anesthetized basis. I tried for edge and delicacy, she too, and it did not bring it through. We both forced ourselves a little, not badly except that at all is badly, through a gently strong 69, and I realized it had slightly queered her. Shortly before we were ready for a fuck which could have been quietly sound & which could have ended in quiet, mutually kind and impassionate depression, I asked her how she was. She was kind and very slightly guarded—guarded in the sense that she could & would carry the slight burden of slight depression. She asked me, I was the same, and answered the same. I asked her if she wanted to go on with it. She said I don't know I suppose so. I said that as long as there was any doubt at all about it it was certain we shouldn't, so long as we well understood each other. I got off her and got her pajamas back on her and we both felt so fine at having used our heads and drawn a right distance between us that it was a matter of amused discipline not

[7]

to go through it all over again on a much better plane.

This morning she woke very strongly in love and I was happy chiefly in her happiness. We woke and slept and woke from 9.30 till about noon. Touching her breasts I realized, in remembrance of early Saturday morning, how much edge I had lost. I was quietly sad in undertone, with the feeling, this is what happens and what you lose but can hope with care to regain and sustain; but I don't now feel I want children of you and a lifetime with you, and all your gestures and your face, both conscious and unconscious, are those of a happy wife; you realize this some, but it is even more than you know; and right now, I know we shall not spend our lives together. I knew too, I would have to hide it from her. Her depression would exceed mine and both exceeded the bounds of sense.

Otherwise I was strongly well and we were both fine. We got up short of our habitual danger of loafing and took a shower together, keeping our hands off each other. I suggested we stay apart till our weekend Saturday and this was solidly and in good understanding agreed on, happily. We ate a slow

[8]

breakfast about two, and bought notebooks in the 14th St Woolworths.

I would like to have in stock about a dozen at a time of these, without any words on the cover. I wish they fit them with blank paper.

All this time I was getting back to work in my head, and looking forward to a hard afternoon of it at Bank Street,[9] and would see Brick[10] or Helen Levitt[11] tonight and sleep alone and she too, a fine re-charger when you miss the other. It was hard to leave her though I was in other ways eager to. I am very attached to her mouth eyes and body. Though

---

9. Bank Street, in Greenwich Village, presumably the location of the studio apartment Agee rented in the fall of 1937.

10. Wilbur Merrill "Brick" Frohock. See J 2.9, note 23.

11. Helen Levitt (1918–) was a photographer whom Agee met through Walker Evans, at the time her mentor. Agee later wrote the foreword to *A Way of Seeing,* a book of her photographs not published until 1965, and collaborated with her on two films, *The Quiet One* (1949) and *In the Street* (1952). In 1941 Agee's second wife, Alma, left him and went with their son and Levitt to Mexico.

I was hoping with some regretful doubt whether we would be sharp for each other by Saturday, I was already looking forward to it.

I left her at 11ᵗʰ & 6ᵗʰ and walked over to Bank. In an apartment court of cement and dirty yellow brick, against one wall, a hearselike black and empty baby carriage without today's bright sunlight anywhere near it.

[9]

I realize that subconsciously I was very relieved that Via and Walker[12] were away, and had made that a strong part of the shape of my peace of mind and anticipation of work, for when I turned into Bank and saw the Ford my first feeling was loss of work and solitude; disappointment. My second and third, hope that W. was there, and affection for Via.

W. had gone home to work. Via had been there an hour and had phoned me. She was affectionate and more glad to see me than I her. This made me feel badly and unsettled me. She began telling me about the trip. It had been queer, W. very detached & silent; her efforts to bring him cheerful irritating to him. "He is a very difficult person". "I realize I am running away from him like the devil." He too, and says so, he is afraid of women, though he tells me he isn't scared of me; he describes himself as a man in flight. (Thurber).[13]

I felt that my actions of the other morning must have deeply disturbed her, and felt rotten. I told Via I wanted within the next few minutes to clearly decide either to work or to talk to her, not to do so in suspension. It was in its

[10]

quiet way bad, though we were both trying & managing to be direct, clearheaded, and understanding of each other. I lost the focus for work. We came to Leroy Street for mail and I came here, Emma's,[14] 121 is cold and dark, and because I felt incapable of good work, I started this, after answering Margoshes' letter.

---

12. Via and Walker Evans had been having an affair since the summer of 1937.

13. James Thurber (1894–1961), American humorist, often portrayed male characters under the tyrannical thumb of women and investigated their fears, insecurities, and weak, ineffectual rebellions.

14. Agee's younger sister, Emma Agee. According to Walker Evans's extant diaries, he and Agee had met, probably through work at *Fortune*, by April of 1935, when Evans was romantically involved with Emma.

Margoshes[15] was in the mail. Adam Zion. Liked my lyrics in transition & P[artisan] Review[16] & did I have anything for Konkretion[17] a Danish magazine of world culture, dominantly surrealist, an American #? Told him I hoped so and will look & see. K is a good consonant. It is funny if I am a surrealist.

This is a day like spring. I wonder if there is a regular January equivalent to Indian summer, a pre-spring. I remember other Januaries even more itchy weather than this. Alma and I both hoped Saturday was this sort.

[11]

[J 4.3: Journal Entry: "All right, yesterday was the 6"]

Friday 7th

All right, yesterday was the 6. not the 5.

To 121 at 6.15, pulled the bed straight, lighted gas oven & called Walker. Brick came, knowing nothing of Via's having moved until I told him. He was very concerned and I knew I would tell him more about it during the evening. We laid off it during supper at Lynch's in idea it should take longer, unbroken talking, not to be overheard. Emma & Alma came in when we were nearly done and we drank more whisky while they ate. Then we bought a quart of 7 star[18] & went to Emma's. Seeing Alma in Brick's context of non-knowledge and his style of bleak criticism in the back of his brain was a little tough but soon wore off. We loafed around hearing radio & talking; Brick's & Emma's looseness of language being to me partly pleasant and partly a pain in the ass. It was thoroughly pleasant to be with Alma with other people

---

15. Adam Zion Margoshes. See J 4.1, note 1.

16. The poems Agee had published in these journals as of January 1938 are as follows: "Lyric" and "A Song," *transition* 24 (June 1936): 7; "In Memory of My Father (Campbell County, Tennessee)," *transition* 26 (Spring 1937): 7; "Lyrics," *Partisan Review* 4 (December 1937): 40–43.

17. *Konkretion*, a Danish journal of culture edited by Vilhelm Bjerke-Petersen, had a run of six issues from 1934 to 1936, including a final double issue on surrealism in Paris. Margoshes's connection with *Konkretion* is unknown, but he may have been associated with an attempt to resurrect the journal with, as Agee's comments imply, an issue devoted to American surrealists.

18. Metaxa Amphora 7 Star brandy.

who were friends and easy; it is in these occasional breaks of it that I realize how lonely a life we lead. As we got a little tighter Brick and Emma, who have a strong fond undertone of unconsummated sex towards each other, began dancing and Alma, very loose & cheerful, asked me to dance. I did very wide burlesque sex dancing, to which

[12]

she was replying, and we were very conspicuous and laughing. All this got hotter and broader for the next half hour and I was putting on the sort of crazy show I used to when I was drunk. Brick said he hadn't seen me act that way in years. (Emma later in the can said the same to Alma.) They have not been much around me but I am much less frequently that loud and gay. I know that to both Alma & me there was a great exhibitionistic pleasure in it and that doubled in knowledge of their enjoyment of the comedy. But we were also familiar as no parodists could be, but only those who knew each others bodies by heart. Alma was not only innocent & unaware but oblivious of her giveaways and I became too amused to try to conceal it, even when I realized it had come far through to Brick and tied in with Via to him. When they were in the can later we talked a little. It's none of it any of my business. Sure, in a sense it's not, but it would come natural to me to communicate it to you. Christ you don't need to communicate a damned thing (waving his hand towards bathroom door) I know all anyone needs to know about it. I'm not so sure you do. He didn't want to stay with it, got up & yoohooed at bathroom door.

[13]

Emma started, then improved on & did, first stages of a strip tease. Alma got into riding pants. I did an extremely poor, incomplete male strip tease. (A good piece of comedy could be made of a stripper whose zippers & snaps stick.) An hour of very juicy music very quiet, gypsy stuff, [Anton Rubinstein's] Kamenoi Ostrow, [Franz Liszt's] 2nd Hungarian Rhapsody, old movie theatre romantic Numbers. We were somewhat comically but deeply moved by it. Brick took Emma on his lap & they lay with their eyes shut feeling each other out. I sat in chair and poured drinks, Alma lay on floor and I knew she was feeling bad. After a while I sat down next her. The music was working very strong. We talked extremely low, against the ear. She was in a deep melancholy and wanted to be dead, and had felt that way nearly all the time for the past 3 years, and pitied anyone who wanted to live. I told her I knew too well her feeling to try to get optimistic; what she felt was true; other things were true too said it was important to know them in proportion. She was crying silently. She took my wrist hard and put her face close to me and said Jim: Love God. / I will, and you do that too. / I do. / Don't ever

[14]

forget to, and when you feel this way, don't dodge it but all the same let yourself relax on the thought of him.

Jim. Do you suppose I could stay with you tonight.

I want you to very much.

About 2 we went over to Leroy Street and I undressed her.

Her tiredness had made her look fully like a woman the past two days; 25–30 rather than her other demeanor, 20–25. She was extremely sad and clear, and deeply in love in a way she had not been before, except in little shows and flashes, a way totally unguarded and defenseless, a whole consigning of her life to my care. It made me sorrowful and heavily responsible and I tried to explain to her why. She disliked the fact and I told her I believed it was inevitable of certain complete kinds of love, chiefly because they are undefended and unqualified. I saw and loved her in our mutual terms and at the same time in total detachment, even more, as if I were a spy on both of us: so, the sharp lines at the left end of her mouth were beautiful and tragic to me. This plane of love I care more about for itself, and it seems also the most

[15]

true and the most valuable to the other planes.

It is troubling and angering to me that deep and true feeling, such as she was having when she wanted to die, seems impossible to reproduce unless the importance & symbolic value of the Feeler is swollen beyond ordinary human proportion. If there is callowness in her wish for death, there is in Hamlet's too, not more nor less. She was at the center of her universe. It should be possible to make the faithful record of any pair's love as exquisite, painful and life-and-death important to others as it is to them. If this can't be done (I've not seen it done) then literature and art are more limited than I care for anything to be, and the hell with them. (It is accomplished by the way in letters, such as Dorothy Carr's[19] to me.)

It is pretty useless about places to eat. One neighborhood contains only one or two that are any good. Getting tired of them and trying others almost invariably is a mistake. Better resign beyond point of Resignation, better clearly accept this

[16]

and quit resenting the beaten tracks to the old places. Take them as you take a subway and the same with the food, especially breakfasts. There are only 4 or 5 breakfasts and it is nearly impossible not to get sick as hell of them. But you'd better adjust yourself to them. I don't ever want to see another egg. Coffee is the only reliable. They shd be more often skipped and reduced to coffee; varied and sharpened by abstinence, like sex and like anything else.

This noon we had Cocanut Waffles. I was surprised they were so good. But I don't want another for a good while.

Singing Bach, clear again, German is a basic language for <u>simple</u> emotion, faith's splendor and guts. Again; slow-paced; chorale-paced; short-worded lyrics.

We are fringing that dangerous (how much avoidable?) stage where 2 people begin to get on each other's nerves, and again I am the more nervous. I'd like to see what a strong dose would do to me of being the one to irritate a

[17]

woman.

The little black shoes under the nightgown still give her the delight that is truly in them. Me, no longer as much, or not this morning; and this sad mechanics: that her own delight, though I know it is unaffected, can increase my lack of delight out of: a fear of the danger of whimsy & cult; a regret at our inequality of feeling; a regret at lying lightly (by not letting her down); and my love for her happiness and determination not to let her down.

---

19. See J 2.2, note 9.

Such reactions are much less heavy-hearted than they sound when laid out on paper.

There is also the salvation-chance of <u>knowing</u> the mechanics of an equation as inevitable: that can relieve you of the pushovers of bewilderment and reduce regret to its true size.

Even such a simple 4 seconds as the above takes all that time to put down, and even then I know I have not put it down even as clearly & fully as I understand it.

[18]

No wonder people and psychologies in even good fiction seem so unsatisfactory. The wonder is that any illusion is created at all. Even Proust and Joyce seem overselected and simple, and Lord knows I can fall for every Literary & human idea of such as the above as too unimportant to bother with. It isn't though. Nor should it be selected and nearly lighted. In actual life there are a hundred similar cases to the one selected which convinces in fictions. Why is reading that much more intense & exhausting than living. The most ordinary breathing of the brain is carried on at musical or poetic intensity if not more; and is not at all tiring. Why is it exhausting when it is put down on paper. The repeats and near repeats would kill with boredom and weight on paper; we sustain them in common life without effort. The exhaustion of common-life written would be false to the non-exhaustion it writes of. The non-exhaustion of fiction is true to the paces of common life but is true through a dozen eliminations and dilutions, which are falsehood. Selection,

[19]

symbolization etc etc are among the first inexorables of art. Then in certain senses something is badly wrong with art.

[J 4.4: Journal Entry: "Two magazines"]

Monday 10.

Friday afternoon-evening-night.   Saturday morning frustration.
        Atlantic City.   Sunday night.   Picture detective.

Two magazines: Picture Detective and another.[20] They have revived the old gangster pamphlet idea of police photographs and taken it into more general crime. The other devotes itself to women in crime. I bought this instead (lacking money for both) for the picture on the cover. As Walker says they must be thoroughly aware of the pathological public they feed & count on. From circulation it might be possible to estimate sadistic population but not really: buy enough stares [?] of it so that a huge crowd wd buy one issue in three. Part of my own interest is that. I'm not made sick by the worst of these as Via is. It is of greatest good for true sets and properties surrounding the murders and crimes—and for various faces. The lunchroom street scene dominated by Indian Simmons; and inside. The bathroom linoleum and sink where the

[20]

cop dies. The desk, radiator and shirt. Even the dark paint around the latch and handle of the door. The 2 cars. The lunchroom with the corpse, and dawn outside.[21] The bare hallway to Weir's room and the carpet on it.[22] The room where all that desperate, cramped and lonely fucking took place. Its wallpaper. The Kentucky road. All the Kentuckian faces. The Armstrong Hotel.[23] Marie Solfa. Hoover and the cowgirls. The Laundry. All indoor details. The 2 hatchet men. The faces & figures of Harley and Green. Hahn's old men. The smart doctor. The field of burial. Hein's talking. Detective. Prosecutes. Bringing up a body.

---

20. The second magazine is *Actual Detective Stories of Women in Crime*, which covered the Denhardt-Taylor murders (see note 30) in its December 1937 issue; no copies of *Picture Detective* could be located.

21. On February 14, 1937, Harry Simmons and Albert Faria were arrested for the murder of policeman Thomas Ennis after robbing the Hi-Hat Restaurant in East Orange, New Jersey. William Chadwick, who worked at the restaurant, was later charged as an accomplice.

22. In Newark, New Jersey, on July 10, 1935, Richard Weir, a thirty-five-year-old soda jerk, walked up to a patrolman and calmly stated, "I've just cut my sweetheart's throat." Mary Louise Rogers's body was found in his room at 79 Court Street. Weir, who had several drinks at a nearby saloon before approaching the police, was later sentenced to life in prison.

23. General Henry H. Denhardt was shot in front of the Armstrong Hotel in Shelbyville, Kentucky, on September 20, 1937. See note 30.

Hahn and her boy. Hahn before. Hahn after; and the man with her.[24]
The 2 cops. The Maine baby & the trooper. The cop looking at the
corpse. Mrs Shaffer & child. Shaffer's hat. Dalhover.[25] The 2 fat wives.
W[m] Smith. The Princess. The knife. Her body. The bathing beauty.

The cover picture, disembodied from any content, is one of the
most frightening I know. The completely savage world. The hard flash
does a great deal. 3 kinds of idiot cruel laughter. None of them look
like cops. They look like special appointees

[21]

of a Kafka but American second-world disguised as cops. The one at
the left I have seen his kind several times, oversized, milk skinned, soft-
jointed adolescent, usually a not well liked clown, who looks like his
mother and masturbates a great deal. Always blond; always that kind
of teeth. Smiles always and laughs very frequently. The middle one is
close to one kind of stage cop: the kind a Flaming Youth[26] girl has to
do with, Leatrice Joy[27] causes his death. He is very conscious of his
looks. The third cop would look like that telling a sex joke or hearing
one, or fucking a whore. His hand is vital with sadism like the balancing hand of a toddling baby. The man is a natty dresser. Foulard tie.
The always new and light colored hat of every city criminal. That his
tie is disarrayed and his hat battered is almost the cruellest thing in the
picture. He could be badly wounded and in great pain but more likely
it is only his pride that is outraged, and his futile hatred and defiance
and his futile cursing. His guts to keep calling them sons-of-bitches is
the last life he has and he is desperately trying to turn their laughter into
anger that would bring him back a little dignity. They are on to this,
too. They may even have known his weakness from before.

---

24. Anna Marie Hahn, the first woman executed in Ohio, was convicted on
November 6, 1937, of poisoning several elderly men for their money. Her
twelve-year-old son, Oscar, testified in court on her behalf.

25. On October 12, 1937, gangsters Al Brady and Clarence Lee Shaffer were
killed in a gunfight with G-men in Bangor, Maine. James Dalhover was wounded
and captured and later executed.

26. *Flaming Youth*, a 1923 film starring Colleen Moore, was the first "flapper"
movie and became synonymous with Jazz Age debauchery.

27. American actress (1896–1985). Agee is referring to Cecil B. DeMille's
Manslaughter (1922), in which Joy plays a wild society girl whose carelessness
results in the death of a motorcycle policeman.

page 4. The inset of Indian Simmons over the place of climax, to date, of his life and of his friends, and of the cop, and of the lunchroom boys, is good. This smiling picture could easily as not have been made after the crime. Again the pearl hat and the smart angle. They are so smart they always, even in the flesh, look as if they had been pasted in by a retoucher; they never quite fit on the face.

Reversed negative? The handkerchief is on the right. He would have a handkerchief and would long ago have graduated beyond wearing it with the 3 or four corner-points showing flat. The lapel and long collar fit the nose and long V mouth and probably the cock as well. Foulard tie again.

The damp street is fine and the whole overexposed quality of the picture; the bricks have delicacy; the pallor makes the whole thing historic as well as present. All the good people who never did this sort of thing, backed into line; nearly every face, cops and all, turned toward the lens with a certain sense of history and of self-importance.

The interior is fine. Day after the murder? The waiters have been ordered to turn their faces away? By whom? Or is one

[23]

of them, still unsuspected, Chadwick? I like the reversed 5¢ and the 5 across the street, the neon Hamburgers to ogle and again the 2 faces looking at the camera. Unposed faces looking at a camera have a special human expression nearly unprecedented. (Not quite; some paintings show these faces). Of this in its varieties & of its uses there must be investigation analysis and study.

Rain in all these pictures. Top coats, and chilly; wet hats and in #3. Simmons re-enacting.

The dark picture is a damned beautiful still-life. Demure almost in neatness, bachelor pathos of shirt (what is the tie doing there?); small-time pathos craft of hiding surplus in this wooden place. Fruit and bottle crates; bulletin; license, bareness of desk; bachelor-neatness truck on radiator shelf. Very long-armed man for the shirt. The lined floor is pretty like a drawing.

The uniform height of the rolled sleeves in #2 is touching; and the gauze cap. Biceps pride.

I guess Ennis is not dead but still dying here, of stomach wounds. His pants appear to have been belted together for the photograph. He has the right kind of chest hair for his face and, by appearance,

[24]

the same on his head; and certainly the right build. A specially strong, gentle and dutiful type and totally courageous; these three things very strongly appear in his dying breathing which is that of a gentle bull. Orchitic [?]. Dumb and kind in bed. Loves his wife and entirely faithful to her almost even in thought. Simple and kind though limited sense of right and wrong. This kind of man would be drawn towards policing, too; so much even that he would appear more logically as a policeman than as anything else; and enough of him that I would guess this is one type of cop. There would be rare individuals who would have intelligence as well as his qualities; but he is not exactly an individual; more like a breed of dog; and very much the best by breed or cast type that ever becomes an American cop.

#6. Simmons is certainly enjoying the re-enactment; at the same time, is almost a little scared of it, like a teller frightened by his own ghost story. I guess the complacent portrait was made at this time, after the killing, the hat is so much the same.

(Of course he would be likely always to buy the same hat.) All the scared good-citizen faces behind him, nearly

[25]

every one again watches the camera, as he does. Two keep their eyes on him. They are scared almost to the point of believing he might bust loose right now and get them. The older of them, with the cigar, the peace-loving son of a bitch, I would like to exterminate. The younger is half envious. The professorial type at the extreme right is not looking at anything.

These faces are like words in good poetry. They mean and tell more than can at all be told about them. You get the whole more than double ambiguity of a living individual in each one and in each, recognize a whole human life and a strong shot of the whole of human life.

It must be Fall, by the time such a picture as thus is made.

Most of the faces are middle class and most of the middle class are middle aged. They have in common an animal quality. Herbivorous, gregarious, rather waddling, easily frightened. Fuzzy, if they were furbearers. Each is a carnivore too and they are all pleased for instance that Simmons will burn; but they are here a little tremulously assembled in their nibbling and fluffy state of mind. They all want to protect their

[26]

homes and their businesses.

Disney has not done everything that could be done with animals.

Both the cars, maybe largely because of flashbulb chiaroscuro, are convincing crime cars.

The background for the bigger one is by accident Art-photo focus. Here I think that is right, with the disembodied car and the oil-spotted concrete. A fine a complex atmosphere of dawn and context suggestion of violence.

#7 is pure lyric. Plaster-scattered floor by door. Very slightly disaligned chair seats. Calm light on table. Cop and nightstick. Above all, the quality of dawn in the door glass and the street and opposed storefront. Death and dawn gentle, definitive and monumental. It needs and should have no context.

————

Weir's unpressed and seldom worn coat. It must have been folded for months in a suitcases or bureau drawer.

This case and these pictures take a lot of work. His

[27]

face and figure before the camera. He gives himself whole there. Why can't it be got into words at least in pieces? It is so simultaneous in him. And her face, mouth, dress, legs, angle of right arm and wrist like a killed bird. Was her hair so long?, is that it, from beneath her thigh? I wish the snapshot on the bureau was legible. The crampedness and detail of the room and the awful loneliness of everything they had. This was a Good House. A woman must have kept it and she and Weir must both have thought of it as Good. The hall carpet is still clear; so is that on the rising step. The hall wallpaper is a little stained but it is solid. The bannisters are brightly varnished, otherwise you would get a less strong halation. The paper and rug in Weir's room are both in thoroughly good condition. His shade is solid. The curtains are clean and a lot of care and material went into making them pretty of their sort. The shelves are so cleanly painted the upper one reflects the wallpaper. The bedstead is hotel type and would have a better than average spring; the mattress is thin but not skimped looking and is a little oversize to the bed. Made to be as much like home as a very poor very lonely single man could hope to find at the price.

[28]

The rug appears to go all the way under the bed, to cover the whole floor.

(Here I got tired and restless, and nearly sure to surrender to one form or another of weakness. I felt like the pacifications of masturbating, but knew in advance its probable depressing effect; also that sexual fasting in all ways will be my surest and soonest restorative to more solid love and mental clarity than I have felt for several days. I am very slowly learning in this and in my mind, and still more slowly, and irregularly, beginning to have the intelligence and strength to apply what I have learned. I am not speaking of masturbation but of everything to do with the psychophysiology of sex. I masturbate 'infrequently'; whatever that means. By my own estimate for myself, on average once in 3 weeks.

What I finally surrendered to was reading Gide, the Congo.[28] With about one sentence in every two I knew[29] the mistake I was making [and that] I was doing wrong, for I was disturbed as you are bound to be when you find even minute aspects of your mind, and methods, and technical ideas, anticipated or cut across. I must not touch this book again until I have finished mine, though my own thinking would in some obvious respects gain by it. It causes weakness and paralysis and can indeed suggest death, which it literally is: one 'ego'

[29]

masked by another, the masking of binary stars. Most of the people I would most enjoy reading and most prefer to study, I should not read.)

---

28. André Gide, *Travels in the Congo,* trans. Dorothy Bussy (New York: Knopf, 1929).

29. Here Agee has drawn a single bracket in front of and containing the phrases *the mistake I was making* and *I was doing wrong,* with the former above the latter. A line runs from the bracket to this explanation: *these are nearly always synonymous and the upper of the two I believe always the more nearly true.*

Details here are strongly suggestive, and recessive into experience like faced mirrors. Weir's coat. The coats on the hangers on the middle hook. His mother and childhood are suggested by the room. The glass shade of the suspended light suggests its quality of white light (the bulb naked against the eye) and acutely, the sound as the chain is pulled against the glass to turn the light off, both when he was lonely before he knew the girl, and when she was with him. The cheap alarm. I believe it is cheap by the button on top of it. (It turns out he had a reading light; and probably would seldom have used this overhead.) In the hall picture the carpeting of the rising step looks well cushioned, but suggests the sound it would yield as you started to ascend, wall-papered walls close on either side of you, to your room. The loneliness and home detail and sorrow of this room, how his life must have been before he met the girl, completely suggests how he would go crazy at the first indication he was losing her. It looks to be a body long to its width yet

[30]

full, as in the upper thighs, loose and flexible, and she would have been soft. The mouth is almost Negroid heavy, the lower jaw light. She would have been hot and pliable, and probably for a while very loving to him and much excited by him; the fact of the loneliness of each and of their solitude together, the smallness of the room, would have increased their excitement in each other and would have extended them to 'lengths' they might under more social circumstances have balked at or not imagined.

By the size of head he would be a short man.

He must be looked at a lot more. Exactly why do I think I 'get' so much from his picture, and what is it I think I get.

KENTUCKY.

Verna Garr Taylor.[30] Dirty sex in this face. It is not congruent with fucking or even masturbating but with very vain, cockteasing flirtation.

---

30. On November 6, 1936, Verna Garr Taylor died from a gunshot wound to the heart in a roadside ditch in Henry County, Kentucky. Taylor's fiancé, Henry H. Denhardt, adjutant general of the Kentucky National Guard and former lieutenant governor of the state, with whom she had been traveling, was arrested for her murder. Denhardt claimed that Taylor had taken his service revolver

As if sex, her looks, and your desire (the latter assumed by her) was a joke between herself and you in which, of course, you were bound to be the loser, with a public standing by and catching on, and laughing at you. I hate women who are professional beauties and confident of their beauty. Even so it has

[31]

some peasant in it (it is not refined), borne out much more strongly in her brothers. This is one Southern idea of a lady, a beauty, sexual health. Her feeling is evidently that she radiates all 3. Get then the quality of tension in the smile and in the squinted eyes. It is not far from a leer, though one disguised, even to her.

No she is not flirting here; she's just breaking down and <u>admitting</u> she's one of the most beautiful women in Kentucky.

I believe I would know this for a Southern woman. Why.

The crisscross of peasant (strong neck, kind of face, strong slope of rt. shoulder) and society (hair, skin, again face, dress, demeanor, bad dress),

the ugly tone of sex and womanliness in the smile and eyes
the sex in the tilt of the head and in the contraction of shoulders
these belong in Southern sex and to a lady or imitation lady.

The extreme of this type smile is Jeanette MacDonald.[31] What in the brain and solar plexus causes this relationship of lips over teeth, by which the upper is drawn tight and the lower protruded. It is always insinuative and is nearly always sexual.

---

from the glove compartment of his stalled car and committed suicide. Denhardt's first trial ended in a hung jury. On the eve of the second trial, Taylor's three brothers, Jack, Roy, and Dr. E. S. Garr, ambushed Denhardt on the street in front of the Armstrong Hotel in Shelbyville, killing him. The Garr brothers claimed to have acted in self-defense, and after a sensational trial covered by the national, international, and tabloid press, Roy was found not guilty. (The charges against Jack were dropped because he had not fired a weapon, and E. S. was unable to stand trial for health reasons.)

Agee may have taken his pseudonym for the Tingle family in *Let Us Now Praise Famous Men* from accounts of the case mentioning the Henry County coroner, D. L. Ricketts.

31. American actress (1903–1965). MacDonald adopted a more wholesome image after moving to MGM in 1934.

[32]

The road. If you drove from Nashville to Louisville on a grayly sunlit day you would see just this in about half your mileage. It is right for murder by this ordinariness; as mortal smashups always seem peculiarly appropriate to straightaways. This kind of wide shallow ditch I am fond of. The 2 cars down at the farmhouse look uncustomary as they are and lonely, and important, like the car of a sunday afternoon caller on a farm. A strong feeling here of the walk up the road from the cars, & of the feet & bodies going sensitive and stepping a little light as they press what they judge to have been close to the exact spot.

Except for their look of country-come-to-city, the officials needn't be southern.

E. S. could be New England in his first picture. Tight, mean mouth, self-certain, righteous, hating eyes.

6. Of the daughters the one to the left seems an unusually good girl, though a very limited one. Why limited; how do I get. Her face is balanced and healthy, but clean and blank of more than the very plain forms of intelligence that make is so. She is wearing mourning and it is in

[33]

her class and country's good taste. She carries a handkerchief to cry with (by all obvious rights it belongs to her sister). She gives no appearance of smugness or of inverted immodesty before the camera. She looks intelligent enough not to have been much fooled about her mother. Sexually not a teaser nor even a flirt; clear in that as far as she goes which is not far: one-man woman, modestly but cleanly good at position one, when and not until she marries a genuinely nice and ltd. young man.

Her sister is a horror. The hands fit the face. Anemic. Irregular menstruation. Both jealous and contemptuous of her older sister whom, in her consciousness, she thinks is sweet, and loves. Steep neurotic. Masturbator. Daydreamer of pink & white vanilla flavored romances with marshmallow and whipped cream. Awful camera lust. Mirror gazer. Making the most she can of this tragic opportunity. Self pitier. She practised this in front of a mirror either before or after the picture, or both. She was here taken I think almost by surprise, but her

rarified qualities of bitchiness effortlessly reflexed into immediate &
unanimous focus. Much feeling of how gently aristocratic she is.

They are straight city girls or the <u>nicest</u> people in small-city small-
town. The elder looks clear of Southern woman traits

[34]

at least to point at which she wd not be recognizable as such by appearance alone. The younger I would bet on any day. You would find her
north too; but 5 to one of her in the south.

Her coat & hat are magically appropriate to her.

Their uncles are still peasant, whether or not they live in a city.
These are best clothes for country funeral and you could tell a lot by
the ties alone. The one at left is harder than hell; cruel; cruel to women;
vain. Looks a little like a jazz musician. Most urban of the 3 & most
urbane. Get the right hand & cigaret, too. As Eisenstein said gesture
& expression are meaningless out of context: these eyes could all be
either funeral (fresh grief; suspicion); or trial (an affair of honor; we are
not ashamed of what we have done). I think latter by face at left &
cigaret but in that case the breakdown of E. S. is interesting in relation
to the hardness in his other picture.

3$^{\underline{rd}}$ brother is still pure deep country right to the haircut. His eyes
and vengefulness a different kind from theirs. Kinder than they are,
more brutal to animals, more kind to animals, more impleable. Middle
one: religious-social; social fear; social pride; righteousness.

[35]

Denhardt is a complete son of a bitch and a perfect landlord face. All
the 4 faces in that picture (which is a fine and frightening picture) are
important as of the landowning class; but his is the worst; the subtlest,
the most vital, the most brutal, the most dangerous. Gigantic bull vitality. Much pride in the face and assumption of liking & respect & cen-
trality. His comedy is that of that sort of man. He knows they think
of him as a Jersey bull and likes that. He knows they know he is putting
on a show & he likes that. He knows they think of him, with some envy
and some fear and some astonishment, as not only a rarin hellraiser but
really a good deal of a son of a bitch and that, plus the openness of the
opinion in their faces, plus the fact none of them would say it directly,
is pleasant to his pride too.

I am tired and shall quit this a while.

[36]

[37]

[J 4.5: *LUNPFM:* Draft of Introduction]

In the summer of 1936 the photographer Walker Evans and I spent two months in the South preparing an article for <u>Fortune</u>[x] on an average family of white tenant farmers. Ever since, I have been wanting to give an account of the two months. My difficulty is, that I want to give a complete and true account. Anyone who has seriously considered the meaning of the words complete and true will know that I may as well give it up on the spot. Some of the rest of you will think I am making some graceful literary gestures of humility; the rest of you will wonder what I am talking about.

The difficulty again is this. I want not only to give a complete and true account, but to give it in terms which shall be understandable, and unmistakeable, and inescapable, to any human being who can read this language.

It should therefore be easy for certain of you to understand that I can neither do what I want to, nor give it up, nor find any ease or comfort whatever in yielding even the slightest compromise: and that this situation is sickening, and enraging, and paralyzing, toward the point of death.

---

[x] A magazine.

[38]

I will yield this much because I must in recognition of truth:

It is beyond hope that any human being shall tell the truth about anything.

It is beyond hope that any human being shall perceive the truth about anything.

It is beyond hope that any human being shall succeed in communicating what he intends to any other human being.

Beyond this, I shall not yield, but constantly shall try to force my self and you, whoever you are, who read this, as near the truth as I am able, and without mercy except in the name of truth. Set your sail vertical to the wind, all motion relapses into chaos and disaster. But set it as close as you can get it short of that; be always on the margins. The rough going is in direct ratio.

You cannot have good manners, and you cannot have mercy. It is impossible sufficiently to assume the delusion, ignorance, cowardliness, laziness and selfishness of every human being who reads this, and of myself. You cannot and must not allow this enemy any foothold.

[39]

You will never conquer him; but your force may help hold his teeth from the throat, the bowels, the soul of the human race: where in fact they have had for ever a perhaps mortal and a perhaps unbreakable and a perhaps inalleviable hold.

Enter, mercy, break forth in gentle tears. No man, not the worst, that ever lived, is guilty, not any, ever.

But let no man take any ease of his guiltlessness.

Insofar as we know, we are responsible; and must most strictly of all suspect our knowledge.

We are trapped exactly as narrowly in tragedy as in life itself. We had better never forget that, and we had better learn to breathe it in an out with every breath: and it is also joy: and we had better learn that too.

So it is nothing easy I want to write to you, nor nothing any of you are going to like. What I wish in god I could do with it is blow your brains out with it.

Above all, for Christ's sake don't think of it as Art.

[40]

(3 space)
Above all else; in God's name don't think of it as Art.

Every fury on earth has been absorbed in time, as art, or as religion, or as authority in one form or another. The deadliest blow the enemy of the human soul can strike is to do fury honor. Swift, Blake, Beethoven, Christ, Joyce, Kafka, name me one who has not been thus castrated. Official acceptance is the one unmistakable symptom that salvation is beaten again, and is the one sure sign of fatal misunderstanding, and is the kiss of Judas.

Really it should be possible to hope that this be recognized as so, and as a mortal and inevitably recurrent danger. It is scientific fact. It is disease. It is avoidable. Let a start be made. And then exercise your perception of it on work that has more to tell you than mine has. See how respectable Beethoven is; and what right any wall in museum, gallery or home presumes to wear a Cézanne; and by what idiocy Blake or work even of such intention as mine is ever published and sold. I will tell you a test. It is unfair. It is untrue. It stacks all the cards. It is out of line with what the composer intended. All so much the better.

Get a radio or a phonograph capable of the most extreme loudness possible, and sit down to listen to a performance

[41]

of Beethoven's 7$\underline{th}$ Symphony or of Schubert's C-Major Symphony. But I don't mean just sit down and listen. I mean this. Turn it on as loud as you can get it. Then get down on the floor and jam your ear as close into the loudspeaker as you can get it and stay there, breathing as lightly as possible, and not moving, and neither eating nor smoking nor drinking. Concentrate everything you can into your hearing and into your body. You won't hear it nicely. If it hurts you, be glad of it. As near as you will ever get, you are inside the music, not only inside it, you are it. Your body is no longer your shape and substance, it is the shape and substance of the music.

Is what you hear pretty? or beautiful? or legal? or acceptable in polite or any other society? It is beyond any calculation savage and dangerous and murderous to all equilibrium in human life as human life is; and nothing can equal the rape it does on all that death: nothing except anything in existence or dream, perceived anywhere remotely toward its true dimensions.

—1 space—

Beethoven said a thing as rash and noble as the best of his work. By memory, he said: 'he who understands my music can never know unhappiness again'. I believe it. And

[42]

I would be a liar and a coward and one of your safe world if I should fear to say the same words of my best perception, and of my best intention.

Performance, in which the whole fate and terror rests, is another matter.

(End)

[43]

[J 4.6: Journal Entry: "Love, art and religion"]

late Wed. night 12th Jan 38

Love, art and religion (<u>true</u>) can exist only in insecurity,—in the narrowest security that can be imposed on precariousness. This is not quite so, you would have to add of the security that in our astonishment and gratitude that it has been built upon precariousness this security can be rested on and can appear to fill the universe (it does). But this by imperceptible degrees can degrade into planes of security which are the death of precariousness. If you are lucky, they are then at length the death of themselves too and the precariousness can begin all over.

You cannot go at the long job of learning what is wrong with you without caring strongly enough to; you cannot care strongly enough to before you realize what is wrong with you. This is hopeless. But there can be other inducements to care strongly. One is a clear realization of the cruelty of the trap itself. Another is every ounce of knowledge you have of what is true and right. Another is your knowledge of what we have, and that can only rightly be measured by its best, like the poetry or music a man writes. And the other is religious. None of these things depend on feeling. They are facts. They can be known at any time.

[44]

I am exhausted; headache, lack of sleep, work, concern about Alma. It is 2.30 and I had only 4 hours last night. Every return of insecurity about Alma, and every passiveness from her, makes me crazy, and puts me in love again. Saturday-Sunday, Atlantic City with Alma. We had looked forward to it but had seen each other too much. The deep degree she was in love with me had troubled me and set me out of love with her. It was not a painful but not a very joyful weekend. An extremely passionate and almost loveless fuck. We spent most of Sunday in bed and were very much alive to each other sexually, but not emotionally. A rather depressed drive home. That night we were very tired. I stayed. She played combination slave and mother and we became beautifully and tenderly happy. I realized in a degree I never have before, that all resourcefulness and intelligence could and maybe should be discarded in man-woman relation, that they should be to each other what neither can be toward anyone else, childish, gentle, and simple. It takes pure faith beyond my present power, and a breakage of strong habits. We were much too happy to sleep much. Monday morning I wrote notes on the pictures. All but the toughest 10$^{\underline{th}}$ need discarding and a

[45]

new start made. Monday afternoon, what, writing, I forget what. Yes, more pictures. Saw Via. Supper with her and Tony. Went to see Zola,[32] wishing I was seeing Alma and gladly knowing it was wiser not to, seeing her the next night. Zola stank as I had foreseen. I was so mad at these faked integrities I wrote till 3, a new start on the Alabama book. Stayed at Via's. Tuesday, late morning, got the stove going again. Leroy St very cold, took hours to get even tepid. Had planned to spend this week hunting out what might be publishable, needing money. Nothing looked so. Sat down to start something that might be. Havana.[33] To Gladys L[ea's] for supper with Alma. Rehearsal. Alma emotionally flat. Passive and distressing a little, though we both had control & understanding and parted well, she for 2 hours work. Home, loneliness intensifying, all I love in her also intensified to point of tears of gratitude and confidence too strong to have alone and I phoned to tell her. Naturally enough she misunderstood it and sank me in hell, such that later in kindness she came over, finished her work here, and spent the night. It was sad, for she was still passive though kind, and I cared too much

[46]

for her sleep to try to bring her from it.

Exhausted and sick this morning, could not work. Letter from Franklin.[34] Answered it at some length and told him some about Alma. She was on my mind all morning and I was much in love with her, and wrote her a very serious letter. Lunch with Via. Rewrote the Havana so far, now much improved and nearly right to go on with I think. Alma phoned. I am not sure she fully understood how much the letter meant. After 5, saw her. Not time enough to talk, read to her some. In last

---

32. *The Life of Emile Zola,* directed by William Dieterle (1937).

33. Apparently a reworking of "Six Days at Sea," *Fortune* 16 (September 1937): 117–120, 210–220. Rpt. as "Havana Cruise" in Ashdown, 139–57.

34. Franklin Miner, an older friend of Agee's from Harvard.

moments made mistake of talking a little. At crucial sentences Emma walked in. She has genius for that. I had to leave with all unresolved. Submerged torture all evening. Supper & cig with W[alker] & V[ia]. To Alma's to write & leave a note. Her light on. Foolish enough to ring her bell, knowing she would regret my voice. She did and got over it. We talked 2 hours. No time to record it now.

My spine aches in the large vertebrae at the base of the neck.

This afternoon played 1st mvt of Mozart D minor much better than ever before. Good night my own love.

[47]

[J 4.7: Journal Entry: "I am at a low"]

27 January.

I am at a low. The heart of it appears to be total self-mistrust and weakness of mind and spirit; the at least patchwork cure would be hard work, which I cannot touch. I am frozen not only sexually but in every way of contact with people. I dread people and I dread being alone for I cannot work and cannot stand my own company. I have been trying to trick myself along with parapsychology cards and with a long letter to Franklin. The letter is dead on my dead hands and I am sick of the cards. I particularly need to see Alma and I particularly dread to see her, for she is liable to lack instinct for support in this sort of thing. Even if she had it it would do no good; but her lack does harm. It is entirely my own job and I cannot seem to touch it. I must be really badly sick, somewhere out of reach of myself, in the head or 'heart', or whatever it is. I am at a point with the Havana thing that would require what I can't now possibly give it: 'orchestration', and a big development. I can half-trace some immediate possible causes: a desperate and exhausting weekend with Alma; the impact of the sort of thing, innocence, no mind, true feeling, that Wolfe means; sexual

[48]

drainage; guilt over my concealment from Walker and my postponement of telling him; guilt, pity, uncertainty, over Via and over Alma and over my own conduct; need of money; no home I care to come to; no heat in it; dirty; delays and postponements of seeing Alma; _____. It's enough I suppose. Yet in a 'good' state of mind I carry this and more.

I must get the stove working here again, clean it up, and live here steadily; make getting up at eight more important to me than any other appointment in the day, short on sleep or not.

I know that Wolfe troubles me a great deal. He is a stupid man as well as a good and innocent one, and his stupidity gives me a feeling of cheapness or guilt or shallowness for whatever forms of understanding I have that he lacks. I am fond of him, and would I think like his friend-ship, and exactly in that proportion. I also want to avoid him, and cer-tainly a part of this avoidance is a form of cowardice I cannot afford. In some ways the worst is, I can't take hold of any of these things and even try to understand them better. I know I am wrong to feel regretful of 'intelligence' and weak with lack of innocence, but I can't

[49]

seem to do anything about it.

I know this depression will not 'last', but I also know it will return; depression and distraction and laziness, lack of strength, forms of fear, have occupied most of my life and have interrupted or destroyed nearly everything I have hoped to do. I know a dozen things that are wrong, and I can no more take hold of them as I am now than if they were pieces of hot iron.

Short of real cure, work is the only possible way out, and the only thing which can give any integrity and vitality to anything else in my life.

I guess I will try to write more of Havana.

[J 4.8: Journal Entry: "'JOURNAL' indeed"]

25 Feb.

'JOURNAL' indeed.

So much stacks up, and still more when you abandon it a while, that you feel weak at trying to write or resume such a thing as this.

Trying also to clean the writing in it. My writing of it is soft and affected. I mistrust all my vocabulary: 'indeed'; 'stacks up'; 'you' (but one or I is

[50]

as bad); 'abandon'; fake accuracy of 'weak'; fake accuracy & frailty of 'clean'; whether or not even to complete or uncomplete sentences: In fact Most of my 'problems' are meaningless, mutual negatives, because

I am still on a plane, like the League of Nations, or the controversy between the conservative scoutmaster and the liberal minister, where none of it can make any difference.

Ted Spencer[35] or what he represents is still able to disconcert me; not entirely, unless at all is entirely, but definitively. I had forgotten, maybe preferred to forget, how sharp and how hard such standards can be, much more strict than those I live in now, yet they also appear to me to kill, sometimes, & more often to partly numb, whatever they touch. And where I have a sort of strictness, his kind of mind has nothing, or a formula name for it, or death. And I believe the directions I am working toward are more 'true' and important: But strictnesses in his standards do nevertheless disconcert me: I realize ways I have become flabby or disregarding. The disconcertion is both demoralizing and, if you face it, salutary. But how much besides the work itself should be faced when you are working or preparing to work, I don't know. It can make you incapable of work that might be good.

[51]

Keep making additions to two lists. One: all items, material and psychic, which like a rain impinge on a tenant from birth (or conception) on. Two: All the 'equations' or 'traps', material or psychic, in his existence or environment.

List and invent all possible questions of various kinds of half-informed people about tenants, Negroes, etc etc, the whole south; and answer them one by one.

Definitions; a dictionary; a miniature encyclopedia. (T-F).[36]

In different keys, to different people (T-F).

Straight letters, to for instance her and her.

It can be so easy for my whole life to wrench, dry out and miss itself.

---

35. Theodore Spencer (1902–1949) was an English professor at Harvard and Agee's tutor and friend. He introduced Agee to the Saunders family.

36. I.e., *Three Tenant Families*.

I am aware of this and I have 'intelligence' and 'conscience'; but of these I am more sure of their power to deceive me than of their power to help me.

You can think with illusions of and perhaps at times genuine clarity and disinterestedness of even a difficult situation, so long as you hold it in

[52]

suspension. When you move toward action in it you can literally feel the air change, even as you approach it. You still 'think', 'disinterestedly', but you can see that becoming a set of more and more formal gestures, the nearer on action you close. Is it or not a rationalization, that thought and conscience assumes either a different, then powerfully relevant, relation to action, or no relevance at all, save that of self preservative, conscience salve. Also that if it is this irrelevant, it is ridiculous to value your thinking, or to think at all, approaching that change into action; as ridiculous as to judge an evolving self-adapting organism by its pre-evolving characteristics (or its post-evolving): also, whether, in evolving process, where no point or 'value' is fixed or fixable (except arbitrarily and so, falsely), judgement itself is relevant: whether everything isn't swallowed up into the intensity of evolvement itself.

Whatever I do or do not now, in this situation, I shall among other things half kill myself, to say nothing of another person and the reverberations of their pain on me.

Even if conscience and intelligence are particularly under immediately 'personal' pressures rationalizations and nothing else, they have the virtue of showing you still more clearly which way your wind is blowing—of your compulsions, pulls, desires.

[53]

This phase between suspension and action is the suspect one and the mysterious more it appears ('it appears'!) than any other.

Action itself has still another kind of numbness.

———

First you speak of your desire or tendency all but rhetorically; as if because you were safe to (and had both to masturbate your need and salve your conscience) in secretly knowing no such thing will really happen. 'I want to break with you'. 'I want to marry you'. 'This is neither more nor less permanent than we make it'.

Later (in my present phase), against all your terrific divisions, indeed the more so because of them, you speak implacably and numbly, straight along the line of desire, less and less frequently giving yourself and the others the comfort of the subjunctive.

'implacably and numbly'; 'comfort of the subjunctive'. I am certainly a weak and dirty brain; that is almost womanly wording.

[J 4.9: Journal Entry:
"Decided it would feel good for a change"]

12.30 night

Decided it would feel good for a change to sleep in pajamas. What I brought up, clean laundered, was the orange, black piped ones my mother gave me when I was married; she wanted to get me something gay and splendid. She gave me

[54]

also then, a green pair with embroidered cocks fighting on the chest. They made tears come into my eyes then and have since, and hurt me deeply tonight: taking the laundry paper out restored memory of their newness.

There was a night, not at all long before our marriage, when all doubts of it struck me the hardest they were able and I told Via of them, saying, how do I know what I am doing; and I was deeply sad, for her and for me, and near or in tears. She took my hand, then my head against her, then drew me away and looked at me with all her gentle sweetness and love, and tears in her eyes, and the slightly drawn, radiant smile of her purest emotions, and said, let not your heart be troubled; several times, very gently; and still deeply sad and loving, we both were, I was drawn into this religious faith and peace.

Her picture downstairs, much slenderer and younger, and years less hurt; and so much, then, of her family. About 24 I should think.

And Silvia's[37] with all its marks of fear and sadness.

This is probably one of the last times in my life I shall be in this house. God help and forgive us all.

---

37. Via Saunders's older sister.

[55]

I came up on the train last night arriving this morning 10 minutes before Ted. I will be staying till Tuesday or Wednesday.

There is a lot of genuinely enough interested talking, but also many pauses, and times when there is much talking without any meeting of eyes.

———

I've just read this 'Journal' through from its first entry. I seem to live, think and write on 3 different planes, of which my living, and my living as I write of it, are so immature they shock me. How is it I can have my fairly continuous illusion, from one living hour to the next, of being intelligent, and honest. How is it I can ever entertain hope, much less the kind of dizzying burn of excitement in the thought of work I might do, which I have had for instance most of today. It may be I can hope through this notebook to start to catch up on myself; it makes the evidence of what I am more tangible than I'm ordinarily capable of seeing. I am sure I am better than this or any more careful writing I have done; but evidently not enough better that I need take any courage of that certainty.

Create in me a clean heart O God, and renew a right spirit within me.[38]

Give me also, no mercy on myself, and give me absolute coldness

[56]

against myself.

I don't believe I am consciously conceited, but unconsciously and automatically, showing in my most casual talk, I assume things of myself no human being can have the right to.

To think that I have the gall to judge anyone's ideas or actions.

I am tired, and weak. I started to write 'Well, God help me'. I now put it down because I felt it. But it is a mark of weakness. Until I have more fortitude than now, should I allow myself to pray at all.

I expect I shall pray tonight, though. But not weakly, I intend, if I can possibly help it.

———

38. Psalm 51:10.

[J 4.10: Journal Entry:
"I suppose I will get this book started and done"]

Sunday night.

I suppose I will get this book started and done, but I will make a mess of it.

I am certainly a cheap child. I have had several stretches of bad feeling, uneasiness, listlessness & dejection during the past two days because of things I have written that are important to me, and not being asked to read them. And the cheapest part of that is, that I don't think any too well of them myself: much more ill than good, even of the best.

[57]

I do not often more than half-think of either Alma or Via. When I do, it is seldom with any warmth or happiness of Alma, and it is with sadness and love of Via, but a love a good deal helped by the situation and the imminence.

Some of the conclusions to be drawn from these 2 ¶s are obvious enough; a second ring should be gone into. I feel too lazy. I also feel afraid to, especially on the second; my half-rationalization is that I am not well balanced or intelligent enough to carry either through either to a true end or me I could stand.

The fear you will find you don't want a thing you have been wanting is so powerful it can make you want it.

I don't see why we should stay alive, much less hold ourselves together by the illusion we know what we are doing.

You can use practically any device to hold yourself together. Most, maybe all these pins are false. The worst is, you came so to depend on them that their removal can ruin you.

My dependence on anger and hatred is such, I think I would fall to pieces without them.

The very fact I can write even this 'reasonably' about them may be sufficient proof I am not of the Anger Class and had therefore better not flatter myself that

[58]

I am.

I just thought of writing Alma, and turned to a blank page to start. 'Darling Alma'. Even that much gave my 'imagination' the premonition of a non-physical erection.

I could not get this from starting to write Via, and that is the difference. I had better say, though: I could not get this from Via unless all my center of desire, which probably I have in part deliberately killed, were shifted from Alma and renewed toward her. If there is any dignity and meaning in love, it certainly isn't within the scope of reason or sense.

I am writing at a table and across from me is a mirror. I look at myself fairly frequently at commas and periods, and loathe my face and all I am.

Supposedly such writing as this will be useful to me as a record later on, maybe for more serious writing. God help the truth then. To some extent, even while I'm doing it, I know I am misstating even the simplest things I put down, and they are the least difficult, the least nearly true and important things that are going on in or around me.

[59]

Automatic talking. Looking at myself scornfully but absently in the mirror, and thinking absently of my writing and of those here and of Via and Alma, I heard myself whispering, "Save: there's nothing to save here".

I should begin to learn to realize that I can't do everything at once. Take a given project cold, look at it like a piece of engineering, know not only what can but what can not be done with it, and give it its own size. Only one cutting edge can operate at a time. (This is obviously not true.)

But that reasoned and resourceful, cool way of setting to work nauseates me. It is the sure way to write neatly or even well, and it is also the sure way to reduce yourself. I am no paragon of reasonableness, but I am much more reasonable than I believe in being.

As a matter of fact, in the above, I as usual derailed myself. I am full of shit.

I won't write to Alma because mailing it would be difficult and so elaborate it would surely go foul and hurt them, though I am sure they already know of it.

[60]

So I will now read more of the Congo, Gide, as usual with a streak of guilt just behind my eyes.

God help us and give me guts. Goodnight. Who to, I don't know; God, and Alma.

'God loves blunderers because they are the children of Peter.'
I am one. None of the work I love most is the work of blunderers; conceivably Dostoyevsky.

God help me, the best that I am or 'perceive' is so much better than the best tries in my writing, and if only I could do it, could be work of a sort I love. But I have to write this down, as if in fear that otherwise no one but myself would ever remotely suspect it.

'Remotely suspect'. I had also better quit using 'God help me': even in writing that I had better, I was more interested in it as 'right' and in getting it down, than I was taken in the heart by the fact.

[61]

As a matter of fact I am badly enough off that I had better not throw away my crutch too soon.

[J 4.11: Journal Entry:
"Just as when I was adolescent at home"]

Monday afternoon.

Just as when I was adolescent at home and, after dinner, Sundays, they withdrew from the whole downstairs and slept and the whole house was silent and empty, I am unhappy and restless, and unable to do work or even to take hold of thought.

Dr. Saunders[39] remembers when he was last at the Fosters' [?] by what flower was in seed at the time. Most of my time-identifying up

---

39. Dr. Arthur Percy Saunders (1869–1964), Via Saunders's father, was a professor of chemistry at Hamilton College in Clinton, New York, as well as a respected horticulturalist who developed more than fifteen thousand peony hybrids.

to 20–21 is by movies. Or, rather, I identify the year of the movie by the memory of where I saw it when.

A movie was a more brilliant part of experience than much that surrounded it. It is the only part that can be exactly repeated; except recorded music.

You can have better ideas before you involve yourself. If I got into making movies my ideas would be fewer and less good. Even getting in a given location would reduce them.

[62]

Two suggestions of working method. El Greco first painted accurately and naturalistically; then distorted more and more in successive drafts. The original naturalism was his trellis and his bight.

2: when Eisenstein has exposed a great amount of film, his note-taking is finished and [h]is work is just begun.

Evocation and description. I am dissatisfied with anything in my work short of the evocative, yet all my work, nearly, founders itself in description.

Newsreels recently:

Zimmerman,[40] legless, training for Havana-Miami swim:

Walking out a diving board on his hands; swimming, taken from above; standing on his stump in a tank, eating a banana underwater.

7, 5, and 3 year old children boxing; other children, mothers, watch.

Two wrestlers fight in 2 tons of prepared mud at Richmond. (There must be reels of the 2 female wrestlers, too).

Bathing girls blowtorch a man out of a thin block of ice and take him tumbling in the surf.

Girls in bathing suits play basketball on rollerskates.

[63]

In 'Adventures of a Cameraman',[41] Spanish soldiers ride horses

---

40. Bill Stern's *Colgate Sports Newsreels,* which debuted in October 1937, often featured sensational "true stories" of athletic feats such as Zimmerman's.

41. No film entitled *Adventures of a Cameraman* has been located, but a number of documentaries supporting the Loyalist cause during the Spanish Civil War used newsreel footage. Agee may have one of these in mind.

down a nearly vertical 80 foot embankment; so steep that every horse falls. Repeat this over and over and over or return it contrapuntally.

In U.S. Camera,[42] a vertical picture of Washington made through a 9-lensed camera. This can handle as much as 600 square miles at a time. Right after the movie going straight away from the earth or straight approach.

They already use the camera levelers, for mapmaking.

Clematis twists on its stem & offers itself abruptly, flatupward, kicking out three flat large leaves.

Photographic show on screen, slide lecture. Same ingredients on wall, to preserve their single integrities.

———

Struck 3. Mrs S[aunders][43] came down immediately. I am at diningroom table writing these worthlessly and apathetically, wanting distraction.

'Would it disturb you too much if I put in the Sibelius?'

'Not a bit. No. Not at all.'

[64]

She starts to shut the door. I say, 'No don't bother, I'm not doing any real work at all.'

'There's also the schoolroom if you want real privacy.' She shuts the door to.

There's a chair here against the wall. Chippendale <u>style</u> I think; diningroom chair. : stuffed with brass, redwood; the wall is inchwide cream and silver vertical stripes. Something to 'evoke' which I could only 'describe'.

She calls the centerpiece (moss and moss-plants) a 'little rustic bowl'.

Photograph of Mrs Edith Grant.[44] Head turned to left half low-

———

42. The 1937 edition of the photography annual *U.S. Camera* included aerial photographs of Washington, D.C., taken with a special nine-lens camera developed by the U.S. Coast and Geodetic Survey.

43. Louise Brownell Saunders, Via Saunders's mother.

44. Edith Grant (1908–1967) was the great-great-granddaughter of Ulysses S. Grant and a former live-in student with the Saunders family at Hamilton College.

ered, sun soft and bright on soft summer cloth of shoulder. A bad photograph but here, some more detail of avocation.

I have thought of trying turning parts of the Congo into my own kind. Maybe I will try it.

[J 4.12: Journal Entry: "Evening at the Hudsons'"]

Monday night.

Wednesday is March 1, Ted says.

[65]

Evening at the Hudsons'. Mozart's B♭ Major, D Minor, G Major; a Schumann; Beethoven 18 #2; 1$\underline{st}$ & 3$\underline{rd}$ mvts of 132.

Christine very anxiously and sweetly took me Aside to explain to me a recoil from kissing me the other morning, which evidently I hadn't even noticed, for I didn't remember it. To have told her I didn't know what she was talking about, the truth, would have hurt her. I felt rotten for her and still worse because she was interrupted and I was drawn away by those going home, so that it was unresolved.

Adolphe Borie's[45] drawing of Via. As door was drawn back in schoolroom I saw it for first time in 2 or 3 years and it shocked me with grief, love, pity and guilt. This chiefly I think because though garbled some ways it has, or entirely conveys to anyone knowing it, the one thing Via chiefly has that no one else I have ever seen has; a certain smile and the quality of mind and soul the smile means; and the way of holding her head, like a slightly distraught wading bird. It is a lovely and pitiable smile; stepping up eagerly and gently to be beaten in the face of; by now half sure that will happen, yet not less eager or innocent than ever.

Back here tonight Mrs S[aunders] so anxious to make things right & comfortable for me I nearly went crazy; all over whether I was staying downstairs or going to bed. If downstairs, a furnace, a fire in the fireplace, etc etc; not waiting for answers or listening to them, & my answers more mild & inaudible the more tense I got, &

---

45. French artist (1877–1934).

[66]

the more reluctant to stay downstairs, which finally I was more or less forced to do, short of yelling. So the fire is built. It is not doing very well. 4 above zero out, warmer than all day.

Out of the deep have I called unto thee: Lord, hear my voice.
O let thine ears consider well: the voice of my complaint.
If thou Lord wilt be extreme to mark what is done amiss: O Lord, who may abide it.[46]

I cannot remember this psalm.

I have no structure at all. None of my ideas, or too few, stay with me when I try to write.

Now it is doing better.

I look for the Lord, my soul doth wait for him; before the morning watch: I say, before the morning watch.

For there's mercy in thee: therefore shalt thou be feared.

[67]

And he shall redeem Israel: from all his sins.

Entrance like those in music, especially 3 kinds I think of now: the abrupt and apparently casual; the abrupt full blast, as if unprepared,

---

46. Psalm 130, *De Profundis*, from the *Book of Common Prayer*, which Agee is trying to remember here and below:

1 Out of the deep have I called unto thee, O LORD; Lord, hear my voice.

2 O let thine ears consider well the voice of my complaint.

3 If thou, LORD, wilt be extreme to mark what is done amiss, O Lord, who may abide it?

4 For there is mercy with thee; therefore shalt thou be feared.

5 I look for the LORD, my soul doth wait for him; in his word is my trust.

6 My soul fleeth unto the Lord before the morning watch; I say, before the morning watch.

7 O Israel, trust in the LORD; for with the LORD there is mercy, and with him is plenteous redemption.

8 And he shall redeem Israel from all his sins.

uncontested climax out of silence; and that which cuts the air like the incision beginning a surgical operation.

Structures of words.

Straight solid materials and senses.

But now descriptive if possible.

Extreme.   Threaten.

Slowed and sleaved in the leaves.

Sleaving the branches of leaves, blown the length of the branch, released.

Sometimes, in wood silence, have you seen,
no wind, not a sound, nothing, anywhere in the air,
everything still, still,
on one stem, somewhere, shoulder high,
one leaf, wagging, frantic silence, waggling:

[68]

grueling

near you, a little to your right, a little away, quivering wildly; quieting; trembling only; then taken again; never quite still; quivering:

irregular and ceaseless like the dripping of a tap at night:

waving, as a wild bird, warning, desperate:

is it signaling you?

what is there you must do. or must not do.

or is it signaling you.

then: then: can you dare go on?

then: can you dare stand still?

———

[69]

Evening lay down in their laps like a tired child and they came in to supper. Creamed potatoes, a little scorched, hot cocoa, canned preserves. There was tarnish light on the thinned tines of the forks, and the shape of an iron limned on one fall of the table cloth. The brocade shone in the light.

Liver and gravy.

They all sat at the table in the fading sky.

There was lace at the three windows.

In one small bowl there was left-over spinach; in one small bowl there was left-over pie plant. They ate.

Lima beans.

The light lay dented liquid in the bowls of unused spoons.

The silver tinted, tinked. They talked.

There was a white hatchwork down in the white linen. One of the napkin rings was carved ivory.

[70]

flushing

The slow wave lifted them, their table and their city, upon the extreme pearl of heaven:

They sank; they sank.

So when the leaf had spoken:

————

Stealing, ever, in wood stillness, scope and extension of silence, stillness, nothing in the air, the whole forest musing, have you seen, on one stem, violently, silent, one leaf quaking?

————

The drawing of Via in notes accurate as I thought; the suddenness and recall is what gave it: but the drawing does get some, best from about 8 feet away.

————

If ever you should care to see my wife,
what she was, what it was she looked like in that first year or so
when we believed in each other,

when all our trouble was over, and before new trouble began,
in the time when it looked certain to us that we had a lifetime together
and that that would be good,

I recommend this drawing.

This shows a way she had of holding her head,
and her peculiarly pure smile, and her eyes, as these were, at her best.

Just these things alone, as if there were nothing else, are enough to
break my heart for her, but it makes no difference.

Just these things alone, as if there were nothing else, are enough
almost to make me love her enough to make nothing else matter, but
not quite.

And nothing does. Not five years; nor the thought of the look in
her eyes; nor the look itself; nothing; not anything I can name or dream;
nothing quite makes the difference.

And so it is very probable that when I get back to New York,

we shall concentrate ourselves on determining to get a divorce, as we
planned to concentrate ourselves before I left; and it will be determined;
everything clearly settled; finally; once for all.

Then I will go away with the girl I love, and love to sleep with, and
when the time clears, we will marry, and hope to cure the wounds we
have made in each other in this past year.

And my wife will have gone to Reno, where it is done laughing,
apparently, to get her divorce, and that will be that.

What will become of her; what will become of me; what will
become of this girl I love; I have no idea. But it seems unlikely that any
of us can come to any good.

Perhaps later I shall tell you of this in more detail. Then again, perhaps not.

[73]

[J 4.13: Journal Entry: "To bed very late last night"]

Tuesday 3.15 afternoon.

To bed very late last night; after burning 3 armloads of wood. Ted waked me as I asked him to earlier this morning, around 9.45. I went back to sleep again; up just in time for lunch.

The Structure and Meaning of Psychoanalysis, by Healy, Bronner & Bowers, Knopf 1931.[47]

Any such reading as this makes me feel I have no right to write, or even to try to make deductions in any relevant field: meaning the whole field of motives, ethics, why any person is as he is, what the cause or stature is of belief or feelings.

[J 4.14: Journal Entry: "Butlers to dinner"]

Tuesday night.

Butlers to dinner. Molly, of Durer: "He's a famous artist isn't he?"

G B of J. Roosevelt:[48] They say he's a sensible fella. Has his eye on the dollar—of Edsel Ford's hour with FDR:, Ford said "Oh, he's not so bad." And then he said it again. "He's not so bad"[49]

of Woolcott:[50] "How's he doing, he's doing very well isn't he?"

of 'Jewy' Baruch:[51] I think he's the smartest man alive. . . . started the depression.

---

47. William Healy, Augusta F. Bronner, and Anna Mae Bowers, *The Structure and Meaning of Psychoanalysis as Related to Personality and Behavior* (New York: Knopf, 1930). This book was known as "the Baedeker of the whole psychoanalytical movement."

48. James Roosevelt (1907–1991), son of Franklin Roosevelt, became the president's secretary in 1937. He resigned in 1938, having been widely seen as holding undue influence on the cabinet.

49. On November 24, 1934, Edsel Ford met with President Roosevelt at the Little White House in Warm Springs, Georgia, to discuss business reforms.

50. Alexander Woollcott (1887–1943), drama critic and member of the Algonquin Round Table, was a friend and frequent guest of the Saunderses.

51. Bernard M. Baruch (1870–1965) was a politically influential businessman for many years. Baruch cronies Hugh S. Johnson and George Peek headed the

of Ted's play: 'Imagination!'[52]

Molly wants to play the piano but can't stand to play alone.

[74]

Last night at Hudson's, elderly woman, poor looking, 'So wonderful, these young men come here and bring us <u>their</u> <u>gifts</u>. They come here and bring us their lovely <u>gifts</u>.'

I have some very neat bad symptoms of myself. Ted is not only critical of my writing in the first concentric [?] but in the second: i.e., he will not commit to any 'friendliness', or to any either generalized or particularized indication whether he thinks I am any good. This, thoroughly in spite of my approval of it, gives me extreme insecurity, enough that my stomach is not in good order; much like that of a child who does not feel he is loved by a parent. I get this same insecurity from a lack of goodnights, or from some degree of shyness, offhandedness, or lack of warmth in goodnights, sufficiently that I seek out to some extent Mrs. S[aunders'] warmth for the false security, & really weakening effects but illusion of strength, it can give me. Of course her form of warmth and demonstrativeness must mean she has been sick all her life with insecurity.

In other words I am still infantile. I warm myself at my friends.

An effect of this insecurity is that I become weak in body, spirit and mind. Capable of indicating to Ted, for instance, much less than what I have. But if 'what I have' can thrive only on support it isn't much and can't thrive much.

[75]

In the same way, I believe I am afraid of criticism of myself, that has any sharpness. That is part must be why I so habitually criticize the whole world.

Evidently I have never outgrown the whole meaning of the need to be kissed good night, and will take anything I can get, for it.

New Deal's National Recovery Administration and the Agricultural Adjustment Administration, respectively, both of which were modeled on the War Industries Board, which Baruch chaired in 1918.

52. Probably a reference to one of the satirical productions Theodore Spencer wrote and directed for the Tavern Club in Boston.

Tomorrow is Ash Wednesday. It is already Ash Wednesday.

I must not only not be anything but hard to myself: I must <u>specify</u> to myself all that I can find that is wrong. Take any degree of my work and analyze it in detail, what is lacking, what is wrong, why, what is there to do about it. Most of it is so basically wrong it probably can't be fixed, only scrapped.

With work I am getting ready to do, force myself to <u>specify</u> to myself what I am going to do and why. Again in all possible detail. Every try I make at this reduces me to weakness and emptiness. That means I write entirely by ear and by feeling and that I fear to destroy these because I fear I have nothing else. I have nothing else, until I give it ground to stand on.

[76]

Probably started through the insecurity; pity, warmth, guilt and grief for them.

Write my own, strictest possible, criticism of the book before I write it.

It is fairly clear to me that my standards have slipped or split, so that I am soft toward sympathetic contemporary work.

I am missing Alma, and thinking also, a good deal, with a good deal of remembrance, of Via.

I might as well be made of nothing but water.

Nothing but hard work, knowing how to work, learning how to use my head, and how to take hold of and get into hard form the things that I care most for, can possibly do any real good. Until then the best of love and friendship is so much aspirin and so much weakening, and by this debased use is bound to suffer.

Ted gave me some mild sleeping dope tonight. I hope it takes soon.

[J 4.15: Journal Entry: "The dope is NEMBUTAL"]

_____

Wednesday night

The dope is NEMBUTAL.

Wed. Mar 30

Via down with bad cold. No work in apartment. Restatement of possible-proba-bilities in mutually protective terms of certainties sets Alma back stiff. I cannot stand to be alone 5 minutes. I ask her to talk to Walker and him to talk to her. They are doing so tonight (Thursday). All evening, exhausting to us both, talk with Alma. She shifts to light conception if it's for the summer, dropping from it its most serious "realities", and I can't stand that. We end in extremely niggerly physical love, which for the time being clears the brain into new denominators.

Today.

The Empson poems[53] to Jack Sweeney.[54] Lunch with Robert.[55] See some good but troubling (soft, iridescent, past facile, overfeminine maybe) paintings by Loren MacIver.[56] Can I come along & be idle with him? No I must work at Leroy. We neither go. Talk with Robert about the immediate problem, my trap fears, marriage, woman mentality.

[78]

Today was taking down just now the front room curtains. Jesus is stripped of his garments. Heavy with dust. Via's stitches. Windows dirty. Faded, the strong blue I once wanted and got.

Tuesday. Via and I worked here together. I should here have itemized everything. Wedding silver & fancy napkins. Blankets. Sorting of clothes, books. (She, passionate to get rid of everything.) An album of snapshots of her childhood & adolescence most of which I had never seen. It nearly broke our hearts. She, much harder than I; needed to be.

_____

53. William Empson, _Poems_ (London: Chatto and Windus, 1935).

54. James Johnson Sweeney (1900–1986), art critic and curator at the Museum of Modern Art and associate editor of _transition_.

55. Robert Fitzgerald (1910–1985), American poet and later editor of collections of Agee's poetry and short prose.

56. American artist (1909–1998). MacIver became known in 1935 when Alfred Barr purchased two of her paintings for the Museum of Modern Art.

We sat by the gas stove talking and drank hot whisky & water. "If it's a mistake we'll find it out simply enough."

God bless and help and keep her. I could wish I were dead.

Walker was embroiled and troubled over the lawyer. That, or if, we could not collude directly with her help.

Orange yellow & green curtains in both & hall bedroom (where [at] Leroy Street, have found a separate room for work, I did so little of it). These are Via's colors.

[79]

[J 4.16: Letter to Laura Agee]

written late night, mid April.
Morning revulsion, unsent.

My dearest mother.

Causing you pain or sorrow, I grieve over and dread; I would may be nearly as much even if I didn't love you. So I have delayed writing you of what I will until after Passion and Holy Week and Easter should have passed in their own meanings undisturbed by me. I feel as much reluctance now, but delay and inevitable denouement would give you even worse; and I love and respect you a great deal too much to wish to deceive you, even if the deception would succeed and thereby save you pain.

Via and I are getting a divorce. The final decree (words of law, not mine) will be middle or late in August. At some time after I am free to, probably quite soon, I shall more likely than not marry Alma Mailman. In any case I shall live with her as man and wife in our personal belief of what that is, beginning sooner. (We have already, as well as we might, which until recently has not been remotely toward as well as we could wish, during a little more than the past year.)

That is the main substance of what I have to tell you. There is more, some of which may I hope be of partial comfort, and some more, of clarification, to you.

[80]

Details of the divorce. The suit was filed at the end of March. First action and decree will be in middle May. Then after 90 days, a final decree. I do not appear in court because I do not contest the complaint. Reno and other divorces possible are too expensive and troublesome. This will be a New York State divorce. Here our only possible grounds are adultery. With a contempt for the legality & instutionalisation of marriage, it is needless to say I have an equal, that is total, contempt for divorce. I therefore prefer these supposedly basic grounds to any more genteel. Via feels the same. The adultery is of course real enough but for legal purposes that is meaningless; a story, with friends as witnesses, is faked. The correspondent is not named.

Our permanence was almost at no time a thing we were sure of or even totally, or extremely, hopeful of. During the first two years I believe we thought relatively little in terms of impermanence. During the past three, increasingly. During these latter three years we were little if at all what could be called in love; but we were so deeply fond of each other that we handled our problems slowly

[81]

and reluctantly, long after we should better have settled them one way or another. But for Alma, or for otherwise falling at all so seriously in love, I cannot be sure we would have divorced; but entirely indepen-dent of any other person, I can feel sure that we should have; and I can wish it might have been, for both ourselves, sooner. How much I still love Via can be not much alleviation to you to know, her love also for me; yet we much prefer this love, and its pain, to the apathy or vindic-tiveness that we might have come into. It is love and liking quite suffi-cient I believe, for two sound and good lives to be built on together, but not without a much stronger wish for such living, and belief in it, than either of us has or desires. And without that wish and belief, it would be a sorry life for both of us.

Whether Alma and I are together for life, we have no idea. A great many things must prove themselves. It is nearly certain I think, that I am essentially solitary, though I dread discontinuity and solitude as much as I feel the basic need for them. I love and respect Alma more dearly than I can tell you, and feel we have an almost untouched world to learn what we may of together,

[82]

and what I hope may come of it is our lives together; but not in any betrayal of either of us: and what the nature of betrayal might be, we have still and patiently to try to learn. We are neither of us afraid of whatever outcome.

You know Alma a little, and I believe, like her. I hope you will care to know her better, for I believe you could love her. We are in many ways extremely different to each other. They are ways I love, as fondly as those in which we resemble. Saying a very little I would chiefly say, we are sexually matched as I had not before supposed possible; we learn and increase in religion from each other, as I have never so much before with another; her innocence, and clarity, and utter spiritual honesty, and courage, and all these and many more, in what they are and can increase into, move and excite my faith and love, and my wish for wisdom and for maturing, as no human being as such, ever has, except very differently, in work a few have done or are doing.

I am not so blurred by love as you may well think. These things and more are true of her, known and considered coldly. Love is only the lens I can best see them through and hope

[83]

to be useful to her by: they are true independent of love's or my own existence.

———

Hobson.⁵⁷ Oak Bluffs. Martha's Vineyard. Mass.

———

[J 4.17: "Notes from backs of envelopes, etc."]

Notes from backs of envelopes, etc.

Jules Romains: Donogoo-Tonka, ou, Les Miracles de la Science. [Paris:] NRF November 1919. First scenario written to be read. (?). BFM⁵⁸ (The stills from the play indicate the French (some of them) had at that time a sophisticated appreciation of what was done naively with sets, & with clothing & spatial relation of bodies, in American quickies and comedies).

---

57. Wilder Hobson (1906–1964), jazz enthusiast and first cousin of Thornton Wilder, was a writer and editor for *Fortune, Time,* and *Newsweek.* When Agee and Alma moved back to New York from Frenchtown, New Jersey, in 1939, Hobson offered them the use of the vacant family home on St. James Place.

58. Probably Franklin Miner. See J 4.6, note 34.

BFM: From Memoires of E de Gramont; Au Temps des Equipiges: of Felix Faure: 'Le pauvre Président avait accuelli une dame trop tôt après son déjeuner, il le réspondit sur le tête de la victime et moutet.'[59]

[84]

BFM Historie du Cinéma, Maurice Bardéche & Robert Brasillade; Denoël et Steele, pusl. Now translated by I. Barry,[60] who according to CG[61] masterminds them in bad taste and not always accurately, in two thousand footnotes. He says they try to source everything good in movies, from France.

Some bull moose tries by Hollywood people, and some good never mentioned pictures: The Crowd Roars. Driven (Charles Brabin). The Denial (Hobart Henley). Stark Love (Karl Brown). Anna Christie (#1) (John Griffith Wray). The Crowd (Vidor). The Courtship of Miles Standish (Charles Ray). Salvation Hunters (Joe Stern). Roadhouse Nights. Her Man. The Dragnet. 20ᵗʰ Century. Devil's Holiday, & Shopworn Angel (Edmund Goulding). A Kiss in the Dark (Tuttle). Second Fiddle. (Tuttle).[62]

Salome vs. Shenadoah (Ben Turpin). Married Life.[63]

---

59. *Au temps des Équipages* is the first volume of the *Mémoires* of Elisabeth de Gramont, Duchesse de Clermont-Tonnerre, published in 1928.

60. Iris Barry's English translation, *The History of Motion Pictures,* was published by Arno Press in 1938.

61. Christopher "Goofy" Gerould was one of Agee's friends from Harvard and a writer and editor for *Fortune.* He introduced Agee to Mia Fritsch.

62. Full titles, directors, and dates for the films mentioned in this paragraph are as follows: *The Crowd Roars* (Howard Hawks, 1932); *Driven* (Charles Brabin, 1923); *The Denial* (Hobart Henley, 1925); *Stark Love* (Karl Brown, 1927); *Anna Christie* (John Griffith Wray, 1923); *The Crowd* (King Vidor, 1928); *The Courtship of Miles Standish* (Frederick Sullivan, 1923); *Salvation Hunters* (Josef von Sternberg, 1925); *Roadhouse Nights* (Hobart Henley, 1930); *Her Man* (Tay Garnett, 1930); *The Dragnet* (Josef von Sternberg, 1928); *Twentieth Century* (Howard Hawks, 1934); *The Devil's Holiday* (Edmund Goulding, 1930); *Shopworn Angel* (There are two movies of the period entitled *Shopworn Angel;* neither is directed by Goulding. Agee may have in mind Goulding's *Night Angel,* from 1931.); *A Kiss in the Dark* (Frank Tuttle, 1932); *Second Fiddle* (Frank Tuttle, 1923).

63. *Salome vs. Shenandoah* (Ray Hunt, 1919) and *Married Life* (Erle C. Kenton, 1920) both starred American comedic actor Ben Turpin (1869–1940).

(Are any of the Larry Semons[64] good?)

Also movies by Harry (H d'Abbadie) D'Arrast (Chaplin's assistant on A Woman of Paris): Service for Ladies; Serenade; a Gentleman of Paris; also Laughter, the only recognized

[85]

or remembered one.[65]

I, BFM, W. E., CG, GSR,[66] should list & recall pictures, performances, sequences, single shots, directors, &c &c, of such as these and of more obscure moving pictures.

———

[J 4.18: "Notes remembered to put down late one night"]

Notes remembered to put down late one night: perhaps indicative of what turns up casually and is lost by non-recording:

'advance recalls'. (meaning rather, images, visions, of times and places never seen which have nevertheless the force & taste of a recall. Such as that created in me by West End Blues,[67] particularly by the piano and following trumpet choruses.)

esthetic of stress – Birth of a Nation.[68] (ie, the wild horn call when the Klan rides.)

'esthetic relationship of print quality to metaphoric placement in time'. (ie: some photographs are present, some future, some past, some on several planes at once.

———————

64. Larry Semon (1889–1928), American silent film comedian, directed and starred in dozens of shorts and feature films, including a 1925 slapstick version of The Wizard of Oz.

65. Argentine director Harry d'Abbadie d'Arrast (1897–1968) was a researcher and technical advisor on Charlie Chaplin's A Woman of Paris (1923) and one of Chaplin's uncredited assistant directors on The Gold Rush (1925). His own films include Service for Ladies (1927), Serenade (1927), A Gentleman of Paris (1927), and Laughter (1930), which he also wrote.

66. I.e., Agee, Franklin Miner, Walker Evans, Christopher Gerould, and possibly Selden Rodman.

67. See J 2.1, note 2, and J 5.1.

68. D. W. Griffith's The Birth of a Nation (1915).

[86]

by and large a pale yet sharp print seems to abstract and make 'time-less', 'ancient'; to suspend in history or time. The question is, is there determinable any exact relationship or set of them: or is it pure squishy emotion; and is it valid and if so when and how and why, to govern printing partly by such considerations.

(Also Perdido Street seems ancient; and makes New Orleans in the early 1920's seem ancient and tragic.)

'development of new erogenous zones through concentrations / / yoga: but forms self-invented.' This works well at least in early stages. The idea further is that by mapping and zoning the body, and perhaps by inventing or deducing functions progressions & symbologies, any part of the body could in the course of time be made erotically excitable: as much so as the standard zones are at present; but in, I should hope, dif-ferent terms.

'Invent and use new gestures. formalities'. This will

[87]

take much more thinking, performance and writing than I have time for now.

————

T. E. Polsky. Old Weaverville Road. Route 1. Asheville NC

————

Reading, via OSR,[69] from

John Herman Randall, Jr., The Making of the Modern Mind (Cambridge Mass 1926):

S. Freud: General Lectures of Psychoanalysis.

A G Tansley: The New Psychology.

W L Northridge: Modern Theories of the Unconscious.

F Wittel: S. Freud

J T McCurdy: O. Rank & H. Sachs: E R Groves: E D Martin.[70]

---

69. Otto Shoen-René.

70. The books listed here are cited in John Hermann Randall Jr., *The Making of the Modern Mind: A Survey of the Intellectual Background of the Present Age* (Boston: Houghton Mifflin, 1926). They are: Sigmund Freud, *A General*

[pages 88–90 blank]

[J 4.19: List of Household Items]

| Alma Mailman | James Agee |
| | JR Agee |

WE	THEY
	tan chair
	straight chairs
	large bed
garbage	book case(s)
towel rack ✓ FL	ashtrays
mirror	
medicine chest FL	rugs
bed, mattress ✓	tennis rackets
ashtrays	violin; have fixed: strings—
piano;	music stand & music
iron & board	music
mending materials	BATHING suits
lamps	card table & wood top
soaptray	radio; records; phonograph
	all kitchen supplies; dishes,
	'silver', pots & pans, lares,
	penates, popcorn, coca cola.
	pillow.
	icebox

---

[92]

[93]

[J 4.20: Description of Unidentified Woman]

as a girl, in love with her own handwriting: recopied college notes, pages out of print, in a beautiful standard hand, with engraver's pains. Chastity, syphilis fear, sterility, masturbation. Blond beautiful standard like her hand. Now 28; frigid and tenacious, <u>hoarding marriage.</u> <u>virgin</u>; studying law Columbia. Studies on side. Job, $35 a week; <u>takes out insurance heavily</u>: paranoia: circular madness. Extremely: pathologically: selfish: jealous: envious. Glossy & sweet: sly: deceitful. Spends money only on clothes: quantity: quality (?): sloppy dresser, rather: wear after need cleaning, to get away with. Lives with family. Hated & hates all family except her mother whom she resembles. Polish-Jewish. Strong mother-daughter sympathies. They are, obviously, to their families, not sane.

Specimen of jealousy. Hatred of sister & sister's friends. Hate jealousy: a friend phones: she says her sister is out; tells her sister nothing of it.

Law or usury would be her inevitable studies.
Men: a season's popularity with considerably older man; good deal of money; very eager to marry her.
Seldom brings men home.
Makes show of popularity when there are no men. She has never had a friend.

[94]

Utica Highschool. Strongly manconscious: whole body, demeanor, way of speaking, change if man came by in corridor—

Commodity-aspect of virginity steadily intensifies.

———

hand, careful at first of letter, loosens like a broken pillow.

air, Frenchtown Flemington,[71] hen country, is ditto; blizzards of belly feathers—

[pages 95–96 blank]

———

71. Flemington, New Jersey, the county seat of Hunterdon County, is eleven miles from Frenchtown. Agee and Alma Mailman were married in Flemington December 6, 1938.

Journal 5

[J 5.1: *LUNPFM* Notes: "Under Negroes"]

Under Negroes: quote lists of race records.[1]

We are living in their ancient history. In their histories and social memory, when they are the dominant race and culture, this will be the period of emergence: 1800–2000 A.D.: and these records, for instance, and any movie or written records of their living, will have an almost holy character.

Their mental shape will not be white; the shape won't even be mental at the centre; not on the other hand hindu or any such different organization.

The effort or effect of communism will be to obliterate or in any case poison this character.

The pitiful-to-tragic, and disgusting, quality of for instance the Fisk Jubilee Singers.[2] They are every bit "genuine", but "genuine" like good house dogs. A smugness in it & what is worse a humble smugness. Nothing left in their voices or music but sweetness though this is of a kind that cannot be matched or faked. They are shifted over in their style into effects: pleasing a benevolent white audience in its idea of what negro music should be. Rubatos, held notes, faded chords, etc.; all half deflected towards this. There is not an ounce

---

1. "Race records" were recordings of black artists marketed to black audiences issued by major companies on separate labels, i.e., the Bluebird division of RCA.

2. The Jubilee Singers, an a cappella gospel group composed of students at Fisk University in Nashville, Tennessee, was formed in 1871 to raise money for the school and has toured extensively ever since. Fisk, designed for the education of former slaves, was one of the first African American universities, and the Jubilee Singers were pioneers in preserving and interpreting black spirituals.

[2]

of effect in the Christian Singers,[3] not even at the close, which is always terse. They are absorbed. It is not for publication.

Man woman division in singing. The woman because of her sexual quotient becomes an indoor, dive singer. The man and the guitarist are sidewalk musicians.

In this archaic music a thing that has now been nearly lost, the sweetness and pity of majors in a blues.

More than any other, Armstrong[4] sticks to the source, this back country blues. Not that he doesn't elaborate it; but he elaborates from that source, not from any grandchild or collateral descendent.

————

My letter of statement to Fields; quote and explain.

————

The dialogue I took down of Tidmore and the negro.

————

The night before 4th of July at Selma.

————

The negro at Marion; the clothes of the strolling negroes.

————

The negress who started and ran when I ran.

————

[3]

[J 5.2: *LUNPFM* Notes: "Burroughs Bible"]

Burroughs Bible.[5] Cover: limp and moist-dank brown false leather, feels like a batwing to the hand. The paper thin and moist. The whole vol-

————————

3. Mitchell's Christian Singers, an a cappella gospel quartet from Kinston, North Carolina, "discovered" in 1933 by John Hammond, made a number of recordings from 1934 to 1940. The group's lack of formal training, intense rhythmic style, and unfamiliarity with canonical spirituals standardized by groups such as the Fisk Jubilee Singers were taken as signs of authenticity. In "Notes and Appendices" in *Let Us Now Praise Famous Men,* Agee recommends the Christian Singers' "Who Was John" and "My Poor Mother Died Ashouting."

4. Louis Armstrong (1901–1971), American jazz trumpeter and vocalist. See J 2.1, note 2, and J 4.18, note 66.

5. Cf. the Gudger family Bible in *Let Us Now Praise Famous Men,* 371–73.

ume has absorbed and given off a cold and moist almost insupportable odor of pork, sweat, and human excrement.

    Title Page.
        The New Testament
    with the words spoken by Christ
        PRINTED IN RED*
                (printed in red.)
Malachi. 4, v. 6:
    And he shall turn the heart of the fathers to the children, and the heart of the children to the fathers, lest I come and smite the earth with a curse.

————

ON FLYLEAF:
    PRESENTED TO . . . .
        Floyd Burroughs
           BY . . . Allienay Burroughs

                                      [4]
                                 SEE B

FAMILY RECORD
    PARENTS' NAMES
HUSBAND   Floyd Burroughs
    BORN   September 11 – 1904
WIFE   Allie Mae Burroughs
    b.   October 19, 1907
MARRIED   Floyd B. and Allie Mae B
    was married April 19th 1924
CHILDREN'S NAMES

                                        [5]

[J 5.3: *LUNPFM* Notes: "The frogs in the swamped woods near Tuscaloosa"]

The frogs in the swamped woods near Tuscaloosa.

————

Burroughs visit to his sister.

————

Centerville. Marion. Greensboro. Moundville. Tuscaloosa.[6]
_____

The Shady Grove graveyard.
_____

The chambermaid in the Greensboro hotel, and the bell boy.
_____

Miss Jurdan and assistant.
_____

_____

A photograph arrests and abstracts her most favorable image; that which, in doubt of love, you can look with least uneasiness; that is nevertheless "honest."
_____

Wall wall: wall: wall.

[6]

How to make <u>walls</u> of walls. If they could be photographically assembled but as in an animated cartoon: Here: the scaffold & ledge of a floor: camera at centre. Out there, just beyond the ledge, planks are assembled and stuck together with nails in a sudden clatter. The edge is fitted along the edge of the floor and the whole rectangle is raised abruptly to vertical. This is done again with another wall, that makes a corner with the first. Then again the blank stage of the floor: Four walls are raised at once like a pitcher plant closing on a fly; the roof in cards lays its wings together on top along a ridgepole.
_____

This same, infolded with shots from outside: the outdoors of a wall coming vertical. Two corners meeting up their height, and receiving the driven nails.

From above, looking into the house, a roof laid on.
_____

Perhaps more can sometimes be communicated through describing the problems of communication and its technology, than through the direct attempt.

Also, sometimes, it is possible to make a thing so simply by naming it, & by saying you wish it might be so. Or by saying it exists but is incommunicable, it may be communicated.

_____

6. In *Let Us Now Praise Famous Men*, Greensboro is "Centerboro," Moundville is "Cookstown," and Tuscaloosa is "Cherokee City."

[7]

How are you going to describe an "ordinary" landscape—there are by the way a million kinds of ordinary and relatively few hundred extraordinary. It would be good to present these quite independent of the "sensibility" of an "artist."

The Fields-Burroughs-Tingle vicinity is one kind of utterly ordinary landscape. There is a highway running north-south through entirely ordinary and so non-representative country: at a certain place there is a white church on the left and a rollercoaster dip in the road just before you come to it from the south. At the flat of this; in the trough between in two low waves, on the right, two posts freshly peeled of their bark, as if they were markers. Between them, a narrow clay road leads off at a right angle and almost immediately starts climbing a low hill; not more than fifty feet up; there is an owned farmhouse, cleanly, painted sand-color, on the right: the road then levels off and lies in a lightly curved series of near straightaways between tilled fields broken by growths of pine, brambles, hickory, ravines. Et cetera.

This goes on without incident even of houses, but for one, low on the left, for half a mile. There, on the right, is a no longer used gravel pit, and a road leads off just as you get to it. It leads past a couple of houses (both visible from road A),   So through to Burroughs: then: we have lost timing: and now so through to Fields: Then:

[8]

But the trouble is that words are not simultaneous. These roads are. These things are all there at once; not only these two roads but the highway too; and the county seat at either end of the run. There is rather heavy characteristic swift traffic (and slow) on the highway; but these roads are entirely out of its pace.

Moreover, these are not all that is "simultaneous"; they have been isolated and by isolation made false through incompleteness. This incompleteness is probably not possible to complete in any words: and where, if anywhere, is its center: in any case the least that might be done is to make the whole planet the continuous center; and the planet not in self-relation but in relation to (a) the whole of the solar system; (b) the local "galaxy", (c) the "universe" (meaning the nearest physical approach to the "absolute") and (d) the "absolute," bearing however in mind that this trembles in paradox of not at all necessarily being an absolute; and is trembling in all these its simultaneous forms, which in turn may not at all necessarily be simultaneous: or are simultaneous in so twisted a way as to dizzy any effort of consciousness to grasp it.

––––––––––––

[9]

The "Goodness" or "Evil" of a man makes extremely little difference in the result. None of these three families would be appreciably better off under the most conscientious, benevolent and intelligent landlord available.

Such an observation is commonly taken by both sides as "excusing" the landlord. No "true" observation exists that cannot be made bad use of: and the use is, finally (or even very soon) invariably "bad".

––––––––

The enjoyment of "beauty" (the ability to perceive it); love; much of friendship; nearly all of speculation; are class privileges. That is not to say that all of one class are capable and all of another are incapable; nor am I trying to: I am speaking though of the great majority. The only esthetic remark I heard in the whole time was from Allie Mae, who liked a given sunset. It was of the sort which has appeared over and over in the only "art" she knows: calendar art. Alma said the stars were beautiful. There was not even remotely contempt, or a feeling she was being affected (they were too far removed even from small-town "culture" to assume that all this is "beautiful" is affected and shameful: They simply did not know what she meant.)

[10]

Withdrawn from the environment, however, many or most would feel nostalgia, and on returning, or in recall, would find much to be "beautiful" which they had never suspected of it.

––––––––

A Thing which keeps returning, is rain on the rear yard clay seen sideby from within the Burroughs hall in the middle of a dark warm-cool morning: the multitudinous speckling sticking of the rain; on clay and few weeds; and along the ragged ends of the boards which lie flush to the dirt now gleaming mud.

––––––––

How is the pure physical driving and implanting power of the environment to be made at all clear: and by clear I mean, how shall it be made to weigh the life out of a reader. I would like every item described in this to come through in terms of its continuous impingement upon the naive and defenseless senses first of infants then of a child, so on.

And mentioning a thing only once, is so hopelessly weak, when that same thing is re-registered an almost infinite and certainly a countless thousands of times, under all colorings of all circumstances possible to that place & to that individual, and importantly different to every

[11]

other individual who shares that environment in its total of overlapped items. But this should have two things at once: the casualness, imperceptibility, lack of intensity, in which it is received; and the intensity of the most intense statement conceivable, in any medium".

————

A sudden and unexplained past portrait of Allie Mae in the best hat, young. And embodied, not described or conjectured.

————

The possessions even of the almost most impoverished: say, of all, nearly, who are not wandering: so accumulate that their number at its most sparse seems monstrous, and the people deceptively rid.

————

This could be laid out so simply:

One man, his wife, his family, human existences, now arrived into a certain situation on the face of the earth. What other way of making a living. What are the arrangements. What work does this entail. What are the results. What do they get for it. In shelter. In food. In clothing. What are their possessions. What is their education. What about their leisure.

[12]

What is an overall day like. A week. What are the seasons: a year. What is the "state of mind" of these people: what are they "like": who are they.

But again, all these things are simultaneous, and utterly interlocked. By such a scheme; much, (by the thousands) of the real meaning, or the relatively real, is left out.

————

If it were possible in this limited time to invent a new method of condensation, of the order of music or poetry, the space here allotted me might be enough: but as it is, that is impossible. It becomes more

and more obvious to me that I must for the time being sacrifice a great
deal for the sake of a little.

————

Steady mutual absorption in annoying and dragging physical duties
& difficulties, makes it impossible to maintain "love".

Kitchen work, it is a cliché, reduces to brainlessness, apathy and
stupidity.

[13]

It may be that those forms of egoism which result for instance in
the neurotic bluestocking, and in the possessive mother, can scarcely
come about without comfort, leisure, money, and quite different, and
relatively sophisticated, traditional conceptions of what a woman is.

The "humble" and "meek", the unquestioning & "uncomplaining",
are those who by chance have never perceived anything.

Certainly not all in "poverty" is bad. But its usefulness would be only
to those who took it on by will and preference, in something like full
understanding, or fully unqualified attraction towards it; as with chastity.
And here, too, "understanding" is "inferior" to the intuitive attraction.

Yet you must count in such as Mrs. Tingle who has neither, and
who has the total beauty, and virtuousness-irrelevant-to-will or wish, of
a potato.

————

I see this country as one field, speckled with houses.

[14]

[J 5.4: Journal Entry: "I am far gone"]

27 September.

I am far gone. I not only no longer know how to write it, I don't
even know many of the reasons why. A feeling even at the best of working with only a fraction of the mind: like running a race with both arms
tied to the sides and one leg cut off, or asleep. This too is what I have
against each 'method' or 'tone', maybe especially the rational methods.
Why can I not write it in complete simplicity, yielding notice that of
course it is incomplete, and working only for the completest possible
clarity. Winter scenes. Morning, after the children are gone to school.

In the bureau drawer, papers which have been used at least one christmas before. Clay. The musical and environmental basis. Placement. How to get a road as it is in all seasons, and degrees of familiarity. How to write of their marriages. Why do I feel I lose so much by openness, by saying I don't know how, yet how can I give this up, or why can't I. Many things in it I <u>do</u> know, and in terms beyond apology or personality, or a leverage on personal effort or intelligence.

My ruining need for tension between words, and the procession of all out of one core.

I started a long letter to Franklin[7] today, taking hold harder than I ever have before, but with feelings of danger, ignorance, and inability to say straight even so much as I know. This latter is badly in my way in writing [illegible words].

[15]

I guess I don't care much what I am moved by, so long as I'm moved. There were a few things in 4 Daughters[8] that had tears in my eyes, and I am grateful to have them there. The thought, even, of the [Beethoven's] G major concerto, & of a number of other pieces of music, nearly kills me now, for I know I understand what I want to write of in terms of equivalent planes, and am impotent.

On recording machine: verbal improvisations on a 'state of consciousness' or even a 'situation', might have things which cannot be written. In complete simplicity, scarcely inflected,: 'Everything will be all right. Everything will be all right,' etc etc.

Saturday night we were fine, and deferred it, looking forward to Sunday night. Sunday night, at the Geroulds[9] after a bad day there (Mrs Smith). Alma, a headache. Trouble. She teasingly stayed in my lap when I wanted to get up and help Doris, I was annoyed, she was hurt, it was all killed. Alma stayed over so that we might have Monday night. We ate out and went to a movie, got home late. Uncertainty what time it was;

---

7. Franklin Miner. See J 4.6, note 34.

8. *Four Daughters,* directed by Michael Curtiz (1938).

9. Presumably Christopher Gerould's family. His mother was Katherine Fullerton Gerould (1879–1944), a well-known author and critic.

what time her train today (schedule changed, DST[10] over). Turned on radio to catch time, unpleasing music & voices, a sort of suspension & strain, listening for the time announcement; this

[16]

lost us any desire or gayety, just quiet, amiable, a lot of confusion & discussion of times, trains, whether I was to go out & find the time, whether to wait it out on the radio; I became depressed; and was getting tired. Alma slept in afternoon; the feeling of deliberativeness & of lack of desire together was closing on us. Feeling badly, I went out, hoping I might cheer, and do something to clean things. It seemed a good idea to come silently round to back, undress, knock on door, teasing, kidding dialogue, and enter naked. That she would be frightened of the knocking never of course occurred to me, because my 'imagination' was working on a different thing; but she was, and it shattered me, and then I had to walk in naked, and could see but not enjoy the humor of this. I was unsexed by it; tried to recoup by relaxing and reading, and got too sleepy to be capable of anything.

My lashes touch the lenses and are uncomfortable.

Tomorrow is Walker's show[11] (the 'opening' tonight I suppose). I wish I could see it, and him.

God help me do better with my work and my living, and give me some life and confidence again, any sense of free clear and confident motion.

[17]

I wish I could give up reading entirely.

Last night Alma dreamed, remembering these three parts:
1 With Emma, and another girl, she met a girl she formerly knew, very well dressed (Alma was ragged and sloppy). The other girl became all eyes, greatly enlarged (each c. 2 feet across) liquid shining & glittering soft black: gay, kind, loving & understanding; and in them she felt fully free and unguarded in her conduct, and warmly happy.

---

10. Daylight Savings Time.

11. Walker Evans's *American Photographs* opened at the Museum of Modern Art September 28, 1938.

2 With me, and others, she was chasing, and trying to conceal, a young negro, all over a city, a fugitive from law.

3 We were at a concert, high in a balcony, which began to lift, and lifted higher and higher; there became no roof and a sense of infinite and swift lifting, terror; a voice behind said it was falling: she realized it was falling a terrible speed and seemed lifting only because as it fell the lip was tilting upward: it sank, many hundreds of miles in a few seconds, with a sense of bottom rushing to meet us. If we could leap out over the lip and clear the base we could save ourselves. I leapt a little ahead of her. We came down vertically hand in hand toward a concrete floor. She awoke just as we struck.

[18]

I am reminded.

I was on shipboard with Alma, Via, and many friends. We were rollerskating, by pairs & groups and crack the whip. As we rounded one end the ship became the great plain deck of a plane carrier and we gathered speed, Alma and I, hands together, breaking through a line of facing friends, higher and higher speed (a noise of skates and their vibration in my footbones). The deck sank tilting and showed line of dark sea, then lifted, tilted, showing only sky. As I came near the end, beyond control, I yelled Let Go My Hand (afraid for her) and left the end, alone, anticipating a long arc and splash into the water: but rose in a long curve that bent back on itself so I was vertical above the ship, seeing it (and faces of friends, Via's very clear) shrink very fast to a speck on a round globe of water: reached the crest: I was now in and seeing a plane: it began to tear to pieces and I fell with increasing speed, sure I would strike and sink the boat.

28 September, Wednesday.

[19]

[J 5.5: Journal Entry:
"Mentally I am cold in the morning"]

28 Sept.

Mentally I am cold in the morning, warm & emotional at night. Work I have done at night looks bad to me in the morning. Trying to work mornings, I am bothered with the inability to feel strongly.

I am trying to read nothing, and to write nothing except work or to Uhr [?], except possibly to Franklin. So: the radio becomes my dope: to hear a voice talking somewhere in the house.

[J 5.6: Journal Entry: "Losses"]

Monday, October (5?)[12]

Losses. Excitement in the house, in work around it, in walking, in waking, in breasts, armpits, kissing, music, religion.

Chaplin.[13] He has gone through more phases of art than any other man. Primitive art: as ballads; naive art, into more & more intensely selfconscious art; a peak in City Lights,[14] as intensely selfcentred as the waste land or Troilus & Cressida: and beyond that into Modern Times, in which the same character has an entirely new leverage.

He shares with Blake and Christ this: that he indicates what is obviously the good way to live: to live that way would mean complete 'withdrawal from the world' for each individual; would mean the destruction of the world as is.

At one and same time, in Modern Times, he seriously shows what 'unemployment' means and insists: 'but this idea that people should have work is ridiculous & wrong in itself.'

[20]

There is also in this picture much that is sex education. The minister's wife. His international style. The waterfront street. The placards in languages embracing most of the world. His face itself, which shifts races. The Law: one gray felt, one Panama.

He acts out all parts for the others.

The cleanliness of his light. His sense from the first of setting and landscape. Interiors: steps of buildings, street corners, rough &

---

12. Monday, October 3, 1938.

13. Charlie Chaplin (1889–1977), British actor and director. Agee greatly admired Chaplin as an artist. See in particular Agee's "Comedy's Greatest Era," in *Agee on Film*, 1–19, as well as his three-part review of Chaplin's *Monsieur Verdoux*, 252–62.

14. Directed by and starring Chaplin, 1931. The other Chaplin films mentioned in this entry are *Easy Street* (1917), *The Kid* (1921), *The Circus* (1928), and *Modern Times* (1936).

casual country: they have any amount more 'reality' than almost any 'documentaries'.

The song. The character-within-a character. For the song he creates an entirely new character who is double: he is what the tramp would create in such a situation; and he is Chaplin himself directly speaking. The beautiful laquer [?] skill of having a table full of French sailors loving his act. The skill of setting up the quartet as background for his preparation: in the evening by the moonlight.

The shifts in kind of woman: Purviance;[15] then a long line of strange girls, then Goddard.[16]

Watching them behind the work in Modern Times you see some of the happiest work I know of.

The bow to Mickey Mouse.

City Lights is the cruellest of the pictures, Modern Times is the happiest. The Circus is like a great classical exercise: like Beethoven's even-numbered symphonies.

Modern Times seems the most grandly accomplished. Full of set-pieces, alternated

[21]

with completely new things. He and Conklin.[17] The skating scene.

His minor types like his streets. So sharp they exceed most 'unacted' movies in reality: the woman who tells on Goddard for stealing the bread.

Extremest focus on hatred of law: in M-T. Where, too, it is identified not specifically with money, and as a crusher of life. (The bank is background as Goddard steps into the Maria.[18])

Scenes of police brutalism were cut from it.

One sequence after another is terminated by the nasty whine of the Maria.

Alyosha, or Myshkin: Don Quixote & Panza in one: Hamlet: one

15. Edna Purviance (1895–1958), American actress, was Chaplin's leading lady in more than twenty films, including Easy Street, The Kid, and A Woman of Paris (1923).

16. Paulette Goddard (1911–1990), American actress, starred in Chaplin's Modern Times and was secretly married to him in 1936. They divorced in 1942.

17. Chester Conklin (1886–1971), American actor, played the mechanic whom Chaplin's Tramp "assists" in Modern Times.

18. I.e., Black Maria, or paddy wagon.

of the great central characters. Nothing he does, and nothing that sur-
rounds him, can lack meaning.

A great 'cynicism' in this: that those who are nearest him: the poor
and simple and the young: are cruellest to him; i.e. they laugh at him
with least feeling. But there are worse: i.e., a great crowd of the middle
class, especially women, who have always thought of him as 'vulgar', and
as not even funny. Yet these again; every egg can be candled against him.

To talk about him is as useless and wrong as writing about music,
or paraphrasing a poem.

In a certain important sense he is one of the luckiest of great artists:
i.e., has found himself a relative snap. Everything he has done for years
gives appearance

[22]

of having been planned, to the last detail of background, & the last minor
character; so that his screen constantly and often with great subtlety
flashes illuminations of meanings of existence.

As far back as Easy Street, he was presenting a 'slum' which would
shock the heart of anyone who at all simply looked at it.

The Kid. What is beautiful in the need of those who lead children
into basements with chocolate bars, who are uncomplexly known as
sex fiends. Any amount more powerful than M,[19] whose 'sympathy'
was so praised.

A very great instant in MT: when the girl, caught up with, runs to
him, a picture of him from behind, showing the side of his face, his
cheek, &c: he is in this instant Chaplin himself, managing to step out
of character and to make his comment and the scene's meanings any
amount more poignant.

The singing scene is one of the most dangerous or daring things I
know of anywhere, and is perfectly carried. Including the fact that
through hearing the voice, the tramp & Chaplin together are unified;
and become much more 'human' than before. There is pain and fear
in the voice.

Two stories I remember hearing. I do not vouch for them. But I
do think they are essentially true of him & revealing of him: he could
not stand a bullfight

19. M (1931), directed by Fritz Lang.

[23]

he went to see. Seeing Chinese torture photographs he was first quiet, then burst out, 'that's right: that's the thing to do to them'; & etc.

Mozart's music. The limberness, masculinity, cleanness & lyricism of this.

The whole Lita Gray[20] divorce: by the transition manifesto—[21]

It may be, that he needs to be in love to make a picture.

Ralph Graves,[22] in a bit, more real than he ever had a chance to be, or knew how to be when he had parts.

The ending of City Lights: one of the very great endings, or instants, in any 'art' I know.

He is in a sense even 'purer' than Shakespeare: no ornament at all. By this analogy: Shakespeare, in terms of music, would cover the whole of it: Chaplin never deviates out of popular tunes.

A whole faction of esthetes think little of him since he became conscious of himself: 'he was a good clown'; 'a good naif'. There are things to said for this: but the main thing is, they are snobs. He has lost what has had to be lost, and has done a miracle, of using the character in a different way. Don't let anyone tell you that meanings are 'read into' his work which are not there. They may be misread, in wrong proportions; but there is plenty of meaning.

A movie could be made of his hands alone.

[24]

I understand he is a good, and careful business man: and that certainly he is good and rich. This is a good contradiction, and a sad one. The man who understands both sides of poverty and of vagabondage, as much as Jesus, of Francis of Assisi, in his mind and spirit, is very careful in his physical life.

In any case it has not qualified his work. So far as that is concerned, he seems the artist least hurt by wealth that I can think of.

---

20. Born Lillita Louise MacMurray, American actress Lita Grey (1908–1995) was Chaplin's second wife. After a shotgun wedding 1924, when she was sixteen and he was thirty-five, they divorced in 1927 following a contentious and much publicized trial.

21. Eugene Jolas's "Proclamation: The Revolution of the Word," which appeared in *transition* in 1929, is one of the seminal documents of surrealism.

22. Ralph Graves (1900–1977), American actor.

Only the movies could hold him. He has done in them some of the most beautiful things of this century. Yet his field is narrow; in so many ways he scarcely touches the movies, i.e. all they might be.

The extraordinary and moving thing of seeing genius at work: watching behind his character.

———

———

Dependence-strain. General & localized. Intense concern for others' feelings.
Continuous watching of Alma; stress, in the pit of the stomach.
Split between overconfidence towards 'inferiors', lack of confidence with 'equals', demoralization with 'superiors'.
A particular attitude towards any woman I am close with, which I am sure is pretty bad. Much of it appears routine among husbands. Lack of distance. Loss of humor. Over-open-ness. Loss of focus. Long stretches of nothing today. A kind of domineering.

[25]

Guilt about work they are doing.

My father died when I was 6. 9 to 14 I was subsumed in a 'hard' school. Early childhood on I quarreled almost steadily with my sister, 2½ years younger. With my first girl I was very critical of her, inside myself, and very sensitive to the wish that my friends like her. I am now less critical, far as I know, but still sensitive on this latter.

'Religion'; emotion; idealization; 'reformer'; 'sadist'; 'generalizer'.
Physical symptoms & pains.

———

Sample: now looking back, and wanting to write of this 'dependence', I feel tired, it looks not only hard to do, but impossible to get said straight, and I won't want to do it.
The Chaplin: seeing MT, I know I understand his work well; yet what notes I have written are flat.

JOURNAL 6

[J 6.1: Notes on Books for Review]

called by Mumford "patriotic project"[1]

advantages (unparalleled and of information) and disadvantages of a new & [illegible] very important way of writing: large, anonymous, staff collaborations.

As a source-book, & anthology, of information, wonderful: (though how much is missed can't be told). But deficient in its conception; very uneven, usually second-third-grade, in its perceptions; undiscriminatory in its use of photographs; the kinds of cautiousness which may be expected of democratically, politically produced work. It is thorough enough & useful enough to make it almost impossible that the job be done again: so it is too bad it was done so poorly.

144 – stupid on architecture –

147 – dams –

128 – excellent photograph –

3 – youngest state: 1912

3 – damned rivers to make the deserts bloom - - "

20 – subtropical to subalpine flora –

---

1. Between 1935 and 1943 the Federal Writers' Project, which began under the direction of the Works Progress Administration and was transferred to individual state Writers' Programs in 1939, produced more than four hundred volumes in the American Guide Series, including collectively authored, comprehensive state guides. In a review of several American Guide publications devoted to New England, Lewis Mumford (1895–1990), American social critic and urban planner, wrote: "These guidebooks are the finest contribution to American patriotism that has been made in our generation: let that be the answer to the weaklings who are afraid to admit that American justice may miscarry or that the slums of Boston may be somewhat this side of Utopia. Let it also silence those who talk with vindictive hooded nods about the subversive elements that are supposed to lurk in the WPA" ("Writers' Project," *New Republic* (October 20, 1937): 306–7).

Agee began writing book reviews for *Time* magazine in January 1940, but the review to which these notes refer was apparently never published. The first book is *Arizona: A State Guide, Compiled by Workers of the Writers' Program of the Work Projects Administration in the State of Arizona* (New York: Hastings, 1940); the second, on Texas, could not be located; the third is *Our Southwest* by Edna Fergusson (New York: Knopf, 1941). Only the first is in the American Guide Series.

26–7 – softpedaling on Indians

29 – reservations: concentration camps –

58, 62 &c – some good eyewitness accounts –

69 – wild horses – rewrite –

73 – saddle –

75 – 90% irrigation

95f – labor

127f – Baron of Arizona

Geronimo – called a
"renegade", not "hero"
or "patriot"

254: misprint

[2]

[3]

Texas –

32 – Jim Younger ←

35f – letters –

47 – South Texans –

Ch V – fairly nice Mexican stuff

  a slightly boy-o-boy manner of telling

87 Bozo [?] & Squalus

92 South Tex politics; Tex-Mex

95–6 Lower Rio Grande Valley; "Magic-Valley"

106 – Spanish-English Law; land; oil.

111 – witch doctor 118 yrs old

119 – Psalms in Lockets

127 – Padre island – 'treasure' of Lost City.

131 – Tarpon Rodeo at mouth of R-G.

136 – cotton $1.02 per lb through Brownsville & Bagdad

139 scores of ghost towns –

140 Jay Gould's pictograph & curse –

159 – charcoal burners

  60 – the freed population of Texas

170 – San Antonio: bilingual; exiles

  5 – Lone Star –

176–8 – colonists under Austin –

  9–80 – Alamo

184–5 – very good by Sweet

187 – Tex-Mex High School football
188 – European wreath of S-A
212f – Riley [illegible] funeral oration.
214 justification-vs-purification
216 – quite fair on religion
217 – [Paul] Bunyan & Kemp Morgan
223f Negroes
231 justifying Southern values by pointing out Northern –
240 Populists – consumers' cooperatives: ruined by railroads –
244 Jim Hogg

[4]

257f Chippy –
262 I want a boyfriend
263f – West Texas
   5 Pecos Bill
267 time, space; good but unrealized –
269 Belle Star
   73 Rangers avert strikebreakers –
274 murder rate ←
284f – planes in ranching, crime detection, oil exploration

[5]

Our Southwest
      pretty good maps – (The Guide is deficient in them) –
6 overrates W[ill]. Rogers –
though it doesn't carry it all the way out it indicates what is too easily
forgotten; that there is no substitute: not even fast: for understanding
and treatment.
14 anti-tourist & prostarkness
16 dig for wood, climb for water –
16 – 17 source of comedy, tolerance, friendliness.
17 – chance –
18 – mobility
22 anti-Dallas.
24 no servants in West Texas –
26 cowboy: Nordic: knighthood

[pages 6–8 blank]

[9]

[J 6.2: Review Draft:
"On a number of things about <u>The Grapes of Wrath</u>"]

On a number of things about <u>The Grapes of Wrath</u>—everything he disfavored—I agree with Edwin Locke.[2] On nearly everything about it that he favored, I disagree. I don't want to argue with him, though, or to cast this letter in any such form. My own opinions were not prompted or changed by his article, and a good deal that seems to me most interesting about the film would have to be dragged in by the heels if I went at it in terms of the article. The fact is that the film, and things surrounding it, excited me a good deal. They seemed worthy of very detailed, serious, extensive discussion. It is impossible to handle them as they deserve, even in a fairly long letter: but I hope the editors of <u>Films</u> and its readers will forgive me if I use what space is possible to set down, without form, some notes and suggestions.

———

It seems to me that the film itself, the claims it made of itself, the sort of film it is, or tries to be, the things critics and reviewers have said of it, and its whole reputation with audiences, with amateur, and professional, and merely optative makers of films, and with producers, taken either apart or all together, are all one almost unmitigated misfortune; and are a "document" mainly of a dangerous fact: the terribly relaxed, confused, lenient standards of even the best, or nominally or reputably best, person engaged in making, evaluating, theorizing about, and seeing, moving pictures in this country.

---

2. Edwin Locke was Roy Stryker's assistant in the Farm Security Administration from 1935 to 1937. Agee is responding to his "Adaptation of Reality in *The Grapes of Wrath*," which appeared in *Films* 1.2 (Spring 1940): 49–55. Locke's review is generally positive, singling out screenwriter Nunnally Johnson, director John Ford, and cinematographer Gregg Toland for praise. He is pleasantly surprised that the movie was made in the first place but does not place too much hope in the industry or its audience: "How much longer audiences will continue to gape at the usual run of vapid and distant dreams when they can have, if they support them, beautiful and stirring accounts of reality like *The Grapes of Wrath* is still a matter of speculation." The spring 1940 issue advertised a future essay by Agee, quite possibly this response to Locke, but the journal folded before it was published. See J 2.2, note 4.

If this is true of the best, the most talented, the most intelligent, the most sincere; and if it is true of the more casual newspaper reviewers and private

[10]

[11]

"authorities" who so much more immediately touch the Eyes, and the Judgement, of the fully massive, most confused, most important audience, it becomes as unhappy to think of the future of American films as it is, in general, to look at the present and at virtually every so-called "important" show the last ten years have produced. And it becomes important that at least those who take film seriously, and who highly regard such a picture as The Grapes of Wrath, to put the brakes on sharply, get out, and see how many tires are flat and which road they are traveling on.

There are other movies most of this might be said of, and many of them are worse than this one; but this one has so special a place in history, and so special a reputation, that it seems a symbol for them all; the ultimate, until worse mistakes (proceeding from it) are made still more pretentiously. This is the one of which too many people have said in print and conversation that it is a great work of art, or the best movie yet made in America, or things still funnier. It is the one, also, over which nearly all left-wingers—and liberals, for that matter—are very happy: so happy, indeed, that they can (literally) overlook—or still worse, see and forgive— any number of its merely non-political gaffs. It is the one, also, which so unqualifiedly heartens all those who plug so hard and care so much for the development of "documentary" films: for the increased use of "reality." I submit that there is quite as much unreality in The Grapes of Wrath as in Gone With the Wind (sight unseen),

[12]

[13]

and that is of a far more poisonous order, being both more near the centres of human living, pain and dignity, and therefore far more insulting to them, and being also so successfully disguised as "reality", that it has deceived even its creators. I suggest that it is virtually worthless in any direct way, but endlessly interesting as an encyclopedia of flaws, substandards, inadequacies, self-deceptions, deceptions of the public, opportunities impaired for the future, and, at very best, of painful disappointments. It may be still more interesting, for those with the special

taste for it, to watch and analyze as an elaborate, flawlessly false and logical and vulgar, collective dream: general America's dream of a lot of
things about itself. Such dreams—and every movie and every piece of
advertising art is one, more or less significant—are bitterly beautiful to
look at, richer in meaning and revelation than any but the best art, and
in their own way infallible. On the other hand it is unhappy to reflect
how many farmers, watching these high-paid, earnest, cruelly insulting
oafs embody their self-dream, will be completely flattered of their reality.

But as a moving picture of what it is supposed to be about, it is to
say it most kindly, inadequate. And if one is severe in proportion to the
nobility of the attempt—and I certainly think one must be—it touches
the threshold of goodness about three instants. The rest of it merely
stinks.

————

It is going to be impossible within limited space to

[14]

[15]

present, in any sufficient detail, my reasons for thinking so: and even if
I did I have no reason to think I would persuade more than a few who did
not partly agree in the first place. Even that would require long efforts
to lay out lives on film esthetics and on critical ethics: the ramifications
would be all but endless. But let me set down a few things. To those who
know the film well, I hope they may suggest the hundreds of others.

————

Three good moments. The first is the first shot and I think it is magnificent. The very next shot, through the roadside fence, betrayed the
astonished hope it aroused. The second is certain elements of the scene
of the sloped curve at dawn where they look into the fertile valley, the
bird sings in the silence, and they are told by the mother that the grandmother has died. The sounds, the silences, the kink of brightness in the
air, the road, and the valley, are all good. The people are not, save in
their ways of walking and standing, and their half-successful efforts to
subdue and space their voices right. The third is Jane Darwell[3] walking

————

3. Jane Darwell (1879–1967), American actress, won an Academy Award in
1941 for her portrayal of Ma Joad in *The Grapes of Wrath*. Locke was less appre-
ciative than Agee, writing: "Although she plays intelligently, no amount of experience or artistry could make her look like a woman of the Oklahoma people."

in earlier morning away from the camera, along the housefronts of the camp. Her walk, her body, the houses, the light, the silence, the sound of the rooster, the placement of the camera, its focus on the second house, are all so excellent, so completely successful, that it seems impossible that the people who

[16]

[17]

were responsible could have made the rest of the film and failed to scrap it.

The California roadside where the truck pulls over toward a flat is also good: and there are great numbers of littler things, so compromised in the general inadequacy that they count for little better than anger that they were used, dishonored, and made less available for future use.

[18]

[19]

[J 6.3: *LUNPFM* Drafts: Introduction]

Once I decided a preface would be necessary, it took three months to find I couldn't write the one I wanted to. So this will have to do instead: a few words on what this book is and is not, and on how it got started.

For three or four months now it has seemed to me that in twenty-five hundred words or so I could unify and make clear everything about this book that I wanted to or needed to. I have pretty well given that up now. I will be more than content if in any form I can get down a few of the essentials: information, directives, false scents, and so on.

———

Nominally, the subject of this volume is cotton tenancy in the United States, as perceived in the environment and daily living of three representative families of white tenant farmers.

Actually, this begins an attempt to recognize the stature of a piece of unimagined existence, and to contrive appropriate techniques for its recording, communication, evaluation, and defense.

The book has been designed in two intentions: as the beginning of a more extended piece of work, and to stand of itself, independent of any such further work as may be done. The title of the work as a whole is Three Tenant Families; the title of this volume is Let Us Now Praise

<u>Famous Men</u>. It will be better to accept rather than to avoid or merely to criticize such confusions and the tensions set up between them: for confusion, and conflict

[20]

[21]

are organic to the method. It is perhaps particularly important that the nominal subject be borne steadily in mind, however little it is directly undertaken. For this book is intended, among other things, as an insult, a swindle, and a corrective; and this nominal subject, and the reader's conception of its proper handling, is our leverage.

#

Evans and I were traveling in the middle south of this nation, seeking out these families, and living with them, during the summer of 1936. Evans was on loan from the Farm Bureau Administration to a New York magazine for which I worked, and for this magazine we were preparing an article on this same nominal subject. For reasons which may be examined in a later volume, the article was not published. After a year, however, it was released to us, and in the spring of 1938 an agreement was reached with X_____, publishers, for an amplification of the same material in book form.

Of the problems, economic, psychological and ethical, of negotiation, of composition of the book's ultimate rejection by X___ (or withdrawal by the authors) nothing will be said here, beyond the explicit statement that they are essential parts of the subject as a whole with which it is proposed to deal. It is only fair to add this warning: readers and reviewers as well as publishers and employers are important creatures of this subject; for the defense of an idea (however inadequate) and added concentricities of its fate, are far too significant to suffer the usual neglect accorded them in the name of taste and in the fear of estrangement of libel suits.[4]

---

4. The article Agee produced was too long and inappropriate in style and tone for *Fortune*'s "Life and Circumstances" series, for which it had been intended. After a year, *Fortune* released the manuscript to Agee, and Harper Brothers offered him a contract but in 1939 rejected *Let Us Now Praise Famous Men* when Agee refused to make the extensive revisions they required. In the spring of 1940, Houghton Mifflin agreed to publish the book along with footnotes and a new preface after Agee deleted certain words "illegal in Massachusetts."

[22]

[23]

But these names and much else must bide their time. In this volume, which is a prologue, they are represented only by shadows.*

———

Our subject as a whole might be mapped—very sketchily—as follows:

At the centre, every recapturable instant of those eight weeks spent in the middle south.

Everything that led to those eight weeks.

Everything that has proceeded from or will proceed from them.

Every relevant problem or issue which is raised by this material.

At the centre again: our selves, and our instruments. These secondary instruments are the still camera and the printed word. The primary instrument is individual human consciousness.

Again at the centre, these three families, chosen with such pain to "represent" their kind; with whom, for a while, we intimately lived, and whom we watched.

Their immediate environment: and, insofar as we have perceived it, the general south.

---

* The virtual absence of satire and of analysis and record of corruption is one of our more serious regrets.

[24]

[25]

Now of these families, and what they represent, a word is necessary. We are satisfied that they adequately represent white cotton tenants and much to do (by no means all) with Negro tenants: and as tenants they will in due time be thoroughly examined. But that is perhaps the least of the things that they represent to us and in our treatment. Tenantry as such, in fact, does not particularly interest us, and the isolation of tenantry as a problem to be attacked and solved as if its own terms were the only ones, seems to us false and dangerous, productive, if of anything, chiefly of delusions, and further harm, and subtler captivity.

They represent: they are; not only tenantry, not only tenants. That is of importance in the structure of their lives; but they are other things

as well. They are of the working people of the world. They are members, and representatives, of the human race; and though the forms of
human bondage are innumerable, it seems to us that they represent,
among the two billions not living, those crude (yet subtle) forms of
bondage in which a majority are held. They are also sons and creatures
of God; and they are God; and in essence this volume begins, with what
inadequacy will be naked before you, an enquiry into human divinity, in
its normal circumstance of disadvantage; into the possibilities of its lib-
eration; into the nature, and intensity, of the responsibility, or guilt, which
(it is proposed) each human being needs recognize towards all others,
who shall dare to be alive.

　　Let it be added, that they seem to us neither more nor less important,

[26]

[27]

and meaningful, than you, than ourselves, than every beast and object
within their world and within the scope of creation.

[28]

[29]

[musical notation]
　　　350
　　　 84
　　1400
　　2800
　29,400

[30]

[31]

　　　Thank you, & goodnight. It's very late in the morning.

[32]

[33]

　　　Much has been attempted in this book; yet on the scale of its subject, it is small; and even on its own scale it is obscure and inadequate.
Ultimately a complete exposition of the subject, and explanation of the
method, will be obligatory. Because so much here is unexplained, inadequate and misunderstandable, the temptation will be resisted: but a
few bits of information seem absolutely necessary.

Nominally, our subject is cotton tenantry in the United States, as seen in the environment and daily living of three representative families of white tenants, whom we sought out and lived with for a while during

[34]

[35]

During July and August 1936 Walker Evans and I were at work in the middle south of this nation. It was, even from the beginning, a curious piece of work. Evans was on loan from the Federal Government, and it was our business to prepare, for a New York magazine, an article on the environment and daily living of a representative family of cotton tenant farmers of the white race.

[36]

[37]

Much has been attempted in this book, but it is small upon the scale of its subject, and inadequate even upon its own scale. Ultimately a complete exposition on the subject, and of the method, will be obligatory. The temptation to make a beginning here and now is strong, but will be resisted. Even so, a few pieces of information, and a few directives, seem indispensable.

───────

It began as a piece of work we were doing, in the middle south of this nation, during July and August 1936. Even then, it was a curious piece of work. Evans was on loan from the Federal Government, and it was our business to seek out and live with a representative white family of cotton tenant farmers, and to prepare, for a New York magazine, an article on the environment and the daily living of this family.

[38]

[39]

This volume has been designed in two intentions: as the beginning of a longer piece of work; and to stand of itself, independent of any such further work as may be done.

The title of the work as a whole is <u>Three Tenant Families</u>.

The title of this present volume is <u>Let Us Now Praise Famous Men</u>.

The nominal subject of this volume, and of the work as a whole, is cotton tenantry in the United States, chiefly in terms of a record, in writing and in photographs, of the environment and daily living of three white families of cotton tenant farmers.

The actual subject is so much more serious, and difficult, that no attempt will be made, here, even to define it, far less to discuss it. But briefly, the effort is to recognize the stature of a portion of unimagined existence, and to contrive adequate technologies for its recording, communication, diagnosis, and defense: and this is perhaps most essentially an enquiry into human divinity in certain normal predicaments.

Of such an undertaking, this book (as will readily be seen) is but the crudest and most fragmentary of beginnings.

The temptation to explain, to defend, and to criticize, is almost irresistibly strong. It will, however, be resisted, or in any case postponed, excepting only a few pieces of indispensable information.

[40]

[41]

That "portion of unimagined existence" which is the centre of all our centres was, in time, July and August 1936, in space, the middle south of this nation. There, in those weeks, Evans and I sought out and lived with three families, of whose living we were to prepare an article, for a New York magazine.

.   ———

These families were chosen with no little care, fairly to represent all cotton tenants of the white race in the United States. They also represent, or are, or are living, embodied symbols of, other things, not less important, in our esteem. They are not tenants merely but are of the working and ill-used people of the world; not working people merely but members of the human race; not human beings merely but sons and creatures of God; not merely creatures of God but themselves divine, themselves divinity. In our study we hope to hold these facts in regard, however seriously that may impair the work as a sociological tract.

———

Each is an individual.

———

None is either more or less important, meaningful, "representative," than the authors, the readers, or any conceivable portion of existence, however trivial it may seem.

———

[42]

[43]

———

We, the authors, are neither scientists nor journalists nor politicians nor artists nor humanitarians; nor do we lay claim, or declare allegiance, to any form of authority save one: the authority, and fallibility, of individual human consciousness. This is a record of blindness as well as of perception; no attempt, it is hoped, will be made to conceal the blindness.

———

These are not works of art but documents. In token thereof, most of its violations are intentional.

———

Confusion, conflict, schism, and the tensions sprung between, are integral and intentional parts of this organism and will best be recognized and accepted as such.

———

These were not members of any union, and were in no danger, and were not being conspicuously misused. We were concerned to perceive normalities. Now, with the war, these silent and mild normalities must seem, to most, vacant and insignificant.

Let it at least be stated, as knowledge and as fact, however hopeless that it be recognized under stress: not one peacetime breath is drawn that does not contain a dreadfulness to equal the whole of war. Until this be known obsessively by many, and generally acted upon, the motions

[44]

[45]

of history are of no particular importance.

———

The reader is no less essential a centre of our subject than ourselves and those we tell of; and is no less responsible.

———

There is here no direct attempt, or far too little, to engage and to intensify the reader's conscience, and our own. A sufficient engagement and intensity may in time be attempted; but it will be impossible.

———

The photographs are not illustrations. They, and the text, are coequal, mutually independent, and fully collaborative. Because there are so few, and because eyesight is so weak and so generally corrupted, this statement will be generally misunderstood by those who so much as regard it. In the best interests of fact, however, and of the present and future of photography, it must stand.

––––––

The text was written with reading aloud in mind. That cannot be recommended, but it is suggested that the reader listen to what he sees on the page; for much that is attempted in variation of tone and pace will be impossible to the eye.

The intention was that the text be read not as books ordinarily

[46]

[47]

are but as a moving picture is seen, or a work of music heard: continuously, with only such brief intermissions as are self-evident. It is suggested that the serious reader follow this scheme.

––––––

The shadowiness and slight use of the people is deliberate; this volume is a prologue.

––––––

As such, it lacks full representation of the strains and traits it portends: the absence of satire, poetry, science, and pure record, and indications of a rational intelligence, are particularly to be regretted. The perversities, violations, insults and mutilations are, however, deliberate: deliberate above all are the incompleteness and the dissonance.

––––––

Of any attempts on the part of the publishers or others to ingratiate this volume, the authors must express their regret and disapproval.

––––––

To those to whom this record should belong, if to any: that is, to all those capable of reading or hearing languages and least of all to that educated for whom he has written it, the author of the text wishes to express his apologies.

[48]

[49]

Nominally this volume is a record, in photographs and in words, of the environment and daily living of three white families of North American cotton tenant farmers, with whom, for a few months, the authors lived. Actually, it begins an attempt to recognize the stature of a portion of unimagined existence, and to contrive proper treatments for its communication, analysis, and defense.

Essentially, it begins a lawless enquiry into certain predicaments normal to human divinity: their probable cause; their possible cure.

This volume was made in defiance of its nominal subject, a series of violations & corrections: then the nominal subject was kicked from under. It must now and here be explained.

Actually, it is a defiance and extension of that subject.

[50]

[51]

A record, in photographs, and in words, of the environment and daily living of three families, North American cotton tenant farmers, with whom, for a few weeks, the authors lived:

An attempt to recognize and properly to record, evaluate and defend, the stature of a portion of unimagined existence:

An enquiry into certain normal predicaments of human divinity; their possible causes: their possible cure.

A photographic and verbal record.

Book One: Thirty-one photographs.

Book Two: Invectives and inventories.

A record of the daily living of three families of cotton tenant farmers with whom, for a few weeks, the authors lived:

An attempt to recognize the stature of a portion of unimagined existence: the enquiry into certain normal predicaments of human divinity.

[52]

Evans was on loan from the Federal Government. ["" on next page]

[53]

During July and August 1936 Walker Evans and I were traveling and at work in the middle south of this nation (engaged in what, even from the first, has seemed to me rather a curious piece of work.) It was our business to prepare, for a New York magazine*, an article on cotton tenantry in the United States, in the form of a photographic and verbal record of the daily living and environment of an average white family of tenant farmers. We had first to find and to live with such a family.

We found no one family through which the whole of tenantry could be fairly represented, but decided that through three we had encountered, our job might with qualified adequacy be done. With the most nearly representative of the three we lived a little less than four weeks, seeing them and the others intimately and constantly. (going intensely about our tasks of observation, questioning and record)

At the end of August, long before we were willing to, we returned into the north and got our work ready.

For reasons which will not be a part of this volume the article was not used.

At the end of a year (of vacillation) it was, however, released to us; and in the spring of (the following year,) 1938, an agreement was reached with a New York publisher for an expansion of the same material in book form.

At the end of another year and a half the manuscript was rejected; or, speaking as truly, the authors withdrew it, rather than make certain required changes

[54]

[55]

through which it might become less unpalatable to the general reader.[5]

In the spring of 1940, after somewhat less success with three other firms, it was accepted by these publishers, on condition that certain words be deleted which are illegal in Massachusetts.

The authors found it possible to make this concession, and to permit prominence to the immediate, as against the generic, title.

————

This volume is designed in two intentions: as the beginning of an extensive piece of work; and to stand of itself, independent of any such further work as may be done.

————

5. See Appendix under J 6.3, page [52], for an alternate ending to this sentence.

The title of this volume is <u>Let Us Now Praise Famous Men</u>.

The title of the work as a whole is <u>Three Tenant Families</u>.

The nominal subject is North American cotton tenantry in the daily living of three representative white tenant families.

Actually, the effort is (more considerable if less feasible. It is, briefly,) to recognize the stature of a portion of unimagined existence, and to contrive techniques proper to its recording, communication, analysis and defense. It is, essentially, an enquiry into human divinity, beset by certain normal circumstances of disadvantage.

The immediate instruments are the motionless camera and the printed word. The governing instrument—which is also centre of investigation—is individual anti-authoritative

[56]

[57]

human consciousness.

Ultimately, it is intended that this record and analysis be extensive, with no detail, however trivial it may seem, left untouched, no relevancy avoided, which lies within the power of remembrance to maintain, of the mind to perceive, of the soul to persist in, which lies within the power of the heart to persist in, and or remembrance to maintain.

Of this ultimate intention the present volume is merely portent and fragment, experiment, dissonant prologue. Since the book is intended, among other things, as a swindle, an insult and a corrective, the reader will be wise to bear the nominal subject, and his expectation of its proper treatment, steadily in mind. The surface is hardly scratched. And though much may seem to be explained, nothing is. The nonexplanation is deliberate.

———

The photographs are not illustrative. They, and the text, are coequal, mutually independent, fully collaborative. By their fewness, and by the weakness and corruption of the reader's eye, this will be misunderstood by most of those who don't ignore it. In the interests, however, (of fact, of personal integrity, and) of the history and future of photography, that risk seems worth taking, and this flat statement necessary.

———

(Much that will seem to the reader inadequate is merely that: but much more is deliberate. Thorough analysis and explanation are obligatory; one centre of our subject. But there will be a minimum of either here.)

————

his is a work neither or art nor of science: nor is it a journalistic, scientific or humanitarian tract. We disdain, and contemn, every form of authority

[58]

[59]

save that of individual experience, of individual consciousness. Confusion and weakness are here neither avoided nor disguised: they are integral to our subject as perception and power.

————

Of any attempt on the part of the publishers, or others, to disguise or to integrate, or "sell", this volume, the authors must express their regret and their intense disapproval.

————

The text was written with reading aloud in mind. That cannot be recommended; but it is suggested that the reader attend with his ear to what he takes off the page: for the changes of tone, pace, shape and dynamics are chiefly unavailable to the eye alone, and with their lens, a good deal of meaning escapes.

————

It was intended, also, that the text be read continuously, as music is heard or a film watched, with brief pauses only where they are self-evident.

————

This is a book only by necessity. More seriously, it is an effort in human actuality, in which the reader is no less centrally involved than the authors and those of whom they tell. Those who wish to participate in this subject are invited to address the authors in care of their publishers. In material that is used, names will be withheld on request.

————

[60]

[61]

With so much abortive, deceptive, deliberately incomplete, dependent upon thinking here withheld or upon perceptions in the reader which we have no reason to assume and which we have in no way assisted, the temptation to explain, to self-criticize and to defend is all but irresistible. It will, however, at least for the time being, be resisted.

[62]

[63]

[J 6.4: Letter to the *New York Post*]

New York Post—

Gentlemen:

Mr. Walker Evans and I are completing a book on cotton tenantry, to be published this winter by Houghton Mifflin. We would much appreciate your permission to quote May Cameron's interview with Margaret Bourke-White,[6] (N.Y. Post 20 Nov 1937)?

Yours very truly,

James Agee

[64]

[65]

[J 6.5: *LUNPFM* Drafts: Introduction]

A record in photographs and writing.

A record (in photographs and in writing) of the daily living of three white families of cotton tenant families, with whom the authors lived:

An attempt to recognize the stature of a portion of unimagined existence and to give it the treatment it deserves:

An enquiry into certain normal predicaments of human divinity.

A corrective, an insult, and a swindle.

Images, inventories, meditations and invectives. Findings, records, interpretations and conjectures on the daily living of three white families

---

6. See "Notes and Appendices" to *Let Us Now Praise Famous Men* for Agee's appropriation of this portrait of Margaret Bourke-White (1904–1971), American photographer and wife of author Erskine Caldwell (1903–1987), with whom she collaborated on *You Have Seen Their Faces* (1937), to which *Famous Men* is in part a response.

of North American cotton tenant farmers. An effort to recognize the stature of a portion of unimagined existence. An enquiry into certain normal predicaments of human divinity. A collaboration of writing and photographs.

An attempt to treat a sociological subject seriously.

[66]

[67]

For a little less than four weeks during the summer of 1936 the authors lived among three families of cotton tenant farmers, in the middle south of this nation. It was their business to prepare, for a New York magazine, an article on the daily living of these families.

That is still their subject, but in this volume they have attempted to treat it neither journalistically nor politically nor scientifically nor as artists nor as humanitarians, but seriously.

[68]

[69]

[J 6.6: *LUNPFM* Draft: "Intermission"]

Intermission:

Conversation in the Lobby.

*In May 1939 The Partisan Review sent to a number of writers this questionnaire. It happened succinctly to represent a good deal that made me angry, and I promptly and angrily replied to it. My anger and speed made my answers intemperate, inarticulate, and at times finitely foolish: but my later attempts to do the same job more reasonably seemed, in the very fact of the reasonableness, to do such questions more honor than they deserved. I decided to let it stand: and insofar as it was an image of my foolishness, to let it accuse me.

It was not pleasant to do this, for I knew and liked (and like) some of the editors, and felt, also, some respect for some of what they were doing; and I thought it likely that my reply would be regarded as a per-sonal attack. It was; and the reply was not printed, on the grounds that I had not answered the questions. That I differ with both opinions is a point worth mentioning but not worth explaining.

For "*", see next page.

Readers who think that in printing this here I am (a) digressing from the subject of this volume or (b) indulging in a literary quarrel, are welcome to their thoughts.

I wish (here) to thank (my friend) Dwight Macdonald for his decency in returning the manuscript to me, in knowledge that I would use it; and to express my friendliness, and my regret over every misunderstanding, unpleasantness, and difference of opinion that is implicit in the incident, or

[70]

[71]

that has arisen from it.

————

*I would now have to add to this a belief in non resistance to evil as the only possible means of conquering evil. I am in serious uncertainty about this belief still more so, about my own ability to stand by it. I also question whether a draft—or even registration—should not be resisted on still other grounds: i.e., whether the State can properly require the service, or even the registration, of the individual. Or, put more immediately, whether an individual can in good conscience serve, or register, by any requirement other than his own.

[72]

[73]

[J 6.7: Draft of Proposal: "A series"]

A series: edited by W. E. and J. A.⁷

There is a small but, I believe, quite certain audience, at present mainly national, in peace times international, for which this series would be designed. There is a secondary and perhaps tertiary audience to which no attention or concession would be paid which would, I believe, in time accrete to such a series. (Various subscribers to literary and art magazines, buyers of modern-library and Penguin books, etc etc: the lower rungs of the "intelligentsia".) Ethically, their accretion would be unfortunate or irrelevant. Financially, it would be profitable. Beyond a certain

————

7. Walker Evans and James Agee. See J 1.13.

set salary and expense-assurance, the editors would turn all such royalties not back to the firm, but toward publication of further books.

I do not know but think it at least possible, & worth serious investigation, that audience I would of itself support the project: but it had better be regarded, rather, that it is an inexpensive project whose chief value to the firm is prestige.

Its whole point would be: a hardness of standard, and lack of concession, nowhere else to be found in American publishing. This of itself, though the fact is censorable, would, with its content, be its selling point.

[74]

[75]

General format. Whether flexible or uniform I am uncertain. I suspect a uniform physique could be designed which on the whole could be very satisfactory. Characteristics: absolute absence of ingratiation; excellence of reproductions; plainness; the utmost cheapness wherever possible: a steady correction of every fashion. Government and scientific pamphlets suggest it: this is a library for specialists.

No advertising beyond the most flat announcement of publication.

Generally small: not exceeding 100 pages. If larger works appear, to be published broken into separate volumes.

General content: some text, some pictures. Records, symbols, science, analysis, discussion & criticism.

Examples: W. E.'s subway photographs:[8] 100, with or without introduction. H. L.'s wall-drawings;[9] same. 100 precious objects irrelevant to art (photographs & comment). An exposition of methods by which corruption betrays itself. A sampling of letters. A sampling of news magazine clips. Series: poems: composed of advertisements, news photographs, and photographs, and photographs personally made. A book using advertisements alone for this. Personal science: a form of mythology. (Reprints) Grosz's drawings.[10]

---

8. Eighty-nine of Walker Evans's subway photographs were published in 1966 in the book *Many Are Called,* with an introduction by Agee. See N 7.

9. In the 1930s Helen Levitt took a number of photographs of children's chalk drawings on walls and sidewalks. An expanded collection, *In the Street: Chalk Drawings and Messages, New York City, 1938–1948,* was published in 1987.

10. George Grosz (1893–1959), German expressionist and dadaist artist and writer, came to America in 1932.

[76]

[77]

Translations of Bert Brecht.[11] Unpublishable mss. A book of letters from 50 writers, artists, on whatever subject they please. Inventories of hatreds, pleasures, indifferences. Uncredited quotations (Blake, Whitman, New Testament, Thoreau, &c, mixed with newly invented ones.) An analysis of aphorisms as scientific statements. A record & analysis of one week's work on Time [magazine]. A book of found-objects. A book of sensations & things uncapturable by any techniques of art or record. A book of non-fiction short stories. A collection of dreams.

Plenty of these already imply that they need exceed the 100-page limit. That might at times by done within the series. At other times the small book might introduce the large: the large be published (within-series) as amplification. Letters, for instance. Other things not yet mentioned because they are obviously out-of-scale.

A book on bad and good photography.

A book on how to read records: how to use the 2$\underline{\text{nd}}$-rate and the evil.

[78]

[79]

Two to six such books a year.

An annual, commending and condemning and recording in whatever fields interest the editors.

An attack on the M[useum] of M[odern] Art.

On motion pictures as caught midway in becoming respectable.

A book of games, pleasures and invectives.

Handbooks of useful knowledge. What anyone should know about leases, civil liberties, venereal diseases, the normal ailments, electricity (radio), sexual ethics and their prospects, the situation of the wife, of the artist, of the faithful husband.

An analysis of misinterpretation (a worse) of crime and of excellence, as found in newspapers, magazines, courts & speeches.

A handbook of ethics: questions and answers.

Traveling in America: text and photographs. 60 days traveling: as exactly as possible recorded and analyzed.

---

11. Bertolt Brecht (1898–1956), German playwright. See E 3, note 17.

Journal 7

[J 7:1: *LUNPFM* Notes: "On the Porch"]

On the Porch—
    ending at:
            " . . . prior to the youngest quaverings of creation—
    We lay on the porch

Resuming, after Shelter, and running through to
    "It was good to be (including these words)

Resuming at end of book with
    It was good to be doing the work we had come to do—

Appendix 3, the Bourke-White interview, is from the N.Y. Post for Nov. 20, 1937. Permission will doubtless be needed; I think H[oughton] M[ifflin] can ask for & get it more effectively than I could, though it's getting (they would refuse the ironic use) would be a finesse: merely asking whether it can be granted in full as germane to the subject of our book.

If <u>Clothing</u> will not seriously influence the price I would like to see it back in. I enclose copy; and leave it to your judgement.
    The Preface would I guess immediately follow the title page.

Essays and Drafts

This section contains one finished essay and three prose fragments in various stages of completion. Written in response to the coverage of the 1943 Detroit race riots and not published in Agee's lifetime, "America! Look at Your Shame!" is a polished, powerful, and perceptive treatment of the dilemma of race, the role of the intellectual, and the turmoil of a country at war, both overseas and with itself. In "Nathanael West: A Portrait," Agee poses as a reviewer of West's Miss Lonelyhearts, *but the piece is more of satirical jab at the nature of book reviewing and literary culture. In "Plans for a Journal: 'Brecht's* Almanac,'" *Agee proposes a writing a daybook in the style of German Marxist playwright Bertolt Brecht but realizes the result may be less revolutionary than merely insipid. "The Ordinary Sufferer" consists of the beginnings of an anti-anti-vivisectionist screed in which Agee takes aim at liberal hypocrisy and middle-brow destroyers of culture.*

[E 1: "America! Look at Your Shame!"]

[1]

I keep remembering those photographs of the Detroit race riots[1] which appeared in PM.[2] Pages of them, and that typically PM headline, all over their front page.

AMERICA!
LOOK AT
YOUR
SHAME!

That disgusted me, as their headlines so often do, but as I looked at the photographs I got a good deal of respect for the paper in spite of everything. Then I realized that with a few exceptions PM had cornered the photographs. They were unavailable to any other paper. That was as perfect and typical a low as I had ever seen them touch. I wanted to write them. Or to do them as much damage as I possibly could. The liberals and the left. They had never shown themselves up better.

Look at your shame, indeed.

There was one in particular, that I couldn't get out of my head; one of the less violent of them. It was the one which particularly showed that there were white people who were not only horrified by the riots but brave enough to do all they could for the Negroes. It showed two young men. They were holding up a terribly bleeding Negro man between them, and they looked at the camera as if they were at bay before a crowd of rioters, as perhaps they

---

1. On the night of June 20, 1943, a fight at the Belle Isle amusement park in Detroit escalated into a full-fledged race riot, and for the next two days rampaging mobs swept over the city, with blacks looting and engaging in firefights with police and whites pulling blacks from cars and trolleys and beating them. Thirty-five people were killed, 25 of them black (and 17 of those by police officers), with more than 700 injured and 1,800 arrested. Only after federal troops imposed a "modified martial law" did the violence end, and the army occupied the city for six months afterwards to keep the peace.

2. PM was a left-liberal New York City daily newspaper founded by former *Fortune* and *Life* editor Ralph Ingersoll in 1940. The June 23, 1943, issue carried nine pages of photographs of the Detroit riots. The headline referenced by Agee actually reads "America! Look to Your Shame!"

[2]

were not. The mixture of emotions on their faces was almost unbearable to keep looking at: almost a nausea of sympathy for the hurt man and for the whole situation; a kind of terror which all naturally unviolent people must feel in the middle of violence; absolute self-forgetfulness; a terrific, accidental look of bearing testimony—a sort of gruesome, over-realistic caricature, which was rather, really, the source, of those attendant saints or angels who communicate with the world outside the picture in great paintings of crucifixions and exalted agonies.

The thing that made it so particularly powerful to me was that both these young men, one of them especially, so far as you could judge by study, were of a sort which is often somewhat sneered at, by most bad people and by many pretty good ones: rather humbly "artistic", four-effish[3] people, of whom you might think that any emotion they felt would be tainted, at least, with fancy sentimentality.

It made me ashamed of every such reflex of easy classification and dismissal as I have ever felt—the more ashamed, because I had to wonder whether, in such a situation, I would have been capable of that self-forgetfulness and courage. It made me half-ashamed to keep looking at them, for that matter, as I had been doing again on that afternoon I am especially thinking of now. I care a great deal for such photographs; they do more, in certain ways, than any other art can. But there is also, in proportion to its best use, something criminal and indecent about the camera; and there is a great load of guilt on the eye that eats what it has predigested.

*   *   *

On this particular afternoon, which was the Sunday

[3]

after the riots, I was up on East Ninety-Second Street seeing a friend of mine,[4] a photographer, and we spent quite a bit of the afternoon looking through things he had clipped and a few I had brought along. I had not seen my friend at leisure for a long time and we had a particularly good afternoon of it, in which the photograph I am speaking of turned

---

3. The classification 4-F denotes those unfit for military service.

4. Walker Evans lived at 441 East Ninety-second Street in New York City.

up powerfully but casually, and moved off to become a sort of tinge in the back of the mind. By the end of the afternoon I had the unusual, gay sort of good opinion of myself, my friend, photography and what my senses could enjoy, which you are liable to get out of whiskey and easy pleasure if work causes the latter to turn up seldom enough. By the time I left to go downtown for supper, I was at the high point just short of where intoxication begins to droop into clumsiness or melancholy; and the minute I was outdoors the streets, in the very beautiful late of afternoon weather, improved that if it can be improved, with the feeling of being alone for a little while, and with the sharp, tender enjoyment of a city I am ordinarily tired in.

At Ninety-first Street, on York Avenue, I got on an 86th Street crosstown bus and sat far forward on the right. It started nearly empty, and filled up rather quickly; I did not much notice when, or with whom, because I was looking out a great deal through the front and side windows, especially as soon as the bus swung west onto 86th Street and the street and the bus were filled with the low, bright sunlight. It was a light so gay, generous and beautiful, it was almost as if it tasted of champagne and smelled of strawberries, hay and fresh butter. What it smelled of more, of course,

[4]

was carbon monoxide, which can also be a festal sort of smell, when everything is right, and was now; and the edges of the hundreds of doors and windows, along the street, were cut in a blue-gold, clean compound of sunlight, monoxide and stone. I watched all the people, puddling and straggling along the walks, and as usual, wondered which were the Hitchcock[5] agents and which were the harmless, and what might be going on in each mind as they thought, if they did, of what was happening to Hitler and his idea and his people, over where it was dark now, and they were counting their losses in the East, and giving out modified reports in the middle, and staggering under the bombers from the west. In an easy insensitive way, I began to be very sorry for all those people caught in the hopeless middle; even for Hitler and his damned idea, so monstrous except that they already seemed so hopeless.

---

5. British director Alfred Hitchcock (1899–1980) made a number of films in the 1930s and early 1940s dealing with espionage.

Around me, I realized the bus was thicker and thicker with people, some standing, some packed on the seats, all swaying, pleasant and patient-seeming in the green and gold light which filled the bus. Across the aisle were some sailors, sitting, their faces very young and very red, in their very white uniforms. Halfway back in the bus were some young soldiers; the same quality of variegated physical perfection and of almost indecent cleanness, which so few civilians ever seem to have—like so many priests, or Sunday babies, or little girls in bride-of-heaven regalia, but even more likable; dumb, very likely, cruel, very possibly, developed and perfected for something I feel no trust in; yet about the best thing that ever turns up in human life. I liked them a great deal, and all my doubts of it cleared; I might not be perfectly sure what I wanted, but I was no longer personally sorry that within a week I was coming up for induction;[6] I was almost glad; and if I were taken, many things could be

[5]

worse. One of them, very possibly, would be to come out the other end of the war, still a virginal civilian.

I liked them still better as I watched them and began to hear them. I specially noticed one quite strong young sailor, just across from me; a big boy, bigger than I am, a little; and because his eyes and his face had a good deal in them which as a child I used to fear, and have always been shy of, I now liked him particularly well. It was the sort of face which only turns up, so far as I know, in the South—heavy jaw, a slightly thin yet ornate mouth, powerful nose, blue-white, reckless, brutal eyes. I knew the voice just as well, and the special, rather crazy kind of bravery; they made me feel at once as isolated and as matchlessly at home as if I were back in the South again. Nearly all these boys, it turned out, were Southerners, the soldiers as well as the sailors, and the loud large sailor and the loudest and littlest of the soldiers were just finding this out about each other. One was from Atlanta; the other knew Atlanta very well. They began testing each other out on street names and bars, then on people, which did not go quite so well, and now and then the others chimed in with a wisecrack or an exclamation more simple-minded. They were happy as hell to run into each other like this—not

---

6. In a letter to Father James Flye dated June 14, 1943, Agee mentions that he has been reclassified from 3-A (temporarily exempt) to 1-A (for immediate induction) and expects to be drafted in July or August. He was never called to serve.

even Viennese refugees can lay it on so thick, and enjoy it so much, as Southerners when they meet by surprise in an alien atmosphere. They were drunk, about as drunk as I was, and that helped; but they would have leaned on their dialects like trimming ship in a yacht-race, even if they were sober. It is a very special speech, as unattractive to most Northerners as it is dear to natives, and I will not try to reproduce it here, beyond suggesting that its special broadenings, lifts, twangs and elisions, even if you didn't know the idiom by heart,

[6]

which I do, were as charming and miraculous as if, in the same New York bus, a couple of Parsees had saluted each other according to their own language and ritual.

A part of it, of course, was that they were basically insecure; it was insecurity and the Southerner's incomparable, almost pathic pride, as well as love of country and loneliness, and the aching contempt for the North, which made them so spectacular, made so many Northerners on the bus look warm, cold or uneasy accordingly, and made the young sailors and soldiers begin to vocalize about the niggers on the bus and the God damned niggers in this fucking town and the fucking niggers all over the whole God damned fuckin' Nawth. The word cut across my solar plexus like a cold knife, and the whole bus, except for those two voices and the comments of their friends, was suddenly almost exploded by an immensely thick quietness. I glanced very quickly back; one of the soldiers met my eyes with eyes like hot iron, and two seats behind him sat a Negro (it is a word I dislike, but most of the others are still worse); sat a colored man of perhaps fifty, in nickel-rimmed glasses, a carefully starched white shirt, and a serge suit, managing so to use his eyes that you could see only the nickel rims and the lenses.

The flailing voices went on and on, more and more fanciful, naked and cruel, and though I was listening with great care for every word, and heard every word, I was also so occupied that I heard very little, and remember almost nothing, now. It was all the old, ugly routines; what we wouldn't do to Boy son of a bitchin nigguh that tuck a seat by a white woman if we was in Atlanta; dey would; get a Nawthun nigguh down deah, you'd see what dey'd do; yaanh, reckin <u>dey'd</u> see thang a tyew. Three any ovem tried it, black rapin bastuhds; but there was very little of this I heard,

[7]

because I was too sick to hear much, and too busy. I was trying to think what to do and what to say. I had, repeatedly, a very clear image of the moment I would get up, draw a standee aside, and hit the big young sailor who was, after all, very little bigger than me, as hard as I could on his bright, shaven jaw. I also had, repeatedly, the exact image of what would happen then. Singlehanded, that boy could tear me to pieces; what the crowd of them could do was a little beyond my imagination. I had the image of looking him in the eye; various ways, in fact, of looking him in the eye. One was the cold, controlled rage which is occasionally used to pick a fight and which my kind more occasionally uses to bring a sexual quarrel or an intellectual argument as near to nature as we are likely to go. One was the more-in-sorrow-than-in-anger look which is liable to compound some genuineness of feeling with plagiarisms from photographs of Lincoln and paintings of Veronica's veil; it is occasionally used, and effective, when somebody else's neurosis goes wild, but unless you are too good a human being to know you are using it, there is no uglier or more abject device of blackmail. One, worst of them all, was the blank eye which commits itself to nothing. But none of these, it was easy to see, were of any use unless I was ready to back them up physically, and I could hear, just as clearly as I could visualize, the phonograph-records of talk they would bring on; nigger-lover is the favorite word. I was also trying to think what to say; for I know from the past—and might have known by some of the Detroit photographs if I had thought of them just then—that their kind of talk and even action is sometimes completely quieted by the right kind of talking, and better quieted then into sullenness; quieted into deep abashment. I have a friend, a small and elderly man, who would have brought that effect almost instantly. But his size and his age would have been a part of it; still more, his perfect self-forgetfulness, his unquestioning intrepidity.

[8]

I was neither small nor elderly, nor self-forgetful, nor intrepid, nor single-hearted in any one of my perceptions or emotions; I was simply fumbling at words and knowledges: Look here. What are you fighting this war about. I know how you feel, I know you're from the South,

I'm from the South myself, I know (I may be, but the way I say it makes it a lie.). Things are different there, and all this you see here goes against every way you believe is right. But you've got to get used to it. You've got to know it. This is one of the main things this war is about (is it? is it?). If it isn't about this we might as well not be fighting it at all (we might as well not indeed). You'll ask me where I've got any right to tell you what you're fighting for. I'm not even in uniform. I'm not I know but I'll be in one soon—next week. (Will I? Do I want to be?) But that's not the point anyhow (this is falling apart). Anyone on this bus has got a right to know the point and to tell it to you, white or black (I sound like a Tennessee Senator; race, creed an <u>co</u>luh), we've got to make this a free country where every human being can be well with every other human being, regardless of race, creed or color, we've got to make it a world like that. I don't believe you mean the harm you say, honestly, but you've got to realize it, you might as well be fighting for Hitler as to fight for this county feeling the way you do.

It was all so much cotton-batting on my tongue. I couldn't gather a phrase of it together and make it mean anything, even to myself. Talking to them, talking for the corroboration of most of the bus, unable to talk in my own language because my own language would mean nothing even if I could use it with enough belief to make it mean something to me. All the hopeless, bland, advertising-copy claims of the Four Freedoms[7] was running in my head; all the undersupplying of the Chinese; all the talk of the "magnificent courage" of the Red Army, and all the Rice Krispies which took the place of a second front; all the Bryn Mawr girls, planning to police post-war Europe;[8] all the PM articles and

---

7. Inspired by Franklin Roosevelt's 1941 "Four Freedoms" speech, Norman Rockwell (1894–1978), American artist, painted a series of works on the theme popularized by the *Saturday Evening Post* and incorporated into a massive U.S. war bond drive. The four freedoms are freedom of speech, freedom of worship, freedom from want, and freedom from fear.

8. By the summer of 1943, though the Russian army had made great progress against Germany, including breaking the siege at Stalingrad, chronic food and equipment shortages had severely reduced the fighting ability of the Chinese army, and the Allies feared the loss of China as a front in the war against Japan.

the Wallace speeches[9] and the slogans; I cannot know to this day with how much justice they undermined

[9]

me, and with how much cowardice. I only know I could not believe a word I said; and had images of saying it and having the hell beaten out of me, and other images of saying it with effect; and other images of a fight which could be stopped by cops who are as much a phobia to me as rats; and others of modest and of carefully worded and of modestly rhetorical statements by myself, repeated in the press; a small yet not wholly undistinguished instant in the history of the world's long Fight for Freedom; that hit me with self-disgust like a blow in the belly; and I noticed that the big sailor was now standing, and an elderly Negro woman had his seat.

Whether he had stood rather than sit beside her, or out of an instant genuine courtesy, quickly repented, or out of mock courtesy, I could not tell, from anything he was saying; and this still further per-plexed me. If his motives were the first or the third, then it was more than even I could bear, not to fight him; if he had felt one moment of reflex courtesy, I felt friendliness towards him in spite of all he was now saying. I listened hard, to learn, and could not make out. One reason I could not make out was that I was also listening to the woman. She was talking very little, and crying a little, and telling him, and the whole bus, that he ought to be ashamed, talking that way. People never done him no harm. Ain't your skin that make the difference, it's how you feel inside. Ought to be ashamed. Just might bout's well be Hitluh, as a white man from the South. Wearing a sailor's uniform. Fighting for your country. Ought to be ashamed.

There was an immense relaxation in the quiet through the whole bus; but not in me. I caught the eye, at that moment, of a man about my age, in one of the longways seats across the aisle. He was dressed in a brown, Sunday-looking suit. He may have been a Jew, and more

---

9. Henry A. Wallace (1888–1965) was Franklin Roosevelt's secretary of agri-culture from 1933 to 1940 and vice-president from 1941 to 1945. An outspoken progressive, Wallace supported civil rights legislation and the establishment of the United Nations during the early 1940s. In a speech entitled "America Tomorrow," given in Detroit on July 25, 1943, he said, "We cannot fight to crush Nazi brutality abroad and condone race riots at home."

certainly would have described himself, without self-consciousness or satire, as "an intellectual." We looked at each other and a queer, sick smile took one corner of his face, and I felt in my own cheeks that tickling, uncontrollable, nauseating smile which, is so liable to seize my face when I tell one close friend disastrous news of another.

[10]

I remembered the photograph in PM, and looked sternly at the floor, with my cheek twitching.

That evening I told of the whole thing, as honestly as I could, to several people who were down for drinks. They were quite shocked by it, and seemed also rather favorably stirred by my honesty. That embarrassed me a good deal, but not as painfully as I wish it might have, and I found their agreement that they would have done the same almost as revolting as my own performance in the doing of it, and in the telling.

So now I am telling it to you.

[E 2: "Nathanael West: A Portrait"]

[1]

Nathanael West: A Portrait

(From 'Little Rambles in the American Past', by A Gentleman with a Duster.)[10]

In the spring of 1933, a few months after the publication of 'Death in the Afternoon' had given notice to an unnoticing world that Ernest Hemingway was well into his great middle period, a few months after Conquistador,[11] the first narrative poem of the time, had been so poorly appreciated as to receive the Pulitzer Prize; during those months when most good Americans forgot the lynching of Negroes to inveigh against Chancellor Hitler; when Cummings published the peculiar but excellent journal which should have, but did not, cause the suicide of one

---

10. Harold Begbie (1871–1929), conservative British journalist and novelist, wrote more than twenty books and hundreds of articles under the pseudonym "Gentleman with a Duster." This is apparently Agee's attempt to imitate his satirical style.

11. Archibald MacLeish's narrative poem *Conquistador* won the Pulitzer Prize in 1933.

Henry Wadsworth Longfellow Dana[12] (perverted grandson of a union sonneteer); a few years before William Faulkner settled down to the serious work of his life; before Horace Gregory[13] fell truly into his stride; before Robert Cantwell[14] outgrew Communism and wrote the strange cold novels that outdistanced even his 'Laugh & Lie Down': at a time when the young men who had gone through despair to turn Anglo-Catholic with Eliot were leaving the fold to become Agrarians, Fascists, Communists: at a time, more importantly, when American writers were first, as they quaintly put it, 'feeling their oats'; were deluded by the violence of their reactions against all things non-American, into a rather maniacal preoccupation with and search for and loud shouting about all attitudes and materials truly American: at this time, Nathanael West's 'Miss Lonelyhearts' was printed.

It was not West's first book: already he had written 'The Dream Life of Balso Snell', which, semi-privately published and urged upon that peculiar public which found merit in the writings of James Branch Cabell,[15] had little more success than it deserved. Apparently, most of the readers of Miss Lonelyhearts had never heard of it, for it was generally reviewed as a first novel.

But Miss Lonelyhearts was another story. Bourgeois critics acclaimed it as conscientiously and well written, as if that in itself were something so rare in an author as to be grateful for (as perhaps it was); leftwing critics found all its merit in the fact that it pinned a decaying system to the wall, but decried the lack of proletarian optimism; the American critics were orgasmic in praise of its complete Americanism. Dashiell Hammett

---

12. e. e. cummings's *Eimi*, published in 1933 by Covici, Friede, recounts his 1931 trip, modeled loosely on the *Divine Comedy*, to the "preindividual marxist unworld" of Russia. In the journal, Henry Wadsworth Longfellow Dana (1881–1950), the poet's grandson and Harvard professor who is in Moscow studying Russian theater, serves as cummings's guide to the city, Virgil to his Dante. In the book, cummings depicts Dana as a stalwart defender of Stalinism, frequently contradicting the evidence of his own eyes.

13. Horace Gregory (1898–1982), American poet and critic. Agee's scenario "The House" appeared in Gregory's edition of *New Letters in America* in 1937.

14. Robert Cantwell (1908–1978), American proletarian novelist, published *Laugh and Lie Down* in 1931.

15. James Branch Cabell (1879–1958), American novelist of highly stylized fantasies.

said: 'in his work there are no echoes of other men's books.' Angel Flores remarked Dostoevsky and Cocteau as progenitors. Josephine Herbst observed that it was a sort of morality play. In short, they found it to be totally original, totally untouched, as an American work must be, by all alien influences. William Carlos Williams, writing in Contempo, one of the major organs of expression for both Americans and Amarricans, wrote: 'It's plain American. What I should like to show is that West has a fine feeling for language. Anyone using American must have taste in [illegible] to be able to select from among the teeming vulgarisms of our speech the personal and telling vocabulary which he needs to put over his effects. West has this taste.'

[2]

That not all writers using American did have it, a Mr. Bob Brown, writing in the same issue (July 25, 1933) gave ample proof. Mr. Brown proved more than that. He was, as he himself might anachronistically put it, the spitten image of the American group: that group which spent much of its time despising all other (and particularly the more mellowed and better educated) affectations. It spent the rest of its time gabbling loudly and rawly in words of few syllables, under the delusion that it was thereby honoring the American language. It mistook its contempt for genteel intelligence for strong deep native intelligence. It was unanimously agreed that no writer could be a true writer who did not spend the bulk of his life in hard and extremely varied labor of a sort which should be, preferably, manly; and must above all have nothing conceivable to do with writing.

They amounted to nothing: but they are worth mentioning at length only because, at that time, it was hard to tell an American from an American; because many excellent writers, such as Ernest Hemingway, were perhaps inescapably tinged with the American affectations; because their bellowings and strictures were a source of annoyance to the stronger and of temporary delusion to the weaker of the abler Americans of that time; and because there is, in every literary Trend, Movement, School, a good deal that is ridiculous and therefore to be employed by the times to come.

So, let us recall from oblivion a few words of Mr. Brown. The fine, the exquisitely bad edges of his language may escape us, to be sure: for nothing shifts quite so rapidly as the finer meanings of colloquial speech.

But the true American spirit is there: the love of brashness, of hard work, of 'dis-yer-writin's a tough racket and we do it dis way and dat way and balls to you, keed': yes, the old spirit of 33 is there:

"'He kneaded her body like a sculptor grown angry with his clay', Nathanael West says in <u>Miss Lonelyhearts</u>. And that's what he does to the book. He slaps life into some semblance of shape for us. Makes his clay behave.' (Mr. Brown quotes.) 'Can you tie that, you writing punks?

'West writes pen-driven . . with a tidal wave of ink.'

'Give me the writing gal who will punch out a novel like <u>Year Before Last</u>[16] while juggling a kid on each knee and knitting a shawl for grandma between chapters.

'Give me a guy like West who runs a big hotel, and writes a <u>M.L.</u> with a sweep of heart and hand . . . that's the stuff to feed the typewriter.

'With West, you . . . go lustily night-winding, Lonelyhearting. He passed her in the foyer, she goosed him and laughed!['']"[17]

[E 3: Plans for a Journal: "Brecht's <u>Almanac</u>"]

[1]

A couple of months back, my friend Nika showed me Bert Brecht's <u>Almanac</u>, a German book of the twenties, and translated me some of the poems. They were swell poems; and even better were his lyrics for the Beggars' Opera.[18] Something of the sort ought to be done here and I

---

16. Kay Boyle's *Year before Last* was published in 1932.

17. The June 25, 1933, issue of *Contempo*, a progressive literary journal published from 1931 to 1934, contains an advertisement for *Miss Lonelyhearts* and several short essays under the general heading *"Miss Lonelyhearts* Is Reviewed." The advertisement includes blurbs by Dashiell Hammett ("A new motif in American writing; in his work there are no echoes of other men's books") and Josephine Herbst ("This story, apart from its extreme readability, is a sort of morality play"). The essays mentioned by Agee are as follows: Angel Flores, "Miss Lonelyhearts in the Haunted Castle," 1; William Carlos Williams, "Sordid? Good God!" 5, 8; and Bob Brown, "Go West, Young Writer!" 4–5.

This issue of *Contempo* also contains an essay on cummings's *Eimi* by Paul Rosenfeld and a letter to the editor by Pascal Covici and a poem by Samuel E. Lesser ("Evolution"), both imitating cummings's style.

18. Agee may be referring to Bertolt Brecht's *Hauspostille* ("Devotions"), published in 1927. Brecht's *Die Songs der Dreigroschenoper* ("Songs from *The Threepenny Opera*") was published in 1928. See J 6.7, note 11

wished to hell I could do it. I thought about it some, and decided I wasn't qualified. Then a couple of days ago I was eating lunch in Liggett's [drug store], and on the way out I trailed an eye along their publishers'-remainders counter. One of the things I saw was Christopher Morley's Book of Days.[19] I managed to keep my lunch down and then, remembering the Almanac and my own desire, walked back and looked into it. It turned out that very little of it was written by Morley; the rest was quotations. I felt better, because I felt that, with the whole field of literature behind him, Mr. Morley's tastes and methods of selection might at least be a cut above his own writing. I was right about that. A great many of them were very good or even better, of themselves; and he hadn't busted himself trying for the utterly appropriate to every day; in fact, if you discounted that sort of mellow archness which distinguishes everything the man's hand touches, some of his Occasional selections were quite all right too. In the long run I have nothing whatever against plagiarism, but I had never in God's earth thought that I would plagiarize from Mr. Morley. All the same, it is very likely that I will, in one way and another, before this book is done; if it ever gets done. At any rate I bought the book (49¢; I waited for the penny), and will use any ideas it gives me. My thanks herewith to Mr. Morley, and my regrets for being a little bit nasty to him. I would be ready to defend him on the stand as at heart a good and kindly-intentioned man; but he must also be a smug one; and besides, I don't like his writing.

★   ★   ★

And now about this tomb of mine....

From the Autobiography of U. S. Grant.

[2]

Now something about the book. I carried the Book of Days home, hiding the name of the author, which was a pretty shameful thing to do, and the more I read in it, the more the idea grew on me. I told Nika about it next time I saw her, mentioning Bert Brecht, and she said she thought it would be a pretty tiresome idea; that Almanacs, Daybooks, Calendars and so on were very old and frequent stuff in Germany, and

---

19. Christopher Morley, *A Book of Days, Being a Briefcase Packed for His Own Pleasure by Christopher Morley and Made into a Calendar for Sundry Paramours of Print* (New York: John Day, 1930).

ran very offensively to whimsy. That last was a bellyblow. I very suddenly realized that there would be no way out of it; that whimsy hangs like glue about the very idea. Now I think there is no single state of mind, no single method of literary operation, which I despise more desperately than the whimsical; and I despise a great many a great deal; some others of which I shall be forced into using. But thinking the whole thing over I determined that I should take the whole idea, foul breath and all, and do what I could with it and, if I could bear the sight of it and find a publisher, let it go at that. So if you strike snags and float upon bad smells and hear elfin laughter in the darkest coziest corner, remember, please, that nobody is more embarrassed than me.

Generally before, with writing, I have been too little for my britches, as a young, unsettled, ambitious, would-be entirely scrupulous would-be poet is likely to be. In this job I shall do my best as it comes along, but much more shall I do my best to keep going and the hell with my better judgement. Because I can swear to you that if I were giving my better judgement even its normal breaks, I should never have got this far. Or if it would.

Perhaps my worst trouble of all is this: I am damned self-conscious, and now in this free-for-all, with the bars let down, I am likely to express a good many opinions. That's one way of writing. It is not the way I think most of. What it comes down to is this: that I'm likely to talk a good deal about myself. Herman Melville and I used to call it using one's own sperm to prime one's pump. Now the only people who can talk about themselves and get away with it are people who have a sort of sense of sacredness about themselves which, unfortunately, I am

[3]

liable to lack at the crucial moments. So it is very likely that no good will come of this. It is even likely that you will consider me a conceited and boring young man. I don't give a damn what you consider me. But the point is this: that a good deal of this book will be stuff I will be, for one reason and another, ashamed of. So that you can always remember, when the hoeing is hard, that it hurts me worse than it does you.

And now one last thing. I am in a most unsettled time of life, as menopause to think will realize.

[E 4: Draft and Notes: "The Ordinary Sufferer"]

[1]

Anti-Vivisectionists,[20] &c—Follow-up articles—Forum—in Modern Youth[21]—with something on this general scheme:

Everyone knows well enough that nothing in heaven or on earth should stand in the way of <u>human knowledge</u>. Not even God must stand in the way of that. People have <u>suffered and died before in the cause</u>. (Be it here said that most of them were artists rather than scientists, workers rather than bosses, beasts rather than the men who opened them up.) So the sufferings of a few animals is a small matter indeed to stand against it, and only those benighted folk who still think of man as a thing set apart can raise the slightest objection. Animals, after all, are far beneath us— less complicated organisms, so far as mind and sensitiveness to pain is concerned. (We ourselves would enjoy the great privilege of knowing <u>why</u> we were suffering, under the same circumstance.)

There is nothing to be compared to the pleasure of suffering for a cause. But we must know what that cause is. The beautiful thing about vivisection is that it could supply a clear cause to people who had been suffering for years without one; would intensify that pain into something beautiful, almost mystical (if you'll pardon the word) and would shorten and terminate that pain.

Pain is of no value to animals, who can't think it over and have no mind to improve—it is of infinite value to human beings. Ask anyone— (anyone except those who either deny its existence would put it out of existence). "Pain to end pain"—

---

20. The antivivisection movement, which sought to outlaw scientific testing on living animal and human subjects, had peaked by the 1920s, as the benefits of animal testing became apparent during World War I, and proponents moved to more general concerns involving the humane treatment of animals. Agee satirically takes the anti-antivivisectionist position here, though, arguing that if animal experimentation is good, then human experimentation is even better—and offers a few candidates for consideration.

21. *Modern Youth* was a short-lived magazine edited by twenty-two-year-old Viola Ilma. Though it published two O. Henry Award stories in 1933, the only year of its run, George Orwell, on having a couple of stories accepted, called it "poisonous, but one must live."

II The Ordinary Sufferer. There are millions in this country alone—out of work, hungry, a pest to their neighbors, a discouragement to all right-thinking people. He has no real idea why he is suffering. He needs money. There are too many of him. Technological Unemployment. Pay him at $10 a throw: give his family your address. When their money is used up, another—the next most fit—may come around. You get the strongest first out of the way. When the last and weakest appears, demand of him, for the privilege of dying for you, all the money you paid out. If he hasn't got it, refuse him aid. Doubtless he'll get it by borrowing or stealing. It makes no difference who he steals from. If from the rich, it's all in line with division of property. If from the poor, it brings others that much nearer your knives. You win, either way.

III Then there are the mental & spiritual sufferers. People who don't quite know what to believe. If they have a religion, however, or religious leanings, they are bound to be towards Truth—towards Human Knowledge. Preach your Gospel to them—they'll be intelligent enough to believe every word of it. If they show extra-special intelligence, make them Members. If not,

[2]

fill them with a fervor for the one Big Clean Thing they can do with their lives. Remind them of Christ's death for humanity—of how useless that was. Of how much finer a death this will be. Charge them heavily for it. They'll accept. And, member or victim, they win, either way. So do you.

————————————————

Thus—reduce the population to a chosen few. You're in control of the money. Money is power. Start a new government.

————————————————

There are different kinds of human knowledge. The <u>higher</u> it is, the more useless. There are many things you could find out wholly incidental to your high purpose, which might be much more useful to humanity at large—and to human curiosity, than all you're going after. Remember that vivisection used to be used for much lower purposes, to good effect. The Inquisition, for instance. Our own Third Degree is a naive and poorly controlled & unscientifically managed thing of the same sort.

And so—there are many people one might nominate, whose oracular revelation (under pressure) could be worth hearing. Their bodies, ordinarily, might not be fit for much—but in their own little way they would serve knowledge and humanity itself, far better than they have before.

Nominations:

Jafsie:[22] what does he think of his nickname?

Rockefeller:[23] "The aged philanthropist"—How he got his money. Whether it is worth the candle. Whether he really thinks all his philanthropies since make up for . . . Of course his body would be next to useless under the circumstance. Probably he hasn't known a healthy reaction for the last 80 years. Tap his knee and see whether a dime comes out.

The Editors of the New Republic:[24] ask them what poetry has to do with science. What Science has to do with life. What essential difference it makes to the human spirit what form of injustice it serves under. What their average income is. Why they have not freely divided this with the first unemployed they met on the street.

Mr. Walter Damrosch:[25] whether he thinks the great tone deaf public in general benefits by hearing 2nd, 3rd, 5th rate music called exquisite and celestial; by hearing it vilely played to boot.

---

22. "Jafsie" was the pseudonym of John F. Condon, self-appointed go-between, and later a suspect, in the Charles Lindberg kidnapping case in 1932.

23. John D. Rockefeller (1839–1937), American industrialist and philanthropist. See P 49, note 52, and P 50, note 62.

24. Under editor Bruce Bliven (1889–1977), the *New Republic* was one of the most outspoken liberal journals in America during the 1930s.

25. Walter Damrosch (1862–1950), German-born conductor and composer, was the host of NBC's *Music Appreciation Hour* from 1928 to 1942.

Poetry and
Notes on Poetry

Although his major prose works have received much more attention than his poetry, Agee was primarily interested in establishing himself as a poet until 1936, and the poems in this volume are a substantial addition to his poetic canon, as well as providing a glimpse into his creative process during the early to mid-1930s. Three-quarters of the poetic material is published here for the first time. Of the remaining poems, most were published in Robert Fitzgerald's 1968 edition of Agee's Collected Poems, and while the edited versions of the poems presented here are usually only slightly different from Fitzgerald's renderings, the reader can refer to the "Silent Corrections" appendix for deleted lines, variant phrasing, and other changes from the manuscripts.

This section commences with Agee's introduction to his 1934 volume of poetry, Permit Me Voyage, and is followed by prose material related to "John Carter," a long Byronic satire, and seven examples of automatic writing, along with poems generated from the technique. The large number of new lyric poems and drafts of poems contain many striking lines and images. Overtly political poems from the mid-thirties display Agee's mordant wit and draw on forms of expression as diverse as editorial cartoons and advertising slogans to comment on contemporary issues such as fascism, Communism, and the New Deal. These include "Major Douglas," "Hold on a second please," "Fight-Talk," "Collective Letter to the Boss," "Madam, is baby's evening stool," "Fellows," and "Sweet Anodyne." "Tenant this season of uneasy darkness," written before Agee's trip to Alabama in the summer of 1936, demonstrates that his interest in the plight of sharecroppers predates the Fortune assignment. Also included here is a draft of "Against time," published at the beginning of Let Us Now Praise Famous Men. Other pieces, such as the dialect poem "Ah's jes' a believing chameleon," the misogynistic "So here's to their strychnine tears," and "Muzzy wuvs her Buzzy," written in baby talk, provide insight into Agee's pointed, sometimes wicked, sense of humor.

[P 1: Draft of Preface to *Permit Me Voyage:* "I am young"]

I am young; I am married[1] (happily, thanks, though I don't care for the institution); I lack the very little money which would grant me time for work. All my life would be much too short for the work I wish I were born to do; and I spend some of it in sleep; the whole day at work. Besides this, there are my friends, and there are also my half-friends; and there is my amiability, and my capacity for wasting time when I have none in my pocket. there is also the desperate fact that a human being is seldom conscious; and there is further the very desperate probability that I haven't, in the long run, got what it takes. There is still further the sad and the lovely and the absolute certainty that, as no man has ever learned, far less told, the truth, neither shall I. Here I am brought out upon this earth, my living year still widening that shall close and sink too soon for me, and be forever done. And here about me and throughout me is the matter that is the earth and air and fire and sky, the father of every thing and thought. And here, the things and the thoughts from the holiest to the least, over all of which my lust is more than ever I might say. Here also, not There, for we are among it, however meanly, all the Universe, entirely, the yawn of space and the puzzle of time; and here too, the very nails on my hands are made of it, that which Is: not even the seed of all Truth merely, but the secret in the seed which made this flowering on the skies of time and matter, and man and me, and that made of all within and beyond our knowledge one whole immortal uncreated flower. Fool, child, friend, blood-brother, beast, stone, fire, air, there is nothing mawkish in this but my miserable saying of it, and because I have spoken chiefly of large matters does not mean that, mere generalities, mere abstractions, they do not apply. Let me tell you that God and God's untraceable Father and all that is, let me tell you that these things are no more abstract than your asshole. Keep your asshole; your need is greater than mine; and besides I am busy. My business and my delight and my desire and my despair is to know and to tell, neither of which has man perfectly

---

1. Agee married Via Saunders January 28, 1933. *Permit Me Voyage* was published in the Yale Younger Poets series in 1934 with a foreword by Archibald MacLeish.

learned. But to tell imperfectly is much better than not at all; and that effort has brought better men than me to hell. Poor convictions, poor conclusions, the best I am able, I must make in time or die quite childless, but I am far from them still. So far that in true conscience I cannot write one line but it breaks into disgust; and that not even the largest choices in art are clear to me.

[2]

Therefore in this book, examine for no sort of coherence: the ways are too many, great God, great earth, great mournful idiot man, great self much self-detested, that I would attack and love and show you. Herein I shall not try them well, nor often earnestly, but only as they occur, and chiefly for amusement, such as may be; while hell aches about us, and as wise and botchy heaven gathers strength. There is much that I hate; I hope I may here say some of it. I expect that I shall speak unkindly of you, and delight in the torture, though you will not feel it. Meanwhile, and forever, may God have pity upon us all, and we upon each other. We need it.

And if you say, what God? I must hold back my spit though you say it scornfully; and I must shut up though you say it earnestly.

But now, let me try to say a little. God in the highest that we have supposed him is simply an excuse for the truth, which is, I do not know. And God is a great convenience, an algebraic sign. Those things for instance which I feel, pity and beauty and joy and heart's-kindness; and which I know also in others; such things I concentrate above my ignorance, and they are filled with a greater light than can be borne. God is a good enough name; inadequate, to be sure, but good enough.

Last year I was hunting for a better word. I hunted much more honestly and much farther than the feelings above; and I did not find it.

Very certainly God is ugliness as well as beauty, and wrong as well as right, and very certainly God is every thing. Very conceivably God is very far superior to beauty and to ugliness, to wrong and to right, to all things, though all these are of God. Conceivably God is beyond consciousness. Certainly he is what the scientists are hunting. He is also what poets are hunting. If he is nothing more than a concentration of nothing, then even so that nothing is more worthy of wonder and watchfulness and worship than all matter and mind, hunger and hate, than all vanities and than all Gods which that nothing has bred.

[3]

And the artist comes nearest it by two ways. By intense apprehension and statement; by utter and comprehensive statement of things as they are. Joyce is among the supremest of poets because, more than any of the others, he has given a pure, whole, intense, and passionless statement of things as they are. Pureness, wholeness, passionlessness embracing all passion, are highest among the attributes of God which have yet been attributed.

On the other hand, the work of a "lesser" poet. Confused, incomplete and wholly passionate, yet in some lines Hart Crane has reached an intensity so terrific as to burn apart all the structure of Ulysses. An intensity almost to split the atom. And there also is a high attribute of God.

[page(s) missing]

[4]

has several meanings, only the feeblest and most journalistically self-conscious of which is likely to occur to one person in twenty. A repellent title, but accurate, in its several ways.

But I run ahead of myself. Putting the ms. together in the first place was a good deal of trouble. I had done poems and verse in many kinds and lengths and tones: all put together they would not only burst the requisite limits of the volume; they would jangle more than even I could care for. I had for instance the first chunks of a long, loose, obscure, satirical, moral, dramatic-narrative, metaphysical, lyrical poem which, were I to let it loose at this time, would knock your eye out. (Which is one good reason why I shall probably not keep on with it). I had a long job called a Preface (or at moments an Introit) which most of you would have laid to Gertrude Stein's doorstep—wrongly, of course—and which was both pitifully inferior and considerably superior to most of Miss Stein's work. I had pieces of a play, and pieces of an outlandish Radio Poem which also would have set you on your ear. I also had pieces of straight journal poetry. And it shook down, in the long run, to this: when all's said and done, what I am after in the end is poetry. I will therefore put into the book such things as seem to me, for one reason or another, finished, crystallized, behind me. I shall play the thing absolutely straight, and sober. Most of these poems I no longer give a damn for, whether in manner or in matter. But I tried well as I could at the time, and here they are. And there they were.

One of the heaviest problems and contradictions within me is that of the human being vs the artist. Which resolves itself, ultimately, into the Battle of the Centuries: God vs. Art. Granted that they can be neck-and-neck, and granted that they breed as well as murder one another, I am finally in favor or art, and I believe that in ways, and for reasons, which I shall not enter upon here, they are the same. Yet their struggle is violent enough to blow the brain where it goes on. In the interests of such truth as I was able to apprehend, it was therefore inevitable that both kinds of poetry should go into this volume. A dedication also seemed inevitable—a dedication not of the lousy volume, as any fool should know, but of all I am or can be: to God, to truth, and to art which is both. I knew very well that such a dedication would be impossible to write worthily. I knew very well too, that such a dedication, to people who have never been able to dedicate themselves to so much as the hole between the knees of their women, would seem obscenely pretentious. I knew that if you dedicated yourself honestly as you could to all things as you loved and detested them, you would be making a damned fool of yourself, and a prize target. I also knew that such a dedication was the least a human being could do; that it would be a confusion of the personal and the general; and that in my weakness and ignorance, I would not succeed in giving it serenity, and would have to do as I might (which was poorly) with solemnity. And finally I knew that as a would-be poet, it was an absolutely obligatory job, and that it should have to appear in this first book. So I wrote it, trying to use, as my main basic tone, nothing slick or experimental of my own, but the generalized and impersonal tone of the Litany's General Supplication. The result stinks. But it is not as bad as it has been called.

---

[5]

Well, this preamble was to save you the trouble of buying the book. That's the general build and sense of the book, so far as I can tell; that (with much more specification) is about the way I'd have reviewed it. I would have ended by saying that this appeared to be the work of a young and over-self-conscious and exceedingly ambitious poet whose talents and whose capacities might be considerable, but of whom, because those talents were so involved in imitation and those capacities so clouded and so generalized, it was quite impossible to gauge a prediction. That, if you could judge by the performances of young poets in the past—which you couldn't and wouldn't—this one might just conceivably become a great poet. And that, on the other hand, many faults, dangers & limitations beset him; so that mediocrity or washout were quite as reasonably within conjecture. In closing, I should not, probably, recommend him to the attention of all those interested in the future of poetry: I should rather tell him to work, and them to wait, until he is forty. But I should also, as a matter of general interest to the Book World, be forced by my job as a reporter to remark that as a "publishing event" this book might prove more than all but, say, a dozen others, published during that same year.

But I am not reviewing this book. The reviewers are doing that.

[P 2: Prose Statement of Purpose for "John Carter"]

[1]

J. Carter[2]

I. Start as is.
   insert long love section
   close back in with the spiteful slime stanzas, and
   warning: I've given, &c &c
   which leads to
      for my intention and on to statements of pts of views &c—lots like to take the literary pulse, so—here, square off and start harangue about poetry; possibly beginning "with something say" like Leonard[3]—and possibly with the better guys and closing with Edna—

---

2. "John Carter" is an unfinished extended satire in ottava rima that Agee began in college and continued working on until 1936. Writing a prose draft and then turning it into verse was a common method of composition for Agee. See "John Carter: 1932–1936," *Collected Poems*, 77–122.

3. William Ellery Leonard (1876–1944) was an American poet and classicist noted for treating fairly radical autobiographical subject matter in traditional forms. The other poets next mentioned by Agee are Edna St. Vincent Millay, Robert Frost, Robinson Jeffers, Edwin Arlington Robinson, and T. S. Eliot.

Then: but all that is old stuff, you say.

Whore-worship is more of less a thing of the past. Farmer Frost, everyone knows, is out of date—Jeffers is a hybrid minor prophet & bad tragedian; Robinson is out too—on his ifs. Eliot's just a lousy Anglican metaphysician. Why not be up to date?

What does up-to-date mean?

It means an interest in science, an interest in social & political problems. History is being made under your sniffing poetic nose. These things are the only ones worth writing of: other problems have no bite in them. How can you write poetry of your own unhappiness in love when millions are starving and a Negro is running for Vice-President?[4] How

(Here, make a broken crazy chorus of many voices: quote many critical points of view & non-critical: the poet for the few is —— what is poetry? a toy for the rich! A thing of the past. An art. A sermon.

What is the status of poetry now?

What does it mean to be an American?

To be a poet?

To be an American poet?

                                                                    [2]

Can a great poem have a moral point of view? Obviously it can.

But if you wish to write a poem which shall try to be a record of the human race, what are you after? Not, primarily, a categorizing of good & evil—not any consistent attempt at that—but a poem recording the consciousness of a good, of an evil: the efforts continuing toward good: and of the delusions which take possession of the race as being absolute good—

All the generations marching upward into the darkness which is beyond all their knowledge, all their disbelief, all their faith. Death as the end or death as the beginning, makes no difference in this thing: that they are caught in an absolute fever of good, of evil: of a destiny suspected always and fought out but never understood.

Every human being infinitely nobler than the greatest work of the race: that work—all civilization—merely the immense shifting projec-

---

4. James W. Ford, a U.S. representative from New York, ran for vice-president on the Communist Party ticket in 1932, 1936, and 1940.

tions of a restless, questioning energy that is the mind & soul of the race. It is this energy that is constant: it is this that poetry should deal with, should always try to be sensitive to, to understand, to record.

That is the thing which brackets everything else: all religions, all opinions—general or personal, individual, &c &c.

I shall be, I hope, inconsistent: I shall be constant only to that one thing—When I love a thing I shall say so and when I hate it also—childish prejudice & prejudice deeper than my brain can find out.

[3]

My idea is of a supernatural evil (this to begin is mythical): which shall move among men & institutions seeking what he may devour—and devouring much. He shall fail against (a) complete earth and (b) complete faith and above all through his ?

(He could be defeated by the great scientific Utopia: the Utopia of complete knowledge, infinity either bounded or trained out of people's thoughts: no desire: And this would be a victory for him. This perhaps a dream?)—

By nature as an unmoral thing

Man as set apart from nature: caught in the torture of a mind: ultimate knowledge will restore man to nature.

---

reluctance of completely dishonest people to tell a downright lie.

[P 3: Prose Summary of Christening Scene for "John Carter": Introduction and Two Versions]

[1]

[Introduction]

They agreed to placate Aunt Emma, but privately agreed they should let it make no difference. They weren't social climbers, after all, and they intended to give John a good democratic education, a good scientific bringing up—And then again. They reflected—They were not only baptized, but confirmed and married in the church—and what harm had it done them?

So it was arranged that on the next Saturday afternoon, there should be a quiet christening party at St. Wilfred's. Dr Whitaker let his lip slide up from three highly polished front teeth and said he was delighted to welcome the little fellow. He then ruefully postponed a bridge party.

We have remarked the inward and spiritual grace: let us proceed to the outward and visible signs. For here, I believe, we shall see our religion at its very best; and it is always well to try to understand the best. So, bear with me while I try to tell you all about this church and its great traditions and the charming people who built it and attended it. For if, as some whisper, Christianity is indeed dying, some sentimental soul hereafter may take pleasure in this little vignette.

And before I proceed, reader old boy, let me say that I am the first to admit my own inadequacy for such a task: so, if my little remarks on religion have failed to convince, and my forthcoming remarks on these other matters seem merely fragmentary, blame it not on the subject (which some more able person should treat) but on me: and supply all missing letters from your own experience.

[1.1]

[**Version 1**]

But such miracles were not, of course, what he wanted to do. There never was a more modest and unassuming fellow and he hated to show off. He did these things only when absolutely necessary: for the thing He was really interested in, was his Message. Poor dear—he was so in earnest about this message that it amounted almost to hallucination! His message—as we all know—was one of gentleness and lovingkindness—of man's equality—of the meaninglessness of riches and pride and destruction.

He preached that lust and anger and sloth are comparatively minor sins—which shows remarkable breadth of mind, really. And that avarice and pride and hypocrisy are deadly sins—which was really an awful thing to say, and one would think would absolutely nip in the bud all chances he might have of making a way in the world.

Nevertheless, such miracles and his preaching appealed strongly to the humbler element in the population: fishermen, quacks, whores, countrywomen, and the socially ineligible in general: and He really began to pick up quite a following.

And one of his disciples, Judas, saw that with proper management, this had great, glorious possibilities. For Judas, practical man though he was, admired Jesus, and would have liked nothing better than to promote an enterprise at once idealistic and practical.

But great leaders are often fanatics, and fanatics never know when to stop. Jesus was both a great leader and a fanatic. He was also convinced that he was the Son of God! So such a thing as <u>arbitration</u> and <u>compromise</u> never entered His head!

Judas seeing this saw danger ahead. Judas was a sensible man. He had his feet on the ground. Yet even Judas was swept off his feet when Christ rode into Jerusalem, uncrowned King! Things he had scarce dared to dream seemed ready to come true!

We can understand, then, his astounded dismay when Jesus walked straight to the Temple (something like our Stock Exchange) and brutally insulted the moneychangers— Judas knew that with capitalism against Him from the start, the "game was up!"

[1.2]

He saw that all these simple folk who followed Jesus were simply out of their wits. And much as he admired J's ambition, he was at last firmly convinced that the whole thing was mob spirit. Thoroughly disorderly, and without a chance for success.

His faith in Jesus wavered. But finally, as all fair-minded men will, he asked the Master just what his wildly inexpedient conduct meant. And when the poor deluded fellow coolly and gently told him, "My Kingdom is not of this world"—Judas realized once [and] for all the will o' the wisp he had been fleeting after!

Judas was crushed. His pride was hurt. He was broken hearted. His wonderful vision lay shattered at his feet. Like many another crushed Idealist, he became bitter: and at last, he joined the other side.

So Christ was crucified between two cursing, smelly thieves: and a degrading and terrible sight it must have been, which would be morbid to dwell on further. Suffice it to say that only two friends and his mother stood by him—after all, a mother's love goes everywhere—and that He conducted himself like the true Man of Men he was.

There is a pretty myth about his resurrection—We need spend no time on it—if you're interested, I refer you to Barton and Lawrence and Lake⁵—or your rector will do.

But the crucifixion—gruesome and sad to think of as it was, we'd do well to think of it, at least on anniversaries—or, indeed, every time our own feet get a little off the earth: for it represents the inevitable end of all great and good men who refuse to compromise.

But what of Judas—for, after all, our sympathies are bound to be more with him—we <u>admire</u> Jesus—but we <u>love</u> Judas, as one of us. Judas, having done his best to save Jesus from his own Quixotic self, having in an hour of bitter despair betrayed him—then, in deep, terrible, impulsive remorse, <u>hanged</u> himself!

Judas teaches us a clear lesson: first, that while it's laudable to admire such greathearted ideas, it's a great mistake to <u>support</u> them. Second, while of course it is deplorable to

[1.3]

betray them, it's even more reprehensible to let remorse lead you to such and end.

In other words we learn, from the story of Jesus what is worth even more to the world than Jesus' teaching: that the world is a difficult, thorny place to succeed in: that life is made beautiful by many lofty ideas and creations. One is well within one's rights in appreciating and approving such ideas, even in financially supporting them: but one must, after all, face the facts and keep one's head above water and one's feet on the ground.

One must, in fact, realize that, because of the great strides in civilization, it is even more true now than ever before that, should people really attempt to live by Jesus' teachings, all this great civilization would fall dead at our feet.

Suppose greed, envy, malice, pride, were out of the system.

Wealth would be meaningless: all that it brings would be meaningless: Rain would shear down the skyscrapers: machines would flower into rust. Our great cities—all our great beautiful world would mean

---

5. George Aaron Barton (1859–1942), American religious scholar and author of *Jesus of Nazareth: A Biography* (1922); Brother Lawrence of the Resurrection (1611–1691), French monk and author of *The Practice of the Presence of God* (1693); Kirsopp Lake (1872–1946), British religious scholar and author of *The Historical Evidence for the Resurrection of Jesus Christ* (1907).

nothing to us: we would have to walk hand in hand with the most unpleasant people, and our discourse would be chiefly of love and beauty and of the life to come. — —

But fortunately, nothing of the sort is likely to happen.

God, after all, made us rational men. He wants us to use our Reason. Reason Tempered with Godliness, so to speak. Which of course means that charity begins at home, and never bursts the boundaries of a conscience which are fixed by one's ideas of personal comfort.

It's all really quite simple, if you keep God in His place.

If a man makes god in his own image, and acts in no way to destroy his own self-respect, he can't possibly go wrong.

No respectable person is capable of doing evil: and of course we all realize that judgement and retribution are mere bugaboos—necessary, perhaps, in their rough, lawless day, but totally, ludicrously irrelevant to this, the twentieth century.

[2.1]

[Version 2]

Faith healers do the same job to this day.

Now, through such things, and through his preaching, which made everyone equal, Jesus got quite a following, and it wasn't long before the Pharisees (who were enjoying a good graft) were jealous of him.

Now the trouble with fanatics and great leaders is, they never know when to stop. Such a thing as arbitration and compromise is the last thing to enter their heads.

Judas saw this, and saw danger ahead. Judas was a sensible man— he had his feet on the earth. Yet even Judas was swept off his very feet when Christ rode into Jerusalem virtually king. We can, then, imagine his astonishment and dismay when the first thing Jesus did was to set all the moneychangers against him. For Judas knew that if you're to become king, you've got at the very least to stay in good with capitalism. He saw that all these common, excitable people who followed J. were sentimentally & emotionally out of their wits. And much as he admired J's ambition, he was firmly convinced at last that the whole thing was mob spirit, thoroughly disordered, and without a chance of success. His faith in Jesus' power vanished.

My Kingdom is not of this earth. Poor deluded fellow!

Now as we know, when one loses respect for a Master trouble is ahead. And so with Judas. He was broken-hearted—his lonely vision he could no longer sustain. So—like many another crushed Idealist, he became bitter: and at last, he joined the other side.

So Christ was crucified between two common, smelly thieves—and a very terrible sight it must have been, and one we should think of, at least once a year. In fact, we would do well to think of it every time our own feet get a little off the earth: for that seems to be the inevitable end of all great and good men who won't compromise.

And then again. The end of Judas is worth contemplating: for he had done his best to save Christ from His own better self—and in a moment of bitterness had betrayed Him—

[2.2]

and then, in deepest remorse, had <u>hanged</u> himself!

Judas teaches us a clear lesson: first that while it's right enough to admire such great-hearted ideas, it's a great mistake to support them. And while of course it's deplorable to go back on them, it's even more so to show such violent remorse.

In other words, we learn, through the story of Jesus and of Judas, that the world can be a difficult place to get along in; that it is made beautiful by many elevating ideas; but that one must, after all, use one's head, and keep said head well above water. And because of the great advance in civilization, it is even more true now than then, that while it is all very fine to admire and in a quiet way support the teachings of Jesus, all our great civilization would stop dead if people really lived by such ideas.

God understands our predicament, just as he understood Jesus. God made us reasonable men. He wants us to use our reason. Reason tempered with Godliness, so to speak. Which of course means that charity begins at home, and beyond that extends to the boundaries of conscience—which again are fixed by one's ideas of personal comfort.

It's all really very simple, if you keep God in His place—

No respectable person is capable of doing evil; and of course we all realize that judgement and retribution are simply outworn bugaboos— necessary in their day, but totally, ridiculously out of the question in this, the twentieth century.

It really boils down to this: if a man makes a god in his own image; and then acts in no way to destroy his own self-respect, how can he go wrong?

Of course there are certain differences of opinion: one might be led to think that the Roman Catholic and the Congregationalist believe little in common: but obviously, these are all simply man-made confusions—trappings—of which we must fight clear.

In John's & Helen's[6] church, for instance, there are the

[2.3]

"sacraments": and a few cranks still insist that they mean something. But, after all, in general, these are sensibly observed only in concordance with social welfare: thus Extreme Unction means nothing but the minister's bedside & pulpit manner: penance (always an embarrassing matter) is out; Holy Orders is as always a restricted matter; while on the other hand, matrimony, baptism, confirmation and (sometimes) Holy Communion, are still pleasant and socially acceptable functions between God and man. Of course they mean little or nothing, but, as a matter of good form, this particular church has so managed them as to become the envy of many others.

Of course, some of the more emotional religions are a bit outré; but no man yet has ever failed to profit, socially and financially as well as spiritually, by membership in such a parish as St. Wilfred's.

And now, reader, pardon me for having conducted you through such rarified heights of Theological Exegesis. I did so because somehow it seemed a good idea to set before you something of the essential Christian spirit as it now stands. Of course, one embarks upon such abstractions only too sadly aware that much of the true human warmth is lost: i.e.—religion seems, thus, an otherworldly, over-spiritual matter. You may say—"people just don't believe that way"—

And you are right, as always. What I have here tried to seek out is merely the double-distilled essence of the Christian faith, as interpreted by some of the leaders of our thought. It must be granted immediately that the human race, with its little faults & foibles, rarely lives up to this

---

6. John Carter's parents.

high level. It must further be admitted that most of us don't bother to think the matter out this far.

So it was with the Carters. They were good people—a charming young couple—but really almost totally irreligious, so far as action is concerned. In fact, it took some considerable talk from their older relatives to remind them that it was only proper that John be christened.

[P 4: Automatic Writing and Poem: "Writing first thing comes into my mind"]

Writing first thing comes into my mind. Point being nothing does when you watch for it. Whistle, ok. Heard that outside. Boat— Midnight boats. Never got much of a rise from. more noise. Window problem. Evil. Regnum Malorum. thought for that. Next? What the hell the use? Scavenger. Lone prairie. O bury me not, , , on the loan prayereee, , Get hands & body in for Gods sake. And natural speech. And the hell with this. When will I stop? When will I start again? Thou only hast my heart, Sister, believe. When Eve first saw the glittery day; she sat and cried, to break her heart.[7] What time is coming, and what way, the sun moves up, and falls apart. Stink o. Miner. Pedantic wit. Phooey. spreaded day before her — . From her pillow's height. High. throne. Smiling from her pillows height. I held her from her pillow's height reach down her smile about me, she watched and sweetly grieving said I'll spend this night without ye. I call that woman holy hell that of my heart bereaved me, and laughed my love to let me tell and never once believed me. She left me low for another guy, he loved and left her high and dry, now both are dead, and only I, remain to tell, our story. She left me cold for another guy, He loved and left her high and dry, now both are cold and only I am left to tell the story.
I met her young, in the young green woods, And the day was wild as glory,
And I laid her down, and I got the goods, and that begins, my story.

---

7. Cf. "When Eve First Saw the Glittering Day," *Collected Poems*, 57.

I watched her from her easy bed
Let loose her smile around me,
And on the smile she sweetly said
I'll spend the night without ye.

I name that girl a holy hell
That of my tears deceived me,
And laughed my love to let me tell
And never once believed me.

Make haste if you will help, the time
Is toward to turn when helplessness
Is your disuse as well as mine
And both mislay the old address.

Have it your way; I see a sign
That points the mileage out to where
The cut worm and the clinging vine

Go your own way:

[P 5: Automatic Writing and Poem:
"hideous, crippled & malignant girl"]

hideous, crippled & malignant girl. ?? Absolute dull rather than intense
pain and cruelness. List & thick block of meanness & pain. Pain as a gift
of God. Bad when the mind is in advance of the soul. It can take a fairly
short time for the mind to be convinced of suffering, heroism against, &
victory, say, but it takes the human being years if at all. Pretension, sanc-
timony, ambition, are some of my faults. Some still worse, which are
natural weaknesses, are cowardice, facility, fear, sophistication, cynicism.
Cynicism is a form of cowardice, but when will I really <u>learn</u> that instead
of its being like a quotation to me. And when will I learn "He who knows
speaks not" or is it true. Qualities, faculties. Natural & human-made
energy. Construct a suffering and accept it. Letters to various, direct
speaking. Irvine. Richards. Franklin. Godby [?]. Brick. Mrs. S. myself.
Via.[8] the cogs worn round & don't eat each other. <u>Hardness</u> & <u>coldness</u>
of wrongs kinds in my work, and extreme sanctimonious sentimentality. Who am I to pity people. I am still of the kind who when alone must

---

8. Irvine Upham, I. A. Richards, Franklin Miner, Godby [unknown], Brick
Frohock, Louise Brownell Saunders, and Olivia Saunders Agee.

wash hands after pissing. Still also of the kind who takes a private shower in a bathing suit. I think it <u>must</u> be brought down and over into talk. I write impurely. I have no real idea what self-discipline means. can the pain be "bought" and <u>earned</u> in writing? Alternate movements in speech and "Fany". Preface: Theme & Variations: Scherzo: finale— The great ones in a way blur as much as they clear the whirlpool that involves every-thing in its reach: another white of course may swallow it. If all hate and scorn and reasons for it could be gathered in behind one shell and shot off together and be rid of. I happen to realize bud of condensation first in this. (The notched race. Little ladies walking around with their notches.)

Large shiny black buick (or (cadillac)-sedan: two mid-aged ladies, their chauffeur, in a Bradenton Hotel.[9] A Vision of Fair Women.

[P 6: Automatic Writing and Poem: "Ginseng, rank fennel"]

ginseng, rank fennel, yarb, snakeoil, amulet, rattles, peeled switch, spit on hook, nail clippings, drink whiskey for snakebite, corridors of fire, lattice of fire, silent, eating like soot on chimney wall, cramp the wheels, culvert, whitewashed culvert, staring culvert, the pale fences, broad stripes, dangling in open truck, red faces, young. Embarrassment. Nigger does filling station work, White makes change. If you gave him Ideas, wdn't give enough to do more than get him in trouble. Life is a convulsion. Water a convulsion. Sic that convulsion. Such a word needs everything level to take hold. Put a stick in the snakes jaws. Got a stick in his jaw. Force his head down with a forked stick. Cold of his body in the hot day: cold strength. Strength of a different kind from yours. Seems to borrow & lend from its whole length. Floated the dust. Float (b[ack]ward) the land (mist).

Wake up my — ˘ , it was morning once.   FAMILIAR

ZEBRAS

---

9. The Bradenton Hotel is in Sarasota, Florida, near Anna Maria. See J 1.4, note 3.

So if it must, I would not hinder it;
Shouting at deathbeds is a poor leavetaking.
I have not feeling; I have not wit;
Nor does a sleeper often dream of waking.

So if you must, I must not hold you back:
Bawling at deathbeds is a bad leavetaking:
Though how I shall be living in your lack
Riddles my dreams from now to death or waking.

I had hoped much

[P 7: Automatic Writing: "small turns"]

small turns, tricky & silly. dope "atmospheres"
came into the world with hands over your eyes / the eye, the joints, no
integument. / Why must we leave this country? Things will be different out there. / eat the drill / drilled throat / To ponds their lily pads.
Calm as a board, this water rain [illegible] down on. Rain runs at us out
of the sky, rain runs over us. Loose scrotum of cloud. Strumming her
[illegible] advanced upon the morning, Lord, were you listening then?
The ark: Animals, looking out of their shadows, see their eyes, their
lives are lonely. They run in the earth, they hide; their lives are lonely:
pelicans, their heads slanted like a section of violins. The pale crab sitting in his white sand hole. the bruised smooth, bruised with terror,
terror is a bruise on his brain, his nerves. Iron glances iron, there is
power. Road spilled, holds the cities wired. Telephones have shaken
their lives apart: few of us have close friends anymore. Cities are growing: everyone mistrusts; you can't afford to be too intimate. Grave at
his head yet smiling his dream standing, draws him up chiming buck-
ets to the mouth: The freestone smiles, the secret water chimes: sweet
water, hard and sweet, is on this mouth. His saddened palms, now delicate with living, find the immediate weight, the complete breast:
Smilings are here, there bodies matched and gentle; confidently her
eyes, his won: they rest. Remotely, usually, the evening chimney /
peddles her crippling smoke, the bluing air: the harness marks are

darker than his body; he blows and breaks his bran. The floral brain.
Brotherly. Brotherly knives bring down the easy wheat: it droops and
spills upon the earth a cover. Contemn. Bruises. Bandstands every
Tuesday evening — bring them to the casual square, dumpling drum,
sweet horn commend us each to other, not despair. Bandstands every
Tuesday evening bring us to the drawling square, braid, sweet horn,
blunt drum commend us each to set aside despair. Locusts with enthusiasm celebrate the spended day; in the dappling shadowed porch swing
Love finds out the usual way. Brothering. Dusted trees resume their
breathing: heavy droop the rooted crops: shops. Children are composed this season: there is hope among us yet: hope can thaw the roots
of reason: and the sorrowful man forget. Blundering. Balance by blundering. I am a fouled spring. Why was I opened beneath that privy?
better not drink of me. Artesian love. Broke, and found artesian love.
Drinking at wells sunk beneath privies. Smiling water: where at the
rivermouth the river smiles. Soiling a hundred miles of Gulf. Silted
veins. My silted veins go slow with gold. Do not ˇ — . Blood stands in
his red shaw.
ceremonial (violin, cello, wind on grass). phrase. shadow. myth.
Mythologies, leaves of our wooden house, wooden cards, wooden
leaves. sprung the hinges,
The ceremonial phrase. One, seven, or not too many at a time,
    Crowd at the groin my doubts, my things much loved.
The river, paved with nudging logs, and the key log, jamming the
narrows.
The black mountain river, paved with nudging logs.
Filing from cloud, discharge. cheated. chartered. Glancing closures in
the iron: meshed: Mesh, toothed iron: speak, vapors:
Time whose wheels taste each other: years drift like unshaping snow.
                                        Snow makes shapenings on the earth.

[P 8: Automatic Writing and Poem:
"clouds as if they lay"]

clouds as if they lay on a shelf of glass. Great <u>distances</u>. Avenues. /
on bridge, dinged 25 or so, rollerskated, on lazy legs. Queer comedy. /
loves one & incongruous figures fine for such: 1 oclock; solitary on

bridge. Woman in sedan, / . Strange quality, pimpish, female, of a chauffeur to midaged-old lady types who live in hotels. Very ugly quality to this. / Garden theatre, roomy, empty, lots of lounging space, Spanish orange plaster; Rube, and very nice. / little Cuban girl, sloe mouth: you can already & easily see her as an old woman. Another: are you satisfied? / Can I have a rickey instead of coffee? misunderstanding. / Dograces:[10] very calcium. New green grass a phony color in the light. Big sign tells odds. They are led round their posts (1 pees) naked: long, widestrap leashes. Weigh in quiet. On to stalls. Head & heart felt. Heads are scratched. One very quiet, leans head vs. thigh of handler. Buzzer: they leap & whine. Some are caught up by throat & nearly carried. Wghts. 47–72 lbs. Genitals tucked far in. Great squad rigamarole. Have to lift some into starting stalls. Rabbit like a fair-prize. Goes round once first. They are loose. Called by number. / Pale shell, tissue, membrane of moon. Effaced: stuck. Smell of cold mist on swamp, tilled land. Sound & sight of train, late night, flat land, cars, lights irregular, mail & baggage, dory & pullmans, engine breeches: light under its smoke. Flat grass, sparse trees, big black branches scattered on grass. Am. landscape. Mist & night make Florida more handsome. Antediluvian. / Magazine. Paper. Editorials. Ads. / (Outside races: a nig boy, overalled, leads hound away. No telling of winning. / Crooked shore. Crippled shore. Crippling the shore. / Smell of water hits like sound of weltering tin on iron. Taste & quality, dead, of galvanized iron, of Zinc. / <u>Absolutely</u> necessary cut loose from self. Possibly best is to write voluminously & carelessly. Make writing the living & <u>get inside</u> it as you are inside living. / Frankie Darro[11] swell keep in mind for city Huck Finn stuff.

My Uncle Sammy sent me
and my dear of mammy meant me
and my sweet patootie sent me
    To be blown to hell.

Mother wants a new gold star.
Pop says. Woman in garter belt.

---

10. The Sarasota Kennel Club began holding greyhound races in 1929.

11. One of the Dead End Kids, American child actor Frankie Darro (1917–1976) appeared in a number of movies as an orphan or street tough and later as a jockey.

least substantial elements of population: even the villains are boys who looked in mirrors. "Proletarian"; debutantes don't do so well. / Shawl. / slowed popcorn clouds. / kind of faces bodies voices & brains environment makes. / Shelves of sand under the water coloring it. / Traffic (of cloud) / ANTAGONIZE. ANTAGONIST. / COLLUDE / COLLOP / COLLOID / COLLISION / DIRIGIBLE / BALLOON cloud / PITCH-BIENDE / PITCHSTONE, PITCHED / cows like weary tents; pitched on their bones like tents / ADVANCED / AFTERDAMP / TALISMAN / ANALGESIC (N.) / ANCHORSTROKE / ANKLE / ANOPHELES / APOLOGY / ARC: BRIDGE, bridged w. light / SHOUTS for the PUMP / AWASH / OVAL TURTLE / BUTTERBEAN / VALVE / CLOSURE / FORECLOSURE / NASTY / DECLARE / DUPLE / FRIT (N[oun]. V[erb].T[ransitive].). / STAMEN / GLADRAGS / ECHO / FUSELAGE / BEAT TO DRAW / THE AIR Has a head on it (cloud) / SHOULDERING CLOUDS / . INTINCTION (of the earth or of matter). / ALKALOID / BORDERS (ON) / VIOLATE / OPSONIC, OPSONIN / ROOTED NERVES / RAMPION / RAMP / PURFLING (of crates, turtles, violins) / FLAX / PROSTHESIS / ENDEMIC / baskethilted /. SILLY SEASON / SNOOK / TRYPANOSOME (auger-body) / that won't wash /

A PERFECT SANITARY NAPKIN. / women entering an age when their dresses look alike for yr to year / EGGLAYING / CHARY

So impossible to detach myself. Hammering merciless in Walgreen's. Groveling to give glass of water. Why are waiters so fooled into defense of employers. People at tables are meek. Or attack waiter who is not responsible. Painting in face of Berceuse[12] doesn't seem so good: little glinting pastel strokes, I mean. Must get inside, be lost & digested into matter.

Asylum Ave. Window. Japanese ivory sheathe of sword.[13] Threaded minnieballs. (latter a War word isn't it?) Camel with pale fairy thighs. Veined. Smooth. Sparrowbelly, weaklooking. Wondering lifted snaky head. Split lip like grasshopper, sheep. Sloping, slouching hyena. Frizzy.

---

12. Probably a reference to Vincent Van Gogh's *La Berceuse (Augustine Roulin)* (1889).

13. From *A Death in the Family:* "Ahead, Asylum Avenue lay bleak beneath its lamps. Latticed in pawnshop iron, an old saber caught the glint of a street lamp, a mandolin's belly glowed" (17).

Fuzz. Hair of no certain length. like possum, gives [illegible] & shapelessness. SHAPED geese. Filthy mouths of hyenas. Lantern jawed;
lifted eye. All head & shoulder. little sickly calf (Fla roadside) innocent
face, very long fuzz on sides, unsteady, looking out of a shadow, apprehension / branching horns / branching life, life branching / life branching terribly / birds throbbing in pines, roaring like a motor in pines,
deep trembling / coiled animals, why a coil / oiled shrimp / snails, crabs
in shells, snakes, embryos, seeds, germinal, spiral, galaxy, nebula, coiled
stars, coiling sky, stars run their coils, flow out their coils / coiled like
snails in their shells, nautilus nebulae, build space & turn like a shell
around them / nautriloid /

[P 9: Automatic Writing: "SERVICE IN EXISTENCE"]

SERVICE IN EXISTENCE
ENLIST. FILLET. FLAG.

I WAIT FOR you as on a ship.
The others are shadows of her.

WORLD STRUCK A BERG.

AMMONIA. STANDING (for 2 cows)
Whisked egg. Whisked water, flowers, grass.
You lose the gestures of childhood: they return suddenly with glad-
       ness, etc. & in dreams. the early gestures of childhood.
TWITCH (flowers, column of gnats; legion, flock, squadron,
       regiments of birds in light).
SPRINKLE of flowers. cold flowers.
a dime under the sky.
TWINKLING.   SERVICES
PARTY QUIETED After wedding couple gone. subdued.
ANCESTORS, those in groves, at a wedding.
NOW these we bury away in their love like a seed: what tree stands
       from it.
You hear one you love: you are detached as a spirit. RETRIEVE.
       DISLODGE. HAMPER.
TAMPER. HEMP. TUB of hill. HILL (V.T.) KINDLE. ALL THE
       TUBS Are full.

WE ARE royal a few hours a year. ARTIFICIAL
BODY is different in anger & compassion. SNOW SHUTS.
column of gnats, boiling, hanging and twitching.
We are hung up in history like a column of gnats, boiling and
        twitching.
    the movements are of boiling and twitching. Little companies
        twitch in air.

Geese who in their generation have seen cities come up on the land.
cities like little spreading crusted sores. syphilis.
    stone chancres on the earth.   WORLD BOWLED LIKE
                                A DOLPHIN
    Tetter of trees.   in continuous light.
    And see the darkness (capillary) between his poles
        of vegetation or of desert rain.
            MOTHERS WHO SPEAK PRIVATE LANGUAGES
                WITH THEIR CHILDREN.
serene, guided breasts of geese.
flying duck: head strained forward, throat level with water.
    pelican: head drawn back, baldish; like illfed child or childish
        old man.
Tubby hills.   CHRISTMAS BELLS LIKE
a great enthusiasm of nozzled water   SPONGES.
water blurting from fireplugs into
            the dancing lines of children.   PAPER BELLS.
matter is continually dislodged.   PROSTRATE (A[dj]., V.T.)
earth: dead ash. clinker.   Sun spreading his FAN.
Kindle the tinders of a year.   FANNED SKY. EARTH.
dilates its leaves. dilate a leafage. SELVAGE. STROMA. SCIURINE.
3rd egg of the hawk.
TEREBINTH. TEREDO. TERMAGENT (wandering under 3 names)
TERRAPIN. GODHOUSE. ANNELID. worms filtering the earth.
        filter in earth.
CONSTITUENTS. INCORPORATE.
Longsighted old age. COLONY. PRESCIENT SKIN. LEVERAGE.
                            PURCHASE.

REVERY (use actively)   ACTIVE.
DISEASES DARK VOYAGING IN AIR.   YOU'VE LET IT LIE
IN THE PAN.

[P 10: Notes and fragments:
"I think that in their honey cells"]

PEOPLE getting up from eating, wiping their mouths, silent suddenly.
TRADE.
TRADING ON BEDS. ACCOSTED.   . BRING. SUCKLE.

I think that in their honey cells
In all the earth those tired ones
Lift out tonight their smiles around our bed;

I think that in their honey cells
In all the earth those emptied ones
Lift out tonight their smiles upon us here:
They gathered and here bank their honey. This honey bank:
Stone labels in our memory.

Stone labels them for memory   shelved in the earth in yards,
                                     stone labels them
As short as theirs.   for memory as short as theirs.
Epitaphs efface each other.
Where the dolphin leisurely bowling his distinguished fins

This dolphin bowling in continual light. Dolphins of heaven.
Night, a slow barge starbarnacled, overslides us: we are wiped out.
We are wiped under shadow and we sleep.
Shawled up the cage in silence.

Shelved in the earth in yards behind iron fences,
Looking through fences.
Watching each other through insecure fences.
Laurel / imitates the bee's eye / IMITATIVE

bee / Small, brownyellow bug: when wings lift they are like shirt tail lifting from neat, prim cleft naked bottom (wh is black).

[P 11: Automatic Writing: "THE TINDERING STARS"]

THE TINDERING STARS.   RUSTLING SNOW.   SNOW CREPT.
        WALKING ON Snow as on wheat.   SNOW SHUT THE
        LAND.   SHUT The year.   SHUT AROUND HIM, he walked
        inside a pearl.   TINDER STARS. STORAGE OF STARS.
WATER MILLING & moiling above the fall, calming at the lip in
prescience.
WATER LAY LIKE A BOARD. HAIRY GRASS. WATER LEVELLING
THE FIELD. DARK MOUNTAIN RIVERS PAVED WITH NUDGING
LOGS.   JOSTLING LOGS.   IN THE CLOCK THE JOISTLING
WHEELS (TEETH). The wheels delicately taste each other. Wheels taste
and turn each other. TASTING THE TIME THEY TURN. NATURAL.
THE COIL RELAXES; THE WHEELS DELICATELY TASTE THE
TIME THEY TURN; NEBULAE. SPRING NEBULAE.
SIGHT   HEARING   TOUCH   SMELL   TASTE

TASTING THE EARTH. TASTE EXHAUSTION. ANGER. LUST.
        LIFE IS A WOUND which builds it many scabs.   SLACK,
        CASUAL WING.
        THE world a thimble.   TOUGH LEAVES. AIR.
AS WATER CALMS BEFORE THE LIP of the DAM. SPILLS. CITY
        FEELINGS.
        FAMILY BRUTALITIES.

[P 12: Poem: "Glimmer, glimmer, universe"]

Glimmer, glimmer, universe
Whom storms of mysteries immerse:
Nebulae not grieved for Zion,
Blown seeds of a dandelion:

How I wonder by what rules
Beyond the touch of local fools
In the anarchic spring unborn
Whose front lawn you shall adorn.

What immeasurable child
Shall your burning have beguiled
Before another picks you dry
And puffs your promise down the sky.

In what city shall that be
And in what strange vicinity?
(Hark my friend, we've had our day:
School is out: they're on their way.)

Gods snub each other on our back stairs
The ancient time contemned as snares.
Our galaxy, so runs the hope,
Is mirror for a telescope.

Curved brightness is a beveled jewel
Examining minute renewal.
All things undreamt, one atom's core:
One spark of sand, its endless shore.

There thrive fish the dark sea down
Unsuspicious of our town.
We each are lumps in a same leaven:
And Friday's print amazes heaven.[14]

---

14. Cf. "Lyrics X: A Nursery Rhyme," *Collected Poems*, 64.

[P 13: Prose Beginning and
First Draft of Poem: "I will hear"]

[1]

I will hear. Nor will not all break down in fear. The curtain, how, it moves, the grainy weave, the silent, silent smoke. Here the spanned bars (don't seem to move), the crib (don't seem to watch), and through, chair (watch), chair in corner, pleasant chair (watch, watch, watch, watch),

what beside behind that chair is hulching, watching?
What shape it is? What shivering strength? Where in that dark its glassing eyes. Where in that awful dark the eyes. The eyes that pore me through like fog and what is it wanting, what is it waiting for, what does it want of me, me, me.

And when, breathing, slow and easy,

And when, watching, calm and cold,

And when, gathering round its coupling joints the terrific muscles of the night, shall it come and take me; and do what.

And deep and dim from other room, the light lined under door, a room beyond, slow, deep, growling easy grainy and secure, talk and laughing, not much different from the sweezing of locusts, but of stronger race. And in the street the careless feet, the warm, casual night.

Not be afraid, no need, they all are there.

They all are there, they do not know, they do not care.

They do not dare.

They do not dare.

They do not care.

I am alone.

Alone.

Flat eyes of open shadow, they snicker, bide their time.

It is not long, oh, not long, (they snicker), and we gather up out of the corners and move in and take you.

We lounge across and cloze, and have you.

You can look but we can look deeper. You can think to yourself but we can hear you thinking. You can be still as a mouse but we know you and you are afraid. You cannot live but we own you. We know all about you and you can never hide and all they do is laugh and not afraid they never care not one they cannot drive us out they can't they cannot drive us out.

By this time the chilliness which had been spreading all ways from his navel was cold ice jelly. His eyes in the dark were dark and bulged with dark. He shifted the cold from belly to brain and, trying it there, was frightened more still,

[2]

O if beneath this ward of night
There's any other creature brings
His humbled soul before the stars
And wordless with his weeping sings

Brother, my blood, my dearest soul,
Whatever harm attends the light

Put by

O if beneath this ward of night
There's any other creature brings
There's any other creature brings
His open soul before the skies
And wordless with his weeping
sings,

Brother, my blood, my own
dear soul,
Whatever change attends
the light
Put by, my kin, put by, be glad:
We're very Near to God tonight.

O if beneath this blaze of night
There's any other creature brings
His childliness before the skies
And wordless and aweeping sings,

Brother, my blood, my own
dear soul,
Whatever change attends
the light
Put by for gladness of the

[P 14: Poem: "Theories of Flight"]

James Agee
Anna Maria
Florida

Theories of Flight

How from those birdless heights the air
Plaited upon the miles of wheat.
But there were flattened faces where
Glass dammed away the hungering street.

Kansas and Crimea were
The mileages we understood.
Moscow and Chicago were
The cities where they did no good.

Here, the starving is for hate.
There, to serve the first good State.
In either place, for lack of bread,
You weigh as light: you're just as dead.

[P 15: Poem: "Yet even slaves"]

Yet even slaves lie down and love.
A little while along this bed
Hunger is nothing and proud hate
Spills wholly from the lowered head.

Though soon we must stand up from love
And mercy and all love put by,
Belt our starved guts with wrath, and kill,
We are not sorry we have met.

[P 16: Poem: "Seriously, if that's your vanity"]

Seriously, if that's your vanity, but remember:

We all that work such grievance are less than children
dancing the lengths out of elaborate games
on a warmed threshold, in a safe dooryard:

whom shadows scare; whom the bearing evening
brings in for bed; and whom the dark undresses.

Not twenty have been more. Though more will be,
and all the race be sometime more than grown,

> This summer shall not swing again
> its largeness on the land:
> This summer's leaves you shall not know
> from this disheveled hand.

[P 17: Poem: "Heal, hardy air"]

Heal, hardy air, harm in earth:
And yield these lungs the while to breathe
it takes to whisper out that worth
whose cloudy forehead you enwreathe.[15]

[P 18: Poem: Early Draft of "Lyric"]

Demurely margin of the morning: glows cold, flows foaled:
Fouled in floron: float, float, easily earth before, demurely:
> It is subdued:

---

15. Cf. "Lyrics V," *Collected Poems*, 62

Chiseled gems the leaves their harbor
Sparkling up: whom light lifted:
Drilling in their curly throats
glinting and sweet ordinate phrases:
listening, each forest leaf:
trembling from her nervy root
the spring:
Teaching; touching:
Sinuous disunion:
Drinking: drinking: each of all serenest wonder.

Hark the smooth ancestral phrases:
      It is subdued.
Bring floral earth your breast before her
      Afford your breast before the morning.
Disunion, ancestral harmonies:

Demurely, the early margin:
Fouled is flown: flower, flower, fearless earth before, demurely:[16]

[P 19: Poem: "Now, for one moment"]

Now, for one moment, I have seen my soul,
Have stared its infinite asperity
Full in the eye; and from that sight I stole
Sick with the horror of the verity.
I called on God to grant me to ignore
The feverish foulness that I could not bear,
I termed it courage, falsely thus to soar
Free of the shame and truth and the despair.

---

16. Cf. "Lyric," *Collected Poems*, 153.

Of all men I am cowardliest, least kind,
Most beyond hope befouled and pullulate
With multiplicity vermin of the mind,
Malformed where I would I were most straight.
Even the foulest beggar cannot gain
From truth, who knows his self-inflicted pain.

[P 20: Poem: "Suffer me not, O Lord"]

Suffer me not, O Lord, one inch to yield
To truth and to the cowardliness of reason;
Although my ignominy stand revealed
To all the cackling world, grant me self-treason.
Better than idiocy prolonged, that now
My brain spins face to face with its confusion.
But since complacency and compromise
Darken the very nadir of all shame,
And since the highest and the holiest prize
Only the great-souled and the brave may claim,
What hell in life, whatever hell ensue,
Suffer me to forget the truth, and You.

[P 21: Poem: "Ah's jes' a believing chameleon"]

Ah's jes' a believing chameleon (credit line to Goofy Gerould)[17]
And I dare you to dig up a creed in all the wide wide werruld
That I won't at some fine time (if life lasts long enough) hang my hat on
If only I be caught by the eye of the man behind the baton.

Of course the world grows tired of caring just what such a fellow thinks
But I always say a chain's no stronger than its missing links:

---

17. Christopher "Goofy" Gerould. See J 4.17, note 50.

Speaking of chains, suppose I curl up quiet in the —— gullet
And you, my friends, if you want to clear the air a trifle, pull it.[18]

[P 22: Poem: "And by the bye my pious friends of the reviewing trade"]

And by the bye my pious friends of the reviewing trade
By whose opinion reputations unmade are unmade
Please note well, as you wade your way through the subsequent
      tepid hash
That I was trying this stuff before I heard of Ogden Nash.

[P 23: Poem: "Forsythe and hindsight"]

Forsythe[19] and hindsight
Are helping Europa a lot:
Half-assed reviewers
Are overflowing your pot:

Laura Jean Libbey[20]
Topped off with a jigger of Freud
Served with sour horse-turds
Rates your's truly's Boid.

Numerous Leftists find The Dance
Grounds for going off in their Leftist pants
As for me I think a fart
In a typhoon stands a better chance as art.

---

18. This poem should probably be considered alongside "Period Pieces from the Mid-Thirties," *Collected Poems*, 145–48.

19. "Robert Forsythe" was the pseudonym of Kyle Crichton (1896–1960), who wrote numerous articles for the Communist publications *Daily Worker* and *New Masses* during the 1930s.

20. Laura Jean Libbey (1868–1924) was the author of more than eighty dime novel romances for women.

[P 24: Poem: "Depilatories garter belts and lotions"]

Depilatories garter belts and lotions
Are making mother sweeter every day.
And mother can appeal to my emotions
Just the biggest kind of way.

[P 25: Poem: "Sweet anodyne"]

Sweet anodyne.
My anodyne.
Better than women, song, or wine.
There's no escape
For man or ape
Quite like hewing closely to
The Party Line
      The Par Ty Line.

[P 26: Poem: "What fool would dare"]

What fool would dare
To show he cares
What bastards wreck, a right idea:
I'll save my skin
The world to win
There's no discipline
On earth as strong as fear.

So let the fools
Make us their tools
Eat what they give you at the schools.
Try not to care
How foul the air

Keeps the population choked
　　Stick by the radio.

You have nothing to lose but your brains.

[P 27: Poem: "Major Douglas"]

Major Douglas[21] is the Kind of man
That heaps up the fire in the frying pan
He spares the child and spoils the rod
And he never gives offense to beast, man or God.

He says the world would escape its pickles
If only the world would take wooden nickels:
And Munson[22] and the brighter sort of Harvard boys
Will make the world a safe place for the Bishop[23] and the goys.[24]

---

21. British Major Clifford Hugh Douglas (1879–1952) was the creator of the underconsumptionist monetary theory Social Credit. While balancing the books for an aircraft factory, Douglas noticed that the combined incomes of all the workers at the plant would be insufficient to purchase its combined production. He applied this insight to the economy as a whole and came to the conclusion that banks create a cycle of debt through charging interest: the principal is presumably equal to what is produced, but the interest requires future loans—and future interest. Since the money consumers have to buy products will always lag behind the cost of the goods they produce, countries constantly have to expand their production capabilities, which inevitably leads to international friction and eventually war. Douglas proposed breaking the cycle of debt through a national dividend that would return the amount of surplus production back to consumers rather than banks. Variations of the Social Credit theory, with its convenient application to the mythical Jewish banker, found a number of proponents during the Great Depression, including Father Charles E. Coughlin, Huey Long, and Ezra Pound.

22. Gorham Munson (1896–1969), writer and literary critic, was the editor of the Social Credit journal *New Democracy*.

23. Controversial economic populist and Catholic priest Father Charles E. Coughlin (1891–1979) was the host of a very popular radio show from 1926 to 1942 and editor of the weekly newspaper *Social Justice*. He blamed Jews for the Great Depression and initially supported Franklin Roosevelt's New Deal but turned against the president when he failed to implement radical monetary reforms, eventually accusing him of being part of a Communist conspiracy.

24. Gentiles, a reference to the international Jewish banking conspiracy.

[P 28: Poem: "Dialog"]

[1]

DIALOG

We cannot wait. Our time is nearly gone.
That mood of spiritual desolation
Which Eliot put under glass, carry on
Long as you like. Certain new information
Suggests that that account was overdrawn
About the time the waves of imitation
Thinned from the ninth. Rather than draw a blank
We even must decline to run the bank.

Tell it to Major Douglas[25] and the Rector;[26]
They can restore your appetite for tea.
Tell it to Sigmund,[27] the great dream-collector;
He'll fix you up, for a sufficient fee.
Talk out your troubled heart in any sector,
Only, my sad young friend, don't talk to me:
Unless you find yourself willing to take
Some drastic steps to cure your bellyache.[28]

[2]

You show some hope, and then again some doubt.
Hope's a good sign; the doubt's intelligent
At this stage. Now suppose you spit it out,
The whole damned business. It's spit well spent.
Since, I suspect, it stands to end a drought
Nothing else could, and won't cost you a cent.
And please don't mind if anyone here makes cracks;
Some of them, like yourself, are erstwhile smacks.

---

25. Major C. H. Douglas. See P 27, note 20.

26. Father Charles E. Coughlin. See P27, note 22.

27. Sigmund Freud (1856–1939), Austrian founder of psychoanalysis.

28. See Appendix for alternate second stanza.

"Well, that, as a matter of fact, does bring to mind
One thing that often bothers me. Just when
I try to ask some question or to find
Some sense in this or that, one of your men
Is liable to be pretty damned unkind,
To put it mildly. Time and time again
I've run from cool to warm, almost to hot,
Only to be put off by so much snot.

I don't believe I'm hypersensitive.
I've friends who've had the same experience.
To anyone brought up on live & let live,
A silly phrase, I grant, that gives offense.
If you have everything you claim to give
The world at large, it doesn't make much sense,
(Does it?), deliberately to throw sand
In the eyes of those who are trying to understand."

[P 29: Poem: "Muzzy wuvs her Buzzy"]

Muzzy wuvs her Buzzy,
          mmm, itta oodlums.
Buzzy turn to Muzzy,
          mmm, itta Foodleums.

Muzzy tan I have a cookie?
Come love me first.
Mmm, little lover: pway wiv my nookie,
Zen I'll div oo a cookie.
Muzzy, me wuvs oo.
Muzzy wuvs oo tooo.

More zan daddy, even more than
Untle Charley or that tall dart man,
Oo thrill your Muzzy when oo divs he a kiss
An oo thrill her when she bathes or helps oo piss.

Mah-Mah, I wanna wee-wee.

Oo wanna mate a wivver?
Turn here, tunnin,
We'll sneak behind the flivver
Duss oo and me.

Ooo, such funning.
Oh, witta wuvver
You're donna drow up to be a dreat bid mans.

Bigger than Daddy's
Or untle Charley's
Bigger dan dat tall dart man's.

So way your head on Muzzy's bweast
And suck her if you love her
And Daddycums will do the rest
And bwing oo a witta bruvver.

[P 30: Poem: "Hunched hung"]

Hunched hung above his mild-eyed and wild sighing bride
who brunts the bulk with stiff four posted stride
delves in the cringing warmth that drinks him of his power
the bull, back crackarched: bee trembling rides a flower.

[P 31: Poem: "Somewhat less indiscriminately"]

Somewhat less indiscriminately
Pour love and gratitude around
For parents to lick up like cats
And for the ravenous ground:

daughters your fathers planted you
        only to deflower you:
sons your mothers cooked you up
        only to devour you:

patterned after Stephen's sow
        who breakfast's on her farrow.[29]
Who is not Ireland but the earth
        our birthplace and our barrow.

[P 32: Poem: "Father, mother"]

Father, mother, whom the pleasure
        cheated even while it taught,
Now your child repents at leisure
        what your hasty trading brought.

[P 33: Drafts: "Sweet heart tonight"]

Sweet heart tonight by rights in graveyards
Long since forgotten bones and bran of bones
congratulate:
all that was ardent is now the air
smiles round our wrestling here. I do not think they pity.

---

29. In James Joyce's *A Portrait of the Artist as a Young Man* (New York: B. W. Huebsch, 1916), Stephen Dedalus calls Ireland "the old sow that eats her farrow."

You do, they say, what we are born to do.   Ask the deaf rest . . . .
No matter for the rest.   a season changes in you.
Discharged, at length, now shall your strength recede:

and now, the season changes in your blood.   altering the blood.
                        equinox.

Born as we were, they say, you are brought one,
No matter by what chance, and now are ripe.
You do, they say, what we are born to do,
And what though with this instant you are changed.
What though the season altering in your groin
Possess your blood henceforth.
Waves are not full before they find their shore
And once discharged, recede: and are received.

What wave is full that fails at length the shore:
And what, discharged, shall any wave — recede.
and be received

Only the wave is full that finds the shore:
And once discharged, recedes and is received.
The wave's a fool that would delay before:
After, a miracle not well believed.[30]

[P 34: Poem: "Tonight sweet heart"]

Tonight sweet heart in graves forgotten
Straws of old harvests whom the sun ignores
Bones and their bran congratulate.

I do not think they pity us:
Or pity less than they are glad:

---

30. Cf. "Lyrics IV," *Collected Poems*, 61–62, and P 34.

All that was ardent which is now the air
Smiles round our wrestling here.

Tonight, water finds the shore
And then is water as before.[31]

[P 35: Poem: "Not for your ease"]

Not for your ease or pleasing was the air
Mild, a while past, and loving with the earth:
What for the seethe of health up breadth of summer
I cannot know, but doubtless not for you.

Cruellest and dingiest of the squatters we
Who wring and spoil and craft this earth apart.
From the huge kindness of their kingdom's edge
The citizens watch seldom but to hide.

However, there are harms about the heart
We never dealt us, but can only serve.
Serve them then as we must, to further harm,
And help what can, and meantime let who will
Lift on this glimmered dark his joy, his frail surmise
While, solemn and unregarding, with stiff hands, the heavens
        Rust and unwreathe the world.[32]

[P 36: Poem: "Young yet on your day"]

Young yet on your day
Pledge tall things to your pride,
Brave in thought of war,

---

31. Cf. "Lyrics IV," *Collected Poems*, 61–62, and P 33.
32. Cf. "Lyrics VI," *Collected Poems*, 62.

Walks in the bullet's way:
Murderers for gain
Be gainful while you can;
You that would change that score
Be merciless and destroy:

You lonely that must mourn:
You that are full of cheer:
You that all harms have borne:
You that see no thing clear:

You woman and you man,
Bridegroom and happy bride,
Find out your truest joy
That crests the mortal tide:

That pride and greed and anger,
Bravery and grief and love,
All death has deep in danger
Death shall not quite remove:

So may the race run out its riot
And burst brains for a reason why,
And know two times for quiet:
To couple and to die:

And this ill-sung remark
Of mine and many others
Run light among the living
When I am in the dark.[33]

---

33. Cf. "You in the Young Day," *Collected Poems,* 151.

[P 37: Poem: Draft of "Against time"]

Against time, and the damages of the brain,
Sharpen and calibrate. Not yet in full,
Yet in some arbitrated past
Create some order out of the listless summer.

Spies, moving delicately among the enemy,
The younger sons, the fools,
Set somewhat aside the dialects and the stained skin of feigned madness,
Ambiguously signal, baffle, the eluded sentinel.

Edgar weeping for pity, to the spiral sickness of the bluff
Bring your blind father and describe a little.
Bring him, leaping, fallen among field flowers shallow.
But undisclosed, withdraw.

Not yet that naked hour when armed,
Disguise flung flat, squarely we challenge the fiend.
Still, comrade, the running of beasts and the ruining heaven:
Still captive the old wild king.[34]

[P 38: Poem: "Sun our father while I slept"]

Sun our father while I slept
You lifted like a field of corn
The smiling and the peaceful strength
Of those that are the race new born.

The infant future waked in you
Once more and at the world's rich breast
Drank the day's courage and lay down
In fearless and refreshing rest.

---

34. Cf. *Let Us Now Praise Famous Men*, 4.

And while the Russian field you raised
Dreams in your starflung shadow's keep,
You wake these backward lands to work:
Good work to do before we sleep.[35]

[P 39: Poem: "Tell me must goodness wait"]

Tell me must goodness wait
And kindliness stand by
Till every harm is healed
And every tear be dry?

And since that time is won
By murdering alone
Shall mercy turn to water
That once was made a stone?

[P 40: Poem: "How on the bare brain"]

How on the bare brain
Age, thought, circumstance
Steadily stand up like rain

Now the water's really deep.
Droplet, you default your chance.

Good night. Sweet sleep.
Pleasant dreams. Harm's done.
Past's past. Don't weep.

God, the bare sun!

---

35. Cf. "Sun Our Father," *Collected Poems*, 154.

[P 41: Poem: "Now Lord God"]

Now Lord God keep your weather eye
A while on cabbages and kings:
And if still you maintain it dry,
Then Death has lost some potent stings.

[P 42: Poem: "A low pit and sink of shade"]

A low pit and sink of shade
And funneled dark I find me made:
Long has lapsed my laden sight
Sourceward down that floorless night:
Down the echoing skull's delusion
And the hooded soul's confusion,
Down my marrow into earth
Searching out my nether worth.
Deeper than my breath can follow
Silence falls beneath me hollow.
Naught of all I'd die to do
May I do, who find naught true
That's truly mine: I find me made
A cistern full of standing shade.[36]

[P 43: Poem: Early Draft of "Johannes Brahms"]

The year turns on him and fulfils his worth:
We, too, of many motions in one mind,
No more anatomize our present dearth
But think of one who did the talk consigned—
A century past he drank his first brave breath,

---

36. Cf. "A Low Pit and Sink of Shade," *Collected Poems*, 56–57.

The undeviant, the rich and deep in heart
Who knew his height and toiled it into death,
Humble and honorable in his art.[37]

[P 44: Poem: Two drafts of "Johannes Brahms"]

Johannes Brahms: May   , 1833.[38]
The year turns round him and fulfils his worth:
We too, of many motions in one mind,
No more anatomize out present dearth
But think of one who did the job consigned:
This century past who drank his first brave breath,
The undeviant, the bright and deep of heart
Who marked his way and toiled it unto death
Humble and honorable in his art.
No wildness his, no roaring at the air,
Splendor of honest sound was all his use:
From which intent no envy nor despair
Nor ease of life compacted might seduce.
And we, to all we and the world disclaim
Swear new, single allegiance by his Name.

The year turns round him and fulfils his worth:
We too, of many motions in one mind,
No more anatomize our present dearth
But think of one who did the task consigned.
This century past he drank his first brave breath,
The undeviant, the rich and deep of heart.
Who marked his height and toiled it unto death,

---

37. Cf. "A Poem for Brahms' Death-Bed," *Collected Poems,* 144–45, and P 44.

38. This poem was probably written around Brahms's one-hundredth birthday, which would have fallen on May 7, 1933.

Humble and honorable in his art.
No wildness his, no roaring at the air;
Splendor of honest sound was all his use:
From which intent no envy nor despair
Nor ease of life compacted might seduce.
And we, to all we and the world disclaim
Swear new, single allegiance by his Name.[39]

[P 45: Poem: "Now the steep and chiming coasts"]

Now the steep and chiming coasts
Alaskan lose the final light:
Greenland and Bermuda still
Sleep in the watches of the stars:
And like two leaves upon a lake
From ice to ice along the sphere
Float the Americas in the damp
Complete renewal of the night.

Now those dreadful millions
Who through the day
The poisons of old broken oaths
Take to the love and dreams
Here rest a hundred million souls
Of their indignities:
By day, for want of better food
They drank those deathly poisons up
Of fear and emulation . . .
O might their dreams like water from deep wells
Wash them awake:

---

39. Cf. "A Poem for Brahms' Death-Bed," *Collected Poems*, 144–45, and P 43.

Hear rest a hundred million ruined souls
Of their indignities. All through the day
Wanting the knowledge of a healthier food
They wolfed the special poisons of our air:
Gaining, and hating, fearing and emulating.
Strangling each other in the name of life:
These are good people: how must they thrive in death
And why insist allegiance to despair.
O might their dreams like water from deep wells
Wash them awake and wiser to their living:
Then might the earth be planted toward her joy
Little in Killing and much forgiving.
Or better might they learn, which they can not:
The love of Jesus and the mind of Marx.

[P 46: Poem: "Hold on a second, please"]

Hold on a second, please: there's work to do
And it involves, one way or another, you.
The garbage stinks and it's high time to burn it.
Christ, if you lack the sense, get busy and learn it.
Anyone can, it's obvious enough:
Take a few easy pointers now, on the cuff.

The human race, not to get personal,
Has got, by now, about a bellyful
Of bitching from the few wise guys who bleed it
Into their checkbooks and, on occasion, feed it
Because, they find, they do, in a measure, need it.

It's gone on since the apes talked, just the same,
The old, invulnerable, badger game,
The cat's paw clipped and scorched, the monthly sitting

Tight and the world's best eating in his shitting:
Millions on millions, peoples on peoples born
And fallen like a field of rotted corn,
Their whole lives wrung to the last ruined drop
Merely to live and seed the next year's crop,
Fervently hoping to their phony God
For better luck the seamy side of the sod,
And worshipping that smug and murderous State
Which pays them with an empty dinner plate
And kept, consistently, nine parts stone blind
To every hope and help the eye can find:
And that's the size, to date, of history.
Not, though, the way things ought to, and will, be.

You see, we're catching on to how it goes:
Or spot, if you like, the canker in the rose.
We're getting tired of bleeding out our lives
And those of our children and those of our wives
For less than living needs and for the sake
Of J. P. Morgan's[40] four-ply sirloin steak.
And sick to death of dying in their wars:
Of making our women and our arts their whores:
Of raising corn and wheat and eating shorts:
Of raising hogs and sharing in their orts:
Of mining gold and getting paid in copper:
Of cooking feasts and scraping out the hopper.

It makes some difference, too, which side you take,
Such as the difference between duck and drake

---

40. Either John Pierpont Morgan (1837–1913), American investment banker and one of the world's richest men, or J. P. Morgan Jr. (1867–1943), his son. In either case, the House of Morgan banking empire was extremely powerful in the world of international finance.

Or such, not to waste unnecessary breath,

As all the difference between life and death.

A man is tearing out his brother's throat:

God and the State stand by and hold his coat.

When B[41] looks sore, and makes as if to speak,

God's contact man says, blessed are the meek;

And when he shows more physical kinds of gripe,

The State Massages him with a lead pipe.

I could go on, and tell you what a life

His children lead; and snapshots of his wife

Might, I surmise, help some to serve to move you.

However, what's the point: if you'll look close

At him alone, you'll see, plain as your nose,

That this unfortunate has your own face

And is, to tell the truth, the human race.

[P 47: Poem: "Fight-Talk"]

[1]

Fight-Talk

Pals, have bosses bled on you so

There's no blood left nor place to go?

You find it hard to get a job

Since that cold night you tried to rob?

You're ousted by the rectal grab

Since you were dope enough to scab?

Your father died when that last dram

Of Sterno[42] broke the diaphragm?

---

41. That is, "B man," as opposed to "A man," two lines before.

42. Sterno, a brand of canned cooking fuel, can be drunk for a cheap high, usually by someone who is really down and out. It also releases a high level of carbon monoxide when burned.

Your mother lies & eats her lip?
Her wailing gives your wife the pip?

Your wife is more than half-seas over
With another shoat and no more clover?

Your oldest son is on the bum?
The Amateurs have slupped him numb?

Your daughter walks the easy street
And gathers and dispenses gleet?[43]

Your little children sit around and cry
And cry and cry and cry and cry?

Your priest brings round the Peace of God;
Advises you to carry a hod?

The lights are doused? the gas is dead?
You've hocked the chair and extra bed?

The landlord's issued final warning
Against eight-thirty Monday morning?

Pal, have the bosses bled you so
You've no blood left nor place to go?

O heavens and its angels no!
By Roosevelt's smile it is not so!

Such talk's the ugliest sort of lie,
And all the world is apple pie.

Stand firm, my boy, resist the passes
Launched by the readers of New Masses.[44]

---

43. "Gleet" refers to a non-specific venereal disease.
44. *New Masses* was a Communist journal founded in 1926.

O plug against the Syren song
Of the cuckling priest[45] and hooey long.[46]

Remember too that Hammy Fish[47]
Is victim of a Freudian wish.

The man who ever stops and thinks
Relieves his mind of all such kinks.

So stop a sec and realize:
The men who run this show are wise,

The cards are right, the deal is new,
The aces are for me and you.

They're killing off the extra hogs
To keep clean writing in the logs.

They're cutting down on planting wheat
Lest anyone should overeat;

Or if not to keep the hand-from-mouth,
Then, maybe, hand-in hand with drouth.

And plowing under extra cotton
To prove the tenant's not forgotten.

---

45. Father Charles E. Coughlin. See P 27, note 20.

46. Populist demagogue Huey P. Long, former governor of Louisiana, was elected to the Senate in 1930 and attacked the New Deal as doing too little to redistribute wealth. See P 28, note 20; J 2.20, note 37; and N 23, note 46. Agee's narrator is ironically calling on victims of the Depression to resist the "Syren song" of New Deal opponents from both the right and left.

47. Hamilton Fish (1888–1991), Republican congressman from New York, was a vigorous anti-Communist and opponent of Roosevelt—he thought the New Deal even more insidious than Communism because the former disguised its true intentions. His father, Hamilton Fish, also a U.S. congressman, was assistant secretary of the treasury under Theodore Roosevelt, and his grandfather, Ulysses S. Grant's secretary of state, was the subject of a 932-page Pulitzer Prize–winning biography by Allan Nevins, *Hamilton Fish: The Inside History of the Grant Administration,* in 1936.

Giving us sleep by burning coffee.
Handing out hot horseshit and toffee.

[2]

Selling the auto workers out.
Being photographed among a Boy Scout.

(Probably the only Miner
(Whoever sat in the President's diner).[48]

And wrangling over Bonus Bills[49]
And other mild cathartic pills.

Now, gleaming Capitol Dome,
Farewell, and coming nearer home,

Behold how love outsmarts belief:
We've signed you up for Home Relief:[50]

Don't be afraid: pull in your feelers:
Ward heelers have become ward-healers.

We've broken up the old machine
And now we run our city clean.

Though we tax our people to the bone
We'll take care of our very own:

---

48. A pun on *minor;* that is, Boy Scouts are the only "miners" Roosevelt will have to the White House.

49. In 1924 Congress voted to pay World War I veterans a bonus adjusted for length of service over a twenty-year period. During the depths of the Great Depression, however, many former soldiers found themselves in dire financial straits and demanded immediate cash payment, marching to Washington and camping out in a shanty town just outside the city limits. In 1932 the House of Representatives passed the Veterans' Bonus Bill, but the Senate defeated it. With the support of populist figures such as Huey Long and Father Coughlin, the Bonus Bill was revived in 1936 and passed over President Franklin Roosevelt's veto.

50. The New York City Home Relief Bureau accounted for about 5 percent of the total federal welfare benefits distributed by the Works Progress Administration in 1935.

We've found the solution, we consider it a wow:
It Works: and this is how:

Nobody's any excuse to get sore,
For every dollar is accounted for:

Of every million we are fed
Half of it goes for overhead,

Another half for office space,
Another half to make a place

For Mister Mugwump's Nephew's Wife[51]
Who's grown a trifle tired of life

And still another half to keep
Investigators half asleep,

And still another half to buy
Cars that will match our Chairman's tie,

And still another to make chauffeurs
Out of incipient corner loafers,

And more to lubricate the game
That brings us more whence that much came:

Oh, money charitably invested,
Rest assured, is well digested.

There's precious little wasted and
That falls afoul a needy hand:

---

51. The Mugwumps were Republican reformers who deserted the party during the 1884 presidential election due to scandals involving candidate James G.
Blaine. That a Mugwump's distant relative is the beneficiary of political patron-
age is indicative of the level of corruption in the political status quo.

Twenty-odd a week for me
And food and rent and fare for thee.

I'm overworked and yet fear not
You'll find me Johnny-on-the-Spot

Or vice-versa, quick as one
Can get three dozen families done:

Very soon now, never fear,
By Monday week or month or year

Attention will come your way:
And <u>that</u> <u>will</u> be a Gala Day:

Always oatmeal in the pot,
Always cocoa, piping hot,

Irish potatoes by the peck,
A nice cut off the horses neck

Starchily erected soup,
Split beans to hand you all the poop,

And each fortnight a plug of soap
To keep up appearances, and hope,

And milk for baby, blue as blue,
And broth for me, and gas for you,

[3]

A quarter's-worth at very worst,
Enough to bloat on till you burst:

And everything that gave you fright
From that time on will be all right:

And that's the way the world is run.
Ain't we, or ain't we not, got fun?[52]

So pledge allegiance once again
To Franklin and his merry men.

And demonstrations three times three
In praise of Franklin's Mother's Knee.

And ululations nine-times-nining,
Find in each swine the pearly lining.

No matter how many lives are sperled
God's in his heaven to hell with the world.[53]

(Cartoon: gas stove, man, head in oven, terribly bloated body: child
lying on floor, bloated, dead, wife entering, child at skirt—
    IS IT INFLATION?
ARE WE TO HAVE INFLATION?)

[P 48: Poem: "Minority Report"]

    Minority Report.
In fun with our wives,
Our donations to drives,
Our political lives,
We diverge from the Norm:
But we read the right books
And we know the right folks
And we go to the Acme
    To keep ourselves warm.

---

52. An allusion to the song "Ain't We Got Fun?" (1921), music by Richard
Whiting and lyrics by Gus Kahn and Raymond B. Egan.

53. An allusion to Robert Browning's *Pippa Passes;* see J 1.6, note 20.

[P 49: Poem: "Madam, is baby's evening stool"]

Madam, is baby's evening stool
As smooth (if not as smart) as silk?
Tell me, do his affections cool
At mention of his mother's milk?

(Lady, does your baby tipple
At the O K Feller Nipple?)[53]

Do you find his love grown cold?
Do you miss that ole sensation?
Maybe baby's grown too old
For mother's favorite fixation.

Let our agent drop around.
He'll fix everything up fine.
Baby gains a half a pound,
You drink whiskey beer and wine.

He'll supply that old sensation,
You will never know the diff,
Let him have just one demonstration,
Absolutely free from syph,

Meanwhile see what he's brought Junior!
All to keep his snookums quiet!
A slight extra fee brings you n yr
Husband too the Oyster Diet:

Wait'll baby, (little love):
See's it! Why his little lips'l

---

53. "Rockefeller Nipple," i.e., capitalism, as opposed to various economic reforms.

Fit our product like a glove:
The (Guess what) O Kay Feller Nipple.

Baby's happier at the puss,
Baby's tougher at the stern:
And without a bit of fuss,
While our agent earns, you learn.

(Lady, does your baby tipple
At the O K Feller nipple?)

(How bout it, lady?)

[P 50: Poem "Collective Letter to the Boss"]

Collective Letter to the Boss

Dear <u>Boss</u>:
The little man with the big mustache[54]
And the man with an olive in place of a head[55]
Are making a perfectly hideous hash
Of the prospects for Peace and I wish they were dead.

But that goes too far for the man with the jaw[56]
Like a pickerel winning a merit-badge:
And the man with the moss all over his maw
Whose wife (named Mary) should be named Madge:[57]

---

54. Adoph Hitler (1889–1945), Nazi dictator of Germany, rose to power in 1933.

55. Benito Mussolini (1883–1943), Fascist dictator of Italy from 1922 to 1943.

56. Franklin D. Roosevelt (1945), Democratic president of the United States from 1932 to 1945.

57. King George V of England (1865–1936), whose wife was Mary of Teck (later Queen Mary), favored a policy of appeasement towards Hitler, which his successor continued.

And it goes for the man with the ranch-and-whore
And the gold and the long clothesline of sheets:[58]
And the priest with the champion fan-mail score[59]
And the man with the mug like a row of teats:[60]

And the man with the teeth and the Commodore's hat
And the glasses and the cruiser quarrel:[61]
And the snakeyed man as small as a slat
And men by the hundred thousand barrell:[62]

And every man in fact who owns
And turns the screws to own some more
And malts our blood and vats our bones
Compels our blood & bones to war.

New Paragraph:
Since, sir, that whole machine is set
Beyond your wish to ever change,
Beyond your power should even yet
The wish by chance your mind derange:

---

58. William Randolph Hearst (1863–1951), media magnate and isolationist, owned a 240,000-acre ranch in San Simeon, California, and was married to the much younger Marion Davies, a chorus girl whom he attempted to make a star. The "long clothesline of sheets" refers to his publishing empire, which at its peak numbered twenty-eight newspapers and eighteen magazines.

59. Father Charles E. Coughlin. See P 27, note 20.

60. Unknown.

61. Possibly a reference to Admiral William H. Standley (1872–1963), U.S. Chief of Naval Operations and one of the negotiators of the London Naval Treaty in March 1936. The treaty, signed by the United States, Great Britain, and France but rejected by Italy and Japan, set limits on armaments and tonnage of warships, including a six-year ban on building heavy cruisers. Completely ineffective, it was one of the stepping stones to World War II.

62. John D. Rockefeller, founder of Standard Oil. See P 49, note 52, and E 4, note 22.

Let Us Now Praise Famous Men

Previously Unpublished Photographs
BY WALKER EVANS

The following photographs, made on James Agee's and Walker Evans's 1936 trip to Hale County, Alabama, are provided through the courtesy of The Metropolitan Museum of Art, New York, and the generous help of Jeff L. Rosenheim, Associate Curator of Photographs. Only one of the photographs, selected from the sequence of two men conversing, has previously been published. While a few of the photographs, such as those of interior architecture, find parallels in the published volumes, others, particularly of the African American men and graveyard scenes, expand the scope of Evans's vision beyond what was first presented in *Let Us Now Praise Famous Men* in 1941 and in its enlarged, reissued edition in 1960.

Agee Portraits

Previous page,
[James Agee, Old Field, Long Island, New York], 1937

Below,
[Wilder Hobson and James Agee on Beach, Long Island, New York], 1937

Opposite page, top,
*[Wilder Hobson Playing Trombone and James Agee Playing Piano,
Possibly Old Field, Long Island, New York]*, 1937

Opposite page, bottom,
[James Agee on Beach, Long Island, New York], 1937

Street Scene (Two Men Conversing)

[Street Scene, Greensboro, Alabama], 1936

Graveyard

[Graves, Hale County, Alabama], 1936

Interiors

Left,
[Cabin Fireplace and Mantel,
Hale County?, Alabama],
1936

Below,
[Cabin Bedroom,
Hale County?, Alabama],
1936

Opposite page, top,
[Cabin Hallstand with Mirror,
Hale County?, Alabama],
1936

Farmers

Below, [Farmers, Hale County?, Alabama], 1936

Following page, top, [Farmer, Hale County?, Alabama], 1936

Following page, bottom, [Farmer, Hale County?, Alabama], 1936

Since, in a word, you force our hand:
Since, in a word, it must be war:
Line up your men and guns and be
Advised: you are the enemy:
All human race in every land
Rares up to wreck you from the floor.

[P 51: Poem: "The rootless winds"]

The rootless winds flower wide
    The marl blows smooth in differing green
The world lolls on her springward side
    The seas go smooth as plate between:

This bright this vagrant bubble
Charmed beyond all its charmful kind
Careers superior to such trouble
As makes small moisture of large mind.

[P 52: Poem: Introduction and Two Drafts of "Tenant this season of uneasy darkness"]

[1]

He watches before his God. Then, turning toward the people, he
    speaks to them.
He has made what watch he may before his God. Then, speaking
    inward:
Soul, seamed up in darkness marching my brief way:
Dwell shining in me, be always flat against five windows wide
And in my mind be balancer.
We are brothers: and you the elder: wiser:
Remembering that we shall quarrel and that I may hate,
Shape my ignorance kindly with your hands.
No man but wears a God and King in his flesh:

Soul sewn in darkness who march my short ways
Tenant whose length of lease is in darkness
Live shining in me, be always flat against five windows wide
    And in my mind the balancer.
We are brothers, and you the elder, wiser:
Remembering we shall surely quarrel and that I may hate
    and hope to kill,
Handle the shapes of my ignorance truly in your hands:

Tenant this season of darkness,
Soul sewn up in darkness who go my short way:
Be shining in me flat against five windows wide on world and
    in my mind the balancer.

We are brothers, and you the elder, wiser.
Remembering how surely we shall quarrel I forget hate hope
    to kill,
        My ignorance, vainness and disloyalty,
Handle the shapes of my nature justly in your hands:

Stand strong up in me soul my God my world before
        And, fighting ever with our differing arms
Let us cut out the truth each in our way:
        And fighting die, glad and worshipping.

[2]

Tenant this season of uneasy darkness,
Soul snaffled and sewn up in darkness who go with me my short way:
Be shining in me flat against five windows wide on world and in my
    mind the balancer.

We are brothers and you the elder, wiser.
Remembering how surely we shall quarrel I forget, hate, hope to kill,

My ignorance vainness and disloyalty,
Handle the shapes of my nature justly in your hands.

Stand strong up in me my soul my God my world before
And, fighting every with our differing arms
Let us cut toward the truth each in our way
And fighting die, glad and worshipping.

[P 53: Poem: "When your busy feet have run"]

When your busy feet have run
Seventy laps around the sun
(Granted no harm along the way)
You'll be ready to call it a day.

And when you flop down, breathing hard
And breathe your last, your one reward
Will be remembrance of the race
While cool breezes quiet your face.

Calm: your team will never lack
Runners on that crowded track:
Strict trainers for that curious game
Where all the records are the same.

[P 54: Poem: Two Drafts of "Fellows"]

Fellows, there's no use taking on that way.
finger in nose,
Arabesques of baccy-fumes,
Din inuendoed smoke down corridors of histories exempt,
The conditioned jitter, the drymouthed kiss, implosion
Soaped, of bombed kestrels, Peared, pyloned in insulate light:

Six-sided snow here, Blind, the lesion
Tides till morning taken: we've got your number:
Tramlines bilked, trade burked, unmatched sprockets,
Keep hands out of pockets,

Fellows, there's no soap playing it like that.
  Finger in nose, playfield whistle shrieking,
  Unstable affections deranged over water and gin,
  Black hat for blondeness, thwart our walk not more:
  Sarabeque of Dunhill fume,
  Din inuendoed smoke down corridors of histories exempt,
    redact:
  Conditioned jitter, drymouthed at the kiss,
  Precarious health of special soil, pain-gathered, grown
    glass-green,
  Implode, soaped, of bombed Kestrel Peared, pyloned in
    insulate light:
  six-sided snow here, Blind, lesion
  Tides till morning takes, leashes off:

We've got your number. Tramlines bilked. Trade burked. Ill matched
    sprockets.
  Keep hands out of pockets.
  Hide up the buck teeth from the baker's cozen.
  You can just cut it out this very minute.
  We do not see very much sense in it.
  Men with fine minds good hearts and such a way with words
  Would do better to let loose bigger and better and more
    natural turds.
  No matter at all how powerful their influence,
  No matter at all how right the things they're saying,
  No matter at all how excellent their poems

And no matter how hard they are to parody.
Nevertheless there are better things
Than walking your balance along a rail with tricky pain
Mile on mile when mile on mile on mile
Whole country and all earth is for your taking. Nuff said.

[P 55: Poem: "Twitch off the tune of night"]

Twitch off the tune of night. Discard the season.
Talk in the nude terms of this instant hour.
This is I fear abrupt, not wholly pleasing:
The Muse, mayhap, has gone a trifle sour:
Yet, gentlemen, there is some height of reason
For tossing her no sweetmeats to devour:
Surely the poet knows less than half his bride
Who lays and loves her merely alkaline side.

I hope to hand out quod for quiddity.
I hope, some ways, nobody will be hurt.
I hope to show some moderate validity
Maunders the back porch of this marble shirt
For what may seem inordinate acidity
And may well make me out some little squirt
Drunk with the chance to demonstrate his twot's
Delight in rudeness: which I'm really not.

If gratitude were all, and kindliness,
And self-esteem, and all good sense of taste,
All of which itch me now, I must confess,
But must not scratch in unartistic haste,
I swear I would have found the wrong address,
Mislaid the moorings of my underwaist,

Eaten this poem, or thought up something better
Such as regretful thanks by return letter.

[P 56: Poem: "So here's to their strychnine tears"]

So here's to their strychnine tears (drink deep) and here's to their
       bloody eggs
And here's to their winning ways and the vertical smile between
       their legs.
You can fight, feint, amputate, turn fag, not a man alive can win;
Your deep wet grave is gaping so you might as well dive in.

Using their weaknesses as crowbars, exploiting their natural
       above welts,
sculpturing their corruption behind pink garter belts

[P 57: Poem: "Who was that boy"]

Who was that boy, ranging the ruined hill,
Spine humbled to the horse's huge, light ghost,
Who would not lay his burden down until
He found the place he knew would please it most;
There, opened the rude ground and tenderly,
But without tears, buried the old, great frame,
Masking the grave with leaves, that none might see:
Then, standing up, first saw the eyes of shame?
O it was I; no doubt but it was I;
Nor doubt, I fear, what ghost I put away.
But how I killed my carrier, or why,
I cannot fathom; far less could I say
Where one might seek, who cared to prove such things,
The lost, betrayed, mangled, magnificent wings.

———
———

I bore my bearer on a wasted mountain,

His weight being nothing, though the form stayed whole

(But for the wings); Yes it was to that Fountain

Where first I saw him drink, I took his soul:

So cloyed with clay, so stifled full of stone, I hardly forced it open

       for his rest,

Where once a liquid more alive had grown

Than ever cherished in a mother's breast.

By what cause, right, or means, ever should I

Grieve? The immortal Spring itself is dead.

Tearless I laid my killed soul to the dry

Root of his nurture.

                 Yet the poor place bred

Just damp enough to lift up leaves in time

To mark the grave, heal the wound, and hide the crime.[63]

[P 58: Poetic Fragments: "lights of the universe"]

[1]

lights of the

    universe like a

    drifting thistledown blown in darkness

[2]

fennel (rank, moist pungent)

    apple trees: corky fruit with tarnished juice

    curdled air

    curbed clouds, sledging—sludge

    a snake sleeping in the sun, like a halted brook

    dark swamps in which moths drowse, half awake in one

        deep shadow.

        gnats simmering above the grass.

---

63. Cf. "Sonnets," *Collected Poems*, 68–69.

snap & whir of grasshoppers

grasshoppers flipping on the lawn

birds dreaming in the deep heat: only the hummingbird

lively, like a loose flame, or an electric arc gone wild.

leaves, crops, all, turgid.

A monstrous sunflower glowers, mourns, looks into its grave.

the huge slab, medal of a head, draws its spine into a question mark

above its rooted birth, its vertical grave.

foundered in light. Deeper death than death

deeper death than night

eloquent of death. summer day that stands upon its death.

the million tongues of leaves, flakes of leaves, hang speechless

All that May brought forth hangs ruining in its bounty.

crest of year, the balanced knot of the fountain

the labor of earth at an end, the labor of man

not begun

[P 59: Notes and poem: "For now of the light of day"]

sinister — guy; melancholy — guy;

theme & variation: shd next section drop the classical forms &

progression for free fantasy?

And in close, alternate nursery rhyme things with ever-broadening rhythm enlarging language, but also, always, more & more calm?

And is poem to date, less intellectual language?

In middle, things shd constantly appear & disappear? owl? whippoorwill? And in a mid-section, contrasts, of suspended anima-tion ([illegible] neither day nor night), and cruelty & hunger of night (owl, & small beast impaled on claws). (rats in stable?)

For now of the light of day the utmost remembrance
Fails from the sunflower's helpless foot:
For now quite finished the lionlike flower of day.
>   Its grand, burned eye, one blinded brown,
>   Stares soberly in all its future towards its grave,
>   Its seed stares towards the root;
>   And now:
>   Now of the light of day the utmost remembrance
>   Fails in the sunflower's helpless foot:

Film Treatments
and Radio Play

Of the film treatments included here, "Runaways" is the most thoroughly developed. Although it was never produced, the script outline is interesting for Agee's stated emphasis on the simplicity of its story line and normality of its characters, two young girls who run away, encountering obstacles such as a menacing dog before being returned home. "Runaways" thereby complements his film criticism, which often extols the unpretentious presentation of honest emotion as a virtue. "Twilight," dated to 1952, is a brief overview of a would-be collaboration between Agee and Manuel Conde (see F 2, note 3)set in Polynesia. The drafts of "Boy and Girl and Musician," "Planter's Son," and "2 Soldiers" are very fragmentary but are included for the insight they offer into Agee's methods for developing stories. "In Goblin Land," a radio play from 1935, is less interesting for its subject matter—an introduction of Pittsburgh clubwomen— than it is as an example of Agee's experimentation with words and music in the medium of radio.

[F 1: Film Treatment: "Runaways"]

[1]

NOTES OUTLINING AN ORIGINAL SCREEN STORY by James Agee

This story is based on, and is to follow pretty closely, a news story which appeared in the L. A. Times for Saturday, Feb 29 or March 1.[1] I will first give the gist of the news story.

Diane and Mary are eleven years old. Each is the other's closest friend. They are eminently normal, healthy, essentially happy children of the lower middle class, but each has her troubles. Diane very badly misses her brother, aged 10, who is living in Monterrey; and Mary and her mother don't get along too well. Mary and her mother have a particularly sharp spat; the two little girls have a wonderful idea: they will run away from home together and go up to Monterrey to see Diane's brother. They plan it out with great care and practicality: i.e., realizing it will get chilly enroute, they each dress in 3 to 4 complete sets of clothes, one over the other. Instead of going where they belong, next morning, at St. Thomas's parochial school, they board a street car which takes them to the Union Station. Besides the spare clothing, they are traveling light, taking along only what seems indispensable to them. Mary takes a textbook called Voyages in English and her beloved The Bobsey Twins in the Great West; Diane takes her Baltimore Catechism and six dollars which her Grandma has given her to buy books with. At the Station she blows $1.75 of this $6 on a long distance call to tell her brother what's up. Then they set off for Monterrey.

[2]

They go by railroad — i.e., walking the tracks. The news story doesn't make clear how they get onto the tracks, but it does state that they started off with a fatal navigational error: they head South instead of North.

They have a lot more staying-power than most runaway children. They plug ahead down the tracks in the wrong direction all that day and well into evening. On the way, they have adventures, of which the paper

---

1. No article matching this description has yet been found in the *Los Angeles Times*.

reports just two. They are threatened by a large dog of which Mary soberly says, telling of it: "No, he didn't bite us, but he sniffed at us." And they are so bothered and frightened by a bunch of teen-age boys, that for hours — by their idea of time anyhow — they hide in tall grass.

Chilled and disheartened by nightfall they ultimately break down enough to seek a few minutes' warmth in a service station. They begin to realize they are being looked at oddly, and get out. The next service station they sight is too much for them. They go in and give themselves up and the nearest police station is notified. Of course an alarm has been out for them since mid-afternoon; their parents are notified and come in a hurry. Mary's line in greeting her mother: "I was rather angry with you, but I'm not any more".

★   ★   ★

[3]

Our story is, merely, to watch these children through the following stages:

1) Why Girls Leave Home
2) How They Plan It
3) What they come up against enroute and what happens to them
4) How it all turns out.

The chief problem is to find the most limpid, simple and spontaneous terms possible, in which to watch them through these four stages. I enclose some notes emphasizing the great importance, as I see it, of not bearing down too heavily or seriously on the provocations and motives, and of keeping their adventures unremarkable and the payoff modest in scale; but at the moment it may be better to proceed with rough notes for the development of the story.

WHY GIRLS LEAVE HOME

We begin on the morning before the runaway as the two girls, who are near neighbors, get ready for school. We keep it as near as possible to take-the-average-morning, realistic domestic comedy. In the course of these opening scenes the following points are established:

Diane's parents are estranged. She lives with her father, a kind, lazy man who likes to avoid trouble, and his mother, a hurried, practical woman. Diane's brother lives in Monterrey with the mother. Diane hasn't seen him in months; she loves him and misses him very much. Now she runs into a cruel disappointment: he won't be coming down to see her tomorrow, as had been planned, for her 12th birthday. We realize that the plan needn't have been canceled if any of the older people had realized how much it meant to the children. They feel Diane is taking it too big.

[4]

She takes this as hard as her disappointment.

As she leaves for school her grandmother gives her $5 with which to buy her own birthday present: "I haven't got the time . . you know what you'd like better than I do . . . you're too big a girl to mind about surprises . ." and so on. We see clearly that Diane is not at all too big a girl.

In Mary's home, meanwhile, things are going as usual. Mary and her mother are too much alike; they "get on each other's nerves". By now this has become a vicious cycle; even when they try, they can't break out of it for long. The mother picks at Mary about all sorts of small details; and Mary goes out of her way to give her the cause without giving her the right. The main quarrel this morning, though, is over something more serious: Mary gets caught experimenting with lipstick. Her mother is very hasty, unintelligent and unfair about this.

So, as they leave their homes, both children are ripe for trouble, probably small but possibly large: Diane is heavy-hearted with disappointment and loneliness; and Mary is as sore as a boil. The moment they meet and walk towards school we can realize that each is the other's closest friend. They plunge instantly into a recitation of their grievances. Mary, being the angry one, is the more violent: she says that for two cents she'd run away from home and never _see_ her mother again.

This is, of course, merely the bombast and wishful thinking of a child who is helpless in its anger. But it rings quite a gong, deep in Diane: she wants, more than anything, to see her brother. If they fall down on their promise of bringing him to _her_, why doesn't she go to see _him!_ And in a kind of stillness both children begin to experience one of the crucial

[5]

moments in life — the moment in which you first realize, coolly, that you aren't eternally subject to the whims and commands of other people; that you have a will of your own, as well as just a lot of wishes. It dawns on them, in other words, that the impossible is entirely possible — that they actually can run away, if they really want to. They are astounded, even awed or a little frightened, by this realization — but from the moment they first realize the possibility, they are had. They are had, of course, far less through their reasons for unhappiness — they use these largely to bolster and rationalize their wish to carry out their scheme — than through essential happiness and healthiness — i.e., through the tremendous new vitality, pleasure, excitement, and opening-out of life, which fill them, from the moment they realize they really can and really will do this almost unthinkably adventurous thing.

By the time they get to school they are absolutely shining with all this — and already have taken on the secret, guileful, fake-casual look of conspirators.

HOW THEY PLAN IT

All through the school day they can't so much as glance at each other without bursting into grins. They recite with a very special air about them. And all through school and the rest of the day, with notes and whisperings and, after school, in conference, they develop them to the edge of megalomania: they won't just visit Diane's brother; he'll go on with them from there on out and the three will fend for themselves. When they have amply proved their ability to take care of themselves they will let their worrying families know where they are, and they won't have a leg to stand on.

But mostly their planning is much more simple and to the

[6]

immediate point — for one of their greatest pleasures, now, is in being eminently practical. For money they have Diane's great windfall, the $5 her grandmother gave her, plus the tiny chickenfeed of their pocket-money — a little over five dollars and forty cents. Upon Diane's queenly insistence they divide their funds, exactly equal. They must travel light and make sacrifices — no doll, or puppy, or any of those domestic encumbrances. It's going to be chilly; they must take along plenty of clothes. But of course they won't be such fools as to leave home with luggage: they will put the spare clothes on over each other, hiding the bulk under their overcoats (for it is winter). They must have more to eat than just their school lunches; each, after everyone is asleep that night, discreetly robs the icebox. After supper each leaves home "to do my homework" with the other, and they meet at a nearby drugstore, where Diane, under Mary's supervision, phones the Union Station and asks, in a near-whispered imitation of a mature voice, "Will you please tell me what time the train leaves for Monterrey?" She finally gets it straight — the time of a train in the middle of next morning. When she asks what streetcar they should take to get to the Station, she gets an uncivil answer. They are crafty enough to go a little way out of their neighborhood, to find that out. They part in solemn excitement. They can hardly sleep.

THE RUNAWAY

Diane's grandmother was pretty disgruntled that Diane "just didn't get around" to buying a present; but during the evening she and Diane's father realize, a little better, what a 12th birthday means; and now at breakfast Diane is told to be home right away from school because there's going to be a big surprise. She worms it out of them: no, it isn't her brother; it's a birthday

[7]

party. This sets her so far back on her heels that her purpose all but crumbles; but she recovers; she can't let Mary down; or her brother, <u>or</u> herself. She goes upstairs on a bathroom claim and hustles into four sets of clothes and is almost caught before she gets her big coat on.

Mary meanwhile is doing her own bundling-up. Both girls have a few serious farewells to say — a doll, a picture, a pup, their bedrooms where they have spent their Youth. Mary's mother nags, as usual, but Mary is singularly mature and patient with her. Just before leaving she swipes her lipstick. Finally both girls kiss their elders goodbye, feeling an unexpected moment of terrible sadness, hypocrisy and guilt — and leave their homes, as they suppose, Forever.

If their families weren't four-fifths blind with everyday living they would have noticed that in all those clothes, no matter how well concealed by overcoats, both girls are suddenly as fat as bears. But Mary's mother misses it altogether. And Diane's grandmother merely remarks, casually, as she watches Diane waddle away to meet her friend, that the child is certainly getting awfully hippy.

With their meeting, the runaway officially begins; and in their first moments they are as shy as newlyweds.

They take care to go right towards school by the usual route until they are well out of sight of any who might notice them; by then they are so near they can't resist the thrill of watching, from within precarious ambush, while the last late children hurry in. It is a large, grim, wonderful moment: from now on they are really cut off from the world and are marked women, minor criminals, in for big trouble if and when they are caught.

[8]

But this mainly excites them and makes them feel grown-up. A still bigger moment follows, as they get rid of their excess baggage — i.e., their schoolbooks. These are much too sacred to be chucked in an ashcan; that is why Diane saves out her Catechism and Mary, the one textbook she really likes. They find a place where the books can be hidden without harm to them, and hide them with the solemnity almost of burial. This is an act of profound violation, almost sacrilege: they feel more cut-off and grown-up than ever. They get right down to business — boarding their streetcar; and during the streetcar trip they sit very still and self-conscious, transfixed by that queer feeling of the essentially innocent, that if you are secretly guilty of something, the whole world knows it.

They get to the Station with almost a half-hour to spare, and Diane decides it's high time to let her brother know what's up. (He's still at home; he's on a later shift, in his overcrowded school.) In the booth scene both children get into the booth and shut the door and all but drown in the sweat of their superfluous clothing; we are in with them; and we intercut with the brother, and with his mother, who is curious about the call though not markedly so — it was, after all, Diane's birthday. The brother is shocked: they'd better get right back to school before they run into a lot of trouble. So Diane, with Mary's help, starts embellishing a fantastic tale of woe about herself and her friend Mary (he isn't overjoyed to hear she's coming along, either); and once the brother is convinced, he is all protectiveness and responsibility. Sure he'll help them. Sure he'll do what they say (i.e., run away with them; he's trying to outfox his listening mother). And naturally he won't tell anyone, what do they take him for. They are to phone him

[9]

the minute they get to town — don't come to the house, just phone; then he'll tell them what to do next. How soon will they be there? They are flabbergasted — they realize they don't know how long it takes; but they tell him they are taking the train, right away. Okay, he'll check it from his end.

It all comes to a dollar seventy-five. Urgent, sweating, frantic business of breaking enough change, trying to figure how many quarters, etc. etc. But they feel the call was a grown-up move, and a success, and with seconds to spare, proceed to the ticket window — where for the first time they realize they haven't anywhere near enough money.

They aren't daunted, though: they soon hit on a good scheme. They will invest enough of their money to get them well out past the edge of the city, and then hitch rides. They buy tickets to an outlying suburb and spend their short wait in necessities enhanced by their excitement: going to the bathroom. While Diane goes in we stay with Mary, who is standing lookout, at the main door, her eyes veering about for any possible pursuer; then Diane comes out and we watch her at sentry-duty while Mary goes in. Then Mary comes out; her mouth is a great gash of lipstick. "Okay", she says briskly, and they hurry to their train.

We cut to the home of Diane's brother Tommy; his mother is beginning to lose her natural decency in favor of her curiosity about the odd, long call; she starts a mild, quasi-tactful third-degree. Tommy is holding out all right.

The little girls get off into the quietude of a suburban station; it is late morning. Now their adventure, they feel, is <u>really</u> begun. They buy a few cents-worth of gum and walk

[10]

out through town onto the Highway and, after several failures, hitch a ride.

The minute they are in the car they know they are in danger. It has never until this moment occurred to them that the man who gives them the ride is bound to be rather curious about two children who, before they know better, ask if he is on his way to Monterrey. The driver, luckily for them, is not very smart and not very nosey; his curiosity is exceedingly idle; so that their frantic and not too skilful improvising of lies, for a while, gets by him; but the episode is full of suspense, of a terrible kind for them and an amusing kind for us, and they soon realize they can't get away with this kind of bluffing much longer. They are saved by the gong: i.e., by seeing, not far ahead of them, where the Highway crosses railroad tracks. They bluff their way out of the car, with many thanks, on horribly thin ice, and it goes out of sight, and, with enormous relief, they start off down the tracks of a different railroad line, in the wrong direction. (It is high noon now; how we indicate, as I think we should at this moment, their horrible mistake, I don't yet know.)

They decide to stick to the railroads from now on. Both have that deep romantic idea, of childhood, which applies so much more glamorously still to tracks than to roads — that if you follow the tracks they will lead you anywhere on earth except where you have to take a ship. Also they begin naively to become aware of a great distinction among travelers. Drivers of autos are apt to be respectable, nosey, not of their side but of the opposition. But along the railroad, if they only avoid railroad men, things are different — they will encounter only hoboes, and hoboes will be on their side; they won't ask questions, or tell on them. They even realize that they can hop freights, and this strikes

[11]

them correctly, as a much braver way to travel than by hitchhiking.

The rest of their day, which is from a third to half the picture and is the main substance and fun of it, I have not yet worked out either in continuity or much detail, but here are a few notes on its general spirit and content:

We know, from the start, that they are headed in the wrong direction. They learn this much later, as I will come to; they start out now with the greatest certitude and self-confidence and with a high kind of inner gayety which at times they find impossible to contain within their delight at being grown-up and doing something big-time. Somewhat later on, in addition to the pathos of their wrongness of direction, we begin to intercut the realization, on the part of their parents, that they are missing and are running away; Tommy, the brother, finally breaks down under third-degreeing maybe; in any case by midafternoon, with school out and the party ready except for the guest of honor, things begin to look funny; the whole business spreads, fast, until cops are alerted, it's on the radio, and the general alarm is out. The alarm is of course misplaced in its concentration, because by now it is known that they are headed for Monterrey, but all the same we begin to know that all the brave hope and effort of our friends is doomed, and we know it long before they do.

Of their adventures along the way — let's say for the moment, up to late afternoon, I am sure of this much:

Both episodes mentioned in the news story — the big dog, and the teen-age boys, are worth using. With the dog, we realize almost from the start that he's harmless, affectionate, baffled

[12]

by their fright; that his sheer outlandish size, plus the fact that he's a stranger, accounts for their gentle terror. We watch it thoroughly in their terms, as thoroughly as through our own perceptions, and we know they are not at all cowardly in their fear, just mistaken; nevertheless it is essentially a comic episode.

The teen-age boy business can be quite a little horror-story, of a fairly gentle kind. I am thinking mainly of the terrifying shapelessness and asininity of many boys of that age, especially when, through being parts of a little mob, they are afraid to show their natural good sense and humaneness. One among them should have traces of this, and betray them under pressure; one should be the Born Leader; the rest are neutral slobs. They find some thing, in these younger girls, to scare and bully; that's about all, except that it is enhanced by the relatively genteelness, besides the femininity, of the little girls. Also there is a fierce unconscious or semi-conscious streak of sexual cruelty involved — or merely, of subliminal sexual awareness, on both sides; but this is only very subtly shaded, for those who are interested; for the general reception, these are just rough boys, troubling nice little girls. The girls run and hide in high grass or weeds, as in the actual story, and the boys chunk ricks in after them; and after a while it is safe to come out. "If my brother was here", Diane tells them — and realizes how helpless he would be, and exaggerates his age by a good five years. One thing we do in this episode is to counterbalance our exceptionally gentle picture of childhood, of a certain kind, with a goosefleshy picture of "youth" at its foulest — the foulest, anyhow, that is moderately normal; for these boys shouldn't any more be "delinquents" than our girls are.

In addition to these small adventures I have, mainly, the

[13]

feeling that there mustn't be too many but, if anything, too few; and that they mustn't be too dramatic or extraordinary, or more than a little too many to really happen under these circumstances in a real day. I am equally in favor of there being a roughly balancing number of episodes which have no drama or dramatic shape at all, but are purely genre comedy. Taking these latter first, I think of two:

Once they first get into the swing of things, along the tracks, the girls are feeling so good they forget they are big-shots and express their exuberance as they would naturally as children. They start all of childhood's fascination with walking the rails and with counting and skipping ties, and with how many paces make a mile, and who can walk the rails the longest, and so on; and this only melts out of them as the sun gets hotter and they begin to shed their spare clothes and tie them into bundles and to eat. (This shedding and re-donning of clothes offers convenient devices for dissolve &c.) By the time they are hungry they are ravenous and go through their little lunches, plus their supplementary icebox scavengings, like wild beasts. They suddenly realize something important; they have forgotten to bring along anything to drink, and when you are hot and hungry it is hard to eat that fast without liquid. This brings a stop in which they are as ill-prepared for trouble as they were for the hitch-hike problem: ordering a couple of cokes, at a roadside stand near a railroad crossing, they abruptly find, again, how much they are looked-at; and they know that from here on out their problems of eating and drinking are complicated. The world is shutting down on them.

For another non-dramatic episode, sparked by a trackside billboard or just out of general conversation, they talk a little about the movies. They both love the movies, but they

[14]

love them different ways. The stuff that can be had fun with here is obvious — not just with movies but with these two kinds of innocence. The only sample I have so far, might or might not stay:

MARY: The one I love is Victor Matoor.[2]
DIANE: <u>Honest</u>? The one I love is Bugs Bunny.

---

2. Victor Mature (1915–1999), American actor.

MARY: Gosh. Bugs? Why?
DIANE: Cause he's just like Tommy.
MARY (politely) — Oh.
DIANE (politely) — Why do you love Victor Matoor?
MARY (dreamy) — He's got such dreamy muscles.
DIANE —- Well who wants muscles?

I am not sure but what the more dramatic episodes I think of, so far, are a little too dramatic — or anyhow, pile on a little too heavily, for one day's wandering. But they have the virtue of being what the two might walk into, quite logically, in such a trip.

One is pure melodrama: they get caught in a narrow cut, or on a trestle, with a fast train. In the first case they are not in great danger but they think they are, and are in great terror, through power and momentum and noise. In the second we either milk it for the maximum possible terror and suspense, or spare the children, and everyone else, only indicating what might have happened.

(Before I forget to I will add a couple of other less dramatic incidents:

They really do consider hopping a freight, on the proper up-grade; but are so awed by its majesty and crushing force, as it saunters by, that they put that idea out of their heads. A

[15]

hobo, grinning, salutes them; and they, reduced to size, wave back.

They see ahead of them a section-gang — people who might notice them or tell on them — and elaborately circumvent them. Or before they can hide, a motorized handcar whizzes past them, with every man on it looking at them curiously, and they have the fear: "Gosh, when they get to town they'll Talk."

And conceivably, they become briefly and pleasantly involved with people who live in a trackside shanty.

The other episode: Warned by their shaky experience in a roadside stand, the girls go into a small-city grocery to buy canned food to take on the road with them — good solid stuff like canned sauerkraut, corned-beef hash, and chocolate bars ("it keeps your energy up"). (Later they may or may not confront a cattle-car on a siding and get into an argument on eating meat: "but this isn't meat, it comes from Argentina"); and a moment when, hungry, they find themselves without canopeners and bash the cans open with rocks.) During these scenes of drifting uneasily into the town and shopping, they begin to realize they are being watched and cautiously followed by a man. They are afraid it is a detective or a truant officer; by now they know that, school being out, they are missed and sought-for. Then he catches up. We soon recognize him as something infinitely more sinister than they had feared — a graduate psychopathic pederast, interested in leading little girls into cellars, ravishing them, and dismembering what's left of them. If this is used at all — and it is a logical hazard children-at-large have to reckon with — I feel it should be used very thin and light. There is the chance, of course, of a terrifying suspense sequence, growing most of its terror and suspense on the children's being taken

[16]

in by him — great relief over his not being The Law or such; Gee what a nice man, and so on; and in any case he should be played very nice and charming — a man who in every sense of the word loves children. But I would prefer that, after we have suffered for a very short time our awareness and their innocence of what he is, they themselves become aware, vaguely, instinctively, that there is something terribly wrong with him; that they are somehow in danger. Obviously these two approaches can be combined; it is a question of degree and shading; within the modest and gentle surfaces I imagine proper to the story, we should only breathe cold on the children, and the audience.

As much as anything, through the events of this afternoon, we are centering simply on the increasing tiredness of the children and, as they grow more and more experienced and tired, their increasing devotion to their idea and to each other. . . tremendous and quietly increasing loyalty to each other, as each loses personal heart, and loyalty to their sense of life as, in a sense, they begin to fail that. I think at some latter stage, basically through fatigue, also through a profound difference in kind, through which they could never later on be such friends and helpers, they fall into a quarrel which, under the circumstances, is more than they can bear and through that fact rather than any "incident", reconcile, into the maturest friendship either has ever known.

There does finally come a point though, when the sun has lowered so much that they begin to realize where the shadows are cast. One says to the other: "Look." They both do; and they both realize: all this time they have been going in the wrong direction. They just sit down in silence and put their arms around each other. Then with no words and with a very great and touching courage —

[17]

clearly not at all thinking of giving up and going home, but only of going to Monterrey – they get up and start in the opposite direction. (By the way, a blister on the heel might well enhance their troubles and persistence.)

At this point everything, below the still realistic surface, begins to be strange. The swiftly developing darkness, and the weariness and courage and disheartenment of the children, lends this strangeness even to the surface; but by subtle shading, which we touch in only enough to involve those who are interested in the realization, the children become surrogates for much more than their own predicament: they become all of hope, and youthfulness, and certainty, at that later stage in which these are broken, but a stoic courage and devotion still keeps you moving towards your determined, stubborn destination; and then, gradually, that too alters, and we realize that all of life, in sufficient fatigue, wants more than anything else just to get home again; to hell with the hopes and the goals. Their deep mutual loyalty and their deep inner courage contests this but they very gradually collapse and admit it, and even become shyly articulate, and then frank, about what they want and what they fear. More than anything, they want to give this up, to be home again, to be taken care of. But just as this increases, so also do shame and regret at their weakness increase; and, still more, fear of what they face: fear of failure, fear of their parents, fear of punishment. And in the larger terms — an increasing hunger and fear, combined, for the time we may at last stop trying, and lie down and die; and for Judgement, however harsh.

We use no "incidents" in this sequence; but once we have established their goose-crawly sense of decline and yearning and

[18]

fear, we intercut with what really awaits them — the parents, the Gods, they must return to so inevitably — worried sick, fighting among themselves, the beginnings of a rebirth of love through catastrophe, and so on.

The girls, quite some while after dark, chilled to the bone in spite of re-clothing themselves, sight a service station at a grade-crossing and make for it, for warmth. They can't stand to really go in and give themselves up; they sneak into the Ladies' comfort station and stand close together, their teeth rattling; and are burst in on by a lady driver, and go on their way.

The shining of the next service station is too much for them. They don't even need to consult, more than by shy glance and a touching of hands. They walk right up to the bright lights and in through the door. The man who runs it, an almost boyishly young-looking Mexican, is arguing with someone over the phone. "Well tell him to come around and tell it to me." Pause. "Well just tell him he can —" A glance at the girls . . . "Tell him he knows what he can do with his, with —" Meanwhile his little bakelite radio finishes a Latin-American piece of music and blats out another announcement, the first the girls have heard, about them. Five hundred dollars reward. The young man says to the phone, "just a second. Hey. Hey. Call me up. I mean — I'll call you back. Huh?" He looks at the little girls. They look at him. He phones: "give me the police." The children flinch. The man, gently: "That's all right muchachas, don't be afraid."

Rough sketch of the payoff:

Mother, having broken down Tommy and heard of the runaway and the general alarm, drives down with him in a rush (from a nearer [19] home, presumably, than Monterrey.) Her mother-in-law: "Oh! You brought Tommy?" Mama (snarling): "Well where would I leave him!" Papa: "Honey. Honey."

From the service-man's call to the local police we cut straight to both families, linked like binary stars in 2 cars, driving fast towards the police station. From there we cut to the station: cops, on the whole nice guys, and a reporter, and a news photographer. The reporter asks Mary: "Did he bite you?" Mary replies: "No he didn't bite us, but he sniffed at us." Diane nods gravely. Both are half-asleep, eating hamburgers. The press photographer sets up a picture — now hold the book up, Mary, so's we can see what it says". Mary sadly, uncomprehendingly obliges; their temples lean together over the title, The Bobsey Twins in the Great West. There is a stir; the parents come in fast.

In the last we have seen of them, when they first hear where their children are, all their love and anxiety has been lost in exasperation: just wait till I get my hands on the little bitch; and we, like the children, in front of the cops and press, are extremely shy — quite a surprise to themselves. A little bit of hypocritical sweetness, not much; more of a touch of restrained threat; a shading of strong but indefinable but restrained emotions. The only emotional moment just now is for Diane when, to her amazement, her brother walks in. She looks at him as if he were a ghost and bursts into silent tears.

The reward is mentioned. "Hell," says the young man, "I don't want a reward. I got kids of my own."

It is only after they are all on the way home that they begin to coalesce. Mary, sitting in her mother's lap beside her father, looks up curiously into her mother's

[20]

face, which is far more tender than we have ever imagined it could be. Her mother becomes aware of the look. "Mary", she says — with the edge in her voice — "why on <u>earth</u>!" And Mary says: "I was rather angry with you, Mother, but I'm not any more." Her mother has an impulse to embrace her, which she inhibitedly restrains; Mary, hurt for a moment, on sudden impulse embraces and kisses her, and this is returned with a whole heart, while the father, shy and moved, keeps his eyes on the road.

In the other car Diane and her brother, very drowsy in the back seat, are in each others' arms. They become a little more awake, and smile, in perfect happiness. In the front seat their parents, without looking at them or at each other, are deeply aware of this. The father says: "We've got to do something, honey. I don't know what it is but we can't go on like we've been. We've got to do <u>something</u>." No answer for a moment; then, moved, she puts her hand on his knee. "Well anyhow we can <u>try</u>", she says.

★   ★   ★

[21]

★ ★ ★ ★ ★ ★ ★

The whole charm and quality of the basic news story and of what can best be developed out of it resides, I think, in the fact that these are eminently normal, average children — not delinquents or neurotics. The one exceptional thing about them is that they actually do what most healthy children dream of at some time, but never carry so far. Everything else about the story is, in its best interests, as unexceptional as possible. In their motives for running away, for instance, there should be no enormous social or psychological pressures — only just as much, available and recognizable, as in the average family; to spark the wish and fuel the action. In their adventures enroute, again, it would work against the best spirit of the story if they should encounter anything really improbable in this simple context, or should run into plot complications. So, too, at the end: nothing of major significance, in any customary sense, is to be proved or developed or solved. There should be only the tenderly indicated defeat of a certain high kind of courage and hope; and victory of certain kinds of weakness and need and love (which in the opening sequence were badly at odds, and are now, if only temporarily, resolved).

Unless these children are as normal as Penrod we have no story — or we don't have this story, which on its surface is purely for fun; the pleasure of seeing how much can be made of how little; the illusion of an improvisation — and at the same time so much more.

Actually, we are handling a gigantic theme, very quietly. It is much larger than if the children were mere protagonists for a reproval of divorce, the Pace of Modern Life. etc. We are talking

[22]

more of biology than sociology.

By biology in this context I mean: these children aren't just running away, they are running toward something. In flight they express their whole awakening sense, at their age, of the tremendous potential expansion of life, and self-reliance, and freedom. The comedy and pathos come of their premature bid for all this; and of their innocence, defenselessness and courage in trying to make it work. By the time the darkness settles down they have become universal as well as personal representatives of hope, courage, and the facing of defeat and judgment.

It is for such reasons, and for the delicate tragic-comedy intrinsic in the whole situation, that I want to avoid plowing too deep in the story, or giving it too powerful a frame. Putting it briefly, their unhappy reasons for running away should be as light as possible, not as strong; their adventures should show us the terror and wonder and happiness, not of the exceptional, but of the ordinary; the essential story line is emotional; and the end is not too emphatic or grandscale. We end with a mild, encouraging betterment of what we began with.

[F 2: Film Outline: "Twilight"]

[title page]

TWILIGHT
a short outline of an original story
by
Manuel Conde[3]
and
James Agee
proposcd for a film in
three-dimensional color.

Feb. 22, 1952

[1]

THE PLACE:

A group of Polynesian islands, in the mid-Pacific.

THE TIME:

Early nineteenth century.

THE THEME:

Our purpose is to show one kind of human and natural perfection — one version of the ancient dream of an Earthly Paradise — during the last days before its invasion and destruction.

We show this chiefly through a story of the development to manhood and to heroism of two youths, one European, the other Asiatic. Through them and their experiences, and through a few supporting characters, we show most of the major events and meanings of life as it was lived in this semi-legendary world. Above all we show their mutual loyalty, even under stress of acute rivalry in love; the increase in their mutual affection and esteem, through this honorableness; and their

---

3. Manuel Conde (1924–), Filipino actor, cinematographer, and producer. In 1953 Agee turned down the chance to write the screenplay for John Huston's *Moby Dick* to work with Conde on *Ghengis Khan*.

continual deepening of courage and humanity, against human, natural and supernatural antagonists.

[F 3: Notes on Untitled Film Treatment: "Boy and Girl and Musician"]

[1]

& Parents' quietness & sedateness must be gotten clear. & & & & & & &

---

or the intense & extravagant adolescent love? Sneaking in windows, parental opposition, &c. middle-class boy, lower-class girl, her parents assume

---

his purely rakish & snobbish attitude, her contempt for them; he is excited into thinking they can do anything. Her bedroom, she has sexed up herself. He sees it when she is sick.

Home for Thanksgiving.

"I'll be twenty in two years".

Party for them, which he doesn't want.

Long cold walk.

After all night up, 4 next afternoon. He phones (they are upstairs?) "Hello. Can you talk?" "Sure I can talk. What do you mean?" "I just meant could you—" ["]How do you feel?" "I'm all right how are you" I'm fine. (———). Say. (   ). did you have any trouble?" "Well, some. Did you?" "Some." "Say. I don't think I can get out tonight." "I can't either." "I wish I could." "I wish I could, too." "I love you———." (Quick cut to her.) "I love you too." "I'll get out tonight if I possibly can." "You better not try because I know I can't." "Well: see you tomorrow at — —'s." "Goodbye." "Goodbye, darling." "———" "Goodbye."
at hang up cut, like switching on a light, to after-supper sitting around. Him; mother; father; sister (mad as all hell); clock. Him; father; mother; clock 40 min later; sister (chin trembling); to vibration of clock's pre-striking whir.

8:30. cut to mother. Hands relax.

(night shots, of each, & of parents. "12, I don't want to deprive Emma of going to the movies because of what you've done. &c &c.

But you must absolutely <u>promise</u> me." "Sure I promise." (So, watch in window? get her attention?) & back home, happy as hell. Singing in car; baffled sister & with his mother, that night: "<u>why</u> I <u>wouldn't</u> <u>any</u> <u>more</u> <u>touch</u> <u>her</u> <u>than</u> . . . ! ! !"

(sound of father winding clock)

next night:

> Dear ——. I've been trying half the night to write you a poem, but I couldn't seem to write anything that was worthy of you. I will quote the only lines I think are fit to preserve. They are:
>
> _____
>
> _____
>
> but they don't one thousandth express my emotions about you and what could? Sometimes I wonder whether when people write the great Love Poems they really feel in love at the time [illegible].

with her father: "Mother wanted me to speak to you. (Threat re boy.) Let me tell you and you can tell him from me. If that boy ever so much as touches you, the wrong way, that is, I'll
maybe in bed; he on cheek or burying forehead or lips in pillow;
she, flat on back, eyes open—
after all-night, she makes him leave her around corner (he peers through bush & she goes thru screen door); sudden heroic closeup of both parents; dissolve to his entrance & his parents. Perhaps the first lines of each; cut to bedroom, waking up.
Lonesome & Sorry⁴ is his tune, Hi Ho the Merry Oh⁵ is the other guy's? Party next afternoon, swimming, clambake? evening; drink to me only with thine eyes &c—(He doesn't quite know all words).
later his sister falls; he gives advice?

[2]

"It won't do you any harm to stay in for once anyway."

---

4. "Lonesome and Sorry," music by Con Conrad and lyrics by Benny Davis (1921).

5. "Heigh-Ho the Merri-O," music by Jimmy McHugh and lyrics by Harold Adamson for the film _Youth Takes a Fling_ (1938).

[5]

then the restiveness & unease—the 3 phases of questioning; reading; arguing; discussion of parents ("I think your parents are very nice"); cut to new character; his arrival: beachwagon to meet: &c then to [illegible] meeting with girl?—or, get the suspense the minute he comes in?

"Where's he from?" (Buck)?:(knows). They stage party for him—

(He tests B. out on the party idea. B explains, why do it? Mine never give parties. They give all the parties.)

Start with tennis. She is there. He is nervous, but proud of his tennis. Does well. Tomorrow night at ——'s.

Tennis mentioned. Jim's good. Oh, I'm not so hot. Oh, don't be silly. Jim, you are good and you know it.

> (he had been showing her tennis? Now who is shows her?)
>   Also their mild estrangement is such that when Moor ball—suspects & says "I don't want to muscle in on any-body's woman" They reassure him &c &c. or does the girl who was 1st interested in him? good.

"you take life so seriously Jim, why can't you just have fun sometimes."

3 friends after: "Gee he's quite a nice guy". (1—with difficulty) "Yeah." "Buck. "Aw, I don't think he's so hot." "What's wrong with him"? "Oh he's all right I guess." Slam car door. Cut to slap of ball. J's face. Ready? Girls are playing. J at side, uneasy, watching her. Beachwagon up; Moor, perfectly dressed, good press. English racket, gets out. She misses a ball. He calls out some cheerful advice. She smiles at him nervously. The set ends as she misses another. Now doubles or singles? Or leave out all this and start cold with their singles-match?

"let's play some more sometime." (polite).

"Swell, I'd like to."

(cut to fantasy, heads, umpires, lawn tennis, demoniacal drives, the pleasant grin, J leaps the net, shakes hands, holds the cup, Jim you out-did yourself" (cut to bed). his face, sneering at it all. WHAM. sneer. hand rubs over face in misery & tired sleeplessness.

[6]

End of date. "See you tomorrow night?" "I'm sorry Jim I'm busy". Kiss.

phone call: "Hello——. Whatya doin tonight?" "—— had me up to Camden." "Oh really?" "Sure." "All I mean is that's nice isn't it?" ["]See you tomorra night maybe?" "Gee it's an absolute shame, Jim, but I'm busy tomorra night too. I'm <u>awfully</u> sorry. Let's make it Saturday night for certain. Huh?

(you know, you <u>do</u> talk too much darling.)

"Yeah, I guess I ought to be able to make it all right." Slow slack hangup, sadness, dentist drilling. His assistant. Short episode.

Moor leaves sooner, has meant no harm, but she feels jilted. So, return to J?

Last night of summer? music?

(Also, earlier, has fantasy of Moor there?)

different intensities & size of dissolve, for face?

late summer. "What's become of ——?"

"Haven't seen her for a week." Very empty, sad, sees her out of pure nostalgia, it is not at all good.

J, alone, to place they spent the night?

how end? early morning, train leaving? shots from rear of train, & from track of receding train; face in train; shift of semaphore? start & end with baggage &c.

cut to school. getting a letter, reading it. Empty & gone. Slowly, to library. Double closeup.

3 divisions? June, July, August?

77th Haydn

#3 op 22, Hindemith

Op 74 Beethoven

[7]

musician, adolescent boy & girl, place a few miles down beach? all 3 are new to the place? i.e., there for the summer? No, boy has been there before. girl & musician are new.

———————————

Schubert B♭ Major Trio.

4 mvts to picture. 1st, the hall? Meeting each other? By end of evening it must be definitely cinched?

Intermezzo; development of tension to create plausibility of late-night scene?

2<u>nd</u>: late night—all night. Ecstasy mv't.

Intermezzo; development of rise yet fall of love. sense of need to recapture.

3<u>rd</u>: clearly & fully in trouble; lack of love, change of heart, quarreling, loss of interest, mutual criticism.

Intermezzo; beginning of other interest.

4<u>th</u>: return to hall.

---

the essential emotion, that of ecstatic discovery; the objective emotion, that of pity and of innocence.

first must get intense loneliness of one, emptiness of the other (or her sense of it once they make out).

Combine with Petrouchka?[6] (How get the Moor in, late?)

Any parental or avuncular advice?

(his kind of love wd for a while very much excite her by its new-ness?) Then she wd be bored by it, or see the Moor's much more favorably, or as relief.

Sh'd have operatic or ballet simplicity; broad, limpid movements.

20's or present?

---

shd there be a class-difference in the Moor too? More money? At least, Petrouchka sh'd have that illusion about him?

Moor comes to visit people by whom they are accepted, but the false acceptance of democracy.

Tunes: 1926: <u>Lonesome and Sorry</u>, <u>Bye Bye Blackbird</u>,[7] <u>Little Gipsy Sweetheart (?)</u>,[8] <u>Hi Hi The Merry O</u>,

---

6. Igor Stravinsky's ballet *Petrouchka* (1935) concerns a love triangle involving the title character, a ballerina, and a Moor.

7. "Bye Bye Blackbird," music by Ray Henderson and lyrics by Mort Dixon (1926).

8. "Gypsy Love Song (Slumber On, My Little Gypsy Sweetheart)," music by Victor Herbert and lyrics by Harry B. Smith, from the operetta *The Fortune Teller* (1898).

2 Black Crows.
slang: get letters &c.

---

away 2 weeks visiting friend?

[8]

she goes to party there, invited by Moor, he is invited too but is very unhappy? she is secret & noncommittal? "Is anything the trouble?" "What do you mean?" Where else besides basketball court? dance hall; then lack the basketball, spring dance, so early morning & bright chilly night?
or should the thing die a natural death? If so how? (After all, I never had this experience).

Or another way: whole course of longer affair, 4 years or so, beginning adolescence, on through to where one marries, other is single in New York?
"Did you ever love anyone else?" "No", (a lie). (Silence). "Did you?" "No. That in I've never loved anybody the way I love you." (Silence). "Did you?" (Silence). "No."
      cut. different place.
      "Did you ever kiss anyone else?" (Silence.) "Yes." (truth). "Did you?" "Yes" (a lie). "But it was never anything like kissing you." (silence.) "Was it with you?" "No." (she begins to doubt it.)
      (He watches her. He sees 1, 2, 3, whom he knows, kissing her. He is very unhappy. Unhappily, for reassurance and comfort, he tries to kiss her himself. She does not want him to.)
      "Did you ever, do anything with anyone else?" "I just mean make love?"
      This kind of questioning—i.e., that he can enter no new experience without more curiosity than it will bear, is very destructive to them.
very sincere defenseless talk, very cynical writing. Both make her uneasy.

Or more properly P. shd be so shy of the girl that the Moor has no reason to know he is horning in. He has no quality of, or right to, proprietorship.

---

boy & girl & musician. She goes to musician's room?

---

brother & younger sister.

"I guess there are just some people that don't ever give parties."

They stay around too much, the parents, & everything has a labored & improvised quality. He is intensely embarrassed because of the girl?

His sister cries?

Borrowed records?

[F 4: Notes on Untitled Film Treatment: "Planter's Son"]

[1]

pre-Civil-war child of planters or of visiting Northerners. Not happy with parents but not specially miserable. Or citified; perhaps sissy? Wanders into deep woods out of pure interest. Discovers a mysterious hut, probably deep in swamp. Negroes live there; runaway slaves. They take care of him. They must all live in secrecy & hiding. No dog: he would bark: maybe a hunting cat? Fires, when? Only at night? The light would show. Only by day? The smoke would show. Probably a carefully covered bed of constantly smoldering coals. All cooking on this; & warmth in winter. They have a little girl? And a baby? Or no: he asks: they say: "You can't keep a baby from hollering." Some very old man or woman? [illegible] flashback into [illegible] Voodoo? Or anyhow—yes—they take the sick girl for voodoo.

Process of living; adventures in hunting; emotional developments.

The woman is sometimes homesick? Flashback?

This is during the war? And now, when they are found, the war is over and they are free?

Burial of the little girl?

Story episode? Story by the man? A very dark story?

When he finds cabin he finds the baby? Alone? No. The cabin, empty.

Or, now that the little girl is dead, they start North?

Or how are they found again? How does the little boy reunite with his parents? & what is the payoff?

Fat from animals, for candles.

Or: not slaves: perhaps not even that period: make a mystery of their secrecy & silence.

A big summer storm.   A snowing winter night; essence of security. Any farming?

A hunt passes them by?

Negroes really on their own.

Starry night. One chief episode for each season?

Or, a negro eavesdrops on the voodoo interview? You see his face, at end? He follows & finds where they are?

Is there a fight? Does the boy take part? No firearms on N's side, of course. Primitive weapons.

Why not "little boy we gonna show you your way back?" Why wdn't they? & why wdn't he go?

No: probably no fight: just silence and submission: one of hunters starts to hit: another, a superior, cither says none of that, or hits him down from the side.

Wife of planter offers to buy them? Then tells them they are free? What is the parting scene?

They ask if they can just go back & live where they were?

They are allowed. And corn & a gun & a dog?

He comes running. He never wants to leave them again. They tell him he must. He walks away. "I'll come back. Every summer, I'll come back." Dissolve or cut to his meeting with his parents. Very shy & very silent on all sides. They too have improved in his absence. It must show in all their faces. Train bell, through scene? Evening scene: he is saying he must certainly go back; his mother is [illegible] him he will if he wants. Father [illegible] nothing. Paper announcing the firing on Sumter?

Or, writing a note or letter that night:

April ?, 1861   were letters dated at
                        head or foot? I hope at foot?

Dear Cousin Bess and Cousin Tom:

Our young prodigal arrived this afternoon as per schedule, safe and sound, and I must confess it has been worth every moment of our many months of sorrow and bereavement.

[2]

Start with breakfast on their next-to-last morning. Boy is staring glumly from face to face. Faces shd be not unkindly, but very difficult to sympathize with or feel much warmth from. General quality of discontent on all sides. Introduce the yellow-boy? Has personal servant? This embarrasses him—so, [illegible] relationship?

Don't want to go back? No, sir.

Didn't get much out of life here though, did you?

No, sir.

Why not?   kinda tends to bullying him I reckon

I don't know, sir.

I reckon it's just hard to get used to (cousin Bess); it takes a while.

Yes, ma'am.

(his father): I'm afraid it ain't that. I'm afraid our Johnny is just a very manly boy.

(mother): Phil! (but her face, as J sees it, is utterly inadequate.)

(shot of the boy cousin.) He sure don't take to ridn, worth shucks.

(his father): Beauregard. That's enough out of you, sir.

Yes, sir.

I don't know whose lan' it is, but—

"It's my land."

"I ain't got no money, sir, but if they was work I could do, to go back and have squatter's rights . . ."

"Don't see no need. Tain't worth nothing to me." (offers him corn, a rifle, gunpowder) "Just see you stay away from my niggers so's they don't get ideas (to his slave,) That goes for you too, understand me? I catch you prowlin around out that way, I'll skin you alive."

"Mighty lonesome life you askin for. But it's your life."

N: Yes, sir.

"No decent human wants to break up a family, but you get a good offer, you can't let sentiment stand in your way."

Hitting the guy who was about to strike the N: "That your property?"

To yellow boy: "I don't lose no love to tattletales." (Boy shd look murder. Faces of other N's.)

Fight between cousins? "Livin with niggers." "Say that again." (He does. Too contemptuous to get his guard up.)

(Hero gets licked after a good fight?) (A beats B pretty hard: stops: B continues: is beaten bad this time. A helps him up: respect and liking; which B begins to feel too.) B: " I shouldn't have come at you that second time." A: "That ain't nothin'."

[F 5: Notes on Untitled Film Treatment: "2 Soldiers"]

Field & [illegible] morning.

    Ravine.

    2 soldiers.

ball, beaten mouth, owl's flight, moisture, tree, root, [illegible], water, birds, fight forgotten, stretcher bearers, dead [illegible], lanterns, rain, suffering [illegible]. Leaning over edge of ravine, turning [illegible]: empty field, smell of violence & rain, [illegible] smoke; silence; sound from all sides; || the [illegible] of flesh immediately after surgery; noises multiplying on irregular country, of withdrawal of both armies.

    Fading of sound & its meaninglessness to the soldiers. Sound of raw breath & of its cessation || dying old woman. Running off of rain, bank worse of branch. Last silence before morning, [illegible] single string against it. Field [illegible], roosters in unblemished country like starlight. Silence: emergence of all things from darkness, taking on color. Sunup. Thrush up.

    Close on to 2 soldiers, first clear view. One, limestone head & blowing brown hair. Other, hurt near heart.

    The second hears the thrush & smiles. After a little, he opens his eyes.

    Sings grief, grief, grief; previous, previous, previous; reprieve, reprieve, reprieve.

[F 6: Radio Play: "In Goblin Land"]

[1]

"In GOBLIN Land"

Oct. 29, 1935

STATION KDKA[9]

Good afternoon. How do you do! To Goblin Land we welcome you. We don't serve coffee and we don't serve tea, but we've a surprise, just wait and see. In Goblin land it's always dark, - Hush, here comes our President, Mrs. Stark!

---

9. KDKA Pittsburgh, founded in 1920, is the oldest commercial radio station in the United States. Robert Saudek (1911–1997), Agee's roommate at Harvard, began his broadcasting career at KDKA, where Saudek's father was musical director. Saudek was also the creator of the *Omnibus* television series, for which Agee wrote the script for a five-part biography of the young Abraham Lincoln in 1952.

Mrs. Stark: This is my first visit to Goblin Land, that I'm quite over-come you may well understand. What are all those shadows moving around? Everyone is so quiet, they don't make a sound —-

Goblins — (Give Mrs. Stark the Locomotive)
GGGOOOBBBLLLiiiinnnsss –
Goblins —
    (Sing to the tune of John Brown's body)[10]
We are the Goblins of the Congress of Clubs[11]
We've come to bring you greetings,
And to prove we are no dubs
We bring to you a sixpence
And a pocket full of rye,
And we'll go marching on —-
Success, success, to the Congress,
Success, success, to the Congress,
Success, success, to the Congress,
And a pocket full of Money —- (finish on high key softly)

(Goblins march away from Mike, voices gradually fade out)

Mrs Stark laughs, applauds and says:

If the Goblins wishes just come true, I'll put my worries in my shoe. Look there is a Goblin drifting this way. Shall I ask its name, or what shall I say?

Hully: I'll call it. Here Goblin, do you have a name?

Gertrude: Gertrude Dodds, Goblin Gertie, it's one and the same —

Hully: Goblin Gertie, how quaint, Mrs. Stark, by the way, I'm going to ask Goblin Gertie to play The Witches dance by our friend MacDowell[.][12] You can almost hear the witches howl!

Gertrude: In Goblin land we try our best to grant the visitors request.

---

10. "John Brown's Body" (c. 1860), lyricist unknown, is adapted from William Steffe's camp-meeting song "Say Brothers Will You Meet Us on Canaan's Happy Shore," which later became "The Battle Hymn of the Republic."

11. An association of women's social clubs in Pittsburgh.

12. "The Witches' Dance" (1883) by Edward MacDowell.

Plays.
Applause.

Mrs. Stark: Here's another young Goblin strolling through, let's stop it and ask what it can do.

Hully: Do you whistle Goblin, or do you sing, or do you play on anything?

Helen: I'm Helen Hunt Allen, I fiddle and fiddle, with a string on each side and two in the middle – I'll play you a tune and lively as light – Kreisler's Tamborin Chinois[13]– A Chinese Delight.
Plays.
Applause after playing.

[2]

-2-

Here comes a whimsy as thoughtful as dawn – it carries a sheaf with words written on – Your name is your passport to Goblin Land, it will serve you as well as a magic wand – So who are you?

Mrs. Neff: I'm May T. Neff, I walk by myself and it walks with me but I've brought a poem for Mrs Stark which I wrote especially.
Reads poem
Applause

(Mrs Neff, please slide the "l" so it will rhyme more nearly with Neff – self, se'f-Neff, change voice slightly for the rhyme only)

Hully: We are going to have a one minute reception outside of Goblin Land for Mrs Stark to meet some of the chairmen of the different departments.

Mrs Giese: I am Lulu Giese of Drama, that's easy to remember, come 'round in November, you'll hear Mr. Gihon, that lion, that scion of KDKA, and now Mrs Stark, I bid you good day.

Mrs Rich: How do you do, Mrs. Stark, I am Aida Rich of the Evening Department. Inasmuch as the members of my department are employed

---

13. "Tambourin Chinois" (1910), by Austrian-born composer Fritz Kreisler.

in the daytime, we plan to relax in the evening and visit the most interesting and entertaining institutions in Pittsburgh, that is from our point of view. Of course, this includes the International, and the Cathedral of Learning, and any place that happens to interest us.

Mrs Stark: That sounds exciting. I'd like to follow that department myself.

Mrs Moon: Mrs Stark, you don't know me, I am Margaret Moon of the Department of Education. Our plan for the year is to study "Psychology" and learn something about "Man, the Unknown", meaning of course ourselves.

Mrs Stark: If we all learn something about ourselves, that is a step forward.

Mrs Eckel: Mrs Stark, I am glad you are our President this year. My name is Pauline Eckel (P. J.) of the School of Physical Education. We plan to do a lot of dancing before the year is over.

Mrs Stark: How do you do, Mrs Eckel, that sounds very good.

Mrs Doverspike: I am Mrs Doverspike from the very serious department of Home-Welfare. This year we are going to study family relations.

Mrs Stark: Well, you have a hard job, but it's a very worthy one.

Mrs Sandles: How do you do, Mrs Stark, I am Mrs Sandles of the Department of Music. We hope to develop our appreciation of music and learn a little more about it by the time the year is over.

Mrs Stark: That's a splendid idea. It would be fine if we could all do that.

Hully: Now we're back again in Goblin Land. Goblin Gertie please play the Juba Dance by Nathaniel Dett,[14] I see it at your finger tips, Goblins don't forget.
Plays.
Applause.

---

14. "Juba Dance," from Canadian-born composer Robert Nathaniel Dett's suite *In the Bottoms* (1913).

-3-

Hully: Here comes a tall Goblin, with grace and with ease,
  I'll get it to sing like a bird in the trees.

Elsie B: You've guessed it quite rightly, my name's Elsie Breese, - Mitchell, too, if that's not too long; But I have come here to sing you a song – "The Spooky Night" by Gerturde Rohrer,[15] and she's written many, many more.

Sings

Applause

Hully: Now here is a goblin as gay as a jockey,
  Hi, Goblin, your name?

Norma: Sire it's Norma Knocho. I'll play you a tune on my accordion now, Good luck Mrs Stark and good wishes to you.

Bert Layton – tap – tap

I see a strange goblin dancing around, with its head in the air and its feet on the ground – that's as it should be, its name is Bert Layton, go into your dance, we won't keep you waitin'.

Bert Layton tap dances

Applause

Choral: WE WANT TO SING! WE WANT TO SING!

Hully: Here's a whole group of Goblins, and each has a name, strange as it may seem not two are the same, they're the Congress Club Choral as lively as bees, and the Goblin directing, is again, Elsie Breese – They'll sing Will-o-the-wisp by Albert Sprouse,[16] poor will-o-the-wisp with never a house.

Song

Applause

Close with piano and violin duet.

(BE YOURSELF!!)

_____

15. Gertrude Martin Rohrer, among many other compositions, wrote the state song of Pennsylvania.

16. "Will-o'-the-Wisp" (1909) by Charles Gilbert Spross.

Notes, Fragments, and Outlines

FICTION

Regrettably, Agee never finished "In the White Light a Keener Whiteness Sparkled," a story of infidelity and desire. The fragment included here gives an indication of Agee's gift for short fiction, though, a genre in which, considering the amount of his production in other forms, he is somewhat underrepresented. "Orchard" is an intriguing beginning as well but, like the other fragmentary pieces in this section, more a hint of what might have been than actual accomplishment.

[N 1: Unfinished Short Story:
"In the White Light a Keener Whiteness Sparkled"]

1.   In the white light a keener whiteness sparkled, glanced, hovered in a rich fragrance, and as he lay with his eyes closed he felt in his body great fullness and great fear; candles in sunlight, the almost invisibly lofty glint of a plane; brambles burning, but noiselessly, each thorn a sparkle. Standing in God's holy fire; confined to fast in fires; in peace; almost in ecstasy.

As he came more awake he began to realize that his hands were moving upon his bony body, that he was turgid, and that he had been dreaming; and the terror which lay somewhere in the dream stayed with him like the smell of scorched cloth, and the peace, the joy, like the sparkling of white in whiteness and like the other fragrance which he could not identify.

To remember that he had dreamed; to feel any richness in his flesh; were both uncommon, unpurchasable privileges. He lay beneath the two luxuries, and tried to let himself sink again into the dream. But it was like lying underwater within reach of sunlight, or under the sun with only the eyelids between; and now he saw the pink-grey of his eyelids, and there was no use. As one might try to steal and eat candy in a schoolroom, he tried to reassemble the dream without letting himself or the dream know that that was his intention, or that he was awake to any intentions. He could bring nothing clearer; indeed, as he tried, the fragrance vanished, and the danger and the incredulous wonder, the white joy, filled him like invisible volumes in the air; even the molecular sparkling was altered; it became an invention of the eye, a poor improvisation, a false dream which he refused to accept.

Then he heard her, and a cold resentment flashed across him of which he scarcely knew, and now, almost as swiftly as water into sand, even the pleasure in his flesh was drunk off and drained away.

Subtly, beneath <u>his</u> pale lashes, he looked and saw her.

2.   She moved on her rather heavy heels, in the Japanese straw mules and the open coolie-coat, from the front room across to the chair by the window, carrying the red lacquer, gold-flowered

[2]

box in which she kept needles and buttons and thread and tape. There was no intentional loudness in her walk, but there was also no effort to walk quietly, and in this compromise he felt a kind of bitterness, of quiet contempt, which he could not blame but which he resented no less on that account. The resentment, however, was gone so swiftly that he hardly knew it; it only added its own stain to the inchoate tinges, almost tastes, of fear and pleasure into which he had wakened, and, now irretrievably awake, he set himself without reflection or effort to his customary task, of guarding his privacy, and spying on her.

She sat in the chair, sewing a strap to her girdle. Her stockings slithered at her shins. She was naked under the open coat and he avoided looking at certain parts of her body because he felt that to do so, spying, would be dishonorable and because it was unpleasant to. He watched her breasts and felt rather sadly, as he watched, that if only they had stayed as they used to be, everything might even now be all right. Very likely it was his own fault. He could think of few things, for a long time back, that were not, essentially, his own fault, when he came right down to it. They are not likely to come through an interrupted pregnancy very well. No, nor an uninterrupted one, either, unless you are very careful and very lucky.

Money helps, too.

The percolator gave its aluminum SNEEZE.

Again.

Fut-tut-umpt-trumptrump, tuttutumpflump-flutter.

She paid it no notice; none to the loud clock, either, her accomplice, his enemy too, like a housecat which one person loves, another endures, or the time-forcer, life-trapper, which might have lain in the basket in the hall, bedroom, might have made everything different, or better, or still worse.

Still worse, most likely.

Better for her, though.

He watched her face under the loose hair as she worked. It made him think of the faces in the subways which used to interest him so much when he was still sure he was going to be a great writer. Unguarded, unaware of being watched; unaware of its own content; inconceivably sad.

Nel mezzo del cammina de nostra vita.[1]
Better for her.
Or would it have been.

[3]

Her face was intent as well as sad: still, almost, the look with which she must have threaded the needle. When your face holds looks like that, beyond their cause, there is something wrong. Some kind of setting, or rigidity, as if you were going dead, drying up. He knew it of himself, how often certain kinds of smile stayed on his face, long after its time was up. Her jaw was heavier than it used to be. It was a naturally generous mouth, but it had become unnaturally tight. At the left corner there was a small crease, now, which was never entirely erased except when she was gay, or brightened with sexual satisfaction or with a sudden moment of respect, hope or trust.

None of those things happened at all often, any more, and the face was more and more, not exactly hard, but more habituatedly resolute and unleisured, responsible. More and more masculine (it was not for nothing that she liked to get into slacks when she got home). And as he lay he knew as well as if his fingers touched it, as if he saw it in the mirror, what was happening to his own mouth.

Bad for both of them; and there didn't seem to be much he could do about it.

3.   Two nights before, he suddenly remembered, at that party they had been asked to, and to which he had gone uneasily, scarcely knowing anyone, presented, essentially, as his wife's husband, to people whom she knew hardly better; he had a sense too, all through it, that though she had probably never intended to let it be known, it was generally known that he had no job and that she was supporting him; at this party, in a place and among people a good way out of their depth in the sort of sophistication smart jobs and comfortable money can bring; he had gotten drunker than he meant to and thus more at ease than he had expected to be, out of pure nervousness, and had gone back into the kitchenette to fix himself another and had seen that Frank Cooper, who had asked them there, had obviously just finished kissing his wife; and

---

1. "In the middle of the journey of our life," the first line of Dante's *Divine Comedy*.

by the way they stood apart, and the startled way they looked at him, he was sure that it had been quite a kiss. It had sent a tremendous flashing shock through him which he had been unable immediately to assess, or name, beyond knowing that abruptly, he was brilliantly

[4]

alive has he had not been for a long time. He felt energy spreading like rays through his fingertips.

He had had little or no control over what he had done, but had felt he had done well. He made no pretense of ignorance, only that he was ignorant of any intensity; gave them a sort of parody-gallant, man-of-the-world, salute-without-words, and took his time about fixing his drink, bantering with them, he felt, much above his normal ability, while he did so. It was not false, for that matter; he found that he felt a remarkably exhilarated friendliness towards both of them (though he had never much liked Cooper, the very little he had seen him); and Cooper's odd mixture of coldness with honest discomfiture made him feel all the more friendly; almost protective. He also felt free, he did not know of what; so free, that he looked at his wife's somewhat swollen face almost with delight, almost as if he had just begun to know her and had just now, for the first time, kissed her. This sense of freedom was still strong when he returned to the front room, and he was already hard at work in a flirtation which he had entered almost unconsciously, before he began to recognize that he now felt licensed.

Yet as he lay now, remembering it, he wondered why he had felt so. They had never at any time felt or imposed inhibitions upon themselves or upon each other; so it was a license on a matter already assumed, and permitted. But seldom indulged. Perhaps that was it. Only during the first months, when they had been at their best with each other, had they done much lovemaking, even much flirting, with other people, and that, come to think of it, had been very mild, particularly on her part. As their own pleasure in each other had dwindled, so had all of that; and this incident of the other night struck him as if nothing of the sort had ever happened before.

Perhaps nothing quite of that sort ever had. For what he had felt, he now began to realize, was a licensing not of the right to do likewise, but of the desire by which he might. And yet, he had found, there was nothing which could possibly satisfy the desire; nor was he sure just what the desire was. He had made—to put it kindly—a good deal of a fool of himself with two women he had never seen before (and never wanted to again); the trouble had been, that even midway in his reckless approaches, both women had lost for him whatever illusions of attractiveness had drawn him in the first place, and he had in both cases beaten the sort of quick retreat which is even more unforgivable, under those

[5]

circumstances, than the brash intrusions in the first place. As the evening wore on all he had left, like the ringing of fever in the ears, was an appetite for liquor and a flaring sense of famine which he could not locate, except that it was essentially erotic. The nearest he could come to it was in watching his wife, covertly, and imagining her face and her body in various erotic extremities with the man who had kissed her. It made his own desire for her more intense than it had ever been in fact, and it gave him a quality of admiration for her, of pride in her, no less intense and unprecedented; but when, in these imaginations, he replaced the man, the desire and admiration and pride were nullified. He began to realize that it was his business to disappear, and hers to spend the night with this character in the sports-coat, but in every attempt to imagine that, he knew what would happen. Even if he managed to leave the party without being questioned, and went on home, she would turn up, alone, an hour or two hours later—sooner, come to think of it—she was very careful about getting sleep during the working week—and then they would either talk about it or they would not, it was hard to say which would be more unpleasant. Even if he conspicuously made off with a girl, it would come to he same thing.

On that night he had thought of using the girl without conscience; merely as a piece of strategy. Now, as he thought it over, he began to realize what his wife would think of him if she knew what was going on in his head, and his dread of her contempt was such that he almost felt contempt for himself. But he was spared that as he watched her struggling into the somewhat too narrow girdle; for as he watched the side of the thigh swell below its edge he was filled with absolute distaste. A moment later he realized, also, that the girdle had not been used for a long time, and he knew why it was being used today.

Busy for lunch? he said to himself.

The pit of his stomach felt high and light, as it had that night. Busy for lunch?

[N 2: Fragment: "Orchard"]

Late in the Sunday afternoon they strolled out behind the house and leaned on the fence and looked at the apple orchard. The apples in this part of the orchard were all yellow and russet and the leaves too were russet; the trunks of the trees were grimly and wildly gnarled and were a rough and rusty black. They leaned on the fence talking in deep rusty voices while they looked along an aisle of trees, and he stood with his toes on the lower rail of the fence and his chin on the upper rail. The fence was splintered silver. He ran his tongue along it; its taste was sour. He looked, as they looked, into the orchard. The orchard was one glow of golden light. The sun was down but from every yellow surface of fruit and leaf and turf and from the leafy ground and the red gold of the ground itself the light stood up in quietest splendor of gold, and in this gold, the crippled trunks smoldered their intense black like charcoal. And all the air was ravished with the smell of ripe russet apples, which fell now and again, as wonderful a winter's first few snowflakes, now from the second tree away, now far down the aisle, now two together, the death-drums of the summer. Some were split and rotten, some were whole; on many there were strange, dull, sun-like warts. (growths, blemishes). (like dull suns & stars).

[N 3: Beginning of Story in Dialect: "Unnanstayun yawls viewpoint"]

unnanstayun yawls viewpoint on minny en minny a matter, little beyit bettuh, maybe, dan de averug suthnuh has had optunety, en dat's one reason whah have had de privilege and de honuh to be delegated aw ye maht say depewted to come up yeah n trah ta reach an unnastannin with yall.

Othah reason ah was selected to come up yeah-n' talk to yawl is, well, it may saoun lak just braggin tyuh, though I dont thank ye'd thank dat of me, well, anyhow, de reason is, 'case ahm what ye maht call a lib'ral. Naow dat's a danjus wuhd, folks, ah realize dat, hits a wuhd dat needs qualifyin de minute hits brought aout. Now I aint a-goin t' spin tew much a mah time a-tellin yuns what ah means bah bein a "libal", we got mo 'm'potent thangs t' take up, but dis is a paht a makin thangs cleah, an' we can't just skip over it like it wasn't nothing tall. Naow I jist give yuns one ah two edzamples a what ah mean, an din wull go awn. Naow f'instance mast a yuns probly remimbuh, long about ten yeahs back, a trail dey called the Monkey Trial dat made de Saouf sich a laughin-stock. Now I tell yuns what I thank, n what's mo ah thought it din, even sid it, aout in de open. Ah sid I was mighty sorry dat raow ivah come up dattaways; hit couldn't but do a shole lot mo hahm dan it done god. Fact is, an' ah said it den, I'm a Babtis' in good standin but ah said it den, dey does come a tahm whin ligion jus bettah back daown n en concede a point ah tew tu Synce. Ah wouldn't go fur's to say at mankind az scinded fun the antropoid apes, but Dahwin en all dem signtis, they shore checked up on paowful lot tertorry, an ah all ways say din tellgent man lucks at thangs in dey true pspective.

And so I feel absolutely confident in your confidence in me, in our mutual confidence, when I tell you that the subjeck I'm heah to speak to you abaout tonight, is, the nigrah. (water.)

[N 4: Outline for "Young Man I Think You Are Dying"]

Young Man, I Think You Are Dying

1. dementia praecox.
2. the non-politician.
3. CG.[2]
4. Upham[3] (?)
5. BFM[4] (?) (letters?)

---

2. Christopher Gerould. See J 4.17, note 50, and P 21, note 17.

3. Irvine Upham, a Harvard classmate and friend of Agee's and one of the "unpaid agitators" of *Let Us Now Praise Famous Men*.

4. Franklin Miner. See J 4.6, note 34.

6. Snob – in art & in living; latter overtaking former?

7. The Analyzed?

8. The one who lives through?

9. One to war?

10. Letter to analyst?   religion?   journal-keeper?

centre around 1 woman?   slum = liver [?]; jazz musician?

[N 5: Notes on "In the White Light a Keener Whiteness Sparkled"]

<u>Child-killer</u>

memory of father's discovery of self & older man? Terror & guilt. ill-remembered, disturbing dream, night before murder? Semi-erotic, semireligious? Almost sexless, a long time.   Reading – struggling to keep awake, until sure she is asleep.

small white butterflies, odor of hot old manure?

intense desire for wife, night after? & she capitulates? impregnated? chance for job offered, that night?

Why write it? What does it mean? Any connection between this kind of weakness and weakness of art & thought in general?

Bakelite radio.   WPA writers' project?

Friend-of-friend's opinions.

---

1.   Indefinite sparkle (the butterflies) & strange odor (grass & manure) & lies with eyes shut hearing his wife move around. Sound of percolation begins. Looks out under blond lashes & sees her dressing. She looks dry, as if she might scrape like a leaf if touched. Her face serious & sad. Unshaven armpits. European, & mother – Loud cheap clock. (Alarm off just before it went off.)

Tries to remember dream.

Hears her eating in front room & opens eyes. She will be dressed by now.

She comes in for hat, neither quiet nor loud on her feet. He opens his eyes.

"<u>Do</u> go around today."

"Why don't you phone him and see."

"We'll probably see him tonight at ~ ." People coming there
tonight? Booze from Hearns?

"But you might remind. It's been nearly a week now."

(Yesterday, passed butterfly shop. Or, sudden twinkling draft of
sparkling white cola.)

---

hurries to mirror.
clock.
radio.

[N 6: Notes for Story and Poem: "John Lamar"]

Maybe it's too bad that John Lamar never got around, directly or indi-
rectly, to writing his own life. His life wasn't in most ways extraordinary,
but he saw a lot and took in a lot and a lot happened to him which I think
would be worth getting down. It would certainly have been a much pleas-
anter and a much better story than this is going to be Transmuted into
the various forms, and seen from the various angles, that he was always
messing with, it might even have been better than good. How should I
know: he never got far enough with anything. Then too I suppose it
might have made quite a fair biography. But biographies are written only
of people who manage to get something done.

The tough part of it is that all the really normal and interesting elements
of his life are made irrelevant, or only half relevant, by the thing that
caused him to end it. I don't say for a minute that they didn't all con-
tribute: they did. And yet if you wrote the half million words or so it
might take to bring them into line and to give them their own values,
it seems to me that so far as the essential story is concerned, you would
be just about where you were before: only a good deal more tired and
very possibly confused rather than prepared.

To say it shortly, I'm in a jam. The one thing I give a damn about is to
make this essential story clear: and I don't know how to. I would be
perfectly willing to simplify, or to condense, or to invent, if I thought
that would help: but I can't see in this case that it is half the use that
the facts are.

Four dreams round my bed
Four dreams round my head
Four sentries at my head
Darwin, Einstein, Freud and Marx

spasm

Four angels round my bed   Jesus, Dostoevsky, Blake,
Armed sentinels at my head,   Weeping child and bestial eye,
Darwin, Einstein, Freud and Marx, Sit in shadows, bide your peace
Guard the bed that I lie on.   Till the dreadful morn shall break.

Notes, Fragments, and Outlines

MISCELLANEOUS

This section contains a hodgepodge of notes, fragments, lists, and outlines from the 1930s to the 1950s concerning everything from Walker Evans's photographs to gossip columnist Hedda Hopper's influence on Hollywood to family genealogy to a history of the world. Despite the rough and random nature of the material, there are some hidden nuggets. Agee's notes on John Huston for a Life *magazine article read like a self-portrait; a one-page itinerary for his trip to Anna Maria, Florida, is a mine of biographical information. His notes on limiting cigarette and alcohol consumption show a concern for failing health, but honest self-examination seems to rule out the possibility for fundamental change. These fragments are presented as written; readers are invited to make of them what they will.*

[N 7: Notes on Book of Subway Photographs]

[1]

The marks of this city upon them.[1] Marked with this city.

A particular kind of crude and deafening motion.

Hypnosis of the noise and of the motion; influence of being underground, and not only that, but under-city: under the miles-square solid complex-stone of the city.

Elevation, automobiles, trains, (planes?), different hypnoses, & different adjustments; silences.

Used between every form of obligation & desire; seldom casually.

These photographs were made in subways in New York City, in the late thirties and early forties of the twentieth century. There are three main influences: the people; their way of traveling; their degree of awareness (or unawareness) of the camera.

Photographs worthy of their existence need no words, and do better without them, so in writing of these, I am bound to feel apologetic.

[2]

These photographs were made in subways in New York City, during the late thirties and early forties of the twentieth century. They are the author's selection from among the persons he perceived. Every effort was made to keep those who were being photographed as unaware of the camera as possible. This succeeded in varying degrees.

These photographs were made in subways in New York City during the late thirties and early forties of the twentieth century. Efforts were made to keep those who were being photographed as unaware of the fact as possible.

Even these two statements are self-evident in the photographs themselves; in adding anything further, one is bound to apologize.

---

1. Cf. Agee's introduction to Walker Evans's *Many Are Called* (Boston: Houghton Mifflin, 1966). These drafts were apparently written in October of 1940. See J 6.7, note 2.

It is conceivable that words and photographs can be brought into intimate, mutually enhancing collaboration; but that possibility is irrelevant here. Short of that, words can only vitiate any photograph worthy of existence.

[3]

It is barely conceivable that words and photographs might be so contrived as to illuminate and enrich each other; pure information, too, can sometimes enhance a photograph. Aside from those two possibilities, words invariably vitiate photographs; and photographs worthy of existence need no words.

Pure information can sometimes enhance a photograph; and it is barely conceivable that words and photographs might be so collaborated as to enrich and illuminate each other.

I am writing of nothing here that is not self-evident in the photographs; I can say nothing that will add to them, nothing, indeed, that will not reduce them. For no photograph worthy of existence needs words, or can be other than hurt by them. Nevertheless I try, for this good reason: people are much less used to photographs than to words.

There should be no words here at all; and if they manage to justify their existence they can do so only by becoming so transparent that they cease to exist; that only the photographs remain.

[4]

These photographs were made in the subways of New York City during the late thirties and early forties of the twentieth century. Insofar as was possible, those who were being photographed were kept unaware of the fact.

During every twenty-four hours, several million human beings use the subways of New York City. They are individuals, and they differ also, greatly, in race, and class, and work, and destination. But each of them carries the marks of this century and of his city, and each falls under an identical and powerful influence of strong motion and crude noise. Each is, for a

[5]

short while, suspended. And in that suspension, and in the strong hypnosis of that moving noise, each is, in a manner peculiar to the subway, unmarked.

In every twenty-four hours, several million human beings use the subways of New York City. They are of every race, and age, and class, of every sort of work and leisure, of every distinction. Each is an individual, as matchless as his own thumbprint; and each carries on his clothing, in his hands, in his eyes, the marks of the city, the marks of his century, the marks of his induplicable living.

In the motion and noise of the subway, and in its suspension, every human being is in a particular way unmasked, and unaware of being so.

To ride watchfully, in a New York Subway, is a dreadful and piteous act of surreption: for in its noise and motion, in its suspension, almost every human being is unmasked, and unaware of being unmasked, and unaware of being watched. And most are sorrowful; and most are ruined; and one gazes into the helpless nakedness of that sorrow and ruin with its guard down.

[6]

Every form of motion works its particular enchantment:
The pity is in the people.

Even the simplest of beings and the best is hurt; even the simplest has contrived guards and disguises that are never lost: not in the most intimate hurt of another; not alone, before a mirror. But suspended a little while in one place, in the moving noise of the subway, these guards are down: and one may gaze into the core and source of every human wound. They are defenseless; and unconscious.

The pity of those spied on through windows is nothing by comparison.

One classical action irons them flat and reveals them in all their variety.

In just one place, every guard is down. Never in the most intimate trust of another; never alone. before a mirror; there

There is just one place in which the human race is stripped naked. Freud used hypnosis.

Nudes. / A setting as steady and negative as a coffin.

[7]

The masks off in varying degrees. Varying degrees of realization of being watched.

A camera, well-used, is inevitably cruel, in proportion of the imperfections of its subject: it is impossible that it be at same time more cruel and more pitying than in the subway. And the cruelty and pity are not the concoction of an artist: they are forced upon him by the value of his material.

Human beings under a very set, very special, uniform condition. Of this city; of this century; they are all marked; (the clothes alone would be enough); but more: they are under the set conditions imposed by the subway.

Every form of motion induces a kind of hypnosis; that of subway is in one respect peculiarly valuable. Underground; undercity; the noise and violence of the motion; the suspension; upon each individual, it draws his pattern.

When Freud began, he used hypnosis. There are other forms of hypnosis, other & more complete, more subtle methods of looking into the bottoms of wells.

[8]

The inhabitants of such a city as New York cannot be said fully to represent the human race, but short of that they represent a great deal. They are of every race and nation and part of the world; there is no other place in the world where human beings are in so complete a variety, so intense a concentration. Metropolitan living is that sort most characteristic of this century.

———————————

The subway furnishes matchlessly good laboratory conditions for a certain important study: the study of the defenseless souls of human individuals. The five-cent fare, and necessity, insure that the mixture be rich, and insure the least common denominator. The fact of being underground,

[9]

Properly used, no matter where, the camera has an absoluteness of a sort no art can approach. Here, it is used under peculiarly implacable conditions.

The human race:
in every variety
of a certain time and place, every garment and every mark or signature;
of each individuality, every mark, and of what its world has made it: every disguise and defense:
In the subway, each of these is unmasked;
and is unaware he is unmasked; and that he is being watched:
the human being, the human spirit, at its most naked and most defenseless.

At the end of <u>City Lights</u>, in the eyes of the blind girl to whom he has given sight, Chaplin first perceives himself truly as he is. It is one of most terrible and beautiful moments I know of. Less intensely, and still more truly, that is the essence of these photographs.

The 5 cent fare guarantees the great common denominator.
The perfect monotony of underground, and the fact of being there.
Nothing to do. Not long enough for the flowerings and extensions usual to a train.
Laboratory conditions.

[N 8: Notes on *Saturday Review*]

[1]

In twilight a light outside making it's cross on the screen. ✳ You have seen this before but this is keen and bright, crisp.

———

black and white glaze yesterday dusk.

[2]

Hurrah for our Seidel² / Side by Seidel /   oleo   golden mediocrity

———————————

2. Henry Seidel Canby (1878–1961) was one of the founders the *Saturday Review of Literature* in 1924 and an editor until 1936.

Now, with an eye for the side of the bread that's buttered,
Three loud cheers for the Saturday Review,
Which faithfully these — long years has fluttered

The Saturday Review: As the leading organ of U.S. literary criticism during one of the liveliest decades in U.S. literary history, it bears a great responsibility which, with all but infallible consistency, it has met half-way: constantly advancing the mediocre and as constantly opposing the adventurous, the courageous, the high-serious and the good: establishing, in fine, a record which can be approached only by the New York Times.

Now, with an eye for the side of the bread that's buttered,
Three loud cheers for the Saturday review,
Which, with a faith good sense has seldom fluttered
Has plugged the elderly, ignored the new,
Licked every well-shined boot, scratched every back

In the belief that literature has everything to do with life and that the responsibilities are proportionally great on writer, critic and reader, three cheers for the Saturday Review, which, as the leading organ of U.S. literary criticism during one of the most vivid and dangerous decades of American life and literary history, has all but infallibly met its responsibilities halfway: constantly advancing the safe, the cowardly, the dull-hearted and the evil and as constantly opposing the adventurous, the courageous, the serious and the good: blinding and drugging an audience already blind and drugged, praising the easy, encouraging

---

Josie loves the little things
And all the Little Things love Josie.
And every time our Josie sings
Is perfectly rosey-poesy-prosy.

(Quote Edna's[3] poems)
Jesus made it just so good
And not a little better;
For if you play just one more trump
Against this poet, you'll set her.

---

3. Edna St. Vincent Millay (1892–1950), American poet.

—Literary Banquet.—
Mabel, Agnes and Becky,
     Willy and Nilly
Are all at the Pulitzer Brekky
     Gelding the lily.

To Muse: Come Live with Me &c—
Valentine: The Willing Poet.
——————————————   Here, Muse, are planes and dynamos
Happy that type of poet   And here are roses dipt in wine,
Whose Muse is so adroit   Sugarlumps, candy, fancy clothes—
She can bring it in thin as the point of a pin   Aw, Muse, <u>please</u>
be my Valentine.
Or spread it out flat like a quoit.

——————————————

                         Pegasus feed bad [?]
                                  or
                            sugarlumps
     Backfire.

[N 9: Notes on John Huston]

                    sleepwalking
     <u>"No Trouble"—contributing causes.</u>
very much extraverted. unreflective. not "sensitive." no grudge-bearer.
no ego-trouble. no jealousy. no depressions or apathy. no self-pity or
grave self-doubt & no megalomania.[4]
No perfectionist. not an esthete. interest very intense while it's going,
but loses it quickly. Not a man of feeling. Rational & intuitive as <u>vs</u> sensation & feeling.
No theorist: each pic brings its rewards & problems. Interest is in present. Little concern for past or future. chief interest is in action & chief
talent is there: action one of surest ways to a picture both good &
popular.

———————————

     4. Cf. Agee's "Undirectable Director," *Life* 29 (September 18, 1950): 128–45.
Rpt. in *Agee on Film*, vol. 1, 319–31.

Very restive. No time to reflect. Always at something.

No "high sense of vocation", Doesn't take work or self seriously in a way to get hurt is it goes wrong. Found vocation by accident.

Essentially a bum, bummed into it & might as easily bum out of it again. His life doesn't depend on it or on anything it can bring him, i.e., either fame or money or self-esteem.

Add it up another way; no bootlicker; no "artist's" arrogance; an extremely likable guy; reckless; never seeks protection. So he naturally draws protection of the best type.

For another: quickly—too quickly—loses interest. In some ways a sloppy artist & in some ways a shallow one. No great concern re cutting or music or soundtrack. Eager concern to handle ideas but not an equal concern to think them out very far. So: things go wrong with his pix which might greatly worry another of equal gifts & wd certainly seem like "trouble". But not even the stuff he knows as trouble seems like trouble to him. That kind of trouble is his natural climate. And other things, he is simply unaware of.

Quite aside from all this, he never fails to make good entertainment or a good movie.

In no sense self-taught, [illegible] naivety, adventurer

always learning something new, never "consolidating" knowledge

---

his work: general comparative assessment.

The sporadic, semi-quiescent Chaplin is unquestionably greater. Clair has done better pix than H. ever has. So has Dovschenko. But bring it down to regularly productive directors, here & abroad. Rosselini: Huston's better. da Sica. H. is anyhow as good. Olivier: by comparison, a gifted amateur. Wyler: greater range, versatility, poetry & tenderness, but much is semi-commercial & shrewd. Ford: a very fine director who has become more & more a picture man. G. Rouquier: as good or better in a field so different they are scarcely comparable. Dreyer: a master, far out at the edge, where JH is near dead-center.[5]

---

5. The directors to whom Agee compares Huston in this paragraph are Charlie Chaplin (British, 1889–1977), René Clair (French, 1898–1981), Aleksandr Dovzhenko (Russian, 1894–1956), Roberto Rosselini (Italian, 1906–1977), Vittorio da Sica (Italian, 1902–1974), Laurence Olivier (British, 1907–1989), William Wyler (American, 1902–1981), John Ford (American, 1894–1973), Georges Rouquier (French, 1909–1989), and Carl Dreyer (Danish, 1889–1968).

general characteristics.

Transparency; virility; cleanness of line. Cf. prose: Swift, Kafka, Hemingway. Clearly a "people" rather than a "camera" director. But is he really? Yes, in chief sense that he never makes the camera "expressive", like Ford. No "adjectives". Wonderful, clear, characteristic setups: Biz of camera is to be at the right place to be invisible itself & best to reveal what is going on before it. Fine sense of frame, depth & tension, though. Little if any fancy lighting: usual law of lighting is to very slightly intensify the actual. Very little angle shooting. Little if any gag work. Considers the symbolism but symbols very rarely "applied". Little if any shot-for-shot's sake, yet many shots of extraordinary lucidity & power. More acutely than with nearly any other director the object is always to tell the story: though here, again more acutely than most he will break it down into, for instance, a shot purely to establish mood, another purely to establish character. As writer-director, [illegible] on how to introduce character by delay &/or silence &/or mood. Again, the Robinson shot.[6] Very flexible sense of camera: lovely aridity of McCord's work for Treasure;[7] the almost Keats-like sumptuousness of Metty's work in Rough Sketch[8] [illegible]. In R-S: lighting contrasts. Deep dark of tunnel sequence;

[N 10: Notes on Zanuck, Etc.]

(1) Could Emma[9] come down immediately, any time she was wanted?

(2) M Vanaman (call at home). Can I have Morgue folders—will return within week. None of these are of people liable to be wanted. [illegible] cd give to you to bring me.

Folders on:

------

6. In "Undirectable Director" Agee writes: "The first shot of Edward G. Robinson in *Key Largo*, mouthing a cigar and sweltering naked in a tub of cold water ('I wanted to get a look at the animal with its shell off') is one of the most powerful and efficient 'first entrances' of a character on record."

7. Ted McCord (1900–1976) was the cinematographer on Huston's *Treasure of the Sierra Madre* (1948).

8. Russell Metty (1906–1978) was the cinematographer on Huston's *We Were Strangers* (1949), filmed under the working title "Rough Sketch," from the Robert Sylvester novel on which it was based.

9. Agee's sister. See J 4.2, note 14.

Darryl Zanuck.[10]   Lloyd Hamilton[11]   OR John Huston[12]
                                                        (depends on what he   chooses)
Harold Lloyd   Buster Keaton   Harry Langdon
Charlie Chase
Larry Semon
Laurel & Hardy[13]

(3) To Robert Coghlan
  (1) Grateful for his postponement. Will do Zanuck story and
whatever of 2 others he prefers: 1) select comics, 2) John Huston too
closeup (peg on next movie, probably next spring.)
  (2) Has Whitney[14] been briefed on Zanuck? If not I'll write him.
His address?
  (3) Deadline for both pieces? November 9 (Zanuck)
  (4) Expense check. Can Mia[15] cast in N.Y.?

(4) Mia:
my driver's license?
the car?
your license if you drive down?
Teresa?[16]

[N 11: Drafts of Hedda Hopper Essay]

[1]

One morning last Spring there appeared in Hedda Hopper's
Hollywood[17] the following item:
"Q".
To most of Hedda Hopper's 22,800,000 readers this was just

[2]

One morning last Spring the following item appeared in Hedda
Hopper's Hollywood:
Q.

---

10. Darryl F. Zanuck (1902–1979), American producer and cofounder of
Twentieth Century Fox.

11. Lloyd Hamilton (1891–1935), American comedic actor.

12. John Huston (1906–1987), American director. See N 9.

13. The comedians here listed are Harold Lloyd (1893–1971), Buster Keaton
(1895–1966), Harry Langdon (1884–1944), Charley Chase (1893–1940), Larry

The source and nature of power is hard to explain, and harder to believe; doctors and criminologists notwithstanding, people have been brained by a well-aimed blow with an astral plume.

[3]

The source and nature of power are sometimes hard for sensible people to understand, and even harder to believe; but doctors and criminologists notwithstanding, strong men have been brained by ostrich plumes. One morning last spring, for instance, the following item appeared in Hedda Hopper's Hollywood:

Q.

To most of the 22,800,000 readers of Hedda Hopper's Hollywood, this was just one more piece of inexplicably fascinating, if rather lathery trivia, to be taken as lightly as all the rest. But in Hollywood, nothing that Hedda Hopper writes, however trivial, is ever taken lightly. A few often ill-chosen words from Hedda written with the same sweeping abandon with which she selects her hats, can make or break an act or cool or close a deal, and reduce a $250,000-a-year executive to a tarn of sunburned aspic. There are possibly fifty men in H[ollywood] who really count, and faithfully every morning after they have brushed their teeth, eaten their roughage, and prostrated themselves for a few silent moments on those little prayer rugs which face toward Wall Street, they make it their first business to read dashing Hedda Hopper and her archrival, unfair, fat & fiftyish Louella Parsons.[18]

On the morning referred to above, for instance, Warner Bros. director Michael Curtiz[19] arrived at his office promptly at 9[30] in a state of high

Semon (see J 4.17, note 64), and Stan Laurel (British, 1890–1965) and Oliver Hardy (1892–1957). Agee discusses Lloyd, Keaton, Langdon, and Laurel and Hardy in "Comedy's Greatest Era."

14. Dwight Whitney, the *Time* reporter who was Agee's studio liaison in Hollywood.

15. Agee married Mia Fritsch, his third wife, in August 1944.

16. Agee's daughter, Julia Teresa "Deedee" Agee, was born November 7, 1946.

17. Hedda Hopper (1890–1966), radio host and gossip columnist, wrote "Hedda Hopper's Hollywood" for the *Los Angeles Times* from 1938 to 1966. Hopper called her Beverly Hills mansion "the house that fear built."

18. Louella Parsons (1881–1972) wrote a syndicated gossip column for the Hearst newspaper chain.

19. Michael Curtiz (1886–1962), Austro-Hungarian-born director and producer.

agitation and sat staring at his phone as if he were a Geiger counter or better still, unborn. At 9^{45} the phone rang at last; Jack Warner was on it; and Curtiz was on the ropes. At exactly 10, with his remaining strength, he sped a distraught drive to Beverly Hills.

[N 12: List of Movies for Review]

Happy Breed, Stairway to Heaven, Green for Danger,   Musical: Fiesta
Overlanders:—
Favorite Brunette, Dear Ruth, Perils of Pauline, Copacabana,
Ghost & Mrs. Muir, Miracle on 34th St.
"Dramas," Dishonored Lady, Smash-Up, Torment, The Unfaithful, Possessed, Macomber.
Melodramas: 2 Mrs Carrolls, Woman on Beach, They Won't Believe Me, Crossfire, Red House, Repeat Performance.
Murder & Mystery: Brasher Doubloon, The Web, Ivy, Moss Rose,
Comedy drama: Apley, Ghost & Mrs Muir, Miracle, Honeymoon, Dear Ruth, It Happened on 5th Ave., Imperfect Lady
Comedy: Favorite Brunette, Pauline, Trouble with Women.
Musicals: Copacabana, Fiesta, Hit Parade of 1947.   Bob son of Battle
Westerns: Ramrod, Duel, Angel & Badman, Pursued
Unclassified: High Barbaree, Overlanders, Cynthia, Hucksters, Swell Guy, Brute Force.
Good enough for longer review: Macomber (Z Korda), first half of Torment, Woman on Beach, Red House, Overlanders, Crossfire,
Some really old ones which shd particularly be mentioned: Overlanders, Stairway to Heaven, Swell Guy, Stone Flower, Lady in Lake, Most over-rated: Apley, Miracle?, Pauline,
Current or near current: Crossfire, Bob Son of Battle, Perils of Pauline, New Orleans, Hucksters, Ivy, Moss Rose, The Unfaithful, They Won't Believe Me.[20]

---

20. Complete titles of movies listed on this page along with director and year of release are as follows: *This Happy Breed* (David Lean, 1947); *Stairway to Heaven* (Michael Powell and Emeric Pressburger, 1946); *Green for Danger* (Sidney Gilliat, 1946); *Fiesta* (Richard Thorpe, 1947); *The Overlanders* (Harry Watt, 1946); *My Favorite Brunette* (Elliott Nugent, 1947); *Dear Ruth* (William Russell, 1947); *The Perils of Pauline* (George Marshall, 1947); *Copacabana* (Alfred E. Green, 1947);

[N 13: List: "Germans & Japanese in American movies"]

1) Germans & Japanese in American movies.
2) The "common man" in "   ".[21]
3) Steinbeck, Guest.[22]

The Ghost and Mrs. Muir (Joseph L. Mankiewicz, 1947); *Miracle on Thirty-Fourth Street* (George Seaton, 1947); *Dishonored Lady* (Robert Stevenson, 1947); *Smash-Up, the Story of a Woman* (Stuart Heisler, 1947); *Torment* (Alf Sjoberg, 1944); *The Unfaithful* (Vincent Sherman, 1947); *Possessed* (Curtis Bernhardt, 1947); *The Macomber Affair* (Zoltan Korda, 1947); *The Two Mrs. Carrolls* (Peter Godfrey, 1947); *The Woman on the Beach* (Jean Renoir, 1947); *They Won't Believe Me* (Irving Pichel, 1947); *Crossfire* (Edward Dmytryk, 1947); *The Red House* (Delmer Daves, 1947); *Repeat Performance* (Alfred L. Werker, 1947); *The Brasher Doubloon* (John Brahm, 1947); *The Web* (Michael Gordon, 1947); *Ivy* (Sam Wood, 1947); *Moss Rose* (Gregory Ratoff, 1947); *The Late George Apley* (Joseph L. Mankiewicz, 1947); *Honeymoon* (William Keighley, 1947); *It Happened on Fifth Avenue* (Roy Del Ruth, 1947); *The Imperfect Lady* (Lewis Allen, 1947); *The Trouble with Women* (Sidney Lansfield, 1947); *Hit Parade of 1947* (Frank McDonald, 1947); *Bob, Son of Battle* (released in America as *Thunder in the Valley*, Louis King, 1947); *Ramrod* (Andre de Toth, 1947); *Duel in the Sun* (King Vidor, 1946); *Angel and the Badman* (James Edward Grant, 1947); *Pursued* (Raoul Walsh, 1947); *High Barbaree* (Jack Conway, 1947); *Cynthia* (Robert Z. Leonard, 1947); *The Hucksters* (Jack Conway, 1947); *Swell Guy* (Frank Tuttle, 1946); *Brute Force* (Jules Dassin, 1947); *The Stone Flower* (Aleksandr Ptushko, 1946); *Lady in the Lake* (Robert Montgomery, 1946); *New Orleans* (Arthur Lubin, 1947).

21. Although written several years later, this list seems, at least partially, to refer back to Agee's *Partisan Review* article "Pseudo-Folk" (11.2 (Spring 1944): 219–23). Agee writes, extending Louise Bogan's statement in "Some Notes on Popular and Unpopular Art" (*Partisan Review* 10.5 (September–October 1943): 391–401) that the folk tradition in America has become "thoroughly bourgeoizified": "Indeed we have a tradition for this sort of badness. . . . [T]here are not many of us who realize that Irving Cobb, C. B. Kelland, Edgar Guest and John Steinbeck have a great deal of shame in common; that the 'talk-American' writer, the Common Man as normally represented in left-wing, liberal and tory fiction alike, and the pseudo-Biblical diction which chokes so much of our writing once we try to 'dignify' the vernacular, are all at least as dangerously 'literary,' snobbish, affected and anti-human as the mock-Mandarin prose and mock-Oxford speech of the self-caricatured Seaboard Anglophile."

22. Agee says in "Pseudo-Folk":

> On page 134 of *The Pocket Book of Quotations* you may read:
> "I'm learnin' one thing, learnin' it all a time, ever' day. If you're in trouble, or hurt or need—go to the poor people. They're the only ones that'll help—the only ones."
> On page 136:

4) Dennis re Liebling.[23]

5) Bogan:[24] Middle-class folk,[25] Southern Exposure,[26] Leftist songs, Ballad for Americans,[27] etc.

6) H. Miller (Walker)[28]

7) "Close to me, Frankie".

8) Hall of Shame (?)

[N 14: List: "Write David Selznick"]

Write David Selznick;[29] Guggenheim re Mike de Capite;[30] Marled [Marlee?]; J. C. Ransom sketched; Stevens (sketched)

"It takes a heap o' livin' in a house t'make it home
A heap o' sun an' shadder, an' ye sometimes have t' roam
Afore ye really 'preciate the tings ye lef' behind,
An' hunger fer 'em somehow, with 'm allus on yer mind."
The latter passage is by Edgar Guest and is quoted from his poem, *Home*. The former is by John Steinbeck and is quoted from his novel, *The Grapes of Wrath*. The very small body of writing you might find which would not incriminate itself by comparison, which attempts to use the vernacular, and which at the same time shows good judgment both in using and in depriving itself of the Mandarin manner, is the prospect we have for the development of a popular literary art which I join Miss Bogan in looking towards.

23. Probably American journalist A. J. Liebling (1904–1963), whose *The Road Back to Paris* was published in 1944.

24. Louise Bogan (1897–1970), American poet.

25. I.e., folk art that has become "thoroughly bourgeoizified."

26. Stetson Kennedy's *Southern Exposure* (1946) recounts his infiltration of the Ku Klux Klan.

27. From "Pseudo-Folk": "Paul Robeson, I am sure, is essentially a good man, and he has sometimes used his fortuitous powers bravely and well on behalf of his race. But what can one think of the judgment of a man who, over and over and over, to worse and worse and worse people, has sung the inconceivably snobbish, esthetically execrable *Ballad for Americans?*" "Ballad for Americans," by Earl Robinson and John LaTouche, was recorded by Robeson in 1939.

28. Presumably a Henry Miller book by way of Walker Evans.

29. David O. Selznick (1902–1965), American movie producer

30. Michael DeCapite (1916–1957), American novelist.

[N 15: Fragment: "Odd Man Out"]

"Odd Man Out" is an extremely ambitious movie by Carol Reed, who seems to me the most gifted man in England at making films. It is not as satisfying a movie as G[reat] E[xpectations], but in most ways I think it is a better and more hopeful one. Reed takes aboard, here, the problem of turning the vicissitudes of a fugitive revolutionist into a morality play about modern civilization. The film seldom bites deep and direct to the problem, but its constant presence, and the [illegible] of themselves[31]

[N 16: Notes from
"John Carter" Notebook: "Uncle Tom"]

[1]

Uncle Tom—Smart boy—wrong side of street—dime a dozen—out of line—fronted for me—what was back of it—lampblack Englishman—wrong—land wrong—What-Are-We-Good-For? spade—Sugar Hill—cold steel—black money—don't start anything you don't mean—stick out like a hanged man—strike sparks off you—

[2]

Critical & political limericks—

Hall of Fame.

Sketches for pictures

The logical end of the sacredness of property in an individualistic era is that no property is quite sacred as your own.

Even twisting heats it.

On the northern hill.

Re the new generations of poetry: one summer does not make a swallow.

Angling a story.

fronting for—

Columbia signs so & so.

book me for—

---

31. Cf. Agee's double review of *Great Expectations,* directed by David Lean, and *Odd Man Out,* directed by Carol Reed, in the *Nation,* July 19, 1947. Rpt. in *Agee on Film,* vol. 1, 266–69.

Ballads.
A pretty day. pretty boy. Whoops my dear.

---

affiliate / subsidiary / vacate injunction / negotiate
        corecian / yardstick /
panorama and
        [illegible] interlarded w. newsclips etc etc.

---

    shaled to the stone / closely self-cornered
the loose beasts preying in the brain / straying brain

Not strong enough to knock a sick whore off a piss pot.

BFM Gitlowites:[32] letter re play . . . . .

                                                    [3]

Streamlined brain; streamstyled.
milestoned—millstoned
Radio—racheting sounds in: montage of sounds in movies
Weekly, mimeographed reviews.

Interpolated Rim & other ads:
    You know what pops into my mind when I hear   They Satisfy.[33]

    The political smile.
        Rhythms: short turns & encores. A magazine.
    Mutuality of the unmutual.
        Amiable.
    The money-touch. In prose, in poetry. A study
    Polite as a whore at a wedding.
    Cute as a shithouse rat.

---

32. Benjamin Gitlow (1891–1965) was arrested on charges of criminal anarchy in 1919 for publishing and distributing copies of the "Left Wing Manifesto," which called for the establishment of revolutionary socialism through violent means. Gitlow spent three years in prison, and in 1925 the U.S. Supreme Court upheld his conviction. Gitlow was presidential candidate William Z. Foster's running mate in 1924 and 1928 for the Communist Party USA but later became an outspoken critic of the Left. BFM is Franklin Miner. See J 4.6, note 34.

33. "They satisfy" was the advertising slogan for Chesterfield cigarettes.

Watch rain stride the ridge.
Shaken rusty barleyhusk.

---

barnacle: the forcing central teeth:

[N 17: Fragment: "A secular requiem"]

A secular requiem.

Darkness, with our little lights, trembling continually in your strong wind, we acknowledge and salute you.

As children into a cave with candles, so we come into your vault, lifting our little lights, which tremble continuously in your unfathomable breath, seeking, with awe, what little we may find,

And find so little: the lift of one curve of what may be an arch; but not its key;

Unexplorable and original darkness

———   cataract.

Is there a bend in time.

Now let those who can supplicate no God   The wheat acknowledges
                                            the wind,
                                            So we acknowledge you.

Many have died, in the way of this world, since the first that had its form and its breath; and of these, most have had mourners, who could commend them to God.

But what of those who died Godless, and what of survivors who can beseech no God on their behalf.

Many have died since those first who lived, whom the heart cannot reach nor the mind imagine, and of those, most have had mourners who could commend them to God.

Likewise there are those who die fatherless, and those who mourn, who can beseech no God on their behalf.

And those also who scorn all mourning, wonder and venerability; yet they too die, and those who survive them, they too mourn in their hearts.

Since those first who breathed as men, for whom the imagination of the heart hardly avails, many have did, and of these, most have left mourners who could commend them to God.

But there are those also who die fatherless, and there are those who mourn, who can beseech no God on their behalf.

They too lived, and live no longer: we too mourn, but have no song.

Mute as the hesitant fawn, sniffing the humiliated antlers, we stand bemused beside our dead; less articulate than birds in their bereavement, whose only persistence is the brisk ancestral phrase.

One lies here dead whom we would acknowledge as dead, whom we would commend to the greater portion of creation: Our hearts are open, but we have no song.

[N 18: Fragment: "dew, utter vanishing of all light"]

dew, utter vanishing of all light; darkness against darkness against darkness; [illegible] stars; coldness; the steady threshing of water grows louder; crickets, frogs; round eye of owl (moon); whippoorwill, serenading, heralding the moon; various trees; thrusting branch; mist off water; larger animals? or all or many, to water? hooves and on quietest feet? And occasional crosscuts to the sleeping beasts and birds; whole riddle of hushed birds in tree owl moves through, sighing of a shadow among shadows, the darkness clearly planted in the noon of his unshining golden Eye: (rats among great hoofs)

opposite—sun: the fist, the sunflower's noon, the feeding and the dying;

[N 19: Fragment: "Camera"]

The camera can be used, I believe, on as wide a range as that of language. It is as seldom as language so used that the result requires to be described and evaluated as a work of art. The words "work of art" are used here with a good deal of diffidence, for they are almost always applied with a looseness or arrogance which can only further offend the skeptical or the hostile, not to mention those who feel that the words can still have a dignified meaning.

[N 20: Notes on Trip to Anna Maria]

Anna Maria[34]

Structure and placement on Fla Coast.

We start down from St Andrews on Thanksgiving morning.[35]

road cleans and widens into Grundy (Marion?) county.

thru Monteagle & down into the valley.

Right branch & to bridge 50¢ toll; we take ferry 25¢.

Into this side of Chattanooga c. 1 oclock. Barbecue sandwiches; bad coffee.

Straight through Chattanooga, single out road to Atlanta; through tunnel.

lose hills behind, flatten out into red clay pine country; bedspreads blown in wind from every house: prevalence of bad peacock; tufts; pastel colors, sun thru them like a wave.[36]

To Atlanta about dusk. Inimicalness of large unknown city; complication of traffic; Marx Bros are showing. At filling station, excessive politeness & service. Herndon, Roosevelt to speak tomorrow.[37] Eat on far side of town: poultry there. 2 women, 2 men, marine songs; on to Macon: wrong road; stuck in ditch turning round; have to piss; fight; help.

Macon. The feeble little boy. Hal Egclaw. White Houses. Bill Robinson.[38]

Think of the pecan country. Sell in too much bulk for roadsides.

---

34. An island off the west coast of Florida where Agee and Via spent a six-month leave from *Fortune*. See J 1.4, note 3.

35. November 28, 1935. Agee and Via also stopped at St. Andrew's School, near Sewanee, Tennessee, to visit Father James Flye and his wife on their return trip to New York.

36. Highway 41 in northwest Georgia was known as Peacock Alley for the colorful display of homemade tufted bedspreads along the roadside.

37. In 1932, black Communist Angelo Herndon (1913–) was sentenced to twenty years of hard labor in Georgia under a slave insurrection law for leading a protest of unemployed workers. The case attracted national attention and the services of the International Labor Defense of the Communist Party. Herndon's conviction was overturned by the U.S. Supreme Court in 1937. President Franklin Roosevelt gave a speech in Atlanta on November 29, 1935.

38. Bill "Bojangles" Robinson (1878–1949), American actor and dancer, is best known for his roles in Shirley Temple movies.

On into Florida; to Hillsboro (?); trouble, right there, pine fire, 1 black boy, builds it, wants to handle baggage, waits on table in morning; <u>very</u> black. Temptation to question him. Style of native painting on dining room wall.

Over to Homosassa; ballplayer; long sand road; convicts (white); over by camp; then swamp; out to road. Eat at —— Springs. (Filling station woman.)

On to Tampa. Marx Bros. Hotel what. That night the flogging.[39]

[N 21: Notes on Schubert, Etc.]

Broad eight-beat rhythms. Schubert.

———

Words widely spaced as in painting and music.
Key words set simple, edge against edge.

———

The writer whose tragedy shows in his handwriting. We wear the exact shape of our weaknesses on our face.

———

Man is changed by his actions. Men are changed by their actions.

———

Times when the best things seem possible, potential, and yet I can't write even a common sentence, or finish one small thought.

———

These things. Expanse and detail of frosted clay. The extensive notes of a wooden flute. Wet wood. Ploring; sporling, Marling. Moral. Exploring. Spelling.   The clay is softening. Relaxing. Like a great muscle that has been tight and now lies loose.

———

Slippery weather. Fluent. Soft. Amorphous.

———

39. In Tampa, Florida, on November 30, 1935, police raided a meeting of a nascent party called the "Modern Democrats," which was attempting to organize citrus workers, and arrested six leaders, three of whom were driven to a remote area and delivered to the Ku Klux Klan. Sam Rogers, Eugene Poulnot, and Joseph Shoemaker were brutally flogged, then tarred and feathered; Shoemaker died from his wounds nine days later. Five former Tampa policemen were convicted of kidnapping, but the verdicts were overturned, and further attempts to prosecute them were unsuccessful.

With words I lose: "science". Resourcefulness. Variety. I become soft. Side at the stomach. Hardness. Coalness. Association. This I'm likely to have best when most casual.

All these losses would in a way guarantee, that I am at least reduced to myself and by myself, so that if I had any force left, force enough to bring through, it would be mine and would be new. But I have at such a time no force left at all, and am made weaker still in the memory of good people.

I am made sick by the wish for nothing less than absolute writing and thus lose every resourcefulness by which I might do relative: and through the help of which only, is it possible to do absolute.

Had I better, then, with every serious thing, do purely "scientific" and even "unscrupulous" versions first? Completely examine each idea.

In part I am afraid of just those things I should have most confidence in in myself?

[N 22: Notes on the Universe]

1. The universe. A little about its size and scope in time. What we know of its origin.
2. The sun. How big is it. How much does it weigh. How much is it worth. Efforts to mine it. Is the sun necessary?
3. The best of possible worlds: i.e., The only possible world.
4. It is draughted away from the sun. Things fall away; things fall back. There remained, the planets. Their names.
5. This planet: earth. A flame, that cooled around itself: scabs over a wound. Cooling, "Stone." "Air." "Fire." "Water". A phase of space. The stone moon slung away. Earth and its moon. Steaming stone to vapor: which on the colder air became water: which fell: and falling, took apart the stone: earth: and was on all the earth a swampy sea. (why is the sea salt?)
6. How otherwise "life" could not have occurred. Between what temperatures: what altitudes: what depths: between what gases: life feeds only on itself: without "earth": nothing but fish: without water, not even that: we are not necessarily "relatives" i.e. we are not necessarily of the same cell. But, if you want to get either hard of sentimental about it, we are all creatures of the sun.

7. Where else may life be? So far as we know, nowhere.

8. Well, how about it here?

> Out of an infinite # of chances they all crossed right here: a bombardment out of the whole "universe": and there was "Life." Once there, the rest was _easy_.

9. We cannot even call life "conscious" as it begins: except that it is that which _is_ whose entire force of existence is concentrated upon not ceasing to be. If you grant that: you must grant also that that force is continually outreaching itself _against_ _death_: i.e. _into_ _life_. Its very existence pens it in a mold: air & height & heat: a wide mold: which continually it forces & splits & takes a new form: If there is one word the word is hunger. The amoeba was always certain to die. Having no other way of living, it tore itself in two. When one died, another was left, which tore itself in two. Et cetera—idem.

10 (Upon space: a field of grass: on which winter follows spring: life in balance.)

11. Life is a thing which _will_ _live_, straining & pouring & wringing itself through narrow & labyrinthine molds: pressure against each other: blind hands which have one brain: Live.

12. And in each phase: a strict ritual (elections in their dances & the simplest forms): which, in moving to another, must be broken up: only to become another: you can apply this to anything under the sun and to everything known beyond it.

13. Does the faculty of life seem to hasten this ritual? & these changes?

14. From jellyfish to Uncle Frederick.

15. Now here we are at man, the crossroads of the world. We have no reason whatever to believe he is the last thing Life will evolve. The evolution will come through "consciousness" $\rightarrow$ "mind" $\rightarrow$ "spirit" $\rightarrow$ "knowledge"? Maybe most likely: in evolution a chain is no weaker than its strongest link. The thing most peculiar is often the most developed: all other things shape to it: as: breathing air, we ceased to be fishes: as, needing speed, we grew light of bone: as, flying, we shaped ourselves to flying. Possibilities of increase in mind. In knowledge. Learning of alphabets. Gestation of child. Religion: science: "society": "art".

16. So far, however, we have not exceeded ourselves. And have reason
     to be most interested in ourselves. The earth is our livelihood
     our learning and our decoration.
17. Childhood—maturity: sun masks everything out.
18. 2 characteristics of man: he is like all else a ritualist. (2) the greater
     part of him is & always will be lunkheads: the work is done by
     a few who often suffer the consequences.
19. He like all else is hungry and in danger. And he is capable of love
     and of wonder. Out of all this: his societies &c &c.
20. There are very good reasons why he may be loved: despised: felt
     "nothing" & "everything" about.
21. This will be chiefly an exercise in hatred, and the dice will be loaded.

[N 23: Notes on the Universe and World History]

Wedding. Prayer Book. Parody of Mags. Daily Colyum.
Alsop. Jewish wedding. Poem Re teeth (June 25? 28?) Table Talk. 43
positions for versifying. Black & White dance. Louisiana hayride (lynch-
ing; baritone). Girl eats flower out of lapel. Guignol of child [corner of
page torn off]
Throwaways & 2nd class mail. Spare morgue stuff. History of America.
He rediscovers America. He talks with Angelo Herndon.[40] He talks of
Clifford Odets.[41] He tells of his acquaintance with President Roosevelt.
He takes his hair down. He is an Anglo-Catholic.

1. Our little story has no discernible beginning, so we may as well
    begin with the sun.
    descrip of universe
    Our little story begins with the sun.
        Once upon a time by some odd chance some celestial body
    swam past the sun so fast and so near that it drafted off a flock
    of fire as an auto draws leaves in its wake and the [planets] were
    hung, several of them, upon the sky and upon the mercy of the

---

40. See N 20, note 36.

41. Clifford Odets (1906–1963), American playwright, most notably of
Waiting for Lefty (1935), and a member of the Group Theater.

sun and there in the force of their motion they swung upon themselves and turned, and turned and rounded as they turned the rounded sun, and turned, and took their shape as bullets from a shot tower falling.

There were eight of these floats of flame and they were in due course of time to be called Mars, and Saturn, and Jupiter, and Venus, and Neptune, and Uranus, after the Gods of the Greeks and Romans, and Percival,[42] after the brother of Abbott Lawrence Lowell, President Emeritus of Harvard University and fearless mediator in the trial of Sacco and Vanzetti.[43]

And the eighth was to become known as Earth, a planet often written of by Shakspere, Thomas Wolfe, and Paul Engle.[44]

2. Let us now devote our attention to the Earth.

In the beginning, earth was not, properly speaking, earth. It was just a blur of flaming gases.

Leonardo Today (Why: What: How: Why) An American Anthology.[45] (teeth poem) (Cong. Record: Long: Bilbo, Johnson[46] &c).

---

42. Percival Lowell (1855–1916), astronomer and brother of poet Amy Lowell, wrote three books on Mars arguing that the planet's canals had been constructed by intelligent beings and devoted much of his career searching for "Planet X." When the ninth planet was discovered in 1930 at Lowell Observatory in Arizona, it was named partially in his honor, the *Pl* in *Pluto* standing for his initials. Why Agee omits Mercury is unknown.

43. After anarchists Nicola Sacco (b. 1891) and Bartolomeo Vanzetti (b. 1888) were sentenced to death in April 1927, Governor Alvan Tufts Fuller of Massachusetts appointed Abbott Lawrence Lowell (1856–1943), president of Harvard and brother of Amy and Percival Lowell, to head a commission to determine the probity of the verdict. The Lowell Commission upheld the conviction, and Sacco and Vanzetti were executed August 23, 1927.

44. Paul Engle (1908–1991), American poet. In 1932, Engle's master's thesis, *Worn Earth*, was selected for publication in the Yale Series of Younger Poets, and two commercial volumes, *American Song* and *Break the Heart's Anger*, appeared in 1935 and 1936, respectively.

45. Edmund Clarence Stedman's *An American Anthology, 1787–1900*, published in 1900 and containing 1,740 selections of poetry, is a major document in American literary culture.

46. In 1935, Louisiana Senator Huey P. Long campaigned in Mississippi for Paul B. Johnson against Hugh L. White in that state's gubernatorial election until Mississippi Senator Theodore G. Bilbo warned him away.

In History.   Contemporary Art: Contemporary Literature: Journalism: &c &c.

This is the nationalistic decade: and I would be the last I assure you not to take advantage of that.

[N 24: Notes on World History]

(As contemporary history: a brief anthropology.)

(A) A short history of the earth: [illegible] the swatch of sun. Water: continents: mountains: cysted wealth: huge continents "undiscovered" by "civilized" man.

(B) A short history of the human race.

The cell wriggles & wrenches & fears & fights its way through and produces, at length, a thing which can be called man.

Men developed an impassioned genius for self-deception, and depended more & more on it.

Ideas of God, of possession, of art, of law, of govt, must have developed together—along w. language.

[] Basis of society: of the family: of religion: of art: of invention: of language.

Primitive societies.

Egypt. Made much of the lotus. Most of its people were owned by a few of its people. Nobody much cared. Spent immense labor raising hunks of stone to commemorate a "king". Believed in life after death. Wheat. The sun. Wood & stone.

Babylon & Assyria: checked on the sun, the moon, the stars. Kalendar. Lions & wings. (sun?) sacred whores. Curled beards. Hanging gardens. Slaves. Kings.

Greece. The dead present. Optical illusions. No zero. Clear heads (good air). Homosexual. Women. Slaves. Blues [illegible]. War over a woman: glorious. There have been sillier causes.

Jews. To avoid dirty pricks in hot weather, lopped them off in Name of God. Were carried thru 40 yrs wondering in name of damned lie. Great prophetic literature: more lies.

Rome. Hard-headed: "virtuous": "Will To Win". Law. Discipline. Moved in on Europe &c & took it. Republic. (Slaves). Empire. (slaves). Movt from land to city. Bread & circuses. Decline.

<u>Christ</u>. Socrates. Budda. Confucius. Christ. Mahomet. X's[47] teach-
ings to have considerable power & effect for next 2000 yrs.
Short biography. Plain. Burning. Radical. Sexual prig. Naturally,
crucified.
<u>Western Europe</u>.

[N 25: Fragment: "O my ancestral land"]

O my ancestral land, my tired old friends, my veterans:
How little light there is, in so much darkness.

You lived, as hungrily as I live now, and grew tired, or sorrowful, or
Darkness suddenly grew tired of seeing you in the light; and where are
you now.

There are records of most, traditions and legends of many, genealo-
gies for some; where are you now.

There is imagination. It is possible to imagine you as you may have
been before there was language. It is possible to imagine you as you
were when Egypt was failing, when Rome was shining, when you still
were savage: Druids and Gauls, Teutons and Scots, the people of amorphous Western Europe.

It is possible to imagine those of you who were contemporaries of
Charlemagne and of Shakespeare, to imagine you in the hovels and the
strange ways of dressing which are hardly more than archaeology, than
theatrical property, to me, but were your homes, the clothes you put
on when you got up in the morning. One of yours is said to have been
Wat Tyler.[48] One of you was Archbishop of Canterbury under
Elizabeth.[49] Some of you

&c   &c.   Some of you were among the Huguenots who took
refuge in Virginia and in the mountains below Virginia. It is possible
to imagine you, it is possible to realize that every one of you existed, as

---

47. Christ's.

48. Wat Tyler (1325?–1381) led an abortive peasant revolt, during which he
was killed, in southeastern England in 1381.

49. Edmund Grindal was the archbishop of Canterbury from 1576 to 1583,
during the reign of Elizabeth I. Agee's mother was descended from Elizabeth
Grindal, his sister.

fully as I exist, as fully as all those of whom I will try to write; but that is all that is possible, and where are you now?

[N 26: List: "Leon Trotsky's History of the Russian Revolution"]

Leon Trotsky's History of the Russian Revolution.[50]
Stag Dinner.
Amateur Nite.
Paris Commune.[51]
Lonigan's Wake.[52]
Serial.
White House.
Gatsby.
Campaign.

[N 27: Notes on Postwar Politics and Economy]

[1]

Ralph E Flanders Pres.[53]
    expand market for all kinds of mfg goods
    NX Laxes
Wilkie—[54]
    "Lend principle" re war taxation
    reduce taxes after war
    create biggest possible natl income

---

50. Trotsky's *History of the Russian Revolution,* translated by Max Eastman, was published by Simon and Schuster in 1932.

51. Probably Vladimir Lenin's *The Paris Commune* (New York: International, 1931.)

52. Presumably a conflation of the titles of James T. Farrell's *Studs Lonigan* trilogy (1932–35) and James Joyce's *Finnegans Wake* (1939).

53. Ralph E. Flanders (1880–1970), U.S. senator from Vermont (1946–59), was president of the Federal Reserve Board of Boston from 1944 to 1946.

54. Though Wendell Wilkie (1892–1944), a Republican utilities executive, ran for president against Franklin Roosevelt in 1940, he later supported some of Roosevelt's initiatives, such as the Lend-Lease Act.

Wallace[55] (eyes!)
>Important smell biz
Baruch—& his Boss Byrnes J is F.[56]
Demobilization & Industrial [illegible]
>biz & labor
[illegible] consumers market
>get statistics
>>glamour &c
>1 billion for household equipment—
>television ("thousands")
>helicopters on golf links
backlog of what?
150 orgs—Comm for Ec Development—Hoffmann
jump output 30-45% over 1940
>grassroots mvt (1300 VS towns)
also world-rebuilding
>Europe, China, Asia & Africa
>>raw materials
>principal market will be domestic but—

[2]

MOT [?]
Postwar Jobs?
Industrial concentration
contract canceled? layoff
"We all knew it had to come sometime"
spot unemployment—
War Manpower Comm.
>70,000 per month discharge veterans
army men & jobs—
>"never had a job"
50,000,000 civ employees   11m soldiers
8m [illegible]
>3 + 9 (army)—

---

55. Henry Wallace, Roosevelt's vice-president. See E 1, note 8.

56. Bernard M. Baruch, political consultant and financier (see J 4.14, note 51), was special adviser to Senator James F. Byrnes, Roosevelt's "assistant president" and head of the Office of War Mobilization and Reconversion.

Ser George (Ga).

    Dewey[57]—cash surplus for postwar reconstruction fund

140m $

great plant can beat anything yet

    filling [illegible]

Depression—good sheet Springfield Vt.—machine tool town

    hillmen; rootless war workers

    Jones & Lamson (1876)

3 yrs jobs for all.

    retooling to mass production, Cancellations

        for Boeing, helped

Confident that p-w orders (engineering dept)—

    [illegible]

[N 28: Notes on India-Pakistan Conflict]

daily income of 100,000 rupees; now it averages 40. The N Western Rway, which serves all W Pak & in mileage is one of the world's great systems, has suffered during 6 weeks [illegible]. There is absolutely no Xch of goods betw Ind & W. Pakistan today.[58]

Lahore is now normal xcpt that only 1 or 2 banks are open, few big insurance co's are operating, and stores selling durable consumer goods such as textiles, glassware, silver & gold jewelry are not functioning.

Karachi, no violence, a quiet steady exodus of Hindus, about 3,000 daily, by ship for Bombay; after selling to [illegible] Mu's at excellent prices. All thru West Pak a shortage of sweepers & sanitation workers, mostly Hindu. Pak auth great efforts to persuade them to remain. Security badge: [illegible] for these & other Untouchables.

A group of Muslim [illegible] came to a Hindu Sikh camp and with many assurances invited, virtually entreated, the merchants and financiers, to return. They stayed where they were.

---

57. Thomas E. Dewey (1902–1971), Republican governor of New York (1943–55) and presidential candidate in 1944 and 1948.

58. Virtually all the information covered in these notes on sectarian violence following the partition of Pakistan following Indian independence appears in a *Time* cover story for November 3, 1947, entitled "India-Pakistan: The Trial of Kali."

<u>Ind Pak Relations</u>: steadily worsened.

1) Question of a cession of princely states. 3 are above contention: Kashmir, which Pak has been pressing, & which announced this week that it aspired to be Asian, [illegible]

2) Hyderabad; State of Minister Patel has been pressing, without success, devout Muslimization

3) Junagadh, whose dog-[illegible] Nawab announced for Pak against will of Hindu [illegible] (80%). Pak is sending arms, even police; Patel has moved strong armed forces to the borders, very possible casus belli.

2) Difference on refugee question. Pak, hard pressed for cash, announced this week refusal to accept any further pop. xchange after the East Punj Moslems. India can see only way to handle question is to swap Delhi & [illegible] Muslims. A growing suspicion that some Hindu extremists like Patel intend to force them on. Not enough room in all Pak.

3) Property xchange. M refugees from Ind have been poor; H & S left behind prosperous landholdings & businesses. Nehru [illegible] and wd insist on adjustment of this very unequal xch of property. Sikh leader Tara Singh, rep for violent words, an easy solution. S & H of WPJ left 6m acres; Ms only 2, he advocated putting more M off land in other provinces to balance situation.

India holds whip hand: most assets still awaiting division. Pak must defend in future Ind goodwill to provide overland comm betw 2 parts of her strangely shaped Dominion.

<u>Women</u>: In Northern India, where the fiercest rioting took place, there are fewer women than men. Sikhs, whose religion forbids their marriage to Moslem women, apparently does not forbid rape followed by torture or release. Moslems, who can marry whom they please, steal women. inestimable # which round into the tens of thousands have been kidnapped during the riots. [illegible], and locked in Purdahs, they will not be easily found. The Indian Government has spoken severely to the Pak govt of this & the Pak gov't has severely requested that they be returned. But even if they are returned, nothing is more sacred to the H & S than the chastity of their women. Hinduism, hard pressed in battle, used to build fires in which their women might commit <u>Seti</u> rather than be captured; Sikhs, in a similar predicament during the past

weeks, are known to have slashed the throats of their wives & daughters. So, although G & others have urged that abducted women, if returned, be taken completely back into the fold, it is clear that the [illegible] of kidnapped women will have only begun.

[N 29: Fragment: "Bomb"]

BOMB

This is the worst single event in history, and I should think also the greatest.[59] We have it as immediately now as in our hands, to destroy ourselves, or to learn how not to. There is no longer any possible alternative.

[N 30: Proofing Notes]

✓ → stretched against that clear face his serpent's smile

✓ gold-white on gray-white, and in one place a rigid shaft of metal radiance almost pierced the fabric.
                    56. brave patterning: valiant: barbaric?: ✓
✓ p 13, shaft.
✓ p 15. his Aunt Patty
✓ 49. bleed, and many.   ✓ dancing trees 50
✓ 51. immortal patience   one [illegible]
✓ 56—becharmed for Enchanted

✓ fluid hieroglyph	—frowning	pale
✓ change on set hand free	angry	✓ limpid
✓ 56-7—flame & blossom?	scalding	clear
✓ p 20—gutter around mothery lives.	fiery	✓ crystal
	brassy	lucid
	—flaming	pure
		p 35—whiskey
✓ –11—exiled; now,	shivering	

------

59. Cf. Agee's "Victory: The Peace," *Time* 46 (August 20, 1945): 19–21. Rpt. in Ashdown, 160–61.

✓ –11—tenderly reveling &c.
   kind and sufferance / endurance? ? ✓
   10—
            brave

                         56 — valiant
                              valorous
                          ✓ barbaric
                              warlike
                                        50
                              X plum tree
                              50—dancing?
   spilled
   56—becharmed?   flirted around his hand
p 11 ✓ flowers: flicked
   flaming;   flickered
   may-apple—
35—whiskey

[N 31: Notes on Health Regimen]

tobacco—is it the nicotine or the tar?[60]
   Any filters take out nicotine?
   maximum c. 6? i.e. smokes only so much as 1 so long?

alcohol—
   what is the maximum? | fancy mxd drinks—
   tight? drunk?, ever?
gradual erosion? through alc. & tobacco
minimum sleep I shd have? 8 hrs.? 9?[61]

---

60. On January 15, 1952, Agee suffered the first of several heart attacks, and a second in late October of the same year.

61. In his foreword to *Agee of Film,* vol. 2, John Huston writes: "I can hear myself uttering some nonsense about doing things in moderation, like sleeping eight hours every night and smoking say half a pack of cigarets a day and only having a drink or two before dinner. Jim nodded his head in mute agreement with everything I said, or if not agreement, sympathy. And he went on nodding until I faltered and finished. Then he smiled his gentle smile and, after a decent interval, changed the subject."

not too many eggs—esp yolks—veg & meat fats; candy—
rest in middle of day? sh'd not stay up <u>far</u> <u>beyond</u> <u>my</u> normal
bedtime? i.e., a good night's sleep gives me a surplus of energy—I
can go 20, rather than 16—in fact it is hard to go 16 instead.
exercise & exertion: tennis doubles? (about 1/3 to 1/4th) the exertion
of singles.

The warnings are clear and, if heeded instantly, safe?
short of breath; palpitation; congestion; pain.
what type of pain in legs means embolism?
I think one trouble was, my wind got too good—
lifting; climbing.

_____

<u>non-physical</u> sources of trouble.
My work as a rule involves a lot of tension. Not as a rule when it is
going best—but distinctly so, on the way there, & sometimes there.
It can be very important sometimes to ride a spell out, and I've always
done so: have good stamina for that. Dangerous now?
one safety valve: If I feel too sick, or too exhausted, it usually
lowers the quality of the work so that I quit anyhow.

"emotional" stuff, personal relationships; my whole machinery of
relations & thinking &c, much like that of my work—
It is extremely unnatural to me to <u>avoid</u> strains, strong feeling, what
is known as trouble   should I try to?

[N 32: Columns of Figures (Bills)]

			.30
99.75			26.56
35.06			5.13
58.90			7.50
29.88			6.70
$223.59	11.25		6.70
	11.38		✓ 52.89 ←
	2.69		
	.10		
52.89	7.53	.10	.10
56.40	3.13	2.70	9.14
18.60	20.22	1.19	.50
30.43	56.40 ✓	.20	11.95
27.32	23	.10	5.63
12.03		3.14	27.32 ✓
197.67		23.00	2
221		30.43 ✓	
		1	.20
223.59	1,130.94		8.75
197.67	421.26		.10
421.26 (phones)	709.68	(Hospital bill.)	2.98
through Feb 13			12.03
463.59	(to Feb 15)		
421.26			

42.33 phone since Feb 13 (This is Friday

APPENDIX

Silent Corrections in the Reader's Text

KEY

{ } = interlinear insertion by Agee

{{ }} = marginal insertion by Agee

[ ] = editorial insertion

$\frac{J\ 1.2}{[3]}$ = Journal 1, entry 2, manuscript page 3

Please see "A Note on Editorial Matters and Methods"
(pages xli–xlv) for further details.

LET US NOW PRAISE FAMOUS MEN:
JOURNALS AND DRAFTS

Journal 1

[Brown spiral notebook, 8" x 5"; "The SPIRAL NOTE BOOK, No. 581-S"; lined pages; doubled-headed arrow in top right corner on back cover.]

J 1.1

[1]

[circled *2* in top left corner of margin]

[2]

. . . this creature, ~~and the trip was familiar to them in idioms of their own, so that the lines of rail split and unfurled ahead of~~

~~them the was the~~ and every quarter . . .

. . . crop, the ~~life~~ city and town . . .

[3]

[in top left margin: *as out of a tunnel.*]

———

. . . starting {in summer} at dusk . . .

. . . images are ~~multiple. I shan't pretend to give all mine, only a few.~~ likely to multiply . . .

[4]

. . . and ~~for~~ on its own merits . . .

. . . from all else it [something lined through] lay out there ahead of me {faintly shining in the night}, a huge . . .

[5]

. . . sensitive, {globular}, amorphous . . .

. . . to be played ~~when the needle has eaten an inch into~~ beyond . . .

. . . the disk) ~~this sperm~~ carrying . . .

. . . strong-headed {, infinitesimal} train . . .

. . . infinitesimal {yet absolute} terms . . .

. . . it brought ~~com~~ the complete . . .

. . . good friend.

~~I thought also in more plainly movie ways.~~
Then there were other ways.

[6]

. . . they sliver ~~their way~~ and sometimes . . .

. . . along the [something lined through] unfurlings over space . . .

[7]

. . . the {intense} sharp glands . . .

. . . and the clay {trackside} weeds shudder, {{insert from left margin: *like a sped-up movie shot*}} and with a reduction . . .

[8]

. . . a child ~~in bed~~ awake . . .

. . . has never ~~extrick~~ extricated . . .

. . . music, and {{insert from bottom margin: , *above all, after the preparation of the two long, lifted notes and the short note, in the lingering, softening, mournfully land-caressing falling and failure of the {iron yet} streamlike last note,*}} is one . . .

[9]

. . . the shaded {, peopled and sleeping} earth opening . . .

. . . lost, ~~in the~~ out . . .

. . . like ~~those~~ the speculations . . .

[10]

. . . you hear {the metal noises} its wheels . . .

J 1.2

[10]

. . . is not [something lined through] solemn but is [something lined through] {a} vigilance . . .

[11]

It is [something lined through] likely to be capable . . .

The [something lined through] satisfactory feeling . . .

[12]

It took me {suddenly} by train . . .

. . . obstructs it. [something lined through] By mere tricks . . .

. . . as it is now, [something lined through] thinking . . .

[13]

This [something lined through] can so easily slacken . . .

J 1.3

[15]

{{insert from left margin: *In*}} Much of this trip . . .

J 1.4

[17]

. . . old friend of mine [something lined though] {at the} school . . .

. . . Tennessee. {{insert from top margin: *I mention these places because.*}} We needed money . . .

[18]

... one I have {{insert from end of sentence: *a hundred per cent*}} worked ...

... September {or} October ...

[19]

... but ~~it is seldom you get paid for doing anywhere near exactly that, and the chance opens~~ as a rule ...

... a good deal about ~~this country in terms~~ the south ...

My father ~~had~~ died when I was six and {{insert from left margin: *though I spent some lucky years in a mountain school*}} most of my life ...

... this fact [something lined through] than not ...

... cheated and ~~crippled~~ irreparably crippled ...

[20]

... unable to ~~use the wor~~ hear ...

[21]

I intended ~~to write~~ to research ...

[22]

... all of which {of course,} when ...

My mind ~~was~~ became capable ...

... strongly mannic ...

J 1.5

[23]

... to exercise [diagonal line running right to left from the end of *exercise* in the middle of the line across the next line to the left margin before *the*] the word ...

... vase &c, [something lined through] putting ...

... and as Ive said ...

[26]

[*or is it.* a few lines beneath the closing with a line indicating the phrase refers to *of course I mean my life, but I retain just sense enough to know that is impossible*]

J 1.6

[27]

. . . that the {stretched} skin burned . . .

[28]

He {had never been south but had organized the Defense Comm.} [and] could . . .

[29]

. . . had ~~also~~ been absorbed . . .

. . . which {badly} embarrassed him.

. . . plate, ~~and they cleared ab It lasted~~ The meal alone lasted . . .

[30]

. . . were not such ~~phonies~~ {{insert from left margin: *utter*}} {frauds} but . . .

. . . tuned in {and kept quiet and listened,} all of course . . .

A {serious} rather complacent . . .

[30-31]

. . . with a ~~fair but overdramatic voice led off with a number called They Burn Babies in Alabama~~ fair baritone . . .

[31]

This {hot tip} was ~~given out~~ {passed} in ~~the sort of Darky dialect that white men affect~~ {the dialect affected by {the sort of} whites who call Negroes darkies.}

. . . with lots of {cultivated} discords . . .

. . . let ding {fortissimo} on some {dialect} word . . .

[32]

. . . wish, ~~dissatisfied~~ bedroom eyes {which dissatisfaction} with {had given} a class angle . . .

{{insert from left margin: *When all was said and done this* ~~bellyful~~ *{5-hour plethora} of tortoni* [sic] *{and political bellyrubbing} cleared about twenty-nine dollars in at best indirect behalf of 9 million people who have never eaten fresh meat.*}}

. . . Alabama [something lined through] so you bitches can sit around and smell {*sniff* above *smell*} the bacon.

J 1.8

[38]

. . . we need {better} understanding . . .

[39]

. . . worry {{insert from left margin: *nor assign it great power of meaning*}} over feelings . . .

[40]

. . . communication from me will ~~vitital~~ vitiate . . .

[41]

. . . may dull it. also . . .

. . . will become less [something lined through] eager . . .

[43]

. . . than I can [something lined through] tell you . . .

[44]

. . . so much. [Agee's brackets follow:] [that again is assuming you could wish it, which I have no reason to assume & do not assume or dream of; I'm only again telling what I feel.]

J 1.10

[49]

. . . thoroughly successful {and thoroughly} communist . . .

. . . in proportion to the {{insert from bottom margin: *relative*}} strength . . .

[51]

. . . seeing {and reading} here: is one {thorough and} entirely . . .

J 1.11

[53]

. . . in Jesus name . . .

J 1.12

[57]

. . . in Jesus name . . .

J 1.13

[89]

. . . basic, [something lined through] and not to be . . .

[**93-95**]

    (Again, they might not.[)]

[**95**]

    . . . bye-lined . . .

Journal 2

[Brown spiral notebook, 8" x 5"; "The SPIRAL NOTE BOOK, No. 581-
S"; lined pages; *C* on front cover; damage to bottom right corner of cover
and first 8 pages.]

J 2.1

[**1**]

    [circled *3* in top left margin]

[**5**]

    [something lined through] "Forgotten Men" film.

[**7**]

    . . . unresolved guitar {chord}.

    . . . descent. [something lined through] Heavily leafed . . .

    . . . trees of [something lined through] houses . . .

[**9**]

    ~~Katov and Kyo are lying side by side, close together; separated
by the vast expanse of suffering~~

    Katov is lying . . .

J 2.3

[**31**]

    . . . most uneasy {over} if . . .

[**35**]

    . . . and feel its ~~varite~~ variety . . .

    . . . and [something lined through] drags the rest down . . .

[**37**]

    . . . life.

    [two long boxes]

XXXXXXXXXXXXXXXXXXXXXXXXXXXXXXXXXXXXXXXXXXXXXX

J 2.4

[37]

. . . along the rails {{insert from left margin: *in a steady shuffling, creaking, leaving,* [something lined through] *decorated by bells, whistlings and brief stops,*}} the train . . .

. . . next day: ~~hot summer;~~ the strong {June} light . . .

. . . buildings, ~~and~~ the people . . .

[37-39]

The taxi driver {, who said he} was the youngest in the city, ~~He~~ took me a short cut across the {bumping} railroad tracks . . .

[41]

. . . busses {{insert from top margin: *, the asphalt, blue in shadow, pale grey-gold in the slicing sunlight; the orchestration of motors; the sharp hiss of air brakes.*}}

. . . came out {at five,} ate a hot dog . . .

. . . 7 oclock . . .

. . . night on ~~the~~ a bench . . .

[41-43]

. . . green with a [in top margin: *All hotel carpet feels richer than it looks.*]

sober, small black pattern.

[43]

Under the [something lined through] glass top of the narrow desk ~~are~~ is a [something lined through] calendar . . .

[*fan.* in left margin] The fan swirs at the centre cieling.

. . . thought of {cheap to middle-price} hotel rooms . . .

[45]

. . . a huge ~~house~~ {and} unknown house . . .

. . . this on ~~new,~~ back roads, new to us, west {and south} of Tuscaloosa . . .

[47]

. . . stood up ~~well spaced~~ thickly . . .

. . . stagnant looking) ~~red water~~ deep . . .

. . . but ~~the leaves of the~~ the foliage . . .

J 2.5

[51]

 . . . the letter ~~contain~~ returning Burroughs letter. . .

J 2.6

[53]

 . . . keep going on {{insert from top margin: *all in one unbroken breath,*}} and would . . .

J 2.7

[53]

The fox. ~~Some t~~ The noise . . .

 . . . like ~~an~~ furred animal . . .

 . . . understand why you are [something lined through] sure.

[55]

 . . . implicit, though, {not real; it is} like seeing {into} the secret life . . .

Stacatto.

[Line from *Set up as musically or artificially, as you like.* indicates this direction refers to the previous three lines from *Silence* to the dashes.]

J 2.8

[57]

 . . . whom through, I [something lined through] was in love . . .

J 2.9

[59]

 . . . wanted to stay, and ~~for~~ {were} for that matter . . .

 . . . to tell you [something lined through] latter . . .

 . . . part new. ~~But~~ Also am . . .

J 2.10

[62]

 . . . live up to {{insert from left margin: *toward*}} it . . .

[64]

 . . . ~~Puskin's~~ Pushkin's writing?

J 2.11
[65]

. . . before I know [something lined through] what . . .

J 2.12
[67]

. . . my kind, [*truest* above *kind*] my transient . . .

~~If we should~~
O if we should . . .

[69]

If we should [something lined through] wake

J 2.13
[71]

Out of the [something lined through] wish . . .

J 2.14
[75]

~~Though this lies down as all things wide~~
~~Into the~~
Though this lies down as all things do
~~In the earth at length~~
At length in the large earth, the true

J 2.15
[77]

. . . as I do {of} this . . .

. . . Tranquillity . . .

J 2.17
[81]

. . . in effect: ~~depending on circumstances, I have~~ "generically, I
have sympathy with labor and its difficulties, and [something
lined through] agree . . .

. . . collective bargaining {, and picketing.}

[82]

. . . every right to ~~do this~~ call . . .

. . . protect ~~the~~ rights . . .

[84]

And if {great sections of} the law-abiding populace . . .

J 2.19

[87]

. . . a long [here Agee has drawn a long strip] strip . . .

Aron this earth right to left in continuous repeated freize . . .

[88]

. . . leaves. ~~Then begin again shots~~ {Stills} either . . .

Then: ~~small town~~ camps . . .

[89]

A big section on [something lined through] <u>mothers</u>.

. . . children at ~~work & play & scho~~ at [*sic*] play . . .

. . . class prejudice and [something lined through] americanism.

[89-90]

Hcrc might be chamber [in top margin: *This all might be run on Food Clothing & Shelter,* → *WORK and LEISURE.*] of Honors.

[90]

Men Who Govern Us: [something lined through] mayors . . .

[91]

. . . cops, criminals, [something lined through] Natl Guardsmen . . .

. . . of law; [something lined through] recapitulate . . .

J 2.20

[93]

Its ~~speed~~ combination . . .

. . . and ~~its~~ the slenderness . . .

. . . the ~~ease~~ almost slippery ease . . .

. . . of [something lined through] the new length . . .

. . . as the [something lined through] side streets diminished . . .

[94]

. . . through ~~now~~ surroundings now . . .

. . . beautiful ~~low-buildinged~~ low-built city . . .

. . . the green ~~side of~~ flank . . .

. . . sharp-edged ~~white~~ pure white . . .

[95]

. . . red-brown {, islanded,} Tennessee river . . .

. . . tilted in a ~~left~~ long left . . .

. . . the sudden [something lined through] lifted lean . . .

. . . beautiful, ~~psy~~ physical curve . . .

[96]

. . . riversides are very like{ly} to look . . .

[97]

[in top margin:~~are those who fight it. Are you for it or against it.~~]

. . . bridge. ~~This was badly burnt land~~ This country . . .

. . . and ~~the~~ weeks of rainless sunlight . . .

. . . stone loose in the [something lined through] sunlight.

[98]

. . . are still {shyly} making [something lined through] intimate . . .

. . . cottonwoods {lifting their sporadic waves nearly to bridge level,} rows of brittle . . .

. . . and [something lined through] foolishly narrow . . .

[99]

. . . upon our narrow {{insert from top margin: *business of driving.*}}

. . . country that was ~~of no century~~ a certain . . .

. . . too. ~~And yet not only ma~~ Others had built . . .

. . . as most ~~city people do~~ cities and city people do.

[100]

[vertical line along left margin down this page with a large *X* to its left]

[101]

. . . cross bridge; {georgia line}: to right . . .

. . . due west; [something lined through] branch to Scottsboro; the courthouse town; ~~decline sou~~ spilling off . . .

. . . town around you is is [*sic*] physically influential as is for instance the ~~pull~~ centrifugal pull . . .

. . . and the {strong} sense . . .

. . . you are going: ~~so that in all~~ the [something lined through] minor curves . . .

[102]

. . . a broad reach ~~instea~~ as compared . . .

. . . chiefly into ~~two thin~~ three things . . .

. . . phrase in ~~directions~~ the sum . . .

. . . undergone; {specially clear} recalls . . .

J 2.21
[107]

. . . dry. ~~Though~~ Figure that out for yourself. ~~I have~~ I take . . .

. . . any such job here. {{insert from left margin: *in too many other ways*}} I simply do not think . . .

[111]

. . . So, {then,} inevitably . . .

. . . attempt to give [something lined through] any experience . . .

[113]

. . . the experience is ~~not my fairly accurate memory of~~ neither . . .

. . . the amount I ~~have~~ am talking about . . .

Journal 3

[loose pages in "John Carter" notebook]

J 3.1
[1]

[circled *1* in top right margin]

The [something lined through] death of the kittens.

[2]

[circled *2* in top right margin]

. . . (blue notebook B[])]

clay; Lucile – [circled *A*]

Journal 4

[Brown spiral notebook, 8½" x 7", with plain cover; "University, Genuine Pressboard, No. 400" on bottom right inside cover; lined pages.]

J 4.2

[3]

. . . Delaxroix . . .

. . . Blitzsteins show . . .

[4]

. . . to get anything {new to her} into her head . . .

[5]

. . . your {lack [of]} understanding . . .

[6]

. . . fine, steady, {human-}animal . . .

[8]

. . . Brick or Helen Leavitt . . .

[9]

. . . Vi had been there. . .

J 4.3

[11]

. . . Vias . . .

. . . Lynchs . . .

[13]

. . . old movie theatre {romantic} Numbers.

Brick ~~lay~~ took Emma on his lap . . .

. . . you do that to.

[14]

She was [something lined through] extremely sad and clear, and [something lined through] deeply in love . . .

[16]

. . . Cocanut [*sic*] Waffles.

[17]

    . . . (by ~~not~~ not letting her down) . . .

    . . . that can ~~make~~ relieve you . . .

[18]

    . . . similar cases to {the} one selected . . .

    . . . which are [something lined through] falsehood.

J 4.4

[19]

    . . . the old gangster {pamphlet} idea . . .

[20]

    Mrs ~~Dalhaver's~~ Shaffer & child.

    The cover {picture,} disembodied . . .

[23]

    . . . the neon ~~Frankfurters~~ Hamburgers . . .

[24]

    . . . type; {(and totally courageous)} these three things . . .

    I guess the {complacent} portrait . . .

[26]

    . . . the oil-[something lined through]spotted concrete.

[28-29]

    [Agee's brackets around the next two paragraphs:] [Here I got tired and restless, and nearly sure to surrender {to} one form or another of weakness. I felt like the pacifications of masturbating, but knew in advance its probable depressing effect; also that sexual fasting in all ways will be my surest and soonest restorative to more solid love and mental clarity than I have felt for several days. I am very slowly learning in this and in my mind, and still more slowly, and irregu{l}arly, beginning to have the intelligence and strength to apply what I have learned. {{insert from top margin: *I am not speaking of masturbation but of everything to do with the psychophysiology of sex. I masturbate 'infrequently'; whatever that means. By my own estimate for myself, on average once in 3 weeks.*}}

What I finally surrendered to was reading Gide, the Congo. With about one sentence in every two I knew I was doing wrong [Here Agee has a single bracket in front of and containing the phrases *the mistake I was making* and *I was doing wrong*, with the former above the latter. A line runs from the bracket to this explanation in the left margin: *these are nearly always synonymous and the upper of the two is I believe always the more nearly true.*], for I was disturbed as you are bound to be when you find even minute aspects of your mind, and methods, and technical ideas, anticipated or cut across. I must not touch this book again until I have finished mine, though my own thinking would in some obvious respects gain by it. It causes weakness and paralysis and can indeed suggest death, which it literally is: one 'ego' masked by another, the masking of binary stars. Most of the people I would most enjoy reading and most prefer to study, I should not read.]

[30]

. . . they might ~~other~~ under . . .

J 4.5

[37]

. . . some graceful {literary} gestures . . .

[38]

. . . what he intends to [something lined through] any other human being.

It is impossible sufficiently to assume the ~~cheated and the ignorant and the coward and the~~ delusion . . .

[40]

[in left top margin a circled *5* is scratched out; *(3 space)* is top center; between *(3 space)* and top line is '¶ *Above all else; in God's name don't think of it as Art.*]

[arrow indicating indent in left margin] ¶ Every fury on earth has been absorbed in time, as art, or as religion, or as authority in one form or another. The deadliest blow the enemy of the human soul can strike is to do fury honor. Swift, Blake, Beethoven, Christ, {Joyce, Kafka,} name me one who has not been thus castrated. Official acceptance is the one unmistakable symptom that salvation is beaten again, and is the one sure sign of {fatal} misunderstanding, and is the kiss of Judas.

See how respectable Beethoven is; and {by} what right any wall in museum, gallery or home ~~has to wear~~ {presumes to wear} a Cézanne; and by what idiocy Blake or work even of such intention as mine is ever published {{insert from left margin: *and sold*}}.

. . . a phonograph capable of ~~extrem~~ the most extreme . . .

[41]

It is {beyond any calculation} savage and dangerous {and murderous} to all equilibrium . . .

[41-42]

And ~~I do not~~ {{insert from top margin: *I would be a liar and a coward and one of your safe world if I should*}} fear to say the same words of my best perception, and of my best intention. ~~Performance is another matter.~~

Performance, in which the whole fate and terror rests, is another matter.'

J 4.6
[43]
. . . to add ~~that~~ of the security . . .

[45]
. . . loneliness intensifying, ~~her~~ all I love . . .

J 4.7
[48]
. . . I can't ~~get~~ take hold . . .

J 4.8
[49]
. . . ~~27 (?) Fe~~ 25 Feb.

[50]
. . . none of it ~~makes~~ can make . . .

. . . strictneses . . .

[51]
keep .making additions . . .

[52]
. . . that thought {and conscience} assumes . . .

. . . conscience and intelligence are {(particularly under immediately 'personal' pressures)} rationalizations . . .

[53]

. . . between ~~sup~~ suspension . . .

J 4.9

[56]

I [something lined through] now put it down . . .

J 4.10

[57]

. . . a thing {you have been wanting} is so powerful . . .

. . . and had [three-dot triangular symbol for *therefore*] better not . . .

[59]

. . . and {so} elaborate . . .

[60]

. . . the work I love {most} is . . .

. . . interested in it as 'right' [something lined through] and in getting . . .

J 4.11

[61]

. . . Fosters . . .

J 4.12

[65]

. . . Hudsons . . .

. . . Mozarts . . .

. . . not waiting for answers or listening to them, & [something lined through] {my} answers more mild & inaudible . . .

[66]

. . . the morning watch{:} I say . . .

[67

. . . one [something lined through] leaf, wagging . . .

[69]

Creamed potatoes, a little ~~scho~~ scorched, hot cocoa, canned
~~preserv~~ preserves. There was tarnish light on the {thinned}
tines of the forks . . .

[70]

The slow wave lifted them {, their table and} ~~in~~ their city . . .

[squiggly line beneath *Stealing, ever, in wood stillness*]

[71]

. . . when all ~~the~~ {our} trouble was over . . .

. . . her peculiarly ~~shining~~ {pure} smile . . .

[72]

. . . this {past} year.

J 4.13
[73]

. . . motives, [something lined through] ethics . . .

J 4.14
[73]

. . . play: [something lined through] 'Imagination![']

[74]

. . . Hudson's, ~~mid~~ elderly woman . . .

. . . <u>gifts</u>.[']

. . . critical {of my writing} in the first . . .

. . . commit to any 'friendliness', ~~This~~ or to any . . .

. . . Mrs. S.'. . .

[75]

. . . I am ~~afraid~~ afraid . . .

. . . to my self . . .

J 4.15
[77]

~~Wednesday~~ [series of 8 dots beneath ~~*Wednesday*~~] night

~~The~~ Restatement . . .

She ~~shilf~~ shifts . . .

. . . the ~~imed~~ immediate problem . . .

[78]

. . . its a mistake . . .

. . . have {{insert from left margin: *Leroy Street*}} found a separate room . . .

[79]

. . . remotely {toward} as well as . . .

[81]

. . . alleviation to you to know, [something lined through] her love . . .

. . . vindictiveness that {we} might . . .

J 4.17

[83]

[*BFM* in left margin] [Agee's brackets follow:] {The stills from the play [something lined through] indicate the French (some of them) had . . . American quickies and comedies}.

[*BFM:* in left margin]

. . . apres . . .

. . . moutet.[']

[84]

[*BFM* in left margin]

. . . The Crowd roars . . .

. . . Chaplins . . .

[85]

. . . of {such as} these . . .

J 4.18

[85]

. . . when the Klan rides.[)]

[86]

[Agee's brackets follow:] [Also Perdido Street seems . . .
ancient and tragic.]

J 4.19
[91]

[in the top margin are three signatures:] Alma Mailman
James Agee   JR Agee [in a different hand]

WE	THEY
~~dust pan, brush~~	tan chair
~~broom~~ [something lined through]	straight chairs
~~waste basket~~	large bed
garbage ~~basket~~ {CAN}	book case(s)

. . . piano; ~~music~~ . . .

. . . ~~swim~~ {BATHING} . . .

J 4.20
[93]

[—*x*— doodle in top margin]

. . . <u>hoarding</u> {{insert from top margin: *marriage.*}}

. . . sister & s' friends . . .

Journal 5

[Brown spiral notebook, 8½" x 7", with plain cover; lined pages.]

J 5.1
[1]

. . . for instance, ~~will~~ and any movie . . .

Rubato's . . .

J 5.2
[3]

~~by~~ BY . . . Allienay [*sic*] Burroughs

[4]

SEE B [*B* circled]

. . . October 19, 197

. . . Floyd B. and Allie [*A* and *O* superimposed] Mae B

J 5.3

[7]

. . . angle and [something lined through] almost immediately . . .

. . . and lies in {a} lightly curved ~~near-straight~~ series . . .

ET cetera.

. . . on the right, is an [*sic*] ~~unused~~ {no longer used} gravel pit . . .

[8]

. . . but in [something lined through] relation to . . .

. . . the local "~~gla~~ galaxy" . . .

. . . paredox . . .

[9]

~~The~~ The "Goodness" or "Evil" . . .

. . . extremely little ~~of~~ difference . . .

. . . what she meant.[)]

[10]

. . . Burroughs hall in the [something lined through] middle of a [something lined through] dark warm-cool morning . . .

. . . the ragged ~~edges~~ {ends} of the boards . . .

. . . senses first of ~~an~~ infants . . .

. . . colorings of all ~~possible~~ circumstances possible . . .

[11]

. . . that environment [something lined through] in its total . . .

. . . people deceptively [something lined through] rid.

What about their ~~lie~~ leisure.

[12]

What is an ove{r}all day like. ~~What are the sex~~ A week.

. . . possible ~~to invent~~ in this limited time to invent . . .

[13]

. . . quite different {, and relatively sophisticated,} traditional . . .

J 5.4

[15]

. . . were fine, and ~~diff~~ deferred it . . .

[16]

. . . Walkers . . .

[17]

. . . remembering these ~~two~~ {three} parts . . .

[18]

. . . reached the crest: [something lined through] I was now . . .

J 5.6

[20]

. . . setting and landscape. [something lined through] Interiors . . .

[24]

. . . Assissi . . .

. . . hold him. [something lined through] He has done . . .

Journal 6

[Brown spiral notebook, 7" x 5", with plain cover; lined pages.]

J 6.1

[1]

. . . damned [*sic*] rivers . . .

[line drawn down middle of page between first column and *Geronimo* and *254*]

[5]

[something lined through] though it doesn't carry . . .

[7]

(—

[   ] [These are Agee's brackets.]

1,2,3,4,5,6,7

———

———

J 6.2

[9]

. . . tries to be, ~~and~~ the things ~~that~~ critics . . .

If this is [something lined through] true of the best . . .

[11]

. . . overlook{—or still worse, see and forgive—}any number of {its} merely . . .

[13]

. . . human living {, pain} and dignity . . .

. . . richer in meaning {and revelation} than any . . .

. . . within limited space to [something lined through] . . .

[15]

. . . through the [something lined through] roadside fence . . .

[17]

. . . littler things, so ~~lost in the general~~ compromised . . .

J 6.3

[21]

. . . Farm Bureau Administration {to a New York magazine for which I worked, and for this magazine} ~~and~~ we were preparing an article on this same nominal subject. ~~for a New York magazine~~ For reasons which may be examined . . .

[23]

. . . must bide their [something lined through] time.

[25]

That is of ~~casual~~ importance . . .

[33]

~~So much has been attempted in this book, so inadequately, and so small upon the scale and requirement of the subject, that the temptation is strong~~
Much has been attempted . . .

. . . so much {here} is unexplained . . .

[35]

~~During July and August 1936 Walker Evans and I sought out and, for a few weeks, intimately lived with, three white families of tenant~~

~~This began a piece of work for a magazine and for the Federal Government, during July and August 1936. During these~~
During July and August . . .

[37]

~~Ultimately, a complete exposition of the subject, and a thorough examination and explanation of the method, will be obligatory.~~
~~So much has been attempted in this book, and it is so small on the scale of its subject, and so inadequate even on its own scale, that~~
Much has been attempted . . .

. . . indispensible . . .

[39]
. . . the stature of a ~~piece~~ {portion} of unimagined existence . . .

. . . indispensible . . .

[41]
They {also} represent, or are . . .

[43]
. . . to any {form of} authority save one . . .

. . . this organism and ~~had~~ {will} best be recognized . . .

[47]
. . . pure record, and [something lined through] indications . . .

. . . violations, [something lined through] insults . . .

Of ~~All~~ {any} attempts . . .

. . . to all those ~~who are~~ capable . . .

[49]
{Nominally this volume is} a record . . .

[illegible word written slantwise in indentation space]
Essentially, it begins a lawless enquiry into ~~human divinity under circumstances of normal disadvantage,~~ {[illegible]} ~~predicament,~~ certain predicaments . . .

. . . its nominal subject, [something lined through] a series of violations . . .

[52]

*Evans was on loan from the Federal Government. [on top line; refers to asterisk on page 53]

, or withdrawn, in the interests of personal integrity as opposed to the comfort of the general reader. [at the bottom of the page; alternate completion of *At the end of another year and a half the manuscript was rejected* on page 53]

[53]

~~During July and August 1936 Walker Evans and I were at work in the middle south of this nation~~

During July and August 1936 Walker Evans and I were traveling {and at work} in the middle south of this nation [Agee's brackets follow:] [engaged in what, even from the first, has seemed to me rather a curious piece of work.]

. . . tenant farmers. ~~It was our business also~~ {We had first} to find {and to live with} such a family. ~~and to live with its members.~~

. . . could be {fairly} represented . . .

. . . intimately and constantly. [Agee's brackets follow:] [going intensely about our tasks of observation, questioning and record]

At the end of a year [Agee's brackets follow:] [of vacillation] it was, however, released to us; and in the spring of [Agee's brackets follow:] [the following year,] 1938, [something lined through] an agreement . . .

[54]

[at the bottom of the page 54 across from the sentence beginning *It is, essentially* on page 55 is written *certain normal* [something lined through] *predicaments of human divinity.*]

[55]

. . . beginning of a [sic] ~~much~~ extensive piece . . .

. . . work as may ~~(or may not)~~ be done.

. . . the effort is [Agee's brackets follow:] [more considerable if less feasible. It is, briefly,] to recognize . . .

. . . to contrive ~~pro~~ techniques proper . . .

The immediate [something lined through] instruments . . .

The ~~more essential~~ {governing} instrument{—which is also centre of investigation—} is individual . . .

[56]

~~of what inadequacy the reader may, or may not, dis~~
      ~~The normal subject, and~~
      ~~The reader will do well to~~
[arrow indicates to insert the following before *The surface is hardly scratched* on page 57:] Since the book is intended, among other things, as a swindle, an insult and a corrective, the reader will be wise to bear the nominal subject, and his expectation of its proper treatment, steadily in mind.

[57]

. . . it may seem, left untouched, {{insert from top margin: *no relevancy avoided, which lies within the power of remembrance to maintain, of the mind to perceive, of the soul to persist in,*}} which lies within the power . . .

Of this ultimate intention the present volume is merely portent and fragment, experiment, ~~and~~ {dissonant} prologue. {{insert from page 56: *Since the book is intended, among other things, as a swindle, an insult and a corrective, the reader will be wise to bear the nominal subject, and his expectation of its proper treatment, steadily in mind.*}} The surface is hardly scratched.

. . . by the weakness {and corruption} of the reader's eye, this will be {mis}understood by most . . .

In the interests, however, [Agee's brackets follow:] [of fact, of personal integrity, and] of the history . . .

[Agee's brackets follow:] [Much that will seem to the reader . . . minimum of either here.]

[59]

. . . for {the} changes of tone . . .

. . . that the ~~book~~ {text} be read . . .

[61]

[seven doodles in top margin]

With so much abortive, ~~so much~~ deceptive, ~~so much~~ deliberately incomplete, ~~so much~~ dependent . . .

It will, ~~be resisted~~ however . . .

J 6.4
[63]

Mr. Walker Evans and I are ~~preparing~~ {completing} a ~~volume~~ book on cotton tenantry, to be published this winter by Houghton Mifflin. ~~We want to obtain permission.~~ ~~May we have~~ {We would much appreciate} your permission to quote ~~an interview~~ May Cameron's interview . . .

J 6.5
[65]

~~To whom it may concern:~~

A record [Agee's brackets follow:] [in photographs and in writing] of the daily ~~living~~ {living} of three {white} families . . .

~~Photographs~~ {~~Records~~ Images,} inventories, ~~remembrances~~ meditations and invectives {{insert from space in the middle of the page: *Findings, records, interpretations and conjectures*}} on the daily living . . .

J 6.6
[69]

It happened [something lined through] {succinctly to represent} a good deal . . .

. . . reasonableness, to ~~give the~~ {do such} questions more honor . . .

. . . I knew and ~~felt affection for~~ {liked (and like)} some of the editors . . .

. . . and I ~~felt sure~~ {thought it likely that} my reply . . .

. . . and ~~my~~ {the} reply was not printed . . .

. . . opinions is ~~part of a worth~~ a point worth mentioning . . .

I wish [Agee's brackets follow:] [here] to thank [Agee's brackets follow:] [my friend] Dwight Macdonald . . .

[71]

. . . add to this~~, though I am~~ a [something lined through] belief in non-resistance to evil . . .

. . . about this belief {{insert from bottom margin: *still more so, about my own ability to stand by it.*}} I also question whether a draft ~~should not be resisted~~ —or even registration—should not be resisted on still other grounds: [something lined through] i.e., ~~question whe~~ whether the State . . .

Or, put more [something lined through] immediately, whether an individual can in good conscience serve, or register, by any requirement {{insert from bottom margin: *other than his own.*}}

J 6.7
[73]
     . . . art magazines, [something lined through] buyers of modern-library . . .

[79]
     . . . normal ailments, {electricity (radio)} sexual ethics . . .

Journal 7

[loose page in Texas Box 12, folder 7]

J 7.1
[1]
          [10 circular doodles in top margin]

     . . . enclose copy; ~~you use your~~ and leave . . .

ESSAYS AND DRAFTS

E 1: "America! Look at Your Shame!"

[Tennessee folder 4, loose pages in "John Carter" notebook]
[1]
     . . . who were {not only} horrified . . .

[2]
     . . . were of ~~the~~ {a} sort . . .

     . . . with [something lined through] fancy sentimentality.

     . . . the eye that ~~follow~~ eats . . .

[3]

~~The~~ I had not seen . . .

. . . if work ~~deprives~~ causes . . .

[4]

. . . blue-gold ~~monoxide~~, clean compound . . .

~~All around me, in the bus~~ I watched all the people . . .

. . . as they thought {, if they did,} of what was happening . . .

Across the aisle [something lined through] were some sailors . . .

. . . but I was ~~glad that~~ no longer . . .

[5]

. . . voice just as well, and [something lined through] the special . . .

. . . the other new Atlanta . . .

They were ~~pleased as~~ happy . . .

. . . as it is [something lined through] dear to natives . . .

. . . special ~~p~~ broadenings . . .

[6]

. . . each other {according to} their own language . . .

. . . the ~~nig~~ fucking niggers . . .

. . . fuckin~~g~~' Nawth.

. . . like a ~~knife~~ cold knife . . .

Three ~~tyew~~ any ovem tried it . . .

[7]

. . . or more abject ~~piece~~ device . . .

[8]

. . . I know {(I may be, but the way I say it makes it a lie.)}.

. . . this war is about {(is it? is it?)}.

. . . fighting it at all {(we might as well not indeed)}.

I'm not I know ~~but I'm~~ but . . .

(will I? . . .

[9]

. . . a small yet {not wholly un}distinguished instant in the ~~long~~ history of the {world's} long Fight for Freedom . . .

. . . and {an elderly} Negro woman had his seat. ~~W~~

[10]

So ~~kn~~ now I am telling it to you.

E 2: "Nathanael West: A Portrait"

[Tennessee folder 18, white pages 2–3]

[1]

[Agee's brackets follow:] [From 'Little Rambles in the American Past', by A Gentleman with a Duster.]

~~At the~~ In ~~1933,~~ the spring of 1933, a few months after ~~Ernest Hemingway had added~~ the publication of 'Death in the Afternoon' had [something lined through] given notice . . .

. . . after ~~the first~~ Conquistador, the first narrative poem of the time, had ~~receive~~ been so poorly . . .

. . . when ~~Mr.~~ Cummings . . .

. . . Dana ({perverted} grandson of a union sonneteer) . . .

. . . before ~~Michael Gold became~~ Robert Cantwell . . .

. . . at a time when [something lined through] the young men who had ~~turned Anglo-Catholic with T. S. Eliot were leaving~~ gone through despair to turn Anglo-Catholic with Eliot were leaving the fold to become Agrarians, [something lined through] Fascists, Communists: at a time, more importantly, when American ~~lit~~ writers were first, as they quaintly put it, 'feeling their oats'; ~~were making a rather outlandish pose of having no pose whatever~~ were ~~persuaded by the violence of their reaction~~ deluded . . .

. . . Nathanael West's ~~published~~ 'Miss Lonelyhearts' . . .

~~West had already written~~ It was not . . .

. . . which, ~~wa~~ semi-privately published and ~~advertised~~ urged . . .

. . . Miss Lonelyhearts ~~never~~ had never heard . . .

. . . acclaimed it as ~~carefully~~ {{insert from left margin: *conscientiously*}} and well written, as if that in itself were something ~~to be grateful for~~ so rare . . .

. . . leftwing critics ~~were happy to find that it pinned a decaying system to the wall, but regretted that West had~~ found . . .

. . . language. [something lined through] Anyone using American must have taste in [illegible] to be able to select from among the teeming ~~vulgarities of~~ vulgarisms . . .

[2]

[rectangular doodle in top left corner]

. . . group which ~~as few will have reason to recall, made a fetish of fetishes such fetishes of See Seeing Raw and Talking Rawer, of Living Hard and~~ spent much of its time despising all other (and particularly the more mellowed and better educated) affectations. ~~and the rest of the time mistaking raw loud gabble for the American language, a contempt for genteel intelligence for strong deep native intelligence, and a hard-working and varied life~~ It spent . . .

. . . rawly ~~under~~ in words of few syllables, under the delusion that ~~this~~ it ~~was {the} American~~ was . . .

. . . they are ~~perhaps~~ worth mentioning . . .

. . . many ~~wr~~ excellent writers such as Ernest Hemingway, were ~~at least tinged~~ perhaps inescapably tinged with the American affectations; ~~and~~ because ~~there is~~ their bellowings . . .

. . . abler ~~writers~~ Americans . . .

The fine, ~~points~~ the exquisitely bad edges of ~~the~~ his language . . .

. . . you ~~not only~~ . . . go lustily . . .

E 3: Plans for a Journal: "Brecht's <u>Almanac</u>"

[typescript, Tennessee folder 18, orange pages 10–12]

[1]

[*Agee* in pencil in top right corner]

. . . Liggetts . . .

I was ~~rih~~ right about that.

. . . he hadnt busted himself trying ~~to~~ {for} the utterly appropriate to every day; infact, if you discounted . . .

~~I had never in God's earth thought that I~~ In the long run I have nothing . . .

. . . on the stand as {at heart} a good . . .

[2]

. . . embarrassed . . .

. . . too little for ~~the~~ {my} britches, ~~of~~ as a young . . .

[3]

. . . of this book will be stuff I ~~would~~ will be . . .

E 4: Draft and Notes: "The Ordinary Sufferer"

[Tennessee folder 17, blue page 1, front and back]

[1]

Anit[*sic*] [Anti]-Vivisectionists . . .

. . . with ~~a~~ something on this general scheme. . .

. . . <u>suffered</u> and <u>died {before} in the cause</u>.

. . . the men who opened them up.).

. . . the same circumstance.[)]

~~Besides, people must suf~~ There is nothing to be compared . . .

. . . and would ~~ultimately relieve~~ shorten and terminate. . .

. . . (anyone except those who {{insert from left margin: *either deny its existence*}} would put it out of existence) . . .

~~Pay them~~ When their money is used up . . .

. . . it brings ~~that~~ others that much [something lined through] nearer . . .

II [*sic*] Then there are the mental . . .

[2]

. . . ~~make~~ fill them with a fervor . . .

. . . how much finer a ~~thing it is to~~ death . . .

. . . which might ~~not~~ be much more useful . . .

The ~~Inquis~~ Inquisition, for instance.

~~If~~ Tap his knee and see . . .

. . . whether he thinks [something lined through] the great tone deaf public . . .

POETRY AND NOTES ON POETRY

P 1: Draft of Preface to *Permit Me Voyage:* "I am young"

[Tennessee folder 18, orange pages 5–9]

[1]

. . . thanks, ~~but~~ {though} I don't care . . .

. . . the work I wish ~~I could~~ I were born to do . . .

. . . aimiability . . .

. . . there is further the very ~~sure~~ desperate probability . . .

. . . as no man has ever ~~thou~~ learned . . .

. . . throughout me ~~are the~~ is the matter . . .

. . . blood-brother, ~~stone,~~ beast, stone . . .

. . . asshole; ~~yo~~ your need . . .

My business and my ~~desire~~ delight . . .

~~I am~~ Poor convictions, poor conclusions . . .

[2]

. . . torture, though ~~it~~ you will not feel it.

I must ~~shut though you say it scornfully~~ hold back my spit . . .

. . . simply an excuse for ~~saying, I do not know~~ the truth . . .

. . . pity and beauty and joy and ~~I hea lovingkindness~~ heart's-kindness . . .

. . . much farther than the ~~thi~~ feelings above . . .

~~Conceivably he is beyond what~~ Certainly he is what the scientists are hunting.

[*Joyce*— and spiraling arrow to nothing in left margin]

[3]

~~And the nearest~~

And the artist comes nearest . . .

. . . pure, whole, {{insert from left margin: *intense*}}, and passionless . . .

. . . embracing all passion, are ~~among the~~ highest among . . .

Confused, ~~passionate~~ incomplete and wholly passionate, yet in some lines Hart Crane has reached an intensity ~~which~~ so terrific . . .

[in left margin: *different quality of intensity—neither higher nor lower but different—*]

[4]

. . . why I shall ~~not~~ probably not keep on . . .

. . . superior to ~~Miss~~ most of Miss Stein's work.

. . . and sober. [something lined through] Most of these poems . . .

. . . in favor or art, and ~~truth But both are~~ I believe . . .

~~It also~~ A dedication also seemed inevitable—a dedication not of ~~this volume, as~~ the lousy volume, as any fool should know [something lined through], but of ~~my~~ all I am or can be . . .

. . . people who have ~~been~~ never been able to dedicate . . .

. . . as you loved ~~them~~ and detested them . . .

So I wrote it, ~~using~~ {{insert from left margin: *trying to use*}}, as my main basic tone . . .

[5]

. . . the trouble of [something lined through] buying the book.

. . . appeared to be the work of ~~an~~ a young . . .

. . . considerable, ~~bu wh~~ but of whom . . .

. . . young poets in the past, ~~this one might~~ —which you couldn't . . .

. . . mediocrity or washout were ~~almost equally~~ quite as reasonably . . .

P 2: Prose Statement of Purpose for "John Carter"

["John Carter" notebook, Tennessee folder 4, pages 1–5; pages 2 and 4 are blank]

[1]

. . . pts of views &c— ~~on through~~ lots like to take . . .

. . . with the better ~~gy~~ guys . . .

~~Tell us~~ These things are the only . . .

[Agee's bracket follows:] [Here, make a broken crazy chorus of many voices: ~~qute~~ quote many critical points of view & none-critical [*sic*]: the poet for the few is — — what is poetry? a toy for the rich! A thing of the past. An art. [something lined through] A sermon.

[2]

~~This poem~~

[something lined through] Can a great poem have a moral point of view?

. . . caught in a [*sic*] an absolute fever . . .

. . . one thing— ~~W~~ When I love . . .

[3]

. . . seeking what [something lined through] he may devour . . .

[Agee's brackets follow:] [He could be defeated . . . perhaps a dream?]

P 3: Prose Summary of Christening Scene for "John Carter": Introduction and Two Versions

[Tennessee folder 3]

[1]

~~Of course they consented, with little ado, agreeing that it was proper, and privately agreeing that it of course made no difference~~

They agreed to placate . . .

They were not only [something lined through] baptized . . .

~~What manner of church was St. Wilfred's~~

~~Here, my readers, we are privileged to see American religion at its best: not merely in inner belief, but in outward manifestations~~ We have remarked . . .

. . . seem merely fragmentary, ~~I beg you to~~ blame it not . . .

[**1.1**]

[*Summer 32* in left margin]

~~Though~~ But such miracles were not . . .

~~The poor dear was really~~ [something lined through] ~~alm~~ Poor dear . . .

. . . and lovingkindness—of mans equality . . .

He preached that ~~the minor sins~~ lust and anger and sloth . . .

Nevertheless, ~~through~~ such miracles and ~~through~~ his preaching . . .

. . . nothing better than to ~~be~~ promote . . .

But ~~the trouble with all fan~~ great leaders are often fanatics, and fanatics never know when to stop. ~~Such a thing~~ Jesus was both . . .

. . . and ~~se~~ brutally insulted . . .

[**1.2**]

. . . his wildly ~~incautio~~ inexpedient conduct . . .

. . . will 'o the wisp . . .

. . . that only ~~one~~ {two} friends . . .

~~And again—the end of Judas is worth contemplating.~~

But what of Judas . . .

[**1.3**]

. . . that ~~it~~ {life} is made beautiful . . .

One is [something lined through] well within one's rights . . .

. . . world would [something lined through] mean nothing . . .

[*build-up on civilization.* in left margin]

. . . judgement and retribution are [something lined through] mere bugaboos . . .

[2.1]

~~Nevertheless, Jesus managed the ride into Jeru~~

Now the trouble with fanatics . . .

[The paragraph *My Kingdom is not of this earth. Poor deluded fellow!* was originally beneath the next; an arrow indicates to move it here.]

. . . we should think of, ~~every time~~ at least once a year. In fact, we would do well to think of it every time ~~we get~~ our own feet . . .

. . . save Christ from ~~this~~ His own better self . . .

[2.2]

. . . while ~~it's is w~~ it's right enough . . .

. . . the world ~~is a d~~ can be a difficult place . . .

And {{insert from left margin: *because of the great advance in civilization,*}} it is even more true . . .

. . . Jesus. ~~And we can be sure that if we~~ God ~~want~~ made us reasonable men.

. . . if you ~~don't let God into it.~~ {keep God in His place—}

. . . person is capable of ~~comin~~ doing evil . . .

~~As for all the "trappings"~~
Of course there are certain differences . . .

[2.3]

. . . "sacraments": [something lined through] and a few cranks . . .

. . . are still pleasant and ~~accepta~~ socially acceptable . . .

. . . little or nothing, but ~~they,~~ as a matter of good form . . .

~~There is n~~ Of course, some of the more emotional religions are a bit outré; but no man yet has ever failed to profit, ~~to~~ socially and financially . . .

. . . pardon me [something lined through] for having conducted . . .

. . . essential Christian ~~religion~~ {spirit} as it now stands. Of course, ~~I am not here to when~~ one ~~goes into~~ {embarks upon} such abstractions . . .

. . . tried to seek out {is} merely . . .

. . . it took some ~~remind~~ considerable talk . . .

P 4: Automatic Writing and Poem:
"Writing first thing comes into my mind"

[Tennessee folder 18, orange page 1]

She left me low for another guy, he loved and left her high and dry, now both are dead, and only I, ~~am~~ remain to tell, ~~the story.~~ our story.

I met her young, in the young green woods, And the day was wild~~, in the warm green woods,~~ as glory . . .

[*Spread* above *Turn* in left margin with bracket around stanza beginning *I watched her from her easy bed*]

Make haste if you will help, the time

Is toward to ~~top~~ {turn} when helplessness

~~Is your will as well as mine~~

Is your disuse [*disuse* superimposed over *disguise*] as well as mine

~~And both have lost the old address.~~   And both mislay the old address.

~~And corn and larch and columbine~~

~~Obliterate the old address.~~

[*Letter to a Friend.* in left margin]

[*shall put your opinions on the air* in left margin]

P 5: Automatic Writing and Poem:
"hideous, crippled & malignant girl"

[Tennessee folder 17, brown page 1]

[Agee's bracket follows:] [The notched race. Little ladies walking around with their notches.

[in left margin: *Mrs. Chapman Mrs. Taylor Casa de Rubyat (Mrs. Daniels) arrived Saturday 4 yr old brat.*]

P 6: Automatic Writing and Poem: "Ginseng, rank fennel"

[Tennessee folder 17, brown page 3]

~~Poetry less familiar than my hand~~   ZEBRAS

So if it must . . .

Bawling at deathbeds is a ~~poor~~ {{insert from right margin: *bad*}} leavetaking:

P 7: Automatic Writing: "small turns"

[Tennessee folder 17, brown page 4]

The pale crab sitting in his {white sand} hole.

[*avid* in left margin]

[*worth the bother* in left margin]

. . . bring them to the casual [*drawling* above *casual*] square . . .

. . . the spended day; ~~on the~~ in the dappling . . .

ceremonial (violin, [something lined through] cello, wind on grass). phrase. shadow. myth.
Mythologies, leaves of our wooden house, wooden cards, {wooden leaves.} sprung sprung the hinges . . .

[*ceremonial how the gods* written vertically in right margin]

P 8: Automatic Writing and Poem: "clouds as if they lay"

[Tennessee folder 17, brown page 5]

Head & heart felt. ~~Buzzer~~ Heads are scratched.

Pale shell, tissue, membrane of moon. ~~Smell~~ Effaced: stuck.

Hammering merciless in Walgreen's. [something lined through] Groveling . . .

Painting in face of Berceuse doesn't seem so good: little glinting pastel [something lined through] strokes . . .

. . . birds throbbing in pines, [something lined through] roaring like a motor . . .

. . . coiled stars, coiling sky, [something lined through] stars run their coils . . .

P 9: Automatic Writing: "SERVICE IN EXISTENCE"

[Tennessee folder 17, brown page 6]

[spiral doodle] _____

SERVICE IN EXISTENCE

[curved line from *I WAIT* to *AMMONIA*.]

(flowers, column of gnats; legion, flock, squadron {regiments} of birds . . .

cities like {little} spreading crusted sores.

TERRAPIN. GODHOUSE. ANNELID. worms {filtering the earth.} filter in earth.

P 10: Notes and fragments: "I think that in their honey cells"

[Tennessee folder 17, brown page 18]

Where the dolphin ~~slowly~~ leisurely bowling . . .

. . . starbarnaled . . .

. . the ~~ey~~ bee's eye . . .

like shirt tail lifting from neat, {prim} cleft . . .

P 11: Automatic Writing: "THE TINDERING STARS"

[Tennessee folder 17, brown page 7]

[bracket beneath *SIGHT HEARING TOUCH;* bracket beneath *SMELL TASTE;* arrows from *SMELL* and *TASTE* converge beneath brackets]

P 12: Poem: "Glimmer, glimmer, universe"

[Tennessee folder 17, brown page 8]

P 13: Prose Beginning and First Draft of Poem: "I will hear"

[folder 18, white page 5, front and back]

[1]

Nor will not ~~break~~ all break down in fear.

[2]

[left column]
~~If in the~~
~~If in the hold of night~~
~~If within the watch of night~~
~~There is a creature of my kind~~   under the watch of heaven

~~If in this holy height of dark~~
~~There's any creature whom the night~~

~~If in the range of this wide night~~
~~There's any creature~~

~~If within this ward of night~~
~~There's any creature~~

~~If beneath the watch of heaven~~
~~If under hold of heaven's height~~
~~There's any creature lifts his soul~~
~~In tears before this holy night~~

~~If in the watch~~
~~If under~~
~~O if within the~~

O if beneath the ward of night
There's any other creature brings . . .

[right column]
Brother, my blood, my own dear soul,
Whatever change attends the light
Put by, ~~put by,~~ my kin, put by, be glad:
~~We're For~~
We're very Near to God tonight.

P 14: Poem: "Theories of Flight"

[Tennessee folder 14, typescript]

P 15: Poem: "Yet even slaves"

[Tennessee folder 17, typescript, brown page 9]

P 16: Poem: "Seriously, if that's your vanity"

[Tennessee folder 17, typescript, brown page 10]

We all that work such grievance are less than children

~~playing~~ {{insert from left margin: *dancing*}} the lengths . . .

P 17: Poem: "Heal, hardy air"

[Tennessee folder 17, typescript, brown page 20]

P 18: Poem: Early Draft of "Lyric" (*transition*)

[Tennessee folder 17, brown page 24]

[*subdued
disunison* in top left corner]

[*tussling / swindle
out of the frying pan
into the foyer* in bottom margin]

P 19: Poem: "Now, for one moment"

[Tennessee folder 17, brown page 11]

Now, for one moment, I have seen my soul,
Have stared its ~~full and deep~~ infinite asperity
Full in the eye . . .
I termed it ~~int~~ courage, falsely thus to soar

Free of the shame and truth and the despair.
Of all men I am cowardliest, least kind,
~~Most beyond all redemption weighted down~~
Most beyond hope . . .

P 20: Poem: "Suffer me not, O Lord"

[Tennessee folder 17, brown page 12]

> To all the cackling world, grant me self-treason.
> ~~I know weakness gathers on my brow~~
> Better than idiocy . . .
>
> Only the great-souled and the brave may claim,
> ~~How will my life,~~ What hell in life . . .

P 21: Poem: "Ah's jes' a believing chameleon"

[Tennessee folder 17, brown page 17]

> [*Forsythe & hindsight*
> *You have nothing*
> *to pull but your chains* in right margin]

P 22: Poem: "And by the bye my pious friends of the reviewing trade"

[Tennessee folder 17, brown page 17]

P 23: Poem: "Forsythe and hindsight"

[Tennessee folder 17, brown page 17]

P 24: Poem: "Depilatories garter belts and lotions"

[Tennessee folder 17, brown page 13]

P 25: Poem: "Sweet anodyne"

[Tennessee folder 17, brown page 13]

> Sweet anodyne.
> My anodyne.
> Better than ~~whiskey, beer and~~ {women, song, or} wine.
> There's no escape
> For man or ape

Quite like ~~closely hewing~~ hewing closely to
The Party Line
    The Par Ty Line.

P 26: Poem: "What fool would dare"

[Tennessee folder 17, brown page 13]

[left column on bottom half of page]
~~It makes no idea~~
~~What sort of gods~~
~~Who wants to care~~
~~Who wants to care~~
~~And who would dare,~~
~~What bastards wreck a right idea:~~
~~Who gives a damn~~
~~Who wants to care~~
~~And who w~~
What fool would dare . . .

[right column on bottom half of page]
So let the fools . . .

You have nothing to lose but your brains.
I do not dare
To show I care
What

P 27: Poem: "Major Douglas"

[Tennessee folder 17, brown page 14]

. . . nickles . . .

And Munson and the brighter sort of Harvard boys
Will make the world {a} safe {{insert from right margin:
place}} for the Bishop and the goys.

Look at Alberta
The people of Alberta
They haven't got a shirta
To cover their backs.

So here's a sneer
For the New Frontier
&c. . . .

P 28: Poem: "Dialog"

[Tennessee folder 17, brown pages 15–16]

[1]

& so to bed
soberly,
~~bring us a quiet mind~~
bring us a quiet mind

DIALOG

We cannot wait. Our time is nearly gone.
That mood of spiritual desolation
Which Eliot ~~established~~ {{insert from right margin: *put*
     under glass}}, carry on
Long as you like . . .

. . . Rather than draw a blank
We even ~~decline~~ must decline to run the bank.

[alternate second stanza]
Tell it to major Douglas and the Bishop.
They'll give you <u>such</u> an appetite for tea.
Tell it to Sigmund, who can dig a wish up
And make it call you Uncle—for a fee.
Try any kind of spiritual pushup
From Body-on-the-tongue to Ether-spree:
But don't try us: unless you're willing to take
Some rational steps to cure your bellyache.

[2]

You show some hope, and then again some doubt.
~~The~~ Hope's a good sign; the doubt's intelligent
~~Just at this stage~~
At this stage. Now suppose you spit it out,
The whole damned business. It's spit well spent.
Since, I suspect, it stands to end a drought
Nothing else could, and won't cost you a cent.
~~If any one here laughs,~~
~~And please don't mind if anyone here laughs~~

And please don't mind if anyone here makes cracks;
Some of them, like yourself, ~~have~~ are erstwhile smacks.

"Well, that, as a matter of fact, does bring to mind
One thing that ~~bothers me.~~ often bothers me. . . .

. . . live & let live,
A silly phrase, I grant, that gives offense.
~~If anyone has all the strength to give,~~
~~All the right answers, all the open sense~~
~~You claim for yours,~~
If you have everything you claim to give
The world at large . . .

P 29: Poem: "Muzzy wuvs her Buzzy"

[Tennessee folder 17, brown page 14]

Paraded W[oo]den Soldiers tune. Muarch . . .

Mamma can I have a cookie? Come love me first.
Ah, little lover.

Children going through sexual stage routines.

Muzzy and her Buzzie speak a language all their own.

Muzzy wuvs her Buzzy . . .

. . . even more than
Untle Charley or that ~~dark haired~~ {tall dart} man . . .
Bigger dan dat tall dart mans.

P 30: Poem: "Hunched hung"

typescript, Tennessee folder 17, trypescript, brown page 19]

Hunched hung above his ~~mis~~ {mild} eyed . . .

P 31: Poem: "Somewhat less indiscriminately"

[Tennessee folder 17, brown page 21]

[squiggle in top left corner]

~~I would~~ {Somewhat} less indiscriminately

P 32: Poem: "Father, mother"

[Tennessee folder 17, brown page 21]

P 33: Drafts: "Sweet heart tonight"

[Tennessee folder 17, brown page 22]

>   all that was ardent ~~that~~ {which} is now the air
>   smiles round [*on* above *round*] our wrestling ~~bed~~ {here}. . . .

. . . the season changes [*alters* above *changes*] in your blood. . . .

>   ~~The wave is only full who finds the shore~~
>   Only the wave is full that finds the shore:

P 34: Poem: "Tonight sweet heart"

[Tennessee folder 17, brown page 23]

P 35: Poem: "Not for your ease"

[Tennessee folder 18, typescript, white page 10]

>   While, solemn and unregarding, with stiff hands, the heavens
>   {Rust and} unwreathe ~~and rust~~ the world.

P 36: Poem: "Young yet on your day"

[Tennessee folder 18, typescript, white page 12]

>   When I am on the dark.

P 37: Poem: Draft of "Against time" (*LUNPFM*)

[Tennessee folder 18, white page 11]

>   Disguise flung flat, squarely we challenge the feind,
>   Still, comrade, the running of beasts and the ~~extreme~~
>   ~~{ruined}~~ {ruining} heaven:
>   Still ~~captive~~ {captive} the old wild king.

P 38: Poem: "Sun our father while I slept"

[Tennessee folder 18, incomplete transcription of white page 16]

P 39: Poem: "Tell me must goodness wait"

[Tennessee folder 18, incomplete transcription of white page 17]

P 40: Poem: "How on the bare brain"

[Tennessee folder 18, white page 18]

[*18* in top left corner]

Good night. Sweet ~~sleep~~ sleep.

P 41: Poem: "Now Lord God"

[Tennessee folder 18, white page 19]

P 42: Poem: "A low pit and sink of shade"

[Tennessee folder 18, white page 20]

[*staunch the wound with shadow* in left margin]

And funneled dark I find me made:
~~Long I let my weighted sight~~
Long has lapsed my [something lined through] laden sight

P 43: Poem: Early Draft of "Johannes Brahms"

["John Carter" notebook, Tennessee folder 4, page 11]

The year turns ~~roun~~ on him . . .
The undeviant, the rich and deep ~~of~~ in heart . . .

P 44: Poem: Two drafts of "Johannes Brahms"

[Tennessee folder 18, white page 9]

We too, ~~Let us~~ of many motions . . .

A~~~~ {{insert from left margin: *This*}} century past ~~to~~ {{insert from left margin: *who*}} drank . . .

The year turns round him and [*proclaims* lined through; *approves* and *attests* in left margin with line to *fulfils*] {fulfils} his worth:

This century past he drank ~~the~~ his first brave breath,
The undeviant, the rich and deep of heart.
Who marked his ~~way~~ {{insert from bottom margin: *height*}} and toiled it unto death,
Humble and honorable in his art.
No wildness [line from *wildness* to *slyness* in left margin] his, no roaring at the air;
Splendor of honest sound was all his use:
From which intent no envy nor despair
Nor ease of [something lined through] life compacted might seduce. . .

P 45: Poem: "Now the steep and chiming coasts"

[Tennessee folder 18, white page 21]

Night overmasters us:
Enamored of their poisoned dreams
~~Now we are under night: Alaska's~~
~~Now the cold~~
Now the steep and chiming coasts . . .

From ice to ice ~~upon~~ along the sphere . . .

~~And~~ Take to the love and dreams . . .

~~Lord~~ O might their dreams like water from deep wells . . .

They wolfed the ~~poisons~~ special poisons of our air . . .

And why insist ~~them~~ allegiance to despair . . .

~~With~~ Little in Killing and much forgiving.
Or better might they ~~know~~ {learn,} which they ~~will not~~ {can not:}
The love of Jesus and the mind of Marx.

P 46: Poem: "Hold on a second, please"

[Tennessee folder 18, white page 22]

> [left column]
> Hold on a second, please . . .
>
> Merely to live and seed the next year's crop,
> ~~Hoping to God, out of this hell on earth~~
> ~~He runs a heaven that will half be worth~~
> ~~The~~
> Fervently hoping to their phony God
> For better luck the seamy side of the sod,
> And worshipping that smug and murderous State
> Which [something lined through] pays them with an empty
> dinner plate . . .
>
> You see, were catching . . .
>
> Of making our women and our arts their whores:
> ~~Of mining gold~~
> Of raising ~~wheat and eating~~ corn and wheat and eating
> shorts:
> Of raising hogs and sharing in their orts:
> Of mining gold and getting paid in copper:
> Of cooking ~~banquets~~ feasts and scraping out the hopper:
> Of laying ~~roads and~~ tracks ~~where they ride and we walk~~
> {and hobbling the rails,}
>
> [right column]
> Involving, whether you like ~~it or n~~ or loathe it, you.

P 47: Poem: "Fight-Talk"

[Tennessee folder 18, orange pages 2–4]

[1]

> [line down middle of page; left column]
> <u>Fight-Talk</u>
> ~~Son~~ Pals, have bosses bled . . .
>
> You're ousted by the rectal grab
> ~~You once~~ Since you were dope enough to scab?

[right column]
~~Son~~ Pal, have the bosses bled you so . . .

O plug against the Syren song
Of the ~~coughlin~~ {cuckling} priest and hooey long.

They're cutting down on planting wheat
Lest ~~we should get too much to~~ anyone should overeat;

Giving us sleep by burning coffee.
Handing out ~~applesauce~~ {hot horseshit} and toffee.

[2]

[line down middle of page; left column]
Selling the auto workers out . . .

~~And And,~~
~~Now~~ Now, gleaming Capitol Dome,

Farewell, and coming nearer home,

Nobody's any excuse to get sore,
For every dollar is accounted for:

~~We've got a solution, we think it's a wow.~~
~~This is how~~
We've found the solution, we consider it a wow:
~~The and is~~ It Works: and this is how:
[mark indicating to transpose stanzas *Nobody's . . . accounted*
for: and *We've found . . . this is how:*]

———

[couplets not separated for the next six lines:]
Of every million we are fed
Half of it goes for overhead,
Another half for office space,
Another half to make a place
For Mister Mugwump's Nephew's Wife
Who's grown a trifle tired of life

[right column]
[couplets not separated for next eight lines:]
And still another half to keep
Investigators half asleep,
And still another half to buy
Cars that will match our Chairman's tie,
And still another to make chauffeurs

Out of incipient corner loafers,
And more to lubricate the game
That brings us more whence that much came:

Irish potatoes by the peck,   Argus eyed
A nice cut off the horses neck

[3]

[line down middle of page; left column]
A quarter's-worth at very worst . . .

[Agee has written *ITALICS* in left margin indicating the next
three couplets:]
So pledge allegiance once again
To Franklin and his merry men.

And demonstrations three times three
In praise of Franklin's Mother's Knee.

And ululations nine-times-nining,
Find in each swine the pearly lining.

[right column]
    is it inflation?
No matter many lives are sperled
God's in his heaven to hell with the world.

(Cartoon: gas stove, man, head in oven, terribly bloated
body: child ~~looking on, crying~~ lying on floor . . .

P 48: Poem: "Minority Report"

[Tennessee folder 18, orange page 13; in box in left corner]

P 49: Poem: "Madam, is baby's evening stool"

[Tennessee folder 18, orange page 13]

[line down the center of page; left column]
Madam, is baby's evening stool . . .
As smooth (if not as sweet [*smart* above *sweet*]) as silk?

~~If~~ {Do} you find his love grown cold?

Let him have {just} one demonstration . . .

Meanwhile see what he's brought ~~baby~~ Junior!

Wait'll baby, [something lined through] (little love):
See's it! Why his little lips'l
Fit our product like a glove:
The (Guess what) O Kay Feller Nipple.
(over) □
{{insert from back of page:

   Baby's full

I'ts a bran new lease on life
Baby's happier at the stern {puss,}
Baby's tougher at the stern:
And without a bit of fuss,
While our agent earns, you learn.}}
[also on back:
   Luther Gulick
Natl Municipal League
and doodles]
   (How bout it, lady?)

[right column]
Baby, how's your baby?
face like a sow's belly—
(His socio-politico-economic life isn't what it ought to be.)

Now We Are Sixty

P 50: Poem: "Collective Letter to the Boss"

[Tennessee folder 18, orange page 13]

   Collective Letter to the Boss
~~The little man with the big mustache~~
~~And the man with the head like an olive~~
<u>Dear</u> <u>Boss</u>:

And the man with the mug like a ~~pair~~ {row} of teats:

And the man with the teeth and the Commodores hat
And the glasses and the the ~~naval~~ cruiser quarrel.

And turns the screws to own some more
~~And drinks the blood~~
And malts ~~the~~ {our} blood and vats ~~the~~ {our} bones
Compels ~~those~~ {our} blood & bones to war.

<u>New</u> <u>Paragraph</u>
~~And since~~ {Since, sir,} that whole machine is set
Beyond ~~his~~ {your} wish to ever change,
Beyond ~~his~~ {your} power should even yet
The wish by chance ~~his~~ {your} mind derange:

~~Since, in a word, your very life~~
~~Since, in a word, it must be~~
Since, in a word, you force our hand:
~~And~~ Since, in a word, it must be war:
{{insert from below: *Align* [*Line up* above *Align*] *your men and*
guns and be
Advised: you are the enemy:}}
All human race in every land
~~Rears~~ {Rares} up to ~~rage you to~~ {wreck you from} the floor.

P 51: Poem: "The rootless winds"

[Tennessee folder 18, orange page 16]

[*10* in top left corner]

This [something lined through] bright this vagrant bubble

P 52: Poem: Introduction and Two Drafts of "Tenant this season of uneasy darkness"

[Tennessee folder 18, orange pages 18–19]
[1]
~~to justify man's ways to God.~~
~~Before God: the dedication; then, turning toward the people,~~
~~he speaks to them sincerely.~~ He watches before his God.
Then, turning toward the people, he speaks to them.
~~He has made what celebration~~ He has made what watch he
may before his God.   Then, speaking inward:
~~I my soul who have this little while put on darkness~~
~~My soul who march this little way~~
~~My soul dressed up in darkn~~
~~Soul who march dressed up in darkness~~
~~My short ways~~
Soul, seamed [*sewn* above *seamed*] up in darkness marching
my brief way:

And in my mind be [*the* above *be*] balancer.
We are brothers: and you the elder: wiser:
~~Remb~~ Remembering that we shall quarrel and that I may hate,
~~Be kind~~ Shape my ignorance kindly with your hands.
No man ~~that~~ but wears ~~his King~~ a God and King in his flesh:

Soul sewn in darkness who march my [something lined through] short ways
Tenant whose ~~lease~~ length of lease . . .

~~Shape my ignorance~~ Handle the shapes of my ignorance tryly [*sic*] [truly] in your hands:

~~Tenant of leased darkness~~
    Tenant this season of darkness . . .

Handle the shapes of my nature justly in your hands:
[*up in* in left margin]

Stand ~~straight~~ strong up in me soul my God my world before . . .

[**2**]

~~Friends: brothers in more than blood (for God is thicker than blood): enemies:~~
Tenant this season . . .

P 53: Poem: "When your busy feet have run"

[Tennessee folder 18, incomplete transcription of orange page 20]

    ~~The~~ When your busy feet have run . .
    ~~When~~ {And} when ~~there~~ you flop down, breathing hard . . .
    While cool ~~winds~~ breezes quiet your face.

P 54: Poem: Two Drafts of "Fellows"

[Tennessee folder 18, orange page 17]
    [*Nuff said.* in top right margin]
    Fellows, there's no use taking on that way.
    ~~The~~ finger in ~~the~~ nose,

~~The~~ Arabesques of baccy-fumes,
Din inuendoed [something lined through] smoke down corri-
dors of histories exempt,
The conditioned jitter, the drymouthed kiss, ~~the~~ implosion
Soaped, of bombed kestrels, Peared, pyloned in insulate light:
Six-sided snow ~~is~~ here, ~~white~~ {{insert from left margin:
Blind}}, the lesion . . .

[*listen*
 to this one in right margin]

Unstable ~~wat~~ affections deranged over water and gin,
Black hat for blondeness, thwart our [something lined
through] {walk} not more:

Conditioned jitter, drymouthed ~~true~~ {at the} kiss . . .

Men with [something lined through] {fine} minds good
hearts and {such} a way with words

P 55: Poem: "I witch off the tune of night"

[Tennessee folder 17, blue page 2]

[*I could not come and fail to speak my mind* in right margin]

Delight in rudness . . .

Eaten ~~my~~ this poem . . .

P 56: Poem: "So here's to their strychnine tears"

[Texas Box 1, folder 2.2, page 10]

. . . exploiting their [*they* above *their*] natural . . .

P 57: Poem: "Who was that boy"

[Texas Box 1, folder 2.1, page 1]

Who was that boy, ranging the ~~ravaged~~ {ruined} hill . . .

But ~~why I~~ how I killed my carrier, or why . . .

P 58: Poetic Fragments: "lights of the universe"

["John Carter" notebook, Tennessee folder 4, pages 6–7]
[1]

universe like a ~~flight~~

[2]

[three pairs of horizontal brackets doodled in left margin]

fennel (rank, moist {pungent})

a snake ~~like~~ sleeping in the sun, like a halted brook
dark swamps in which moths drowse, half awake in one deep
shadow.
    ~~a~~ gnats ~~sizzling~~ {{insert from right margin: *simmering*}}
above the grass.
[*deep of the day* in left margin]
snap & whir of grasshoppers
grasshoppers [line from *grasshoppers* to *skip* in left margin]
flipping on the lawn
birds dreaming in the deep heat [line from *heat* to *light* in right
margin]: only the hummingbird
lively, like a loose flame, or ~~a wild~~ an electric arc gone wild.
A monstrous sunflower {glowers, mourns} looks into its
grave.

[triangle doodle in bottom left margin; two square doodles in
bottom right]

P 59: Notes and poem: "For now of the light of day"

[Texas Box 1, folder 2.1, page 8]

And in close, alternate nursery rhyme things with ever-
broadening rhythm [something lined through] enlarging
language . . .

[brackets around next two lines:]
For now of the light of day the utmost remembrance
Fails from the sunflower's helpless foot:
For now quite finished the lionlike [in right margin: *that which
turned like a lion*] flower of day.
    Its ~~burned~~ grand, burned eye, one blinded brown,

{{insert from right margin: *Stares soberly in all its future towards its grave,*}}
Its seed stares towards the root . . .

Film Treatments and Radio Play

F 1: Film Treatment: "Runaways"

[Tennessee folder 19, typescript, pages 1–22; pages 21–22 are on a different typewriter and paper]

[1]

They areeminently normal . . .

. . . a wonderful idea: they will run~~aw~~ away . . .

. . . i.e., realizing~~g~~ . . .

. . . indispensible . . .

. . . she blows in $1.75 of this . . .

[2]

They plug ahead down the tracks in the wrong direction ~~for~~ all that day . . .

[3]

I~~n~~ enclose some notes . . .

In the~~se~~ course of these opening scenes . . .

[4]

The moment we meet and walk towards school . . .

. . . whisful thinking. . .

. . . to see <u>him</u>!.

[5]

. . . that they actually <u>can</u> run away, if they {really} want to.

. . . worrying families know where they are, and they won't have~~a~~ a leg . . .

[6]

. . . the %$5 her grandmother gave her, plus the tiny chickenfeed of ~~her~~ {their} pocket-money . . .

Upon Dian'es queenly insistence. . .

When she asks what streetcar the y should take . . .

[7]

If their families weren't four-fifths blind with everyday l living . . .

It is a large, grim,wonderful moment: from now on they are really cut-ff from the world. . .

[8]

. . . that if you are secretly guilty of something, the whole qorld knows it.

. . . it as, after all, Diane's birthday.

. . . protectiveness and responsibility[comma lined through].

[9]

. . . the minute they get totown . . .

Urgent, ~~seating~~ sweating, frantic business of breaking enough change . . .

. . . success, and {with seconds to spare,} proceed to the ticket window . . .

. . . necessities enhanced by their excitement: ~~the~~ going to the bathroom.

. . . senry-duty while Mary goes in.

. . . beginning to lose her natural decency in vafor of her curiosity . . .

[10]

. . . before they know better, ask is he is . . .

. . . and not too skilful improvising of lies, for a while, gets buy him . . .

. . . and they soon realize they can't get away with this kind of bluffing~~m~~ much longer.

. . . so much more glamorously still to travks than to roads . . .

But along the railroad, if they only avoid railrad men . . .

[11]

 . . . we begin to intercut the realization, on the part~~e~~ of their parents . . .

The alarm in of course misplaced. . .

 . . . but all the same we begin to know~~n~~ that . . .

 . . . let's say for the moment, up to lare afternoon . . .

[12]

 . . . the fact that he's a stranger, accounts for their gentle ~~trt~~ terror.

 . . . how helpless he ~~is~~ {would be}, and exaggerates his age by a good five years.

[13]

feeling that there mustnt be too many. . .

By the time they are hungry theyare ravenous and go through their little lunches, plus~~t~~ their supplementary ~~school~~ iceboc scavengings . . .

they talk a lt little bout the movies.

[14]

 . . . Bugs Bunny~~?~~.

One is pure melodrama: they get caught~~n~~ in . . .

They really do~~o~~ consider hopping a freight . . .

[15]

 . . . "but this isn't meat, it comes from Aggentina". . .

 . . . and it is a logical hazard children-at-large have to reckong with . . .

 . . . on the childrens' being taken . . .

[16]

Obviously these two approaches canbe combined . . .

 . . . which, under the circumstances, is more than they canbear and . . .

O ne says to the other . . . [Extra space is Agee's typo.]

[17]

Their deep motual loyalty . . .

. . . and even become shily articulate . . .

. . . lie downand die; and for Judgement, however harsh.

[18]

. . . fear, we incercut with what really awaits them . . .

. . . worried sick, fighting smong themselves . . .

The girls, quite some while after dark, chilledto the bone . . .

. . . by a lady ~~passenge~~ driver, and go on their way.

AAglance at the girls . . .

Meanwhile his little bakelite radio finishes a ~~radio~~ Latin-American . . .

Rough skeatch of the payoff . . .

[19]

There isa stir; the parents come in fast.

. . . all their love andanxiety has been lost in exasperation . . .

. . . more of a touch of restrai ned threat . . .

. . . they begin to ~~coaleas~~ coalesce. ~~Diane and her brother~~ Mary, sitting . . .

[20]

Her mother becomes awareof the look.

In the other car Diane and her ~~btoer~~ brother . . .

F 2: Film Outline: "Twilight"

[Tennessee folder 19, typescript]

[1]

We show this chiefly through a story of the devlopment . . .

F 3: Notes on Untitled Film Treatment:
"Boy and Girl and Musician"

[Texas Box 1, folder 2.2, pages 1–8]

[1]

"Goodbye, darling." "——" "Goodbye."
{{insert from ms. page 2: *at hang up cut, like switching on a light, to after-supper sitting around. Him; mother; father; sister (mad as all hell); clock. Him; father; mother; clock {40 min later}; sister (chin trembling); to vibration of clock's pre-striking whir.*
    8:30. cut to mother. Hands relax.}}
    (night shots, of each, & of parents. "12, [something lined through] I don't want to deprive Emma of going to the movies because of what <u>you've</u> done. &c &c. But you must absolutely <u>promise</u> me." "Sure I promise." (So, watch in window? get her attention?) {{insert from bottom margin: *&* *back home, happy as hell. Singing in car; baffled sister &* {{insert from bottom margin: *with his mother, that night:* {{insert from page 2: *"<u>why</u> <u>I</u> <u>wouldn't</u> <u>any</u> <u>more</u> <u>touch</u> <u>her</u> <u>than</u> . . . ! ! !"*
    (sound of father winding clock)
    next night:
Dear ——. ~~I tried to make you~~ *I've been trying half the night to write you a poem, but* ~~I didn't~~ *I couldn't seem to write anything that was worthy of you. I will quote the only lines* ~~one~~ *I think are fit to preserve. They are:*

---

but they don't one thousandth express my emotions {about you} and what could? Sometimes I wonder whether when people write the great Love Poems they really feel in love at the time [illegible].}}
with her father: "Mother wanted me to speak to you. (Threat <u>re</u> boy.) {{insert from page 2: *Let me tell you and you can tell him from me. If that boy ever so much as touches you, the wrong way, that is, I'll*}}
maybe in bed; he on cheek or burying forehead or lips in pillow;
    she, flat on back, eyes open—}} }}

Party next afternoon, swimming, {clambake?} evening . . .

[2]

[see insertions on page 1]

[3]

[see N 31: List: "Germans & Japanese in American movies"]

[page 4 is blank]

[5]

"Where's he from?" (Buck)?:(knows). They stage party for him—

[line to *Buck:*] (He tests B. out on the party idea. B explains, why do it? Mine never give parties. They give all the parties.) Start with tennis. She is there. He is nervous, but proud of his tennis. Does well. ~~Next night~~ Tomorrow night at ——'s. [line to *They stage party for him*] Tennis mentioned. . . .

Cut to slap of ball. {J's face. Ready?} Girls are playing.

. . . Jim you were <u>wonderful</u> [*out<u>did</u> yourself.*"" above <u>wonderful</u>] (cut to bed). ~~WHAM~~ his face, sneering at it all. WHAM. sneer. hand {rubs} over face . . .

[6]

See you tomorra [something lined through] night maybe?"

[Agee's brackets follow:] [you know, you <u>do</u> talk too much darling.]
"Yeah, I guess I can [*ought to be able to* above *guess I can*] make it all right."

[Agee's brackets follow:] [Also, earlier, has fantasy of Moor there?]

{{insert from a few lines above: *J, alone, to place they spent the night?*}}
    how end? early morning, train leaving? shots from rear of train, & from track of receding train; face in train; shift of semaphore? {{insert from below: *start & end with baggage &c.*}}
    cut to school. [something lined through] getting a letter . . .

[7]

the essential emotion, that of ecstatic discovery; [something lined through] the objective emotion . . .

[line between *class-difference* and *Moor comes to visit*]

[8]

[passage from *"Did you ever love anyone else?"* to *is very destructive to them* is bracketed down the left margin:] . . .

~~bandleader~~ boy & girl & musician. She goes to musician's room?

F 4: Notes on Untitled Film Treatment: "Planter's Son"

[Texas Box 1, folder 2.1, pages 6–7]

[1]

Some very old man or woman? {{insert from left margin: [illegible] *flashback into* [illegible]}} Voodoo?

[in left margin: [illegible] *in furs as much as cloth?*]

[in left margin: [illegible] *the guy for the planter?*   [illegible] *in* [illegible].   How.* [illegible] *swell comic—shd here play very straight.*]

A snowing winter night; essence of security. [*story, that night?* above *essence of security*] Any   farming?

[in left margin: [illegible] *Papa a clergyman?*]

He walks away. {{insert from left margin: *"I'll come back. Every summer, I'll come back."*] Dissolve or cut to his meeting with his parents. Very shy & very silent on all sides. They too have improved in his absence. It must show in all their faces. Train bell, through scene? {{insert from left margin: *Evening scene: he is saying he must certainly go back; his mother is* [illegible] *him he will if he wants. Father* [illegible] *nothing.*}} Paper announcing . . .

. . . 1861 [circled] . . .

Johnny {Our young prodigal} arrived [something lined through] this afternoon {as per schedule,} safe and sound, and I must say [*confess* above *say*] it has been worth every moment of our many months of sorrow and bereavement.

[in right margin: *almost windlike war music*]

[2]

[in left margin: *white cousin, about his age, contemptuous of him?*]

[something lined through] "I ain't got no money . . .

. . . about to strike the N: ~~Whose property you think you're~~ "That your property?"

F 5: Notes on Untitled Film Treatment: "2 Soldiers"

[Texas Box 1, folder 2.1, page 9]

. . . flesh immediately after [something lined through] surgery . . .

Sings grief, ~~grif~~ grief, grief . . .

F 6: Radio Play: "In Goblin Land"

[Tennessee folder 10, typescript, pages 1–3]

[1]

We do don't serve coffee . . .

In Goblin land its always dark . . .

. . . John Browns body . . .

. . . Cingress of Clubs . . .

And a pocket full of tye . . .

Look there is a Gobline drifting this way. Shall I ask it's name . . .

. . . Gertie, its one and the same —

[2]

Here oomes a whimsy . . .

I'm May T, Neff . . .

It would be find if we could if we could all do that.

. . . please ~~pla~~ play the Juba Dance by Nathaniel Dott . . .

[3]

Now here is a gobline as gay as a jockey . . .

Notes, Fragments, and Outlines: Fiction

N 1: Unfinished Short Story:
"In the White Light a Keener Whiteness Sparkled"

[Tennessee folder 4, "John Carter" notebook, loose pages 59]

[1]

    1. ~~In the white light whiteness sparkled~~

    In the white . . .

. . . he felt in his body great fulness . . .

. . . in peace; almost in estasy.

. . . were both ~~rare luxuries~~ uncommon, unpurchasable privileges.

. . . it became an [something lined through] invention of the eye, a poor improvisation . . .

. . . in the Japanese straw mules and the ~~coolie~~ open coolie-coat, from the front room across to the chair by the window, carrying the ~~cigar box in which~~ red lacquer . . .

[2]

    She sat in the chair, ~~and sewed~~ {sewing} a strap to her girdle.

. . . unless you are very ~~lucky~~ careful and very lucky.

Unguarded, unaware of being watched; ~~inconceivably sad~~ unaware . . .

[3]

. . . beyond knowing that ~~he was suddenly he was~~ abruptly . . .

[4]

. . . parody-gallant, {man-of-the-world,} salute-without-words . . .

. . . was ~~not~~ a licensing {not} of the right to do likewise, but of the desire by which he might.

[5]

[several doodles in left margin]

Busy for lunch?

4.

N 2: Fragment: "Orchard"

[Texas Box 1, folder 2.2, page 16]

> [something lined through]
> Late in the Sunday afternoon they strolled out behind the
> house and leaned on the [something lined through] fence . . .

> . . . now two together, [something lined through] the death-
> drums of the summer.

N 3: Beginning of Story in Dialect:
"Unnanstayun yawls viewpoint"

[Tennessee folder 18, white page 4]

> ~~Fact is,~~ Fact is, an' ah said it den . . .

> . . . mankind az [something lined through] scinded fun the
> antropoid apes . . .

> . . . all ways say [something lined through] din tellgent man . . .

> [Agee's brackets follow:] [water.]

N 4: Outline for "Young Man I Think You Are Dying"

[Tennessee folder 4, "John Carter" notebook, loose page 3]

N 5: Notes on "In the White Light
a Keener Whiteness Sparkled"

[Tennessee folder 4, "John Carter" notebook, loose page 4]

> . . . untill sure she is asleep . . .

> [arrow indicates *small white butterflies, odor of hot old manure?*
> refers to *memory*]

> She comes in for hat, ~~He opens his ey~~ neither quiet nor
> loud . . .

> [*"We'll probably see him tonight at ~ ." People coming there
> tonight? Booze from Hearns?* has a box drawn around it]

> [Agee's brackets follow:] {Yesterday, passed butterfly shop.
> Or, sudden twinkling draft of sparkling white cola.]

N 6: Notes for Story and Poem: "John Lamar"

[Tennessee folder 17, brown page 2]

>   Really the only damned thing I care about here is to get it out
>   clearly: to give it the kinds of bitchy intensity it must have
>   had for them.
>   Maybe it's too bad . . .

. . . that the facts are.

>   ~~But then again, there are disadvantages in sticking to the facts.~~
>   ~~{To} mention just two. A man has an intense and desperate~~
>   ~~quarrel with his wife, the sort that lasts from bedtime till five~~
>   ~~in the morning. Such a quarrel, recorded, would certainly be~~
>   ~~Something. But it is just one of many all but identical quar-~~
>   ~~rels. If one just by chance happens to lead to say, a murder or~~
>   ~~a separation, does that really make it much more important~~
>   ~~than its carbon copies? Are you to record all the quarrels?~~
>   ~~Hell no. Then why draw one out of line.~~

[left column]
Four dreams round my bed
Four dreams ~~round my at~~ {round} my head [*bed* above *head*]

[right column]
Four angels round my bed
~~Four~~ {Armed} sentries at my head, ?sentinels

Weeping child and ~~compound~~ {bestial} eye,

NOTES, FRAGMENTS, AND OUTLINES: MISCELLANEOUS

N 7: Notes on Book of Subway Photographs

[Texas Box 12, folder 7, pages 1–17; even-numbered pages are blank
except for two doodles on page 6]

[1]

>   Used between every form of [something lined through]
>   obligation . . .

. . . the people; their way of traveling; their ~~consciousne~~ degree . . .

[2]

~~Photographs which deserve to exist can only be vitiated by words.~~

It is conceivable that words and photographs. . .

[3]

There should be no words here at all; and if they manage to justify their existence they ~~will~~ can do so only . . .

[4]

~~There should be no words here; and if they manage to vindicate their existence they can do so only by becoming so transparent that they cease to exist, and leave only the photographs.~~

   [box around this paragraph:] ~~Photographs worthy of existence need no words, and can only be harmed by them. There should be no words here. They are here guiltily, and as a form of assistance to those who do not yet know how to see what is in a photograph. If they are other than evil they will become transparent in~~
   ~~These photographs need no words.~~
   These photographs were made in the subways of New York City . . .

[4-5]

Each is, ~~suspended~~ for a short while, suspended.

[5]

To ride watchfully, in a New York Subway, is a dreadful and piteous act of surreption: for ~~almo~~ in its noise . . .

[6]

   . . . even the simplest has contrived ~~disguises~~ guards and disguises that are never lost . . .

Never in the most intimate trust of another; never alone. [something lined through] before a mirror . . .

[7]

Human beings under a very {set, very} special {, uniform} condition.

[9]

At the end of <u>City Lights</u>, ~~Chaplin first perceives himself~~ in the eyes . . .

N 8: Notes on *Saturday Review*

[Tennessee folder 18, white pages 7–8]

[2]

As the leading organ of U.S. literary [something lined through] criticism . . .

. . . as the leading organ of U.S. literary criticism during one of the most ~~violent~~ vivid and dangerous decades of American life and literary history, has all but infallibly met its responsibilities halfway: constantly advancing the ~~mediocre and~~ safe, the cowardly, the dull-hearted and the evil and as constantly opposing the adventurous, the courageous, the serious and the good: blinding and drugging an audience already blind and drugged, [something lined through] praising the easy . . .

	[Agee's brackets follow:]
~~Joes~~ Josie loves the little things	[Quote Edna's poems]
And all the Little Things love Josie.	Jesus made it just so good
~~And every word that Josie writes~~	And not a little better;
And every time our Josie sings	For if you play just one more trump
Is perfectly rosey-poesy-prosy.	Against this poet, you'll set her.

———————————

—{{insert from right: *Literary Banquet.*}}—

To Muse: Come Life with Me &c—   ~~Muse~~

[*Pegasus feed bad or sugarlumps* circled]

N 9: Notes on John Huston

[Texas Box 1, folder 2.1, page 5]

[circled *1* in top right corner]

[*free/energy* in left margin]

In no sense {*self-taught*}, [illegible] naivety, adventurer always learning something new, [insert something illegible] never "consolidating" knowledge

Wyler: greater range, {versatility} poetry & tenderness . . .

But is he really? {{insert from line below: *Yes, in chief sense that he never* [something lined through] *makes the camera "expressive", like Ford. No "adjectives".*}}

Little if any fancy lighting: [something lined through] usual law of lighting . . .

Again, the Robinson shot. [something lined through] Very flexible sense . . .

[*H & audience* in left margin]

N 10: Notes on Zanuck, Etc.

[Texas Box 1, folder 2.1, page 3]

[*Mrs James* [?] *O'Gorman.* below *M Vanaman (call at home).*]

Charlie Chase [?]   ~~Mack Sennett and his comedians~~
                         ~~Snub Pollard, James Finlayson,~~
                         ~~Fatty Arbuckle~~

Larry Semon

2 others he prefers: 1) [something lined through] select comics, 2) John Huston too closeup (peg on next movie, probably next spring.[)]

Deadline for both pieces? [something lined through] November 9 . . .

[box around *the car? your license if you drive down?*]

[several doodles in bottom and right margins]

N 11: Drafts of Hedda Hopper Essay

[Texas Box 1, folder 2.2, pages 20–22]

[2]

. . . people have been brained by ~~an astral~~ a well-aimed blow with an astral plume.

[3]

The source and nature of power ~~is~~ {are} sometimes hard {for sensible people} to understand . . .

A few often ill-chosen words {from Hedda} written . . .

and reduce a $250,000-a-year executive to a ~~pool~~ {tarn} of sunburned aspic.

. . . eaten their roughage, and ~~spent a~~ {prostrated themselves for a} few ~~minutes alone on those~~ silent ~~minutes~~ moments on those little prayer rugs which face toward Wall Street, they make it their first business to read {{insert from left margin: *dashing*}} Hedda Hopper and her arch-rival, ~~Louella Parsons~~ unfair . . .

. . . at his office promptly at 9$\underline{^{30}}$ [something lined through] in [something lined through] [a] {state of high} of [*sic*] agitation and sat staring at his phone as if he were a Geiger counter {{insert from left margin: *or better still, unborn.*}} At 9$\underline{^{45}}$ {the phone} rang at last; ~~and~~ Jack Warner was on it; and Curtiz was on the ropes. At exactly 10, with his remaining strength, he [something lined through] sped a distraught drive to Beverly Hills.

[in bottom margin: *Since Quakers don't have preachers, it is conceivable that Hedda has never bothered to check very carefully on her childhood, but the story is nonetheless in the proper spirit.* [bracket around previous sentence; line to:] [illegible] *the scratching,* [illegible] *& preachers, then* [illegible] *then say, in any case, she was* [illegible] *to the limelight of history.*]

[in bottom margin: *Careful in their facts, astute in their judgements, honest in their allegiances.*]

N 12: List of Movies for Review

[Texas Box 1, folder 2.2, page 14]

"Dramas," {Dishonored Lady}, Smash-Up . . .

~~Comedies: Apley,~~
Comedy drama: Apley . . .

. . . Ruth, {It Happened on 5th Ave.} ~~Trouble with Women~~
Imperfect Lady . . .

{{insert from top right margin: *Westerns: Ramrod, Duel, Angel & Badman, Pursued*}}
Unclassified: High Barbaree . . .

N 13: List: "Germans & Japanese in American movies"

[Texas Box 1, folder 2.2, page 3]

N 14: List: "Write David Selznick"

[Texas Box 1, folder 2.1, page 2]

Write David Selznick; <u>Guggenheim re Mike de Capite</u> [?]
[checkmark over *Mike*]; ~~Herbert O. Sackler~~ {Marled
[Marlee?]} [checkmark over *Marled*]; [*sketched* over J. C.
Ransom] <u>J. C. Ransom</u>; <u>Stevens (sketched)</u>

N 15: Fragment: "Odd Man Out"

[Texas Box 1, folder 2.2, pages 11–12]

[manuscript page 11]

~~Most movies, including many of the best ones, have been
made our of those fragments of the movie alphabet which
were developed between roughly 1912 and 1925. Eisentstein
and Dovschenko each developed a few more letters, and some
incredibly powerful ways of using them, which are now in
neglect; the man who came somewhere near completing the
alphabet was Jean Vigo. His masterpiece, in my opinion, was
"Zero de Conduite"; solid inspiration from start to finish.~~
[something lined through] ~~In "L'Atalante", he applied his dis-
coveries (and in process made a few more) to a more conven-
tional kind of film.~~

~~Most of the main things Vigo has done are not brand new
with him, not his personally, nor do they belong peculiarly to
movies.~~

~~To see "objectively"; to see "subjectively, through the eyes
of one of your characters; to see~~

[manuscript page 12]

"Odd Man Out" is an extremely ambitious movie by Carol
Reed, who seems to me the most gifted man in England at
making films. It is not as ~~good~~ satisfying a movie as GE, but ~~I
like it better~~ in most ways I think it is a better and more hopeful one.

N 16: Notes from "John Carter" Notebook: "Uncle Tom"

[Tennessee folder 4, notebook pages 12–15; page 14 blank]

[2]

> [three square doodles in top right margin]
>
> ~~18 Grove St. R. Elliott~~
>
> ~~12.30 Friday~~ ~~bottom—Lobby~~
>
> Critical & political limericks—

[3]

> Aimiable.
>
> Shaken rusty barleyhusk. [line to *barleyhush* in right margin]

N 17: Fragment: "A secular requiem"

[Tennessee folder 1, page 4.3]

> And find [something lined through] so little: the lift of one
> curve . . .
>
> [in left margin: *of what light may you be the shadow are you cast
> as the light of truth strikes our delusions?*]
>
> ~~Much has died, in the way~~
> Many have died . . .
>
>   . . . survivors who can [something lined through] beseech no God
> on their behalf.
>
> ~~But what of those who die fatherless, and of those who~~
> ~~mourn, who can beseech no God on their behalf~~
> ~~There are~~
> Likewise there are those . . .
>
> And those also who scorn all [something lined through]
> mourning . . .
>
> Mute as the hesitant fawn [*The fawn, hesitant before the humili-
> ated antlers,* above *Mute as the hesitant fawn*], sniffing [*nudging*
> above *sniffing*] the humiliated [*humbled* above *humiliated*]
> antlers, we stand bemused beside our dead; less articulate
> than birds in their bereavement, {whose} ~~which are~~ only
> {persistence is the} ~~persist~~ brisk ancestral phrase.

One lies {here} dead whom we would {acknowledge} ~~know~~ as dead . . .

N 18: Fragment: "dew, utter vanishing of all light"

[Texas Box 1, folder 2.2, page 13]

dew, utter vanishing of all light; darkness against darkness against darkness; ~~until the moon~~ [illegible] stars; coldness; the steady threshing of water grows louder; crickets, frogs; ~~whip~~ round eye of owl (moon); whippoorwill, {serenading,} heralding the moon; various trees; thrusting ~~brooks~~ branch; mist off water; larger animals? or all or many, to water? [something lined through] hooves and on quietest feet?

N 19: Fragment: "Camera"

[Texas Box 1, folder 2.2, page 17]

N 20: Notes on Trip to Anna Maria

[Tennessee folder 18, white page 1]

N 21: Notes on Schubert, Etc.

[Tennessee folder 18, white page 6]

With words I lose: [something lined through] "science". Resourcefulness. Variety. I become soft. Side at the stomach. Hardness. Coalness. Association. [line from *Association* to circled in left margin: *This I'm likely to have best when most casual.*]

. . . relative: and ~~only~~ through the help of which only, is it possible to do absolute.

N 22: Notes on the Universe

[Tennessee folder 18, white page 13]

It is draughted away [line from *draughted away* to *enlisted* in top left corner] from the sun.

Steaming stone to vapor: which ~~became rain: whi~~ on the colder air . . .

. . . <u>we are not necessarily "relatives"</u>: ~~except t~~ i.e. we are not necessarily . . .

We cannot even call life "conscious" as it begins: except that it is [something lined through] that which <u>is</u> ~~which is deter-mined~~ whose entire force of existence is concentrated upon ~~continuing to be~~ not ceasing to be. If you grant that: you must grant also that that force is continually outreaching itself <u>against</u> <u>death</u>: i.e. <u>into</u> <u>life</u>. ~~Molded~~ Its very existence ~~is any~~ pens it in a mold ~~wh~~: air & height & heat: a wide mold: which continually it forces & splits & takes a new form: If there is one word the word is hunger. ~~The amoeba having no other way of continu~~ The amoeba was always certain to die.

(Upon space: ~~creatures are~~ a field of grass . . .

Life is a thing which <u>will</u> <u>live</u>, straining & pouring {& wringing} itself through ~~molds~~ narrow & labyrinthine molds: pressure against each other: ~~hands~~ blind hands which [something lined through] have one brain: Live.

And in each phase: ~~a ritual~~ a strict ritual . . .

Now [something lined through] here we are at man . . .

. . . all other things ~~sp~~ shape to it . . .

~~16.~~
~~16. But so far we have not come~~
16. So far . . .

The earth is our livelihood our learning and [something lined through] our decoration.

. . . the work is done by a few who {often} suffer the consequences.

[in left margin: *Life has an "infinite" capacity for more of the same.* and *Small-town story.* Also, three spiral doodles.]

N 23: Notes on the Universe and World History

[Tennessee folder 18, white page 14]

[circular squiggle in top left corner]

[*poem* circled in left margin]

He tells of his acqua[intance; corner of page torn off] with President Roosevelt.

~~Our story begins with the sun. Something swam past it so fast it drafted off~~

1. Our little story has no discernible beginning, so we may as well begin with the sun.
{{insert from left margin: *descrip of universe*}}
    Our little story begins with the sun.

[*pickerel* in left margin with line to first two sentences of next paragraph]
      Once upon a time by some odd chance some celestial body swam past the sun [something lined through] so fa[st (corner of page torn off)] and so near that it drafted off a flock of fire as an auto draws leaves in its wake and the [planets; (corner of page torn off)] were hung, several of them, ~~a few million miles apart, and they were caught up in the force of the~~ upon the sky and upon the mercy of the sun and there in the force of their motion they swung upon themselves and turned, and turned~~, and turned,~~ and rounded as they turned the rounded sun, and turned, and took their shape as bullets ~~in a shot towe~~ from a shot tower falling.

It was just a ~~lot~~ blur of flaming gases.

Leonardo Today {Why: What: How: Why:} An American Anthology. (teeth poem) (Cong. Record: Long: {*Bilbo* above colon} Johnson &c.)

This is the ~~decade for~~ nationalistic decade . . .

N 24: Notes on World History

[Tennessee folder 18, white page 15]

A [circled] ~~A short history of the human~~
A [circled] A short history . . .

[*you cannot think too ill of man.* in left margin]

Spent immense labor raising ~~pyrami~~ hunks of stone to commemorate a "king". Believed in life after death. Wheat. The sun. [something lined through] Wood & stone.

Blues [illegible]. [insert *glorious* from after *woman*] War over a woman.

N 25: Fragment: "O my ancestral land"

[Tennessee folder 1, page 4.2]

You lived, as hungrily as I live now, and and grew tired, {or sorrowful,} or Darkness {suddenly} grew tired . . .

. . . in the morning. ~~The clothes you were bur~~   One of yours . . .

Some of you ~~came with~~ were among the Huguenots who took refuge in in Virginia and ~~were~~ in the mountains . . .

. . . as all those [something lined through] of whom I will try to write . . .

[in left margin: *The old. The old people.*]

[in left margin: *Rest in God, if God there be, / Rest, rest.*]

N 26: List:
"Leon Trotsky's History of the Russian Revolution"

[Texas Box 1, folder 2.2, page 9]

N 27: Notes on Postwar Politics and Economy

[Texas Box 1, folder 2.2, pages 23–24]

[2]

Depression—{good sheet} Springfield . . .

N 28: Notes on India-Pakistan Conflict

[Texas Box 1, folder 2, page 19]

[written vertically in left margin: *A group of Muslim* [illegible] *came to a Hindu Sikh camp and* {*with many assurances*} *invited, virtually entreated, the merchants and financiers, to return. They stayed where they were.*]

. . . Patel has moved strong armed forces to the borders, [something lined through] {very possible} casus belli.

M refugees {from Ind} have been poor . . .

Women: ~~The Sikh~~ In Northern India, where the fiercest riot-
ing took place, there are fewer women than men. Sikhs, whose
religion [*The religion of the S, which* above *Sikhs, whose religion*]
forbids their marriage to Moslem women, apparently does not
forbid rape followed by torture or release. Moslems, {who}
can marry whom they please, steal women. [something lined
through] inestimable # which round into the tens of thousands
have been kidnapped during the riots. [illegible], and locked
in Purdahs, they will not be easily found. The Indian
Government has spoken severely to the Pak govt of this & the
Pak gov't has severely requested {{insert from left margin: *that
they be returned. But even if they are returned,* [something lined
through] *nothing is more sacred to the H & S than the chastity of
their women. Hinduism, hard pressed in battle, used to build fires in
which their women might commit* Seti *rather than be captured; Sikhs,
in a similar predicament during the past weeks, are known to have
slashed the throats of their wives & daughters. So, although G &
others have urged that abducted women, if returned, be taken completely back into the fold, it is clear that the* [illegible] *of kidnapped
women will have only begun.*}}

N 29: Fragment: "Bomb"

[Texas Box 1, folder 2.2, page 15]

N 30: Proofing Notes

[Texas Box 1, folder 2.2, page 18]

✓   gold-white on gray-white, and ~~the rigid~~ in one place a
     rigid shaft of metal radiance ~~tightened~~ almost pierced . . .

✓   p 15. his Aunt Patty   ~~1923~~

          ✓ 49. bleed . . .   ~~p 22, 1923~~

✓   56-7—flame & blossom?   {scalding}
     clear

     [*gold* after bracket from *frowning* to *furious*]

✓   –11—tenderly reveling &c.   ~~shuddering~~

~~quavering~~

[*flowers?* after bracket from *shivering* to *quavering*]
kind and {*sufferance* above *endurance* in bracket}? ? ✓
10 ~~satanic~~
   ~~wasn't~~
   ~~thought~~
   ~~replied to~~
[*patterning* after bracket from *brave* to *warlike*]

N 31: Notes on Health Regimen

[Texas Box 1, folder 2.1, page 4]

[*moderate* in left margin]

[*1-2-3* in left margin]

rest in middle of day? sh'd not stay up <u>far</u> <u>beyond</u> ~~norm~~ <u>my</u>
normal bedtime? [in right margin: *not to* [sic] *many eggs—esp
yolks—veg & meat fats; candy—*] i.e., a good night's sleep gives
me a surplus of energy—I can go 20, rather than 16—{{insert
from left margin: *in fact it is hard to go 16 instead.*}}

The warnings are [something lined through] clear and, if
heeded instantly, safe?
short of breath; palpitation; congestion; pain.
what type of pain in legs means embolism?
[line to *short of breath*] I think one trouble was . . .

My work as a rule [something lined through] involves a lot of
tension.

one safety valve: [something lined through] If I feel too sick . . .

~~"emoti~~
"emotional" stuff . . .

. . . what is known as [something lined through] trouble—should I
try to?

N 32: Columns of Figures (Bills)

[Texas Box 1, folder 2.1, page 10]

~~6.25~~	~~.10~~	~~.10~~	~~.10~~
~~16.35~~	~~3.75~~	~~8.58~~	~~14.44~~
~~8.88~~	~~16.91~~	~~12.90~~	~~8.48~~
~~13.50~~	~~10.06~~	~~8.95~~	~~12.88~~
~~16.25~~	~~.20~~	~~4.63~~	~~23.00~~
~~61.23~~	~~31.02~~	~~35.06~~	~~58.90~~
~~31.02~~			
~~7.50~~		~~13.13~~	.30
99.75		~~2.19~~	26.56
		~~14.56~~	5.13
		~~29.88~~	7.50
			2.98

INDEX

James Agee Rediscovered was designed and typeset on a Macintosh computer system using QuarkXPress software. The body text is set in 11/14 Dante MT Regular and display type is set in Diotima. This book was designed and typeset by Liz Lester and manufactured by Thomson-Shore, Inc.

matter how much I bashed him – he wouldn't let go.

I pulled the knife from my back pocket and plunged it into his shoulder once – twice – three times until he let go of my neck. He stepped back. I was mad. Bloody mad. I went berserk – stabbing him in the head again and again until he finally fell backwards. He was in a sitting position with his legs outstretched. He put his hands over his head, trying to defend himself from the blows that I was raining down on him. All the time he was crying out, 'Oh, my head! Oh, my head!'

But I didn't care. I straddled him, sitting on his legs. I held the knife with both hands and plunged it into his heart. The five-inch blade went through his chestbone like butter. Blood splattered everywhere and he gave out a gasp. The noise was so loud it brought me back to my senses. I jumped up. For a moment I stared at his blood-soaked body. He didn't move. Blood pumped from the wounds in his head and chest. I dropped the knife and ran.

My legs felt like lead as I ran down the gravel drive. As I reached the end of the path, I turned and looked back. It was like a dream. He was standing in the doorway clutching his chest. He tried to call out, so I stuck my fingers up and ran.

I couldn't believe it. I had beaten him, stabbed the old git in the head and heart and still he wasn't dead. He was like Superman – indestructible!

I looked down at my hands – they were covered in blood. I had to try to wash it off before I got home. I knelt down in the gutter at a big puddle and washed my hands and face. I knew I had to be home by seven or Auntie would be cross.

I slammed the front door – dead on 7 p.m. My frenzied attack had taken less than an hour. Auntie looked up at the clock on the mantelpiece. 'Only just!' she smiled.

I ran straight upstairs and locked the bathroom door. I looked in the mirror. My shirt was covered in blood. I ripped it off, the buttons popping as I did so, and stuffed it in the laundry basket.

As she left for the school meeting, Auntie called upstairs: 'Don't forget to check on Gerry, Ricky. There's plenty of cold meat in the fridge if you're hungry, I won't be long, love!'

I peeked into the nursery. Gerry was fast asleep in his little bed. He looked so peaceful, so innocent, tucked up in his Thomas the Tank Engine duvet.

I flicked the lights off, closed the door behind me and crept out of the house to look for Barry. I hadn't a clue where he'd gone. I went to all his usual haunts but he was nowhere to be seen. I met another friend of mine from school, he was a bit younger than me, 13. I asked him if he'd seen Barry anywhere but he hadn't seen him all evening.

We were standing on the corner chatting when, out of the blue, an ambulance whizzed past us with its lights flashing and its sirens blaring. It was heading straight for the vicarage.

'Come on,' the youngster squealed. 'Let's follow it and see what's happened!'

I was a bit wary of going but the boy insisted, so I tagged along. We ran along trying to keep up with the ambulance. It didn't have to go very far.

As we approached the vicarage there was already a crowd of onlookers standing on the pavement outside the house. The whole place was crawling with 'cozzers'. I was a bit nervous but I thought to myself, 'The tough old bastard can't be dead 'cos I saw him standing in the doorway.'

My mate pushed his way through the crowd to get a better look. 'Come on, Ricky – let's see what's happening!'

But I didn't need to get a better look. I had bashed his head in and I knew exactly what he looked like. I left my mate gaping, trying to get a better look at the grisly sight. I said nothing – there was nothing to say. Barry was nowhere to be seen so I decided to go home. Maybe he was waiting for me there.

The house was in darkness. Auntie still wasn't home from her meeting. I ran upstairs to check on young Gerry. He was fast asleep. I opened a tin of Coke and sat outside on the doorstep, listening to my cassette player, waiting for Barry. I couldn't have been sitting there for no more than ten minutes when I glanced down the road and noticed four plain-clothes 'cozzers' walking up the street. Straightaway I knew they had come for me.

The front door was wide open so they couldn't see the number of the house. They walked past, then stopped. They turned and looked at me. I didn't run. What for? I didn't think he was dead. One of the 'cozzers' opened the gate. 'Are you Richard John Dennick?'

'That's right,' I answered confidently.

'You're under arrest,' he snapped.

'What for?'

'Murder!'

I didn't say anything. I just looked at him. I wasn't shocked. I didn't feel sad. I felt surprisingly cool. One of them snapped, 'Get your things, you're coming with us.'

I explained that I was looking after a little boy and that he was asleep upstairs. 'Never mind that. We'll look after him'.

I was bundled into the back of a waiting police car and taken to the local police station if you can call it that. It was one of those council houses turned into a police station. Nothing much ever happened in the small village so I don't suppose they had any need for a real one. Once inside, I was taken to a small room upstairs – the interview room. I sat down at the small table and one of the officers offered me a fag and said, 'Come on, lad – why did you do it?'

At first I denied it but they said Barry was downstairs singing like a bird. I wanted to smile and say, 'Hope it's not a Beatles song he's singing' but it was no laughing matter and it was no use denying it either. So I put my hands up. I told them the truth. The whole sordid story. All about the pervy vicar. I thought they would be shocked but they wasn't. Seemed the Canon Alan Jones had convictions already.

Later that night I was taken to Carmarthen police station to see a doctor. He examined me, taking blood and samples from under my nails. He didn't say a word to me, not a word. I remember thinking at the time I bet he's a mate of that perv, 'cos he fucking hurt me jiggling the needle in my arm.

Later my aunt was allowed in to see me. When she walked into the small, cold interview room, it was obvious she had been crying. I didn't look up. I couldn't look at her. I didn't say anything. There was nothing I could say.

The next day the cell door opened and three officers handcuffed me to take me to Carmarthen Magistrates' Court.

'Can I have a fag?' I asked.

One of the officers in the back of the police car broke a cigar in half and handed it to me. I was driven to court to be charged with murder smoking a cigar and I didn't give a fuck. It was like one of those Hamlet cigar adverts. I was remanded in custody and taken to Risley Remand Centre in Warrington. Better known as Grisly Risley.

Risley is a terrible place. It has the highest suicide rate among young offenders in the country. When you're banged up there, you know why. It's a nightmare. As soon as I walked into the reception the screws started slapping me about. They made my life hell. They taunted me, saying I wasn't the usual scum bag murderer, I was worse – much worse. I had killed a vicar. For that I would rot in hell – or jail.

I stayed at Grisly Risley for six months. My trial at Chichester Crown Court lasted two weeks. I was completely lost. I didn't understand anything that was said in court. I tried to explain. I didn't deny it. I told them the truth about what happened. The police or barrister, I don't know which, stood up and said the vicar was a known homosexual with convictions, but then someone else stood up and said: 'Ah, my right honourable friend, but not with children!'

Even though the police found photos and videos of naked kids in the vicarage, they didn't want to know. The trial went on and on. In the end the judge, Mr Justice Mars-Jones, said that I was 'evil' and that I had killed for gain. But that wasn't true. 'You will go to prison for life. You will be detained during Her Majesty's Pleasure. Take him down.' It was 30 March 1983. I was 15 years old. I buried my head in my hands and cried.

September 1989

I had been in prison for six years. I'd had enough. I don't know when the idea of getting out first came to me. It wasn't as if I planned it but one day I was padding around the exercise yard, around and around and around. Suddenly the thought came into my mind: ' I could get over that wall!'

Then, just by chance that night, when I was in the TV room, I saw the scaffolding where workmen had been decorating and I thought, 'I could climb that scaffolding. I could get on to the roof that way. From the roof on to the wall.' I didn't plan it properly – no master plan. It just came to me. It was an opportunity waiting for me – begging me to grab it.

I felt sick with nerves but I was more excited than I have ever been. I raced back to my cell to get some things together. I didn't know what I was going to do or what I was going to take but somehow it just all fell into place. My mind was spinning. What if I failed? So what if I did. I didn't have anything to lose. I stuffed a few things into my kitbag and a five pound note that I had hidden in the back of my radio. A few years earlier I had watched an old war movie called *The Great Escape*. In the film the prisoners of war used stuffed dummies to fool their guards. That's what I did. I ripped up sheets and stuffed the pieces into a pair of jeans. I made a life-size dummy and laid it in my bed so that it looked like I was asleep. I took a blanket and stuffed it into my kitbag. I figured I might need that. Then I nipped back into the TV room and waited.

I waited and waited until the last stragglers left the room. There was only me and three cleaners left. I was scared. But I thought, 'Fuck it – it's now or never.' I scrambled to the top of the scaffolding. The cleaners stopped in their tracks and looked in amazement. The oldest of the cleaners, it must have been the supervisor, motioned to the others to turn a blind eye. Quickly they gathered up their cleaning things and scuttled out of the room.

I crouched down at the top of the scaffolding. I wanted to be invisible. As the screw walked in to check the place, I held my breath and closed my eyes tight, trying not to make a sound. All I could hear was the squeaking of his boots on the polished floor and the jingling of his keys.

He paced around the room and stopped at the bottom of the scaffolding. My heart missed a beat. I thought he'd clocked me but he just stopped to spark up a fag. I drew a heavy sigh of relief when I heard him lock the door. I knew then that I had until morning to make my escape.

As quietly as I dared, I tapped on the plasterboard, trying to find the hollow sound between the rafters. With one of the scaffolding clips I started to scratch away the surface of the plasterboard. I started with just a small hole then it got bigger and bigger until it was just big enough for me to squeeze through. Once I was in the ceiling cavity, I prized away the slate tiles. First one, then another, then another. A burst of red hazy night sky shone into the dusty cavity. It was the best sight I have ever seen. I squeezed through the hole on to the roof. I had already ripped the TV cable from the telly and I looped it over the drainpipe. I peered over the edge of the roof. It must have been at least a 45-foot drop but I didn't care. I started to abseil down the side of the building. I heard a creaking noise, then snap! the cable broke. I found myself hurtling through the air, 15 feet to the ground, and landed straight on my arse. I scraped my knuckles on the flint walls as I fell and I hit the ground with such force that I broke my two front teeth.

I picked myself up and scurried across the exercise yard, spitting my broken teeth out as I ran. When I reached the outer razor-wire fence, I threw the blanket and myself over it. One of the razors ripped across my chin, opening it up to the bone but I didn't feel a thing. I could smell freedom. Almost taste it. Nothing was going to stop me.

Suddenly a screw on patrol appeared from nowhere. I froze but he saw me. In a flash, he let his vicious-looking dog off its chain and mumbled something into his radio with some urgency. I scrambled over the rest of the razor fence and ran. I ran and ran as fast as my legs would take me. In the distance I could hear pandemonium.

I ducked down into someone's back garden and changed

my clothes. As I walked down the road my whole body tensed up and I knew exactly how the prisoner in Midnight Express felt. I tried to act normal but after so long in prison I didn't really know what normal was.

I heard loud music coming from a club. I had to get off the street. I figured my best bet would be to mingle with other people. I walked into the crowded club house just as the bar closed. 'Time, gentlemen please!' the landlord called.

I pulled the crumpled fiver out of my pocket. 'Pint of lager please!'

'Sorry, mate, I've called time!'

A young bloke who was standing beside me took pity on me. He was obviously a regular and said, 'Go on, give the boy a drink. It's my birthday.'

'Just one then,' the landlord sighed.

The bloke was half-cut and he pushed the pint in front of me. I looked at the cool pint of beer. Oh, how I had dreamed of this moment. Freedom and a pint. The geezer seemed a decent sort of chap. He looked as if he had been around. I had to take a chance. I needed help and he was just the chap to help me.

I took him to one side and whispered to him. I told him I had just escaped from nick. In an instant he sobered up. At first he thought I was bullshitting but the desperate look on my face must have convinced him I was telling the truth.

'You'd better stay with us,' he said. 'It really is my birthday and I've got a coach coming soon to take us to Brighton. Get on the coach with us, that way you won't look out of place.' He explained that he'd done a bit of bird himself and knew what it was like. I didn't tell him I was in for murder and doing life. I just told him I was in for unpaid fines.

The rest of the partygoers on the coach were all pissed and didn't give me a second glance. Someone handed me a joint and a tin of beer. In no time at all I was buzzing.

When the coach reached Brighton, I said my goodbyes and disappeared. I phoned some friends that I knew. To say that they were shocked was an understatement. They agreed to bring me some clothes and money but they said they didn't want to see me or get involved. That was fair enough. I hid in the bushes and waited for their Range Rover to pull up. As it approached, they switched the lights off and the passenger door opened. Nobody got out. They just dropped out a small bundle and drove away. I waited for a moment, to make sure the coast was clear, then grabbed the bundle and ran, ducking down an alley in the shadows.

Carefully, I opened the package. Good! There was £500, some fags and a change of clothes. I changed into the trousers and clean shirt and booked myself into the Metropole Hotel. All night I drank the miniature bottles of spirits out of the bar in my room and listened to the radio for any news of my escape. I must have fallen asleep in a drunken haze.

The next day I woke early. Was I dreaming or was it real? I looked around the hotel room. It was real all right. I paid my bill and headed for London and some friends. Most of my so-called friends gave me a blank. A couple of them agreed to give me some money as long as I fucked off and didn't come back. I couldn't blame them really. I was on every news bulletin on the TV and in every newspaper.

I ended up staying in Southwark, South London. Just by chance I had met an odd sort of a couple and they said I could stay with them for a while, just until I got myself sorted. They didn't know who I was and they were too drunk most of the time to recognise me. It was brilliant. I would walk for hours with their dog in the park. I even went to clubs. It was great. My first taste of freedom.

But I had one big problem – money, or the lack of it. I couldn't sign on or get a job. The money from my friends soon dried up. I had no choice, I had to do a robbery. I spoke to the couple that I was staying with and they agreed to help. He had an imitation gun and she told me about her local post office. 'It's a doddle,' she said. 'Let's do it.'

We drove to the post office in his Mini – what a getaway car! The girl went in and sussed it out but it was too crowded and no good. On the way back home we stopped at a Paki shop to get a cheap bottle of wine. As we walked in, I decided there and then to rob the shop. I yelled at the Paki behind the counter: 'Give me the money from the till!'

He wobbled his head and waved his arms about like only a Pakistani can: 'No, No, No,' he said in broken English.

I pulled the gun out from under my coat and jumped over the counter. I shoved the Paki out of the way and pressed the till open. The drawer flew out and I grabbed the cash. There wasn't much – about £250.

The other two were already in the car with the engine

running. We hadn't got a mile down the road when a police car pulled us over. I was gutted.

I gave a false name – Jason Ward. I didn't think for one moment that they would believe it but they did. I passed all the criminal computer checks, no problem. I was in Pentonville Prison for two and a half months under my false name. I even appeared in court a couple of times.

On 2 November 1989, just after dinner, a screw came into my cell. 'The governor wants to see you,' he snapped.

When I walked in the office, he held up a wanted poster and said, 'I take it this is you?'

I tried to deny it but it was no good. They took umpteen photos of me but, worst of all, I was transferred to a Category A prison. That was that. The game was up. I couldn't stand it being back to a Cat. A, back to square one.

Eventually the court gave me an extra six years for armed robbery and nine days down the block for escaping. The extra six years didn't matter a shit. I already had a life sentence.

After my taste of freedom I couldn't cope with a life inside anymore. I'm not ashamed to say it, but I couldn't take it anymore. I started to crack up. My mental health deteriorated rapidly being banged up down the block. I started to act erratically. At the time I thought I was acting normal. But then I was convinced I was the son of God. Before I knew it I had been nutted off and sent to Rampton. My tariff date ended in 1995, but as I was in Rampton, sectioned, that didn't count. But it's strange. It don't seem to matter any more. You see, I'm working my ticket. It's easier than nick …

Sue
Butterworth

Killers

John Kenny was murdered on 10 December 1991. His body was found in a rubbish skip by dustmen who at first thought it was a mannequin dummy. He had been beaten to a pulp and stabbed. His injuries were so severe that newspapers at the time were convinced it was a Triad murder.

In fact, John, an unemployed alcoholic, was killed by two of his neighbours – Craig Hendley and Sue Butterworth. Craig, a young, foul-mouthed thug, and Sue a 35 year-old brassy, blonde ex-stripper, carried out the killing after a drunken row over a broken video recorder. It was a brutal, vicious and totally senseless murder.

I met Sue Butterworth through Linda Calvey. Linda

had been moved to Holloway Prison for her visits and she phones me every Saturday without fail. 'I've got someone else for your book; someone who has agreed to talk openly. You can visit her tomorrow, if you like.'

The very next day I drove into London. It was the first time I had visited an all-woman prison. Holloway Prison is a big building right on a busy main road. I drove past it twice. It doesn't look like a prison from the outside; it looks more like a Presbyterian church. I went through all the usual security checks and waited in the cramped waiting room. Visits are only an hour at a time. When a man visits a men's prison he has the back of his hand stamped with indelible ink. As I was going into a women's prison, I had the back of my hand stamped. This is done so that the women inmates can't swap places with you and escape.

A butch-looking prison officer allocated me a table – number eight. Being Sunday, the visiting hall was packed with visitors. Patiently, I waited for the screw to call number eight. When she did, Sue came rushing through a door at the end of the hall. 'Hello Kate, glad you could make it!' She was very hyped up and shook my hand hard. 'I'll have a Coke and a Mars, if that's OK.'

I got the Coke and Mars from the small canteen. Sue looked slightly older than 38. She was tall, with short blonde hair, and was wearing a smart navy suit.

'The shock made me lose my baby and my Rocky he's been abused over the last 18 months. He came to visit me and he had cigarette burns all over his little body. I blame myself – I should be there to look after him.'

She explained that while she was on remand she discovered that she was pregnant. As a result, the shock made her lose the baby. Her two small children went to live elsewhere and were abused. Happily, they now live with a family in Kent and are doing well but Sue hopes to get them back when she has completed her sentence. I explained to her all about my book and she agreed to tell me her story. 'I ain't bothered. I ain't got nothing to hide or anything else left to lose,' she said. 'I'll tell you exactly what happened.'

She had recently married an Israeli prisoner inside Long Lartin top security prison. 'Oh, that's nice,' I said.

'No it ain't,' she said. 'As soon as he got out, he buggered off back to Israel and I haven't heard from him since. I don't care. I'll just pick myself up, brush myself down and start all over again! That's what I've always done,' she said.

She started to tell me the horrific story that led her to a life sentence.

★ ★ ★

'You're nothing but a bitch,' he yelled. 'I'm leaving, I'm going back to my mum's'.

That didn't surprise me. It's what Jerry always did when we had a row.

'Go on then, run back to mummy – see if I care'.

I put up a front as if I didn't care but inside I was hurt. That was the story of my life. Most of my relationships had been violent ones and I'd had a few. But I'd cope. I always did. I am a survivor.

John Kenny was different. He was a quiet, straight sort of a guy. He lived in a flat a couple of doors away. It was a rough neighbourhood on the outskirts of Paddington in London. John was a smashing bloke, always eager to please, but he had one failing in life – booze. That's how Jerry and I met him. We all liked a drink and we soon become friends, spending many a night drinking until the early hours of the morning. Right from the start I liked John – and he liked me. We enjoyed each other's company. He was so different from my boyfriend Jerry. John was a bit of a git when he was drunk but always made me feel special. That was something I wasn't used to and I liked that feeling.

Jerry slammed the door behind him as he left, waking up my two kids.

'You bastard,' I thought. 'That's it now, I'm finished with you – for good'. All day I cried. I was so upset. I needed to talk to someone. I wanted to talk to John, he would understand. I got the kids dressed and hurried over to John's flat for a chat. He was such an easy-going bloke and was pleased to see us – or at least he seemed pleased. I cooked us some tea while John played with the kids. I've got a little girl Fiona and a little boy Rocky. Then they were aged only two and three. John was brilliant with them, and my Rocky adored him.

Once we had our tea and bathed the kids, I put them

to bed. At last I could relax. I dropped a couple of sleeping pills and John rolled a joint. We opened a case of Special Brew and had a drink or two or three. It was strong — bloody strong. Before I knew it I was pouring out all my troubles. Poor old John, I really bent his ear. By the early hours of the morning I had said all there was to say. I don't know if it was the drink or not but I remember just wanting him to hold me and to cuddle me. Which he did. Before I knew it we were in bed.

Early next morning John said, 'Get your things. You and the kids can move in here with me.'

I was delighted.

He didn't have much in the way of furniture but that didn't matter. He had a few odds and ends but nothing much; he never was one for material possessions.

So I moved lock, stock and barrel into his flat — the cooker, fridge, furniture the lot. It was great. For the first time in ages I was happy.

Next morning I went to Soho, to see my dentist. Jerry had broken one of my teeth when he bashed me, so I went to have it crowned. It must have been my lucky day. I bumped into my old boss, Charlie. Old Charlie owned a seedy club in one of the backstreets but he was OK. We started chatting and he said that I could have my old job back if I wanted it. I jumped at the chance. A new man, a new flat, a new job, brilliant!

I'd had a lot of jobs in the past, mainly stripping. But the one I earned most money at was in the clip joints in the heart of Soho. The work was hard but it was good fun.

Plus, it left the nights free for me to look after Fiona and Rocky.

I used to work on the doors in the seedy clubs, drawing in the punters. I was good at it too. I'd always wear some scanty-looking number with black stockings and suspenders. I'd stand outside the club calling, 'Rub your tummy, guv'nor! Step inside – live show!' Once I got the punters' attention, I could charge them what I liked. Then I'd send them downstairs to the hostesses. That's how I made my money – good money too.

I used to meet some weirdos I can tell you. Some of the girls would tell me outrageous stories of the things men want done to them you would never believe.

One of the girls at the club, Diane, was a friend of mine. We went way back. She had worked all the clubs and done the rounds, just like me. I liked Diane and it was good to be back working with her again. One evening before our shift started we were having a cup of tea and she was telling me all about the long running saga of how her husband had thrown her out and taken the kids off to Malta.

She was fed up because she had nowhere to live and she had this new toyboy called Craig Hendley – a name that was to change my life. I felt a bit sorry for her and told her she could rent my flat if she wanted to. She was over the moon. 'I'll send Craig over to pick up the keys,' she said. 'We'll move in tonight!' Craig seemed all right – young and fit but nothing much to look at.

A few days later me and Diane went out for a drink.

For a change we didn't have a drink in the club. Instead, we went to a pub in Berwick Street and, to my surprise, who walked in but Jerry. As soon as I saw him I melted. (I couldn't resist him – I never could. He used to laugh and joke with me saying: 'Treat 'em mean and you keep 'em keen!' I made him right. I was keen. I couldn't keep my hands off him.)

After a long chat and several drinks, we sorted out our differences and decided to get back together. He wanted to come back home. I was glad but that left me with one problem – John Kenny.

The next morning I told John that I had seen Jerry and that we were going to give it another try. John shrugged his shoulders and said it was for the best. He was so laid back when he was sober, nothing bothered him – least of all me. The very next day I moved back into my old flat with Jerry. I told Diane and Craig that they could stay but just until they found somewhere else.

It was only a tiny flat and far too cramped for four adults and two small children. Within a day or so we started to get under each other's feet. There just wasn't enough room so I asked John if Diane and Craig could stay at his place for a while. What a mistake.

The next thing I knew John was knocking at my door at eight in the morning. When I opened the door I was shocked. He had an enormous black eye. 'What the hell happened to you?' I gasped. It turned out that Craig had bashed him when he was drunk. I thought that John had done his usual and got all leery after a drinking binge and that Craig had stuck one on him. John always did want to fight the world when he was drunk. He's what you might call him a depressive drinker. He looked a sorry old sight standing on my doorstep. He was skint and wanted to borrow a few quid for a bottle of cider and some tobacco. I gave him some money. I didn't mind. He would do anything for me. He was a good-hearted man. He often helped me out by repairing things in the flat and he never asked for any money.

After the row, John said that Diane and Craig had to go. I couldn't blame him, not after Craig had bashed him. Shortly after that Diane left the club and I didn't see her again for several months. Then, late one night, she came looking for me at the club. She was in a terrible state and was desperate for somewhere to live. She said that Craig had just been released from Armerly Prison and they had nowhere to live.

I felt sorry for her. I didn't like Craig. I knew he was prone to violent outbursts and I couldn't put up with that. After all, I had the kids to think about. Diane pleaded with me: 'Just let us stay for a few days.' She said that she'd had enough of Craig and was going to give him the elbow the next time he started.

I didn't believe a word of it but I agreed to let them stay: 'Just for a few days, mind!'

But a few days turned into a few weeks, then a few months. Craig was a bastard – an out and out bastard. Poor old Diane: she had taken just about enough of him. She confided in me that she was going to escape to Malta to see her kids. She never told Craig. She just disappeared and vowed me to secrecy. When Craig found out he was furious. For a week he stomped around the flat ranting and raving. I daren't tell him where she had gone. He kept phoning her husband's house constantly, day and night, until, finally, after a week, he got an answer – but not one he wanted to hear.

Diane's husband Leli answered the phone and said sarcastically, 'Sorry, Diane's too busy to talk, she's got her mouth full – with my cock!'

Craig screamed out, 'If I get my hands on you or her, I'll kill the fucking pair of ya!'

I have never seen anyone angrier than I saw Craig that day. That conversation changed him. At first he went wild with anger then he just seemed lost. He felt he was nothing without his Diane. Day and night, night and day, that's all he ever talked about. Everyone was sympathetic at first but then he started driving everyone mad, including me.

'What shall I do? What shall I do?' he kept asking. He was inconsolable.

On 6 December, I decided to decorate the flat for Christmas. I sorted everything out but the fairy lights didn't work so I went and knocked on John's door. He looked terrible. He had been having trouble with his ex-wife, and the Old Bill had woken him up at six in the morning to arrest him for beating her up. 'What a fucking day,' he said. 'I need a drink.'

'I've got a bottle of vodka at home, come over and have

a drink and you can fix my fairy lights while you're there.'

He came over and we started drinking. That day and those bloody broken fairy lights were to start a mammoth drinking binge that lasted until Monday 10 December.

I woke up with one hell of a hangover. I felt like shit. Craig was stretched out on the settee. I told him to go to the post office and cash my family allowance book for me. I dragged myself out of bed and picked up a half bottle of flat beer. I was gasping for a drink, my mouth felt like I had pigeons nesting in it.

I swigged back the warm beer and threw the empty bottle on the floor. It tasted disgusting but I didn't give a fuck. Craig came back with my money and more beer and we started drinking again.

After about his tenth beer and countless chasers, much to my disgust he started going on about Diane again. 'Oh, I miss her – oh, I love her.' He was like a long-playing record, going on and on. I'd had enough. I told him she was back with her husband and kids and that was that. He would just have to get on with his own life and find someone his own age.

By tea-time we were as drunk as ten men. I wasn't even dressed; I still had on my T-shirt nightie. For some reason – God knows why – I decided I wanted my video recorder back from John. It had been broken and John was going to fix it so the kids could have it for Christmas. But he'd had it for ages. All of a sudden it just came into my head and I got the needle. 'I'm going over to John's. I want to get my recorder back,' I snapped.

'Yeah, it's a liberty,' Craig said. 'The slag should have done it by now. It's nearly fucking Christmas. The kids will want that. I'm going with ya.'

I slipped on a pair of shoes and opened the front door, with Craig behind me. We must have looked a sight staggering to John's flat. 'It's me! It's Sue! Open the door,' I shouted through the letter box.

John was still drunk. He stumbled to the door and let us in. I sat down on the sideboard and Craig slumped down on the settee next to John.

'I've come for my video recorder,' I slurred. John said: 'Yeah, alright. I'll get it in a minute'.

Craig piped up, 'Never mind in a minute. Get it now!'

John was pissed and instantly got the hump and started shouting at him. 'It's nothing to do with you. Mind your own business!'

After a few minutes of listening to the two of them arguing, I lost interest. The TV was blaring in the corner and *Home and Away* was on. I started to pay more attention to that than to those two silly bastards.

I could hear John slagging off his ex-wife. By this time he was very irate and was spitting as he spoke. He was calling her all the names under the sun and got carried away. He started saying all woman are the same. Then he made a fatal mistake. 'Yeah, they're all the fucking same,' he said. 'Look what Diane did to you. She ain't nothing but a slag!'

For a moment there was a deathly silence. Craig's face changed. I swear I saw the devil reflected in his eyes. He stood up, then went crazy, like a man possessed. At first he started to punch John about the head. Then, when John fell on the floor, he started kicking and kicking him. I just froze. I couldn't move. It was like watching a horror movie.

John was so drunk that he was powerless to stop Craig. I've heard it said before that when a man loses his mind he gains the strength of three men. Well that certainly was true in Craig's case. Nothing could stop him. He was battering the hell out of John. When he had worn himself out beating him, he grabbed a cushion off the sofa and pushed it over John's face. He was screaming: 'Die, you bastard. Die!'

I knew then that what I was witnessing was more than just a drunken brawl. This was different. A sort of panic washed over my whole body, like a rush.

All I could think of was getting my video and getting out of that flat. In blind panic I rushed to the hallway cupboard where John kept the things he was repairing but it was locked. Frantically, I rushed around the room looking for the key but I couldn't find it. I found a tool box and tried to break into the cupboard but it was no good. I wasn't strong enough.

Everything went quiet in the living room so I called Craig to come and help me to get the cupboard door open. When he came out into the hallway he was covered in blood – John's blood. His eyes looked wild, like he was on some kind of drug. In a flash, he tore the cupboard door off its hinges and gave me my video.

After what had happened, the video seemed so insignificant. I walked back into the living room. John was lying on his back on the floor. A vegetable knife was sticking out of his neck. His face was so swollen from the beating that it looked like a big purple balloon. His eyes, if you could call them eyes, were more like slits where his eyes used to be. In the struggle, John's jumper had been pulled up around his shoulders and his jeans pulled down. I could see more stab wounds all over his body. I felt sick. What a fucking mess. I screamed at Craig: 'What have you fucking done?'

'Shut up, bitch!' he snapped.

I was scared to death of what he might do. I had seen with my own two eyes just what he was capable of. I thought it best to humour him and try to keep on his good side. 'You better get out of those clothes. They're covered in blood.'

There was a pair of Craig's old jeans left in the bedroom from when he had stayed at John's. I had to think fast. I ran into the bedroom and dragged down a big old suitcase from off the top of the wardrobe. I was in a total panic. All I could think of was getting everything that belonged to me out of that place. I went back into the living room just to see if it was real or I had dreamed it. But it wasn't a dream. It was reality. I looked down at John's body. He was lying in a pool of blood. Craig bent over the blood-soaked body and coldly pulled the knife out of John's neck.

I heard a crack. At first I thought it was his neck

break. But it wasn't, it was his teeth snapping shut. Craig shouted: 'Let's get out of here!'

We grabbed all our belongings, including the broken video recorder, and hurried back to the safety of home. I slammed the front door, as if to shut out the horror of what had happened. Then I locked it. I didn't know what to do next. Quickly, I stuffed the blood-stained clothes into the washing machine. As I did so, I put the keys on top of my freezer.

I tried to act normal so that Rocky and Fiona wouldn't sense anything was wrong. What I needed was a drink — a large one.

Craig wrenched the bottle of cider out of my hand and guzzled it back. He looked like a mad man. I was scared shitless of him but I figured that as long as I was helping him, me and the kids would be safe. I had to keep him sweet so, after the kids had finished their tea, we opened another bottle and started drinking again. But it seemed it didn't matter how much I drank, I couldn't blot out the horror of what had happened.

Something startled me. Someone was banging on the door. 'It's the police. What are we going to do?' I cried.

Craig snarled, 'Shut up, you silly bitch. Go and see who it is.'

Nervously, I opened the door. It was a friend of John's called Pat Brown. 'Seen John?' he said. 'I've been banging on his door for ages but he can't hear me over the telly.'

I had to keep calm. 'Naah, I've not seen him all day.'

He was mumbling on about how he needed to have a

wash and shave. I wasn't really listening; my mind was miles away. I didn't know what to say and I just wanted to act as normal as possible, so I said he could use my bathroom.

Craig was so drunk he didn't give a fuck. 'All right, Pat?' he said. 'Fancy a drink?'

For the next couple of hours the three of us sat in my lounge, drinking. I couldn't get John out of my mind. The thought of him lying dead just a few doors away. I couldn't take it in. Craig was busy bragging to Pat how tough he was. God, I hated him. He was such a bullshitter. I'd heard his stories so often, I knew them off by heart. But he was right about one thing, he needed money. He asked Pat if he was interested in robbing an Indian restaurant later that night. What next?

I looked over at the kids playing happily in the corner with some Lego. I smiled at their innocent faces. Craig stood up, stumbled into the kitchen and returned with the washing up bowl. His trainers were splattered with blood. Coolly, he took them off and started to wash them. I couldn't believe it. He was actually washing them in front of Pat and the kids.

To my horror, someone else banged on the front door. This was it: I felt sure this would be the police. But it wasn't, it was the bloody Avon lady. 'Coo-ee, it's me. Avon calling,' she joked.

Tragedy was turning into an awful kind of black comedy. She just kept talking on and on. I couldn't get rid of her.

Craig pushed past me in the hallway. 'We're going to the pub.'

In the end I got rid of the Avon lady, put the kids to bed and poured myself a drink. Peace at last. I must have fallen asleep in the chair, only to be woken by Craig's gruff voice. 'Wake up, it's time to move the body.'

John's flat was as cold as an ice box. The balcony door was wide open and the net curtains flapped in the breeze. I pulled my cardigan around me to guard against the chill wind. Everything seemed still and quiet. They say you can smell death. They're right — that flat stank of death. John was lying on the floor. It didn't look like John anymore. He was a mess. His eyes were like slits in his bulbous head.

Craig ripped off John's jacket and threw it over the balcony. 'Come on, hurry! Help me fix him up!'

I didn't want to touch him but I was scared of Craig. Slowly, with my fingertips, I pulled down his blood-soaked jumper. The blood from the stab wounds had congealed. Quickly, I pulled up his jeans and fastened them. Craig pulled off John's cheap watch and put it on his own wrist. God knows why, it was only plastic. Then he tried to pick up John's body by his shoulders but he was too heavy. 'Get his legs,' he snarled.

'I can't! I can't! I can't carry the weight!'

Craig got angry. 'Get out of the way. Stand by the door and make sure that nobody comes.'

Half-carrying and half-dragging, he pulled John's body to the top of the stairs. There was no way he could carry him down the three flights of stairs — no way. 'We'll have to drag him!' he said.

He grabbed John's legs and started to bump him down

the stairs. His head banged on each step. It was awful. I had to look away. When we reached the bottom, we came to three brick steps that led outside to the skip. 'You're going to have to help me get him into the skip,' he said.

Together, we dragged the body over to the skip. Craig propped it up against the skip and told me to hold it while he climbed in. He leant John's body against me. It stunk. A mixture of booze and blood. It was horrible. The congealed blood smelt like raw liver. It made me want to vomit. Craig looked over the top of the skip: 'I'll pull. You push.'

What a way to end your life – in a rubbish skip. Poor John!

Craig tore open some black sacks and emptied the stinking trash over the body to hide it.

All I wanted to do was get home and all I needed was more drink. I wanted to blot out what had happened. Craig and I talked to try to get our stories straight. He said that if it all came out, that he would tell the Old Bill that I had nothing to do with it. That was a lie. He never told them any such thing.

That week I took the kids to stay with some friends. I couldn't stay at the flat. I couldn't stop thinking of what would happen to my babies. I couldn't stop drinking. I knew for sure that it wouldn't be long before the Old Bill turned up.

It took them three days. On the 13 December, just twelve days before Christmas, I returned to my flat to get some things for the kids and they burst in. 'Susan Jane

Butterworth, you're under arrest for the murder of John Edmund Kenny!' I didn't say anything. I was taken to Harrow Road police station. I was so upset. Not for myself – but for my children.

I kept telling the police over and over that I didn't kill John. It was a drunken brawl between Craig and John and it had got out of hand. But they didn't believe me. They showed me photographs of John's flat. It looked different. Not how I remembered it at all. The bedroom had been ransacked. I knew it wasn't like that the night I left it.

I was shocked. I didn't know what to say. I couldn't explain it. Someone had really gone to town, taking everything that wasn't nailed down. It looked like John had been murdered, then robbed. But it didn't happen like that. I told the police that I didn't know why the flat had been ransacked. But I could hazard a bloody good guess. It wasn't me who went back and robbed John's gaff. That only left one person. The same person who killed him – Craig Hendley.

In July 1992, I pleaded not guilty to murder, but guilty to unlawful burial. The jury didn't believe me. I was found guilty of murder and sentenced to life.

Also Available by Kate Kray

HARD BASTARDS
Shocking portraits of the twenty-four hardest
men in Britain.
£14.99

HARD BASTARDS 2
The sensational sequel to Hard Bastards.
£15.99

THE TWINS: MEN OF VIOLENCE
The inside story of the Kray twins, as told by the
woman who knew her best.
£5.99

PRETTY BOY BY ROY SHAW
The amazing autobiography of the hardest bastard there is.
£14.99

Send off this coupon with cheque or credit card details to:
BLAKE PUBLISHING LTD.,
3 Bramber Court, 2 Bramber Road, London W14 9PB for your copy.

------ copies of *Hard Bastards* @ £14.99
------ copies of *Hard Bastards 2* @ £15.99
------ copies of *The Twins: Men of Violence* @ £5.99
------ copies of *Pretty Boy* @ £14.99

Either
a) Debit my Visa/Access/Mastercard (delete as appropriate)

Card number: _ _ _ _ / _ _ _ _ / _ _ _ _ / _ _ _ _

Expiry date: _ _ / _ _

b) I enclose a cheque for .... made payable to Blake Publishing Ltd.

Name: ....

Address: ....

....

....

Daytime Tel: ....

PLEASE ALLOW 28 DAYS FOR DELIVERY